MARSHALLING JUSTICE

ALSO BY MICHAEL G. LONG

Resist!: Christian Dissent for the 21st Century

First Class Citizenship: The Civil Rights Letters of Jackie Robinson

The Legacy of Billy Graham: Critical Reflections on America's Greatest Evangelist

God and Country? Diverse Perspectives on Christianity and Patriotism (with Tracy Wenger Sadd)

Billy Graham and the Beloved Community: America's Evangelist and the Dream of Martin Luther King, Jr.

Martin Luther King Jr. on Creative Living

Against Us, but for Us: Martin Luther King, Jr. and the State

MARSHALLING JUSTICE

The Early Civil Rights Letters of Thurgood Marshall

EDITED BY MICHAEL G. LONG

Foreword by Derrick Bell

Amistad
An Imprint of HarperCollins*Publishers*

The author wishes to thank the National Association for the Advancement of Colored People for authorizing the use of letters about Thurgood Marshall that are a part of the NAACP's collection.

HarperCollins books may be purchased for educational, business, or sales promotional use. For information, please write: Special Markets Department, HarperCollins Publishers, 10 East 53rd Street, New York, NY 10022.

FIRST EDITION

Designed by Lisa Stokes

Library of Congress Cataloging-in-Publication Data
Long, Michael G.
Marshalling justice : the early civil rights letters of Thurgood Marshall / edited by Michael G. Long.
p. cm.
Includes bibliographical references and index.
ISBN 978-0-06-198518-8
1. Marshall, Thurgood, 1908–1993—Correspondence. 2. African American lawyers—Correspondence. 3. Race discrimination—Law and legislation—United States. 4. African Americans—Civil rights—20th century. 5. Civil rights movements—United States. I. Long, Michael G.
KF8745.M34A4 2010
347.73'2634—dc22 [B] 2010025097

11 12 13 14 15 OV/RRD 10 9 8 7 6 5 4 3 2 1

For Nate,
who loves to play

One of these days, we will make democracy work in this country.

—THURGOOD MARSHALL

CONTENTS

FOREWORD

Far from Optimism

Derrick Bell

Unjustified optimism in the face of unrecognized obstacles is an ideological hazard that has often afflicted advocates of racial justice. Currently, it is manifested in the view that Barack Obama's election to the presidency marks the beginning of the post-racial era. Manifestations of similarly unwarranted euphoria were expressed when Lincoln issued the Emancipation Proclamation in 1863. The expectation of a race-free America was predicted as certainty when the Supreme Court handed down its school desegregation decision in 1954. The Civil Rights Act of 1964 and the Voting Rights Act of 1965 also prompted grateful prayers by black people that "our day had come." The assassination of Martin Luther King, Jr., in 1968 was too high a price to pay for the widespread adoption of affirmative action programs in the years that followed, but those programs were also deemed certain to curtail if not eliminate still viable racial discrimination across a wide spectrum of American life.

It is significant that in the letters Thurgood Marshall wrote from 1935 through 1940—his early years as a civil rights lawyer—he rarely expressed optimism. This was the period when the lynching of black men and some women was carried out with an awful regularity and the perpetrators were never prosecuted, seldom even arrested. Segregation of public facilities, on a far from "separate but equal" basis, was required and protected by law. The courts could not be depended on to find even blatant violations of black rights worthy of relief. Marshall, barely paid enough to cover basic bills, handled a multitude of cases and causes, and much of this work is reflected in his letters to colleagues, clients, government officials, and business leaders.

Marshall was a fun-loving man who seemed to have remembered every story he had ever heard, but his letters were serious, and purpose-driven. His mission, seldom stated but readily apparent in his writing, was to confront discrimination wherever he found it. All too often, it was a confrontation without either legal or political power to back it up. It was out of this background that his lawyerly skills and tactics were nurtured and matured into the carefully constructed litigation that led fifteen hard-fought years later to *Brown v. Board of Education.*

There were early victories. In 1934, working with Charles Houston, the then lead NAACP counsel, he gained an order requiring the University of Maryland to admit Donald Murray, an Amherst graduate, as the first Negro admitted to its law school. Marshall helped shepherd Murray through the rigors of law school to graduation. Finding clients of Murray's character, though, was not easy. Similarly, the Montgomery County Board of Education in Maryland responded to Marshall's suit seeking equalization of teacher salaries by agreeing to his demands. He felt this victory could be pushed to equalize teacher salaries across the state, even the nation, but he ran into expected opposition from school superintendents claiming black teachers were inferior. Unexpected resistance came from some black communities that, pointing to a number of teachers who had been fired for taking part in the equalization campaign, felt Marshall and the NAACP campaign were not improving their lives but actually making them worse.

His early letters also chided President Roosevelt and United States senators for failing to support antilynching legislation, none of which was ever enacted. He wrote Southern governors urging them to investigate lynchings that transpired in their states, a painful obligation given the predictable response that there was no evidence upon which they could act. They ignored Marshall's offers of information gathered by courageous persons able to provide both details of the murders and the names of the murderers.

Many blacks sentenced to death were victims of legal lynching with juries willing to convict on even a scintilla of evidence. In one case, prior to writing a sorrowful letter to the mother of Oscar Perry, who had been condemned to death, Marshall wrote to a cooperating attorney who had unsuccessfully sought clemency for Perry:

> It is this type of case which tends more and more to bring about a feeling that many of the courts in this country still prefer to permit prejudice to overcome a true sense of justice. However, we are sure that with the ever-growing group of individuals and lawyers in the South like yourself, who are willing to fight for justice, the battle is not lost and we still cling to the hope that eventually we will have justice in this country for all citizens.

Far from optimism, this was a balm for despair. It was an antidote that appeared in many of Marshall's letters. And yet his challenges to racial bias, as recorded in these letters, continued. He complained about a federal program of the TVA that introduced segregation policies in an area where blacks and whites had worked together. He sought the help of local lawyers to challenge the use of extradition processes to prevent the return south of blacks who had escaped from Southern chain gangs, returns that would likely end in their deaths.

Marshall wrote magazine editors who used racially derogatory stories and pictures. He even wrote to the head of Whitman's Candy for calling one of its products "Pickaninny Peppermints—Chocolate Covered." The picture on the box was a total stereotype of black children. The company's attorney responded that he was surprised that the word "pickaninny" was distasteful, thinking it referred to a cute Negro child. After a lengthy exchange of letters and attention from black newspapers, Whitman dropped the offensive name.

The banal complaints based on feigned claims of ignorance were far outnumbered by letters revealing just how bad life was for black people in the early decades of the twentieth century. Consider the tenant farmers and those held in peonage—hardly different from slavery—who with no legal recourse were regularly cheated out of the products of their labor. Or the New Mexico school that because it had few Negro children felt justified in hiring just one black teacher to cover grades one through junior high school, all in one small building. Or the disenfranchised blacks in Texas. Marshall's organizing efforts there were eventually successful in challenging the white primary, which had effectively prevented blacks from taking part in the only election that counted in a state dominated by the Democratic Party.

From 1938, when his mentor, Charles Hamilton Houston, resigned as special counsel of the NAACP, to 1943, Marshall handled all the NAACP matters on his own or with the help of volunteers. The growing number of complaints from Negro soldiers required that he hire two lawyers that year, and it was in 1944 that he hired Robert Carter as his assistant. As he complained to the NAACP leaders Walter White and Roy Wilkins, Marshall's budget was, at best, minuscule. Over the years that followed and despite an impressive list of legal victories, money was always tight. When Marshall hired me in 1959, five years after the *Brown v. Board* victory, he had to stretch to meet the salary I was supposed to earn as director of the Pittsburgh NAACP branch. Even more amazing, I became only the fifth member of the Legal Defense Fund legal staff. As of early 1960, the staff consisted of Marshall, Jack Greenberg, Constance Baker Motley, James Nabrit, and me. Robert Carter had replaced Marshall as NAACP general counsel.

By that point, Thurgood Marshall was a national hero in the black community, but he never lost his folksy touch. He used mock humor when one day I asked how he had fortified himself for his many trips to the South, particularly to small towns where some racial outrage had taken place. "Well," he replied, "when I got off the train and saw and felt all that racial hostility, I reached for my civil rights," illustrating his action by taking out his handkerchief, "folded them up very carefully, put them down deep in my back pocket, and kept them there until I finished my business, got back on that train heading out of that damn place."

I nodded at his story but often thought of it later as I traveled to places in Mississippi and Alabama, less dangerous than in the 1930s but hardly places of safety for blacks not willing to stay in their place, let alone outside agitators who came just to stir them up. On those trips, like Marshall before me, I was buoyed up by the realization that we were visitors providing legal advice and counsel to the local blacks challenging the segregated status quo—the courageous men and women who lived there and would not accompany us as we left by train or plane.

It would be wonderful to urge reading Thurgood Marshall's letters as an informal but quite revealing history of black life, a history now transformed by time and events. But what has not disappeared is the deep suspicion among many whites that blacks as a group, as opposed to those they know well, are not as worthy as and in fact are not the equal of whites. In times of economic crisis, these fears are easily aroused and manipulated into racist attacks on President Obama and calls for a return to the old days. Marshall's letters remind us of what those old days were like. More important, they remind us that there were few voices speaking out against the outrage of injustice, too many rationalizations, too few warnings that the biased attacks against blacks served to shield the reality of the economic and political systems of upper-class domination that disadvantaged most whites.

Considered against current events, the message of Marshall's letters written more than seventy years ago suggests a future that echoes back to the infamous words of Thomas Jefferson: "When I consider that God is just, I fear for the future of my country."

INTRODUCTION

A Young Rebel

The twentieth century saw the emergence of the two greatest civil rights leaders in the history of the United States—Martin Luther King, Jr., and Thurgood Marshall.

While King's legacy is familiar to us—we hear his dramatic dream echoing through history every year—we forget that it was Marshall's shoulders that King stood on when he announced that he had seen the Promised Land.

Commentators often state that the time was right for King to emerge as forcefully as he did, and King himself talked about the zeitgeist of history being far more important than his own role in galvanizing the civil rights movement. But what many of us fail to note is that the time was right exactly because Marshall had already pushed the clock ahead, sometimes single-handedly. For twenty long years before King assumed leadership of the Montgomery bus boycott in 1955, Thurgood Marshall, the young NAACP attorney known to everyday blacks as "Mr. Civil Rights," struggled day and night against racial discrimination and segregation in schools, transportation, the military, businesses, voting booths, courtrooms, and neighborhoods.

Long before King traveled North for graduate school at Boston University, Marshall had already won a case that allowed Donald Murray, a young African American man, to matriculate at a law school *south* of the Mason-

Dixon Line (*Murray v. Maryland*). It was a landmark case that began to open doors, however slowly, for young African Americans who wanted to attend graduate and professional schools in their own communities in the South.

A decade before King gained the right for Rosa Parks and other African Americans to ride the buses of Montgomery without being told to sit in the back—actually, it was Marshall and his associate Robert Carter who filed the suit that led to integrated buses in Montgomery (*Gayle v. Browder*)—Marshall had won a Supreme Court decision that ruled that a state's segregation statutes did not apply to interstate passengers (*Morgan v. Virginia*). This historic 1946 ruling led to the first Freedom Riders, not John Lewis and his colleagues in 1961, but an interracial group of brave young adults who boarded buses in 1947 in order to test the Supreme Court decision. Some of them ended up in chain gangs.

Years before Southern cops dragged a frightened-looking King to jail and snapped his mug shot, Marshall had found himself in the back of a police car in Tennessee, shortly after defending so-called rioters in Columbia, and fearing for his life as the police drove him toward the infamous Duck River. It didn't take long for him to imagine, especially because he had already sought justice in so many Southern lynchings, that he might be witness to his own.

Decades before King delivered the speech of the century—"I have a dream"—and shared his hope that "little black boys and black girls will be able to join hands with little white boys and white girls as sisters and brothers," Marshall had plotted strategy for the desegregation of education, and all that goes with it, including recess on the elementary school playground, in public schools ranging from kindergarten through the university level. As most of us know, Marshall and his legal team had triumphed in *Brown v. Board of Education* more than a year before Rosa Parks refused to surrender her seat. But what most of us still don't know is that Marshall had been plotting the desegregation of public education for two long decades before the 1954 victory (after *Murray v. Maryland*, for example, *Sipuel v. Oklahoma State Regents*, *Sweatt v. Painter*, and *McLaurin v. Oklahoma State Regents*).

Well before J. Edgar Hoover wiretapped King's hotel rooms and used tapes of the civil rights leader's sexual dalliances in hideously threatening ways, Marshall had earned Hoover's wrath by criticizing the inability of the FBI to locate individuals guilty of race-based crimes against African Americans in the South. If the FBI could sniff out communists in the most unsuspecting places, Marshall wondered, why, for God's sake, couldn't it identify whites who committed their crimes in broad daylight?

Fifteen years before King eulogized four little girls who were murdered in the bombing of Sixteenth Street Baptist Church in Birmingham, Marshall had already appealed to the U.S. attorney general to make "Bombingham" a safer place for blacks. In 1949, for instance, Marshall complained directly to the attorney general after three houses owned by African Americans in Birmingham had been dynamited—an act that Marshall believed had the support of Birmingham's thuggish chief of police, Eugene "Bull" Connor.

Two decades before "Bloody Sunday," the 1965 clubbing and gassing of nonviolent marchers by state troopers positioned just outside Selma, Alabama, and the resulting march from Selma to Montgomery, when King led his followers in a protest for voting rights, Marshall had already won a Supreme Court decision against the "white primary," a tool that Southern whites used to prevent African Americans from voting in Democratic primaries (*Smith v. Allwright*). Because the Democratic Party ruled the South at this point, the denial of the right to vote in primaries effectively meant that black voters had no real say in choosing their political leaders.

More than fifteen years before King moved to a Chicago ghetto and decried real estate practices that encouraged segregated neighborhoods, Marshall had won yet another historic decision, arguably his most important victory ever, when the Supreme Court unanimously ruled on May 3, 1948, that racially restrictive covenants—property covenants that prevented African Americans and other racial minorities from owning or occupying real estate in white areas—were legally unenforceable (*Shelley v. Kraemer*). Marshall firmly believed that deep integration would never happen until blacks and whites could not only study and work together but also live together as neighbors.

A generation before King railed against the disproportionate number of African Americans dying on the front lines of the Vietnam War, Marshall had protested the disproportionate number of court-martials against black soldiers during the Korean War. Marshall had flown to Korea and learned firsthand that black soldiers were the first to be sacrificed in the war's most dangerous battle zones. Marshall had also lodged a protest with the army's supreme segregationist, General Douglas MacArthur, about the segregation of soldiers. Had Marshall had his own way, the Tuskegee Airmen celebrated during the inauguration of Barack Obama would never have had the chance to be trained at Tuskegee in the first place. Marshall detested Tuskegee, and he took measures to get the War Department to halt its plans to establish the segregated training base for black pilots.

And long before King led Memphis sanitation workers in their strike for economic justice, their black-and-white pickets proclaiming "I Am a Man," Marshall had lobbied not only welfare agencies to increase payments for heartbreaking cases of poor African Americans but also President Truman to establish a system of universal health coverage. Beyond this, beginning as far back as his student years at Howard Law, Marshall himself had picketed for racial justice. Reflecting on his picketing years later, after he had become a Supreme Court justice, Marshall stated: "I guess I'm an old rebel anyhow."

Unfortunately, this "old rebel" seems to slip from our collective memory with each passing year. Even those who should know better tend to overlook Marshall's civil rights legacy. For instance, a few days before the inauguration of Barack Obama, as planning was under way for "a civil rights victory party on the mall," Jesse Jackson stated: "It is a huge civil rights moment. Barack Obama has run the last lap of a fifty-four-year race for civil rights."

Granted, fifty-four years ago saw the arrival of the Montgomery bus boycott, the heroic movement launched by Rosa Parks, a courageous seamstress with a cause, and E. D. Nixon, the fearless local NAACP leader. But the Montgomery boycott, however earthshaking it turned out to be on the American landscape, was the beginning of the *modern* civil rights movement, not the entire movement for civil rights in America.

Jackson is not the only guilty party of recent times. The famed historian Mark Noll has just authored *God and Race in American Politics*, and Thurgood Marshall, despite his countless speeches before black churches throughout the South in his long campaign for civil rights in the 1930s, '40s, and '50s, makes not even one appearance in the whole book. Martin Luther King, Jr., is a main figure, of course, and even Billy Graham appears several times.

No doubt, it's easier to recall the marches and protests and rallies of Martin Luther King, Jr., than the nitty-gritty work of a civil rights lawyer constructing painstaking, even tedious, arguments to win one civil rights case after another in order to establish a small legal precedent that might yield a victory at the Supreme Court.

Even if we do occasionally remember Marshall, we tend to think of him merely as "the first African American Supreme Court Justice" without considering the monumental civil rights work he undertook during his many years with the NAACP—the exact same work that led John Kennedy to consider appointing him to the federal bench in the first place, and Lyndon Johnson to contemplate elevating him to Solicitor General and the nation's highest court.

The result is a grave injustice to Thurgood Marshall.

Marshall, of course, is not the only significant figure other than King in the three-hundred-year race for civil rights in America. And recent civil rights literature has rightly begun to tend to the contributions of not only lesser-known figures who made King's work so successful but also to those who built the NAACP at the turn of the twentieth century and, before that, who fought slavery, Reconstruction, peonage, and so much more. Both Marshall and King stood high on the shoulders of countless blacks and sympathetic whites, most of them unnamed and unknown, who dared to say "no" to a system that de-Americanized—and dehumanized—African American men, women, boys, and girls.

But I do want to suggest that Thurgood Marshall was the most important, effective, successful, and powerful civil rights leader before Martin Luther King, Jr., came on the scene in 1955, and that the more fully we grasp Marshall's invaluable work in securing civil rights for all Americans, the better we will understand the historical forces that gave rise not only to King as the greatest civil rights leader of the second half of the twentieth century but also to all of the resulting civil rights victories—including the election of our country's first black president.

In fact, it was Marshall's historic work in shattering the backbone of the white primary, not just the explosion of African American voters on the rolls following the 1965 Voting Rights Act, that laid much of the electoral groundwork required for the eventual success of numerous African American politicians, everyone from John Lewis of Georgia, the former president of the Student Nonviolent Coordinating Committee, to Barack Obama.

This is just one facet of the fascinating story of Thurgood Marshall before the advent of Martin Luther King, Jr. The rest of the story is found in the complex maze of documents known as the NAACP Papers deposited at the Library of Congress—thousands upon thousands of memoranda, interoffice notes, and letters to politicians, NAACP supporters, government officials, Southern segregationists, and everyday people in desperate need of legal assistance in the face of a justice system stacked against them.

The NAACP Papers fill out our limited picture of Thurgood Marshall, and in the pages ahead, which are filled with Marshall's own notes, memoranda, and letters, you will encounter him in a new way. You most likely know Marshall as a liberal Supreme Court justice—one who voted to grant criminals the right to an attorney upon their arrest, to assure adults the right to access pornography, to keep even the most vicious of criminals from facing capital punishment, to allow publication of the Pentagon Papers, to give women the right to abortions, to support busing as a tool to end segregation in public schools, to sustain affirmative action policies, and to strengthen the separation between church and state.

While all of this is essential information about Thurgood Marshall, there is so much more to know about him, especially in his early years, and in the pages ahead you will come to a deeper understanding of both Marshall and the radical roots underlying his relentless advocacy for those on the underbelly of society.

You will not encounter the first African American on the Supreme Court, but you will experience the dramatic evolution of a young attorney into a fighter of great courage, a brave young man who kept his eyes on the prize during very difficult times. You will see the NAACP's robust lead counsel loudly criticizing U.S. presidents, business leaders, attorneys general, military generals, school board directors, and anyone else who dared to stand in the way of constitutionally assured rights for African Americans. And you will meet a tireless civil rights leader who lobbied Congress for antilynching legislation, advocated for the presence of blacks on federal courts, threatened businesses that dared to use the word "nigger" when pushing their products, stood shoulder to shoulder with black soldiers accused of cowardice, and sent sympathy notes to mothers whose sons were unfairly sentenced to death.

In short, you will see a brawny young man wielding the U.S. Constitution as if it were a sword intended to cut down the mighty in defense of the weak.

Better stated, you will *hear* this youthful Thurgood Marshall—and in his own blunt words. You will hear a straight-shooting attorney say, sometimes harshly, other times affectionately, but all the time directly, that racial discrimination against any American is always and everywhere unlawful, unjust, and immoral.

It was a message that got him into lots of trouble.

Communists saw him as too oriented toward the status quo, but J. Edgar Hoover, the infamous director of the FBI, saw him as threatening enough to warrant surveillance (although Marshall eventually became an informant for the FBI). Black gradualists found him uncomfortably immobile in his stance against the "separate but equal" doctrine, while other grassroots activists found his legal wrangling to be too lengthy and burdensome for accomplishing immediate goals. At once, Marshall was an "Uncle

Tom" and a political radical, an uncompromising absolutist and a compromising plodder. Indeed, the Marshall who appears in the pages ahead is far more complicated—far more nuanced in his politics—than the one-dimensional liberal that his critics described him as during his years on the Supreme Court.

Expect to be surprised—at his courage, his compromises, his convictions, and perhaps most of all, the scope of his work. When I first started this project, I struggled quite a bit with the question of how best to organize the letters. One of the tempting options was to organize them topically. But it did not take too long for me to settle on a chronological order, partly because I wanted you, the reader, to have a sense of the fullness of Marshall's legal plate throughout his tenure with the NAACP.

His plate overflowed—always.

Consider 1940. In that year alone, Marshall protested, among other things, discrimination in the armed forces, the NAACP's small budget lines for legal defense, the all-white primary in Texas, unequal salaries between white and black teachers in public schools, racial discrimination in labor unions, racially restrictive covenants used by the Federal Housing Administration, the failure of the Dies Committee (what would become known as the House Un-American Activities Committee) to address the violence of the Ku Klux Klan, the lynching of African Americans, the Venezuelan government's refusal to grant landing privileges to black sailors, countless individual cases of discrimination, and so much more.

There was nothing unusual about 1940. Each year saw Marshall addressing a wide variety of racial problems, all of them important and some of them requiring years to resolve. Beyond the issues just noted, the list of race-related problems Marshall dealt with is simply breathtaking. Coerced confessions, mob violence, election fraud, racist politicians, all-white juries, an obstinate FBI, chain gangs, discriminatory insurance practices, the National Association for the Advancement of White People, segregation in blood collection, communist efforts to assume leadership of the NAACP, resistance within the NAACP itself—these are just a *few* of the problems that you'll see Marshall fighting in the letters ahead.

The chronological order of the book will help you sense not only the ongoing fullness of Marshall's legal plate but also the shifting emphases of his career with the NAACP. Although it is clear that sometimes the issues chose Marshall—for example, the arrival of World War II forced him to shift his attention to discrimination in the armed forces, and the bus boycott in Montgomery demanded that he address the surprising tactics of a new civil rights leader energizing thousands in rallies and on the streets—it is also indisputable that Marshall chose his own pet projects. Early in his career, for instance, he selected the desegregation of the University of Maryland's law school as his first major target. Marshall's mother, Norma, had wanted him to attend there, but he never bothered to apply and instead plotted to get even with the school for refusing admission to qualified black students. The equalization of the salaries of black and white teachers in public schools was another major goal that Marshall selected early in his career. Again, the issue seemed personal: Marshall's mother was a schoolteacher, and he wanted to correct an injustice that she and her family had suffered. And Marshall's dogged determination to desegregate public education, as well as the priority he seemed to grant to education-related cases, was no less personal. It was his way of expressing gratitude to his mentor, Charles Hamilton Houston, the brilliant man who taught Marshall at Howard Law, who became the NAACP's first special counsel, and who had the wisdom to arrange for the NAACP to hire Marshall. It was Houston's plan all along to destroy segregation in the United States by attacking, first and foremost, segregation in public education, and Marshall carried Houston's torch every step of the way during his NAACP career.

Nevertheless, even as there were different points of emphasis in the various stages of his career, many issues of racial injustice were evolving simultaneously throughout his career. Indeed, a benefit of the chronological order of his letters is that it reveals Marshall as a juris juggler. Sometimes he kept the balls in the air (as when he argued two different Supreme Court cases in the same week), and other times his clients in the wider NAACP found themselves thinking that he was dropping their cases. In 1941, for example, E. Norman Lacey, the secretary of the Tampa NAACP, dared to suggest that Marshall was not granting enough attention to a Tampa voting case. After he received Lacey's critical letter, Marshall sent this blistering reply:

> . . . No doubt you, as a layman, might believe as other laymen do that the only thing necessary to file and win a case is to draw up a pleading and put it in court. To give you an idea of what is necessary in these cases: We did research for four years before filing our cases to break down discrimination in state universities; we did research for more than three years, and are still doing research, on the cases to equalize teachers' salaries; we have been working on the question of primaries since 1925, and the first real break is at hand as a result of the recent decision of the United

> States Supreme Court in a case involving a primary in Louisiana. This case, however, is a precedent only where federal officers are being voted for in the primary, and we feel it far wiser to stick to our Texas primary case, which involves a primary for nomination of federal officers.
>
> It seems to me that your entire complaint is that we do not understand the situation in your branch and other small branches, especially in the South. I think you should also realize that it is quite evident you do not understand the situation here in this office. There is one fulltime lawyer on the staff of the NAACP. There are 409 other active branches of the Association throughout the country. There are from fifty to one hundred branches which are semi-active. All of these branches consider this office as the headquarters and quite naturally consider me as their lawyer. In addition to these branches, there are hundreds of individuals who are members of the Association who are constantly writing to us for advice. In order that the record may be completely straight, I hope you realize that I have other duties in addition to the legal work which come about because of the fact that we are forced to maintain a limited staff in order to keep within our budget. This should, I feel, give you a fairly accurate picture of what we are up against.

The chronology will help you experience Marshall's building frustrations with the overwhelming nature of his job, but you'll also learn that even after he hired other attorneys to join him on the NAACP staff, his legal plate continued to overflow. It seems that the more successful he became, the more work his office attracted. And let's not forget that while he was fighting racial injustice in all of its various forms, Marshall also had to deal with numerous personal threats to his life—in fact, he was almost lynched in 1946, as you will read in his chilling report of the time white police officers drove him to the infamous Duck River in Tennessee.

But Marshall survived—and flourished—throughout his career with the NAACP. Thanks to the work of Walter White, Roy Wilkins, and Charles Hamilton Houston, the NAACP was already the major civil rights organization in the United States when Marshall began his tenure there. Once ensconced in the NAACP's headquarters in New York, which gave him a national platform for his civil rights work, Marshall then led the Association to heights unimaginable as he and his team won one landmark Supreme Court case after another, culminating in the *Brown* decision of 1954.

Although fringe groups on the left had long considered the NAACP to be too conservative in its approach, it was really not until after King's rise to national prominence that discontent with the NAACP became more diffused throughout the wider African American community. The main criticism was that the Association focused too much on courtroom tactics and not enough on the street tactics that would attract the masses. Interestingly, Marshall was aware of the criticism long before 1957, and you'll learn that he wisely encouraged the NAACP's leaders to take more direct political action while he gave the bulk of his attention to advancing the cause of civil rights through legal action. While he kept his eyes focused on the legal prize, Marshall also kept a foot on the street.

If there is anything crystal-clear in the pages before you, it is that Marshall planted many of the radical roots of the modern civil rights movement as well as ongoing civil rights victories. Equally important, though, is the undeniable fact that his accomplishments with the NAACP help us to better imagine the possibilities for tomorrow.

Once again, in the immediate years ahead, we will see dramatic changes in the makeup of the federal courts, and an important lesson in the pages ahead is that the U.S. president need not choose someone who is politically safe, uncontroversial, unbiased, or broad in professional experience when filling vacancies on the federal benches.

Marshall was anything but conventional when Kennedy appointed him to become a federal judge. Given the power of Southern congressmen at the time, Marshall was a risky choice for the court. Because he could be such a maverick, various constituencies considered Marshall a controversial choice. Given his advocacy work with the NAACP, he was naturally biased in favor of those on the underbelly of society. And because he focused on fighting racial segregation and discrimination during his many years with the NAACP, his law experience was singular in focus.

Yet, when all was said and done, after the Southern segregationists had their say, after Southern attorneys characterized Marshall as "biased and bigoted," after conservative commentators wrote their nasty columns, and after racist whites registered their complaints to their representatives, John Kennedy and, later, Lyndon Johnson stood by their risky, controversial, biased, and singularly focused nominee.

And there's little question we have become a better nation for it—better attuned than we otherwise would have been to the needs of minorities, pregnant women, the underclass, people on death row, criminals subject to overanxious law enforcement officials, and everyday citizens in need of protection from a criminal president.

Yes, the time is ripe for remembering Thurgood Marshall during his tenure with the NAACP, and we can do no better than to hear him once again in his own rebellious voice—unfiltered and uncensored, reasonable and wrathful, passionate and prophetic—for our own operatic times.

A NOTE ON THE TEXT

In editing Thurgood Marshall's letters from his tenure with the NAACP, I have made minimal changes to correct misspellings, typographical errors, and run-on sentences. Because I wish to preserve the cadence found in many of the letters, all of my changes are "silent"; they are not marked by the use of brackets or [*sic*].

Marshall normally typed his own letters when he was on the NAACP circuit, traveling from branch to branch throughout the country, and these are perhaps the most enjoyable letters to look at, primarily because he rarely stopped to correct his many errors. He plowed ahead, typing furiously, and lucky for us, leaving behind documents that give insight into his forceful personality.

In the office, Marshall sometimes wrote letters by hand on yellow legal paper, usually with a blue pen, and then instructed his secretaries to type the letters at a later point. In addition, he often dictated instructions for writing letters, or sometimes the full letters themselves, that his assistants and secretaries later drafted and he signed. In these latter instances, he reviewed the letters that went out under his name to be sure that they were correct and that he could stand behind them. Marshall also occasionally wrote letters that his boss, Walter White, would sign.

Marshall was a devoted letter writer during the early part of his tenure with the NAACP, and most of his letters in the NAACP Papers span the years 1934–1949. The amount of letters Marshall authored and generated is simply breathtaking, especially when one considers that for several years

Marshall was the only lawyer on staff at the NAACP. But his letter production dropped off as he took on more staff members and allowed them to write the letters that he would otherwise have written. It also seems that his letter production dipped markedly as he became consumed by *Brown v. The Board of Education of Topeka, Kansas*, and related cases.

Although he was a devoted letter writer, Marshall did not compose letters about every aspect of his civil rights work during his years with the NAACP, let alone every civil rights issue, or all the personalities he encountered, and if there are apparent gaps in the book, it is most likely because I could not locate letters that he wrote on the subject. Sometimes, rather than sitting down to write or dictate a letter, Marshall would work the phones, as he did frequently with the Department of Justice. I have searched in numerous libraries and archives across the country, from Talladega College in Alabama to the University of California at Berkeley, but I do not claim to have exhausted all possible sources for Marshall's letters during his NAACP years.

Finally, the letters in this volume come from the time period beginning in 1934 and ending in 1957, the last year that Thurgood Marshall served as special counsel to the NAACP.

MARSHALLING JUSTICE

CHAPTER ONE

1935–1936

MARSHALL TO SENATOR MILLARD TYDINGS

Fresh out of law school, Marshall opened a private practice in Baltimore, became legal counsel for the local NAACP, and soon found himself lobbying Senator Millard Tydings of Maryland to support antilynching legislation. Although his earlier correspondence with Tydings was genteel in tone, the following letter is an excellent example of Marshall's fierce opposition to the "states' rights" argument often advanced by pro-segregationists. On a lighter note, the letter also shows that the young attorney could be a bit verbose, especially when dealing with prominent opponents.

Marshall refers below to Charles Hamilton Houston, the rigorous dean of Howard University's School of Law when Marshall attended there from 1930 to 1933. Marshall often depicted Houston, who left Howard to become special counsel to the NAACP in 1935, as his most important mentor. It was Houston who taught Marshall that lawyers should use their skills to eliminate discrimination and segregation—indeed, to transform U.S. society.

MARCH 18, 1935

My Dear Senator:

Allow me to thank you for your letter of February 16th concerning your position on the Costigan-Wagner anti-lynching bill. After careful consideration of the same, I respectfully submit that in view of the facts as they actually exist today, your reasons are unsound.

You claim to be unable to decide because of the fact that you " . . . have been much right of a stickler for local self-government in matters that were local rather than national." Permit me to remind you that this argument is never raised when the dominating element of a state comes to the federal government begging for loans or financial assistance. The local papers have been carrying stories every day of you, with hands outstretched, bending every effort to secure additional funds from the federal government to aid your state, yet when a measure is proposed to curtail the exploitation of the helpless element of the state—to protect them in their lives and property—to merely assure to them what is guaranteed by the Constitution—you raise the same outstretched hands in defense of state rights.

This bill does not deprive the states of a single right which they now have. When the officers of the state either act on behalf of the mob or fail to use reasonable means to prevent them from acting, as was done in the lynching of Claude Neal in Florida; when daily newspapers told of the proposed outrage and invited all to attend; and when after the lynching was over, the lawless element with the sanction of the officials of the state continued to spew their venomous wrath upon innocent, law-abiding, tax-paying Negro citizens; and when after all this the state officials, despite numerous requests from individuals and organizations all over the country, refused to act—how in the name of justice and decency can anyone talk of protecting the rights of such a state when it has forfeited all rights to be classed as a state because of open treason and rebellion?

There is another equally familiar example in the Williams and Armwood lynchings in our state. The attorney general of the state was forced to admit that there was a breakdown of law enforcement machinery—that despite the fact that there were sworn statements of trustworthy witnesses identifying members of the mob—the officials of the county refused to prosecute them. The lynchers received the sanction of some of the "respectable" citizens, and a former Maryland senator in an open letter commended them. The governor and the attorney general attempted to exert the powers of this sovereign state and the troops were routed and the attorney general, representing the governor and the state of Maryland, was set upon and assaulted. Since that time nothing has been done in any way either to punish the murderers or to prevent future outrages. May I ask what you have done either as an individual or as a high official of the state to remedy or alleviate this situation? Because of the inactivity of the judicial, the executive and the legislative branches of this state to function at all, we are driven to the inevitable conclusion that there has been an open and *successful* rebellion depriving this state of its rights to be classed as a "sovereign" state.

. . .

Continuing, you advance the belief that " . . . one of the primary urges in some of the lynchings has been the failure of the courts to function properly and the long delays in bringing the accused to trial disgust the people with the machinery of justice." In view of publications, statistics and testimony at the hearings on this bill last year and this year, I am much surprised that you should advance such a theory. It is an absolute fact that the majority of the lynchings have taken place in isolated remote areas of the Deep South where no persons, not even the bitterest enemies of this bill, would dare assert that when Negroes are accused of serious crimes against white persons there would be the slightest delay in bringing them to trial. . . .

. . . No, my dear Senator, it is not that the people are disgusted with delays, because there have been none; rather, it is an established fact that the reason is the economic exploitation of the Negroes by those in power. This fact is established by the Southern Commission, as exemplified in the Tuscaloosa outrages, the Claude Neal lynching and the Armwood lynching, when, to continue their exploitation, the mob after each lynching went into the Negro settlements and proceeded to cast fear into the minds of the people there. Such an excuse is merely a weak attempt to justify the actions of barbaric "citizens" hiding behind the cloaks of those who will attempt to protect them in a demand for state rights.

. . .

In conclusion permit me to quote from the testimony of Charles H. Houston, Esq., before the subcommittee: "But I think you and the country both should know that there is grave disillusionment and deep distrust among large elements of the Negro population, especially in the South." Others who have investigated these conditions made similar statements at that time. Your Negro constituents know the true facts. They do not want to penalize anyone. The only thing they want is protection. Lynching is not only in violation of the rights of the victim involved, but since the majority of the persons lynched are Negroes, mob violence tends to create a sense of insecurity and a distrust of the law in the mind of the entire Negro population. It is needless to point out the grave concern a nation must feel when a large element of her population can find no sense of security or faith in justice through legal means or through their elected representatives.

Again we ask you to consider this bill and prevent the continuation of this form of outrage, which has its roots in the determination to make the Negro the subject of economic exploitation.

Sincerely yours,

Thurgood Marshall

MARSHALL TO SENATOR MILLARD TYDINGS

As soon as he learned that Tydings had planned a trip to the Virgin Islands during the debate and vote on the antilynching bill, Marshall fired off a short telegram of protest. "Understand you insist going to Virgin Islands for last two or three months of Congress despite the fact that you were absent from early part of session," he wrote. "May we urge you to remain in Washington as our representative until bills of such vital importance as the anti-lynching bill are disposed of?" Shocked by Marshall's indignant tone, Tydings replied: "Please couch your telegrams in the future in more genteel language if you want them answered." Marshall backpedals below, but only a bit.

APRIL 10, 1935

Dear Senator Tydings:

My telegram to you of this date was necessarily short and there are certain additional facts that I desire to call to your attention. This proposed trip to the Virgin Islands while Congress is in session has met with opposition from other members of the Committee on Territories and Insular Affairs, and I understand certain members have stated they must resign.

As citizens of the United States, it appears to us that during the regular sessions of Congress, this government is so constructed as to require the counsel and opinion of all senators. This is even more needed in the present session of Congress when the very salvation of the nation is held in the balance and when we, as citizens, can justly expect our representatives to remain on the floor of the Senate to debate and vote upon issues of vital importance to us all. In view of the fact that you were absent during the first part of this session on business of the Committee, and since the Virgin Islands have gone all these years without such exceptional interest as to their welfare, is it unreasonable for us to request you to postpone this trip a few months and remain in Washington to consider and vote upon such important issues as the anti-lynching bill?

As citizens of Maryland, we have an even deeper interest in having you remain in Washington. Perhaps a senator of one of the states not affected by any lynching stigma could leave at this time, but we cannot see how a senator from such a state as Maryland, with its record of lynching atrocities, would not be on the floor when the Costigan-Wagner bill is voted upon. For not only are the interests of the Negro people protected in this bill but also the welfare of the others if we are to follow the article by Gerald Johnson, in the *Evening Sun* of February 22nd, who states: "There is one feature of lynching, however, which appertains to it in such high degree as to make it unique—it is the apotheosis of stupidity, the carnival of idiocy, the repudiation of brains and the enthronement of the empty skull. And the erection of the low-grade moron into a ruler is, after all, about the greatest crime that can be committed against the laws of God or man." Our state of Maryland certainly needs federal protection to prevent such atrocities, and their only method of securing such protection is through their representatives.

My dear Senator, again we urgently request you to remain in Washington until such bills are disposed of.

Very truly yours,

Thurgood Marshall

MARSHALL TO THE MARYLAND STATE BOARD OF EDUCATION

In the early 1930s, Charles Houston had invited Harvard Law professor Nathan Margold to write a report on the most effective legal method for attacking segregation in education. Margold accepted the invitation and concluded that the best way was simply to insist on what the law allowed for under Plessy v. Ferguson *(1896)—black schools equal to their white counterparts. Because states would be either unwilling or unable to foot the bill for equal black schools, Margold argued, they would eventually agree to admit African Americans to white schools. Like Houston, Marshall found Margold's report compelling and decided to fight Baltimore County on this very point.*

Baltimore County had no high school for blacks in 1935, and Marshall held conversations with local activists, especially Lillie May Jackson and Carl Murphy, about desegregating the white schools shortly after he had begun his private practice. After meeting with Jackson and Murphy in the summer of 1935, Marshall assisted thirteen-year-old Margaret Williams (and others) in applying to the all-white high school in Catonsville, and the letter below is part of the groundwork Marshall laid in preparation for filing a suit.

NOVEMBER 14, 1935

Gentlemen:

The Board of Education of Baltimore County maintains, according to its annual report, twelve high schools designated "white high." No separate high schools are maintained for the education of Negroes in Baltimore County. It has been, and is still, the policy of the Baltimore County Board of Education to refuse to admit qualified Negro students to the "white high" schools of the county. The Negro residents and taxpayers of Baltimore County are without high school facilities in the county where, at the same time, adequate high school facilities are maintained for all other races and classes in said county.

Repeated petitions and requests over a period of years have been made to the Baltimore County Board of Education requesting the establishment of high schools in Baltimore County for the education of Negroes. All such petitions have been denied.

On October 2, 1935, at the regular meeting of the Board of Education of Baltimore County, a petition (copy of which is herein enclosed) was presented. The Board of Education refused to receive or consider this petition, and definitely refused to establish high school facilities in Baltimore County for Negroes.

The decision of the Board of Education of Baltimore County was unlawful, arbitrary and in violation of the Constitution of the United States and the Constitution and laws of the state of Maryland.

Therefore, the petitioners, whose names appear on the enclosed petition, appeal to this Board to hear this petition and a representative of the petitioners, and to require the Board of Education of Baltimore County to maintain the educational system of that county in accordance with the law, and to establish and maintain adequate high school facilities in Baltimore County for the education of Negroes equal to those maintained for other citizens of said county.

Will you please advise me of the date set for the next regular meeting of the State Board?

Very truly yours,

Thurgood Marshall

After Catonsville High denied admission to Williams, Marshall filed suit, in March 1936, with the intention of forcing Baltimore County to construct a separate—and equal—high school for blacks. Murphy, the publisher and editor of the Afro-American *in Baltimore, bankrolled the effort and became Marshall's mentor along the way. During the trial, Marshall sent Charles Houston an update reporting that the opposing counsel "injected prejudice throughout the argument, pleading that there was a Negro girl trying to crash into the white school and trying to break down the traits of the state of Maryland. They did not cite a single case other than the* Gong Lum *case, and we had to tell them the citation of that case." However inept the opposing counsel might have been, Judge Frank Duncan merely ruled that Margaret Williams was ineligible to attend the all-white high school because she had failed to pass the qualifying exam; he refused to rule on the school board's failure to provide a high school for African Americans. A defeated Marshall did not appeal the decision.*

WALTER WHITE TO MARSHALL

Marshall's mother, Norma, had wanted him to attend the University of Maryland School of Law, but the school was all white and Marshall did not even bother to apply. Shortly after graduating from Howard, where he had strategized with Charles Houston about desegregation in public schools, Marshall began to lay plans to desegregate the University of Maryland.

Showing enormous ambition at the age of twenty-six, Marshall wanted to "get even with Maryland for not letting me go to its law school," and in December 1934, more than a full year after he had initially hoped to get the Maryland case up and running, he helped to recruit Donald Murray, a black graduate of Amherst College, to apply to the law school. Predictably, Maryland denied Murray admission because of his race, and Marshall joined Houston, the NAACP's special counsel, in representing Murray in his suit against the university. The suit was filed on April 20 and, with Houston as lead counsel, the attorneys argued in the summer of 1935 that the university had violated the Fourteenth Amendment when it turned down Murray's application. Judge Eugene O'Dunne ruled in favor of Murray, and Marshall's stature rose in both the NAACP and the wider African American community.

Marshall truly liked Murray and took an active interest in his personal success. When the eager student noted that he did not have enough money to pay his tuition, for example, Marshall and Houston successfully encouraged the NAACP to help foot his bills. Marshall also personally escorted Murray to campus and sought out racially progressive students who might befriend the new student, and Houston instructed Marshall to review Murray's notebooks and arrange for tutoring. "Start working on this at once because whatever happens, we must not have this boy fail his examinations," Houston wrote on January 3. "We have got to teach him how to answer questions, too. Impress upon Murray also that from now on, girls are nix until after his examinations."

Maryland appealed—and lost—the Murray *decision handed down by Judge O'Dunne, and in the note below Walter White, the secretary of the NAACP from 1929 to 1955, sends his congratulations to Marshall. White could be rather stingy with NAACP funds, but he was deeply impressed with the young attorney from Baltimore. Less impressed were members of the local Ku Klux Klan. Marshall and Murray had received threatening letters during the course of their campaign to desegregate the law school, and Marshall believed some of the letters had come from local KKK members.*

JANUARY 18, 1936

Dear Thurgood:

Here is our check No. 98 in the sum of $265.00 for services and expenses as noted on the enclosed voucher and on your statement of account. I have never sent a check to anyone accompanied by such sincere congratulations as this one. The victory in the University of Maryland case is epoch making and all of us here join in sending our warmest congratulations. Let us know if the University of Maryland desires to appeal to the United States Supreme Court.

Cordially,

Walter White

MARSHALL TO CHARLES HOUSTON

Marshall kept Houston apprised of his political activities. At the end of 1935, for instance, he informed Houston that he had become active in the American League Against War and Fascism, a coalition of liberal groups opposed to war and fascist movements at home and in Europe. Marshall's active role in the league—he was a member of the commission on minority—is early evidence not only of his liberal stance on foreign policy issues but also of his efforts to draw attention to the linkages he saw between fascism and domestic racial injustice. His public opposition to fascism also appeared three years later, when he signed a petition demanding that President Roosevelt revoke an arms embargo against Spain. Liberals like Marshall believed that the embargo prevented the Republican government from defending itself against General Franco as he marched to victory in the Spanish Civil War.

On a more local level, Marshall held credentials that political leftists in Baltimore found attractive, especially his efforts to help organize black workers at Bethlehem Steel and his willingness to defend Bernard Ades, a white lawyer with communist ties who had accused a local judge of racism. After local activists encouraged him to run for a seat in the U.S. House of Representatives, Marshall grew serious enough to solicit Houston's advice in the following letter. The plan was for Marshall, a registered Democrat, to run as an independent.

JANUARY 21, 1936

Dear Charlie:

The gang that has been trying to get me to run for Congress has just left the office. The fellow whom I thought was a communist has turned out not to be. One of them is a socialist, the other is Jones, I.L.D., of the *Afro*, and the other is a professor at Johns Hopkins University. They intend to call the party something similar to the Independent Voters' League, with the idea of getting endorsements from both the Republican and the Democratic parties for the individual candidate. This will, perhaps, be impossible; yet, on the other hand, there are some members of both parties who will be unable to refuse as individuals.

I am going to talk the matter over with Carl Murphy tomorrow. I have not decided finally as yet and want you to advise me once and for all as to just what you think is best. Of course, your advice will be confidential.

Please let me know before Thursday night what you think best. Perhaps there might be a way to keep the party from being labeled

Communist on the ground that it will be only for the express purpose of electing one man to Congress rather than as a permanent organization.

Ever sincerely,

Thurgood Marshall

Two days later, Houston wired his advice: "Accept candidacy but avoid communism and personal expense." Following part of Houston's advice, Marshall would never align himself, formally or informally, with the Communist Party—indeed, he would later become sharply critical of communism—but contrary to the rest of Houston's advice, he would not run for office.

MARSHALL TO PRESIDENT FRANKLIN ROOSEVELT

This brief telegram is Marshall's first effort to lobby a U.S. president. Roosevelt's failure to speak out against congressional foot-dragging on the antilynching legislation left Marshall frustrated and bitter. "You can't name one bill that passed in the Roosevelt administration for Negroes," he stated years later. "Nothing. We couldn't even get the anti-lynch bill through."

APRIL 22, 1936

The Baltimore Branch of the National Association for the Advancement of Colored People urgently solicits your cooperation toward getting favorable action in the Democratic Caucus of the House on anti-lynching legislation and with particular reference to H.R. 5, H.R. 148 and all identical bills.

Thurgood Marshall

MARSHALL TO REPRESENTATIVE STEPHEN GAMBRILL

Marshall also lobbies Representative Stephen Gambrill of Maryland on the antilynching legislation. Marshall's early lobbying efforts stand in sharp contrast to his later NAACP work, when he focused mostly on legal proceedings and left lobbying to Walter White and his eventual successor, Roy Wilkins, but the remarkable stridency of his tone below would continue unabated throughout his tenure with the NAACP.

APRIL 22, 1936

Hon. Sir:

I received your letter of April 20th concerning the Democratic Caucus on the anti-lynching bills. I have carefully read your letter, and seem to understand some of your views on the matter. In turn I would like to give you our views concerning the same questions.

First, we appreciate your views as mentioned, in that you are bitterly opposed to lynching, but certain groups of American citizens, who have been subjected to this beastly crime, feel that it is no longer adequate to have representatives who are merely opposed to such atrocities unless they are willing to take a stand toward making measures to prevent the same. The time has now arrived when we must demand action.

The Negro people of this community, and other communities in this country, have patiently awaited some form of protection of their lives and property, and are now feeling a certain sense of distrust toward most persons upon whom they should be able to rely.

You also mentioned that you hesitate to give to the federal courts power over such crimes, yet Congress has passed the Lindbergh kidnapping laws, which have the same effect, and the federal government has taken jurisdiction merely on the question of the crossing of state boundaries. To date no question has been raised as to the expediency of such legislation.

From the tone of your letter it seems that you are also numbered in the group favoring states' rights to the bitter end. I cannot, for the life of me, see how a representative from the state of Maryland can raise such a question on lynching in face of the recent occurrences on the Eastern Shore, when that portion of the state was in open rebellion against the chief executive of the state. Neither the law officers nor other law bodies nor the state militia itself could either preserve order or maintain a semblance of justice. Under such circumstances, could the state of Maryland protect its citizens?

. . .

In closing, Mr. Representative, we appreciate your views on the matter, yet we do expect you to consider our views concerning the same questions, and we are repeating that we not only expect our representatives to voice their disapproval of lynching by stating so, but that they take steps to erase this beastly crime from the record of our country.

Very truly yours,

Thurgood Marshall

MARSHALL TO GEORGE CRAWFORD

Roscoe Pound, the dean of Harvard Law School and a frequent guest lecturer at Harvard, had offered Marshall a full scholarship to pursue a doctorate of juridical science following his graduation from Howard, but Marshall was eager to begin practicing law and turned down the prestigious offer. However enthusiastic he might have been, he lost more than $3,000 in his first year as a private attorney.

In the face of mounting debt, Marshall applies to his alma mater for a faculty position. William Hastie, a Howard Law faculty member, wrote a recommendation letter to accompany the application, noting that Marshall was the ranking student of his class. "Mr. Marshall, while a student here, exhibited a scholarly interest in legal literature which was particularly noteworthy," Hastie wrote. "Moreover, as a student assistant to the librarian he showed exceptional ability and initiative in the organization and conduct of the library. Since entering the practice of law both men [Hastie's letter also recommended Edward P. Lovett] have given freely of their time in cases involving issues of general importance in the vindication of civil rights of Negroes through the courts." The following letter, addressed to the chair of Howard's law school committee, nicely captures Marshall's own thoughts about the importance of his early work.

APRIL 23, 1936

Dear Sir:

I have been informed that there is a possibility of certain appointments to the faculty of the Law School of Howard University for the year 1936–37. Under these circumstances, I am making application for a position on the faculty.

It is my belief that there should be, at least, one graduate of the Howard Law School as a fulltime professor on the faculty. I do not believe that there are, at present, any graduates serving in this capacity. There has been, in the past, a bit of opposition to the appointment of law school graduates to the faculty on the basis of "in-breeding." In my case, however, "in-breeding" could not be true because my A.B. degree was obtained from Lincoln University, Pennsylvania, and I have the benefit of college education at one university and professional education at another.

I entered law school in 1930, and was ranking student in my class for the entire three years. I served as student assistant librarian for two years, and created and maintained the card index system now used in the law school library, which compares favorably with the same index systems used in other schools such as Harvard University. I was elected a member of the first Court of Peers, and the next year was elected chief justice of the Court of Peers. In 1933 I was graduated from the law school with a degree of bachelor of law *cum laude*. My record in the law school, I am certain, is available.

In 1933, after graduation in the early part of June, I took the Maryland bar examination within the next two weeks and passed. I was admitted to the Bar of the Court of Appeals of Maryland in October, 1933, and to the Supreme Bench of Baltimore City in November of the same year, after which time I immediately started active practice of the law. Since that time, my experience has been more or less diversified. I have tried many criminal cases including several murder and rape cases. I have received several court appointments to defend prisoners, and in one particular rape case, Judge Owens, of the Supreme Bench of Baltimore City, certified to me the highest fee possible to be paid for a case involving capital punishment.

My civil work has included personal injury cases, property damage cases, contract actions . . . and corporation cases. I am, at present, counsel for the colored laundry in Baltimore city, reputed to be the second largest Negro enterprise in the city, counsel for the only Negro building and loan association in the city, counsel for the colored Funeral Directors' Association and counsel for several prominent individuals in the city. I have also taken part in the trial of several cases of more or less national importance. I was associated with Dr. Charles H. Houston in the case involving the disbarment of one Bernard Adam, a white attorney. This, I have been informed, is the first time Negro attorneys have represented a white attorney in such a procedure.

In September, 1935, I took part in the civil action against a white policeman in Prince George's County, Maryland, charged with killing a

Negro while under arrest, which case resulted in a verdict and judgment of $12,000 in favor of the widow. I was also counsel in the case of *Murray vs. the University of Maryland*, which decided the right of Negro students to attend state institutions. This case went to the Court of Appeals and is being reported in many of the law journals of the country. I am, at present, engaged in a case in Baltimore County involving the establishment of colored high schools.

I am, at present, counsel for the local branch of the NAACP, and chairman of the legal committee. I am secretary of the local bar association and secretary of the National Bar Association. I have also been admitted as a member of the Junior Bar Association in Baltimore City, which is a branch of the American Bar Association. As to my personal history, I am 27 years of age, married and, at present, living in Baltimore City.

If there is the possibility of an appointment on the faculty of the law school, I do hope that this application will be considered, and I stand ready for a personal interview at your convenience.

Sincerely yours,

Thurgood Marshall

Howard did not offer him the job, but Marshall did return the favor to Hastie a year later, shortly after FDR had nominated Hastie for an open seat on federal district court in the Virgin Islands. Marshall asked his friends to lobby senators on the confirmation vote. "Emphasize that the opposition to him on the ground that he is a Negro serves notice to Negro lawyers all over the country that because of color they can never aspire to responsible federal judicial offices, regardless of how superior their qualifications may be," Marshall wrote. On March 26, 1937, after predictable resistance from Southern senators, Hastie became the first African American federal magistrate in the United States.

MARSHALL TO ROY WILKINS

Wilkins, the assistant secretary of the NAACP, visited Baltimore in the early spring to speak with Marshall and the two main leaders of the Baltimore NAACP (Lillie Jackson and Carl Murphy) about plans to hold the Association's twenty-seventh annual convention in the city. During his stay, Wilkins and Marshall frequented a jazz club—and not just for the jazz. When word of their drinking got back to Jackson, she protested to Murphy, and he in turn sent Wilkins a letter condemning the effects of carousing on the local Association's reputation. Marshall was not pleased to learn of the letter, and below is perhaps the most rambling, and unintentionally amusing, letter that he ever wrote on NAACP stationery. Marshall was angling for a job with the national office at the time, and there is little doubt that he must have feared for his ambitions. Marked "personal," the letter is especially fascinating because it adroitly describes the division between the pious members of the NAACP, including many Christian ministers, and the members who were more inclined to take up the sins of the world—like Marshall's smoking, drinking, and nightclubbing. Marshall refers to Daisy Lampkin, the national secretary of the NAACP, and Lillie Jackson's daughter, Juanita.

MAY 4, 1936

Dear Roy:

If possible, will you let me have the letter Carl Murphy sent you about the nite club, and also your replies on the same? It seems to me that if the conference is to come here in June, all personal difficulties should be ironed out long before that time.

I have been attempting to keep peace around here toward the end that everything would move along, but it seems that in order to do this it will be necessary to sacrifice all of my ideas on several matters. One of them is that in view of the fact that you were invited here by the Baltimore branch to talk on that Tuesday, and further, since you were with me at the nite club, it seems that any statement condemning this is an insult to you, the national office, and me. For my part, I am going to take it up at the next executive office committee meeting and demand that the branch officially write you straightening out the entire matter.

I believe we should take a stand on this once and for all, and I shall most certainly insist that so far as I am concerned, I am going to do as I please during my leisure time.

The thought just occurred to me, when I was talking to Daisy Lampkin on Saturday about the whole matter, that, if you remember, Mrs. Jackson was very much put out because you would not consent to have Juanita at the closing of the forum. It seems to me that that forms a basis for her ideas on the matter along with the attempt on her part to inject her personal ideas into the business of the Association. This I am not going to stand for.

I just talked with Carl Murphy and he is of the opinion that since the membership in Baltimore is composed of so many of the element centered around ministers, who are more narrow-minded here than any other place else, it is his belief that those in authority in the Association should be at least careful that these people are not driven away from the fold. As to this statement he is correct on the part of the narrow-minded group exemplified in the president herself. The question is whether we should cater to that group and possibly offend other groups, or whether we should not cater to all groups together. At the same time, I am still of the opinion as set out in the beginning of this letter, and unless I change my mind before the meeting next week, that is the position I am going to take. Or possibly I will just take the matter up with Mrs. Jackson alone now that I have gotten Carl Murphy's views on the matter, which are that he, himself, is not opposed to our actions.

Finally, I am of the opinion that you should not give up any ideas about the conference, and that I guarantee you at least a measured support from my particular group.

Ever sincerely,

Thurgood

[P.S. deleted]

MARSHALL TO CHARLES HOUSTON

In another letter marked "personal," Marshall, who at the time is running his private practice and doing a lot of work for the NAACP pro bono, makes a direct appeal for help in meeting his financial needs. This is one of several letters from this time period in which he wrote of his financial stress—and of his firm commitment to the NAACP. Marshall refers below to his invaluable assistant, Sue Tilghman, who was nicknamed "Little Bits," and to his mother, Norma, whom he fondly called "Mama."

MAY 25, 1936

Dear Charlie:

(2) . . . As it stands, things are getting worse and worse, and first of all, I fully realize that the Association has no money and that there is very little left in the Garland Fund. However, I would like for you and Walter to make sure that there is no possibility of helping me out through here. However, if there is a possibility, I would appreciate it very much if I could be assured of enough to tide me over; then, in return, I could do more on these cases. For example, to prepare briefs and research, etc. on the other cases or any of the legal matters which you would need assistance on.

Just to give you an idea of my expenses, the rent is $21.88 per month, $7.50 per week for "Little Bits" and approximately $6.00 per month for phone bill. Besides, there are, of course, the notes on the car and other items, including stationery and postage.

Personally, I would not give up these cases here in Maryland for anything in the world, but at the same time there is no opportunity to get down to really hustling for business.

In conclusion, I am asking that you see what can be done. Of course, you realize that I know you understand the whole situation, and that you can be perfectly frank, but as the "boys" say, "it has arrived at the point where I just can't take it." Then, too, I must look out for this summer when most of the weight of the house will be on me while Mama is not in school.

Think this over very carefully and do what you can for me.

Sincerely yours,

Thurgood

[P.S. deleted]

CHARLES HOUSTON TO MARSHALL

After the NAACP conference in Baltimore, when Marshall's speech on race and education further impressed Walter White, Houston recommends that Marshall join the NAACP staff. Houston refers to Arthur Spingarn, the president of the NAACP; Warner McGuinn, a prestigious African American attorney who had helped Marshall establish his law practice in Baltimore; and Vivian "Buster" Marshall, Thurgood's first wife. The couple had met in 1928, when Thurgood was a sophomore at Lincoln University and Buster was a first-year student at the University of Pennsylvania, and they married a year later.

SEPTEMBER 17, 1936

Dear Thurgood:

. . .

The Association needs another fulltime lawyer in the national office. I am not only lawyer but evangelist and stump speaker. I think this work necessary in order to back up our legal efforts with the required public support and social force. But it takes me out of the office for long stretches at a time, and slows down the legal work in New York.

There are enough cases in the New York area, New Jersey, Maryland and Virginia to warrant another lawyer, to say nothing of office correspondence, consultation and research. And I will be glad to recommend to Walter and Roy that just as soon as possible they give you an opportunity to come to the national office at $200 a month for six months if that interests you. If so, I suggest that you make a trip to New York to talk with Walter, Roy and Arthur Spingarn, provided Walter writes that there is a remote possibility. I am sending him your memorandum and a copy of this letter.

In case the thing can be worked out, I suggest that you close up the office, simply keeping the room to store your furniture. . . . Leave your telephone on but have a nickel pay telephone installed so that incoming calls may be received. This keeps the continuity of the office and does not make a complete break until the first six months have passed.

I don't know of anybody I would rather have in the office than you or anybody who can do a better job of research and preparation of cases. We have got to contact all the colleges this year, and it is impossible for one person to be in two places at the same time. Two lawyers would always put one in the office, except in rare instances when both might be away for a few days in actual trial.

But before you write Walter about the matter give careful thought to your future in Baltimore. Moving to New York even for six months would mean, even with your office kept open and an arrangement with Mr. McGwinn to take care of your business and calls, almost a total loss of business, and if you returned to Baltimore it would almost mean starting over again.

You have been more than faithful in giving your time to the Association and I know this has meant a sacrifice of private practice, so you can be assured I will do everything in my power to try to make some provision for you; but you know on what a slender financial margin we operate, and Walter knows the finances better than I. So after you have given the matter mature thought, and discussed it with Buster and your family and trusted friends in Baltimore, write Walter. In the meantime he will have your memorandum and a copy of this letter for his own thought.

. . .

Best luck, and here's hoping you every possible success in Towson.

Regards to all.

Yours as ever,

Charlie

MARSHALL TO WALTER WHITE

An eager Marshall thanks White for an offer to join the NAACP as assistant first counsel. Later in the month, Marshall and Buster moved to a Harlem apartment where his aunt and uncle also lived. Accustomed to a sparse office, the twenty-eight-year-old Marshall was struck by the apparent luxury of the NAACP headquarters. "How very tush-tush," he uttered upon seeing his new office space at 69 Fifth Avenue.

The letter below refers to Houston's efforts to desegregate professional and graduate education in Missouri, where he had recruited Lloyd Gaines, a black college graduate, to apply to the state's all-white law school. Missouri was significant because it had no law school for blacks, and Houston believed that if states were unwilling to build separate but equal law schools, judges would force them to integrate their white schools.

OCTOBER 6, 1936

Dear Walter:

Thanks for your letter of October 5th. Might I say that I am very happy about it all, and, further, that I will be indebted to you and Charlie for a long time to come for many reasons, one of which is that I have an opportunity now to do what I have always dreamed of doing! That is, to actually concentrate on the type of work the Association is doing.

. . .

Enclosed is copy of a letter to Charlie concerning my work from now on. To be very brief, I have been arranging to have my private practice, what little there is of it, transferred to Mr. Warner T. McGuinn, who is going to take it over. This is practically straightened out now.

Pursuant to Charlie's instructions, I have been giving almost fulltime work since the first of the month, completing the Baltimore County case, and since Saturday, I have been working on the Missouri case. Let me know whether or not it will be all right for me to finish up this work in the Supreme Court Library on the Missouri case before coming to New York, or if you prefer, I could easily come to New York and run down and finish this work. It seems to me that it would be better to get over with it now. Whatever you advise can be worked out.

I have had several offers to do work in the Democratic Party here in the state, but have declined them in view of the possibility of my getting this appointment. So all in all, so far as I am concerned, I am ready to come to New York whenever you suggest, or to do whatever else is necessary.

Please let me have your opinion on the letter to Charlie, which I am forwarding to San Francisco and, of course, will not be received before Friday. In view of the shortness of time, I want to get started as soon as possible.

Ever sincerely,

Thurgood

MARSHALL TO WALTER WHITE

From his earliest days at the NAACP, Marshall sought to build a good working relationship with Elisha Scott, the president of the Topeka NAACP and one of the most influential civil rights attorneys in the South. The friendly relationship proved especially significant, and beneficial, when Scott's sons, John and Charles, later filed Brown v. The Board of Education of Topeka, Kansas.

NOVEMBER 10, 1936

Elisha Scott, Esq., president of the Topeka, Kansas, branch, is pushing the prosecution of Cleo Mosler, white, who is charged with shooting and killing one Fred Harvey Smith, Negro, aged 15. It appears that Mosler deliberately shot the boy who was coming up the pathway through a portion of Mosler's premises. It seems that he told the boys to halt and they did; but he, nevertheless, shot the boy point-blank with his 12-gauge shotgun. Two boys were together; one was shot.

The theory of the defense is that there had been chicken stealing in the neighborhood and Mosler shot the boy in self-defense claiming that the boy had not halted and had one hand in his pocket. His other theory is that he shot too quickly. It is obvious that the two theories of the defense are in direct conflict.

The boy's family and friends are poor and have only been able to raise $11 up to date.

In view of the fact that Scott has secured permission from the county attorney to enter the case, I suggest that a modest donation be made toward the expenses in the case and that we contact the branches in Kansas and suggest that Scott have the Topeka branch carry the actual burden of the case.

CHAPTER TWO

1937–1938

MARSHALL TO WALTER WHITE

Marshall's early work with the NAACP included criminal cases dealing with racial violence, and here he begins the New Year with a case about "sex-crazed" white thugs who assaulted three African American residents of New Jersey. The end of this stunning memorandum about racial violence clearly shows that Marshall was just as tough on blacks as he was on whites when he found either to be obstructions to racial justice.

FEBRUARY 2, 1937

Miss Willa Hempfield, Miss Ann Tillman, and Edward Thompson, colored residents of the shore area, were returning to Asbury Park from a social affair in Princeton about 12:30 Friday night. A car containing five white youths was driving recklessly zigzagging across the road, and on being remonstrated with by the colored motorists, the white men became abusive and ended by savagely attacking and beating up Thompson, who was driving the two girls.

Beaten into an unconscious state by his white assailants, the five young white thugs threw his crumpled body into his car and in a spirit of sadistic glee decided to kidnap the girls. Their car was too small to hold all of the crowd so they forced by threats and overwhelming manpower

Miss Hempfield in their car and commanded Miss Tillman, who could drive, to follow them. Fearing for her life, Miss Tillman promised to do so, but when the leading car turned off the main road into a lane leading into the woods, Miss Tillman stepped on the gas and raced her car, continuing down the main highway. In the meantime Miss Tillman had noted and jotted down the number of the kidnapper's car, and at the first opportunity she stopped and called up the police station, notifying them of the assault and kidnapping. A radio alarm went out to all the police cars in the county but for four hours were fruitless of any results as the kidnappers had fled to the woods where, according to the story of Miss Hempfield, she was cruelly forced to submit to the most humiliating and beastly treatment by the sex-crazed youth who had abducted her. Two of the original five men who abducted the girl were put out of the car because of their being too drunk, Miss Hempfield alleged, and her captors, now three in number, speeded their car deeper into the woods. The details of her story are revolting in the extreme and unprintable. For four hours she went through a living hell, and she tearfully and hysterically declared, "I never expected to get out of those woods alive."

However, about 4:30, her captors, having finished their fiendish sport, drove back into the main road and tried to dump the girl out. This she refused to permit. She told the reporter . . . "I intended to stay in that car until I saw a policeman and make my complaint for the way they had mistreated me."

They had hardly proceeded a few hundred feet on the highway when one of the state troopers rode up and arrested the men, and at the station house before Justice of the Peace Fred Quinn, the three men were held for the assault on Thompson, the colored male driver, but, according to Miss Hempfield's story, the judge discouraged her from bringing the rape charge, telling her that the story would not sound nice in court and would be embarrassing to her. It later developed on inquiry that the probable reason that the judge discouraged her from pressing the more serious charge of rape and kidnapping was because the accused youth, John Quinn, Jr., was the judge's nephew.

However, when Miss Hempfield's friends heard her story and she was advised of her rights in the matter, she took her attorney and, backed by colored leaders in the county, made her complaint against another justice of the peace, Elmer Wainwright, who rearrested the trio—three men were charged with kidnapping, three for assault, and one, John Quinn, Jr., was charged with rape. Another surprise angle of this sordid story was the development of the fact that Miss Hempfield was a maid in Judge Edward Knight's family, having worked for the judge's aunt, Mrs. Howard Hulick, for over seven years. Miss Hempfield bears a very excellent reputation, being active in the religious and fraternal life of her community. The colored citizens of this area are watching this case and its development with great interest—and also Judge Knight—who has declared himself as an archenemy of rapists. He will have an opportunity to show whether his indignation runs high . . . when a colored woman is the victim.

. . .

Miss Hempfield was approached by Justice of the Peace Fred Quinn, uncle of the accused youth, who requested her to drop the case because of a long sob story about the poor circumstances of the boy and that his life would be wrecked, etc. This to my mind is justification for seeking the removal of this justice of the peace. . . .

The grand jury convened on the twenty-second of December and received a letter from Miss Hempfield requesting them not to proceed and not to indict Quinn for rape. Several people had talked to members of the grand jury prior to this case and they had agreed to do all in their power to indict this boy, so they refused to receive the letter and issued a subpoena for Miss Hempfield to appear before them on the twenty-ninth. She did not appear on the twenty-ninth but sent a much longer letter setting out in detail her reasons for not wishing to prosecute the case. This information was all brought to light as a result of an investigation of the legal committee of the state conference through Mr. J. Leroy Jordan.

The next day Miss Hempfield is reported to have said that she intended to leave the jurisdiction and she had left for Washington. She is now either in Alabama or Miami, Florida. It is very clear that she has been paid off. But, according to the investigation of Mr. Jordan, there is absolutely no way to prove this.

We had a meeting of the New Jersey state conference in Morristown, New Jersey, on Sunday, January 31. Mr. Jordan reported and upon his suggestion, which I agreed to, the only possible method of continuing the case is to have a group of citizens of Asbury Park approach the Supreme Court justice for that circuit and request him to hold an investigation as to the possibility of an obstruction of justice and an investigation of the methods used to have Miss Hempfield leave the jurisdiction.

We are all fully aware of the fact that this might involve Miss Hempfield as a party to the crime of obstructing justice and of leaving the jurisdiction, but we were all of the opinion that a woman of her type should be in jail the same as the people who paid her the money.

Sincerely yours,

Thurgood Marshall

MARSHALL TO WALTER WHITE

U.S. district attorney offices were often indispensable for achieving racial justice through courts in the South, and here Marshall expresses concern that the district attorney's office in the Eastern District of South Carolina might become home to an attorney who was obviously unfriendly to African American interests. Ben Scott Whaley, in spite of his racist comments, went on to serve as both assistant U.S. attorney and as U.S. attorney for the Eastern District of South Carolina. As the following memorandum to White suggests, Marshall kept a close eye on newspapers across the country.

MARCH 25, 1937

According to the newspaper clipping from the *News Courier*, Charleston, S.C., March 13, 1937, Ben Scott Whaley, secretary to Senator Byrnes, is to be appointed assistant United States district attorney in the Eastern District of South Carolina.

The clipping of March 29, 1936, quotes Whaley as protesting against the mixed audiences in Washington, D.C., attending "Porgy and Bess." He objected to the intermingling of the races and stated that he was astonished to see "a generous sprinkling of Negroes in the audience, all dressed up in stiff shirt, tuxedos and some of them with tails." He told the management that it would lose the patronage of many Southerners.

Do you think it wise to send a copy of this and a protest to the Department of Justice and the Judiciary Committee?

MARSHALL TO JAMES DORSEY

Marshall tries his hand at explaining the significance of race and class in relation to mortality tables, and the result is (for his time) a progressive stance on the relation between race and disease. The letter's recipient, James Dorsey, was an attorney based in Milwaukee.

APRIL 27, 1937

Dear Mr. Dorsey:

. . .

As to your inquiry concerning the higher mortality rate for Negroes and a consequent higher rate for Negro insurance applicants, a check of the mortality tables will show a higher death rate for Negroes. On checking the figures from the U.S. Census Bureau, this fact is verified. The truth of the matter is that Negroes as a whole live on a lower scale economically and socially. And for some reason or other the death rates have been separated as to race. The position has been taken that the mortality tables should be based upon economic levels rather than upon race, and on doing this we will find that the Negro death rate is no higher than the white death rate if made on the same economic level. . . .

Many authorities formerly took the position that diseases, especially pulmonary diseases, were peculiar to Negroes. However, this conception has been abandoned by even the strictest insurance companies who realize that disease is not peculiar to race but rather is based upon the social and economic background.

In a short time, I have attempted to find some authorities to back these statements. I have been informed that Dr. Dublin of the Metropolitan Life Insurance, who has done much to create the illusion that Negroes as such have a higher death rate, acknowledged that he was wrong and that it was an economic question. This article appeared in *Outdoor Life* magazine. We are trying to locate this article and have it copied. If we are able to do so, we will send it to you. However, you will find enclosed an article which bears out our position and which I think should be read into the record at the hearing.

I trust this information will be of service to you and will reach you in time.

Yours sincerely,

Thurgood Marshall

MARSHALL TO S. S. KRESGE COMPANY

Marshall knew all too well that racial discrimination at lunch counters was not confined to the Southern stores where young men and women would protest so effectively in the 1960s.

MAY 20, 1937

Gentlemen:

This office has received complaints concerning the operation of one of your stores, 400 Chillicothe Street, Portsmouth, Ohio. . . . According to these complaints, several Negroes have visited this store, and upon applying at the lunch and soft drink counter to be served, they have been forced to wait an unreasonable length of time and then have been served ice cream and soft drinks mixed with salt and pepper.

I am certain you realize that such actions are contrary to the civil rights act of Ohio and are not to be tolerated.

We have been informed further that the matter was called to the attention of the manager, who refused even to consider the complaint. This matter is being called to your attention in order that you may have an opportunity to prevent a recurrence of these actions. . . .

Very truly yours,

Thurgood Marshall

MARSHALL TO GOVERNOR JAMES ALLRED

On July 2, 1937, an inmate in the Texas state prison system sent the NAACP an anonymous letter requesting assistance for combating cruel prison conditions: "Please hear our cries. . . . These official are sure cruel to us, we have in each building two prisoner as building tenders they is allowed to kill you if they see fit. They have whips with iron handles and dirka knifes. Each one of these building tenders are first grade student and they will do what the captains and guards tell them." Marshall dealt with prison abuse claims frequently in his early years at the NAACP, and below is his letter of protest to the governor of Kentucky. It is typical of countless other protest letters he sent during his tenure with the NAACP.

JULY 31, 1937

Dear Governor Allred:

We have received complaints concerning the treatment of Negro prisoners on the Ramsey State Farm, Camp #1, near Houston, Texas.

We are informed that the Negro prisoners are beaten and, in many cases, killed for trivial reasons.

We are informed that on July 28th of last year, one Booker Smith, in charge of prisoners, killed a prisoner and claimed it was in self-defense. We are also informed that Captain Shaw chained a prisoner with a quarter-inch chain around his neck and fastened it to his feet so that his neck was pulled down to his knees and that the same Booker Smith whipped this prisoner, whose name was James Brown, to death.

We cannot too strongly urge upon you the seriousness of such offenses which, even though committed by persons in charge of a prison, are, nevertheless, brutal murders. These are only a few examples of the intolerable conditions reported to us in the prison camps in Texas, and we urge you to immediately cause an investigation to be made.

Very sincerely yours,

Thurgood Marshall

In reply, Governor Allred simply asked for more information and added: "I am sure that neither the Manager of the State Prison System nor the members of the Prison Board, as well as myself, will tolerate any brutality if we can find evidence that it exists anywhere in the System."

MARSHALL TO J. M. TINSLEY

Of special interest to Marshall was the gross inequity in teacher salaries for blacks and whites. Marshall was very close to his mother, Norma, a schoolteacher in Baltimore city schools, and he knew that, like other black teachers, she suffered at the hands of a school board that paid black teachers far less than it paid white teachers. In a letter at the end of 1934, Marshall reported that he had filed a petition on behalf of William B. Gibbs, Jr., the acting principal of a black elementary school in Montgomery County, Maryland, to equalize teacher salaries in the county. Marshall had recruited Gibbs for the suit, and the NAACP explained the petition in a press release: "The petition recites that Mr. Gibbs is a normal school graduate, holds a first-grade teacher's certificate of the first-class issued by the state department of education of Maryland; that he is receiving a salary of $51 a month, or $612 a year, whereas teachers in white schools in Montgomery County with his same qualifications and experi-

ence and performing essentially the same duties are being paid approximately $98 a month or $1,175 a year."

Fascinatingly, the Montgomery County School Board opted to settle the matter before trial, and in the following letter to the president of the Virginia NAACP, Marshall explains the significance of his landmark victory. He took the settlement as reason to press on throughout Maryland as well as in other states. "The breaking down of this differential in teachers' salaries," he argued, "is a contribution toward removing the economic foundation for the perpetuation of race prejudice in the South. This precedent will have a direct application on all public employment, which will incidentally have its effect on the standards of private industry."

AUGUST 30, 1937

Dear Dr. Tinsley:

As you no doubt know, we were successful in the teachers' salary case in Montgomery County, Maryland. I am sending you under separate cover a few mimeographed statements on this case. This particular case will equalize teachers' salaries in Montgomery County within a year.

This case not only means that the salaries of teachers will be equalized and is a definite step in our campaign to equalize educational opportunities but also has a much wider effect on our entire program. This type of case has, perhaps, one of the greatest appeals to a larger NAACP program in Maryland, and this case means that it is the opening fight to give to Negroes a half million dollars a year because that is the amount of the difference between white and colored teachers' salaries in the state of Maryland. Here, we are actually giving a material benefit to Negroes in general. This money will eventually get into the hands of Negro physicians, dentists, lawyers and other professional and business men. It will do much to raise the standard of living for Negroes; it will also break down the age old tradition that Negroes are not entitled to the same salaries as white men, even though equally qualified to do the same work.

We believe this program should go next into *Virginia* and North Carolina. . . .

MARSHALL TO THE NAACP OFFICE

Marshall followed up his letter to Tinsley with a trip to Virginia and North Carolina, hoping to spark cases related to teacher salaries, voting rights, and better schools for African American children. Below are a few excerpts of an insightful memorandum that he sent from Durham, North Carolina. Marshall's report on South Boston, Virginia, gives clear indication of the lethargy that years of racial discrimination created in some communities, and his report on the NAACP in North Carolina provides evidence that at times local African Americans were quite opposed to the NAACP's presence in their communities, sometimes for reasons related to the NAACP's top-down strategy of pushing local cases.

OCTOBER 17, 1937

. . .

South Boston and Danville, Tuesday.

. . .

South Boston very interesting. In the heart of the tobacco growers. At the present time the people are all in town selling their tobacco. School situation is terrible. Principle of elementary school is gardener and janitor for the county superintendent of schools and is a typical Uncle Tom. New addition to high school at Halifax but not equipped. Elementary schools terrible. Question of voting has not arisen because so few register.

Spoke at mass meeting and stressed school questions and voting questions. Negroes in this community very lax and inactive. President of branch fighting almost alone.

. . .

Charlotte, Thursday, 14th.

Conference with Bowser and Harris and people on franchise question. Negroes vote, 3,500 registered. They run a Negro for the city council every year to keep the Negroes interested in voting—a mighty good idea. However, politicians say that there will be a new registration and a definite effort to keep Negroes off the books. The problem presents itself when too many Negroes get on the books.

. . .

Observations on North Carolina:

1. NAACP. The set-up here is very peculiar and needs careful planning. It seems that after the meeting in Raleigh on the University of North Carolina case, when plans were made to equalize teachers' salaries, that the people who were opposed to equalizing salaries put out the statement that the *outside* Association (NAACP) was coming in to take over the state. The idea has been promoted that North Carolina can handle its own affairs without outsiders. That the NAACP was trying to steal the glory. I have had many conferences where the people were perfectly frank about the whole question. There are many angles to the propaganda that was put out. Certain people were ignored—outside lawyers took over the problem without consulting the *proper* local lawyers—we wrote North Carolina branches to push the fight rather than teachers and citizens in general, etc., etc. All in all we have been put in a bad light all over the state.

. . .

MARSHALL TO WALTER WHITE

Marshall refers to the "Scottsboro Boys"—nine African American youths, ages twelve to nineteen, who were tried and sentenced to death for allegedly raping two white women on a freight train in Alabama in 1931. Two years after the sentencing, Ruby Bates, one of the women who had made the rape charge, recanted her testimony and stated that no rape had occurred. It would take fifteen years of appeals and retrials, as well as national and international media attention, before the last of the Scottsboro defendants would be freed on parole. The following memorandum should lay to rest any notion that Marshall favored only court proceedings in the quest for racial justice in the United States. Equally interesting, however, is that the memo reveals Marshall's strategic thinking about taking an idea that originated in the NAACP's national office and making it appear as if it arose from everyday victims of racial injustice.

NOVEMBER 1, 1937

The article in *The New York Times*, October 31, 1937, by John Temple Graves, II, "Alabama May Free Scottsboro Group," revives in my mind an idea which was discussed last week. Since the Supreme Court of the United States has denied certiorari in the Scottsboro case it seems that the legal proceedings are closed, and the only possible recourse for the freedom of the Scottsboro boys rests with the possibility of a pardon by Governor Graves. The article in *The New York Times* gives new hope to this possibility of a pardon.

The particular idea in mind is to have a large group of mothers from Alabama to visit Governor Graves and request him to pardon the Scottsboro boys. It is our belief that this type of approach might possibly influence Governor Graves to pardon the boys and at the same time influence public opinion to the extent that it will cooperate with Governor Graves in doing so.

The idea would have to be very carefully worked out. In the first place, only mothers from Alabama should participate. They could be transported from all sections of Alabama in automobiles and trucks volunteered by individuals. It is very important that no association or organization should sponsor this idea. It should come wholly from within Alabama. The meeting with Governor Graves should be featured by the singing of spirituals, and the mothers should stress the point that they are not there for the purpose of raising any legal technicalities and that they are not criticizing the state of Alabama but that they are mothers of children and boys like the Scottsboro boys, merely there to plead with the governor to pardon the boys. Under these circumstances, there can be no charge that the mothers were prompted by outside organizations and that New York people were attempting to run the state of Alabama or that anyone was attempting to raise legal technicalities. There would only be the question of typical mothers of Alabama pleading for the freedom of the sons of other mothers.

Please turn this idea over in your mind and let me know whether or not you believe it would be a good idea to try.

MARSHALL TO THE *AFRO-AMERICAN*

Marshall occasionally penned letters to build grassroots support for his legal work, and the following is part of a letter he sent to Baltimore's black newspaper. Take special note of Marshall's creative use of a charge frequently leveled by his white opponents in cases related to equitable salaries—that black schools were inferior to white schools. Although his language is rather soft below, a month earlier Marshall had penned a letter encouraging an NAACP leader in Muskegon, Michigan, to protest a plan for segregated schools. "Wherever there are separate schools," he wrote, "you will always find that the colored school is inferior."

MARCH 29, 1938

We are reliably informed that an official of the State Department of Education, several county superintendents and a prominent Negro educator are busy spreading the propaganda that Negro teachers are inferior to white teachers and that they are not as qualified as white teachers and are therefore not entitled to equal salaries. This is one of the most malicious pieces of propaganda ever issued.

According to the laws of the state of Maryland, teachers are rated according to certificates issued by the State Department of Education. Negro teachers meet the same qualifications as white teachers for these certificates, and according to the latest annual report of the State Department of Education . . . Negro teachers as a group have a higher percentage of first-grade certificates than white teachers.

The propaganda also states that colored teachers are products of colored high schools, which are inferior, and are products of Bowie State Normal School, which is inferior, and therefore the colored teachers of the state of Maryland are inferior. It is quite evident that if the colored high schools are inferior, they are state schools and the blame is not on the colored teachers but again on the state of Maryland. If Bowie Normal School is inferior to the three palatial white normal schools, this is also the fault of the state of Maryland and not the fault of the colored teachers.

I am sure that the colored teachers of the state of Maryland are not concerned about this propaganda, and I hope that Negroes in general in the state of Maryland are not taken in by such a vicious attempt to interfere with the cases to equalize teachers' salaries.

. . .

Thurgood Marshall

MARSHALL TO THE NAACP EXECUTIVE STAFF

Marshall's suit to equalize teachers' salaries in Montgomery County, Maryland, sparked a vicious backlash among some school boards in different parts of the state, and here he recounts intimidation and punitive tactics carried out against African American teachers. Of special note is Marshall's curious, if not altogether wrongheaded, claim that the NAACP did not "play politics."

JUNE 23, 1938

. . .

Discharging of Teachers

It is quite evident now that there is a small bloc of county superintendents who are definitely doing all in their power to defeat equalization of salaries. . . . These superintendents have agreed to release as many colored teachers as possible in order to intimidate the other teachers.

In Maryland, teachers who have been teaching more than two years can only be released on cause and teachers teaching less than two years can be released without cause at the end of either the first or second year. All of the plaintiffs in our cases have been teachers who have been teaching more than two years and cannot be released except on cause.

In 1936 Howard Pindelle was a high school teacher in Ann Arundel County with five years' tenure. At the beginning of our fight to equalize salaries he was the first prospective plaintiff. At the end of the school year, 1936, he was informed that he had been offered a position as principal in Frederick County, which was a better job and with more pay. He applied for this position and told the superintendent he did not have a principal's certificate. He was assured by the superintendent that he could obtain his certificate within four years and that this would be agreeable with the board of education. He started in his duties as principal in Frederick County. By moving from Ann Arundel County to Frederick County he lost his tenure and became a probationary principal. His second year as probational principal ended last week and he was told that he would be released.

This to my mind was a most traitorous trick. The authorities wanted to get rid of him for his activities in the teachers' salary cases but could not do so as long as he had tenure. By offering him a better job he lost his tenure and now he has no job. This is a round-about way of putting a man out "legally."

Namon Allen, the leader of the teachers attempting to equalize salaries in Somerset County, was also released.

. . .

All of the Negro probationary teachers in Prince George's County have been released.

There is nothing that can be done legally about any of these cases under the laws of the state of Maryland. The only possible redress is to have the teachers, taxpayers, voters, and patrons bring all possible pressure against the boards of education and against the county superintendents. We have attempted to do this in each of the counties. We have had conferences with these people in each of these counties.

To carry this matter further, all members of the county boards of education are appointed by the governor, and yesterday Mr. Carl Murphy, Mr. George Murphy, Mr. Marse Calloway, a politician of the first water, and I had a conference with Governor Harry W. Nice. Governor Nice informed us that on June 30 he will make a political statement as to his candidacy for office. He quoted to us a statement in the speech to the effect that he is calling upon the next legislature to equalize teachers' salaries and calling upon the people of the state of Maryland to abolish this unconstitutional system, etc. He also wrote letters to the Republican members of the boards of education of Prince George's County and Frederick County urging them to make an immediate investigation of these "deplorable practices" of discharging teachers because of their fight to equalize salaries and has ordered them to take the matter up with the state board of education and to make a report to him. Governor Nice stated that if there was anything further we wanted him to do, he would do it. We told him there was nothing further at the present time and Governor Nice stated his office was open to us and to keep him advised from time to time as to developments in any counties in which he had Republican members of the board of education.

Despite the fact that we do not play politics and despite the fact that Governor Nice's actions are controlled in a measure by his solicitation of the Negro vote, I believe that we must give credit to Governor Nice for what he has done.

MARSHALL TO GOVERNOR FRED CONE

By the end of 1938, Marshall was working with Representative Joseph Gavagan of New York on authoring a draft of an antilynching bill that Gavagan then submitted at the next congressional session. During his early years with the NAACP, Marshall spent considerable time on numerous lynching cases, including the one described below by Dinnah Kirkland of Fernandina Beach, Florida:

> *. . . Please my son has ben misen every since the 24 day of may now he was arested or he was acuse of insulted a white woman but they did not ever make a charge against him so they told me that they would turn him out that night because the white lady she was not*

> *sure he was the one so the sherif told me that he turn my son out at nine or ten oclock that night but I have proof that it was 11 oclock when he turn my son out an it was a crow of white mens out thair an thay carry him of in a car an I have not seen or herd anything of him so thay carry him off and kill him so I go back to the sherif the next morning an ask about my son he says he turn him out now this happon in Marion county Ocala Fla. Why I am here thay run me away because I was trying to find out about my son so if you get any unstandin about it I sure will thank you because thay did me so bad thay drove me away from the jail . . . I do wish you would take this matter up at once an let me here from you at once thay run me away from Ocala Fla. I am just a widow woman no help so I was advise to write you for some help because the sherif in Ocala Fla I do think is responson for my son he was just 18 years old so I will close hoping to get ance soon . . .*

Kirkland's sad letter, which she addressed to the NAACP, ended up on Marshall's desk, and here he sends a letter of protest to Governor Fred Cone of Florida.

JULY 28, 1938

My Dear Governor Cone:

Early in May, 1937, Willie Kirkland, about eighteen years old, was picked up and lodged in jail in Ocala, Florida on suspicion. The sheriff was informed that a Negro boy answering Kirkland's description had attempted to hug a white woman on the streets of Ocala the night before. Kirkland was kept in jail for about a week and sometimes he was questioned all night in an endeavor to connect him with the offense. The white woman was confronted by Kirkland and she said positively that she would not identify him as the guilty party. Court officers who had investigated the case told the parents of the boy that there was no proof whatever that he had committed any crime or that he was the guilty party in this case and that there was nothing left to do except to release him.

On or about May 24, 1937, the mother appeared at the jail early in the afternoon and remained there until about nine o'clock that night expecting the sheriff to release her son in order that she might take him home. The sheriff refused to release Kirkland and the mother returned home a few blocks away to await the release of her boy early in the morning.

However, at about midnight the sheriff of Marion County ordered the boy released. Occupants of the jail saw him leave the jail yard. He was accosted on the outside by some half-dozen white men in a Ford car. The boy has never been seen alive since.

On February 12, 1938, a skeleton was found near Ocala, Florida. Mrs. Kirkland was requested to return, and on or about April 9 positively identified the skeleton as that of her son. Mrs. Kirkland, friends of the family, and interested citizens have been unable to have his death investigated in any manner by the officials of Marion County. Representatives of this Association in Florida have made an investigation and have discovered the above facts which we are in turn forwarding to you.

We most strongly urge you as the chief executive of the state of Florida to cause an investigation to be made by your attorney general into this apparent lynching. In view of your statement to the United States Senate through Senator McKellar, we urge you not only to make an investigation, but also to use all means at your disposal to have the guilty parties prosecuted.

Yours respectfully,

Thurgood Marshall

The governor replied on August 2, stating that his investigation had turned up no indication of foul play. Cone based his assessment, disingenuously but predictably, on the account provided by the local sheriff, who had claimed that "there was no sufficient evidence to hold Kirkland" and "that Kirkland possibly left the city thinking that he might be mistreated by relatives of the young lady."

MARSHALL TO SYLVIA FRANK

By this point, Charles Houston had left the NAACP to run his family's law firm in Washington, D.C., and Marshall had become special counsel to the NAACP, the top lawyer in the Association. Not long before these personnel changes took place, Houston and Marshall had traveled to Tennessee Valley Authority (TVA) sites to document racial discrimination carried out by the federal agency, and in the letter below Marshall writes Sylvia Frank, a student at the University of Rochester, about some of the NAACP's findings. Perhaps most striking about this letter—other than its indictment of the federal government in a shocking case of actively proliferating racial discrimination—is the time and energy Marshall devoted to writing it in the first place. Frank, after all, was an everyday citizen, certainly not someone in a prestigious position.

OCTOBER 1, 1938

Dear Miss Frank:

Your letter of September 20, addressed to Mr. White, has been called to my attention on returning to the office.

The NAACP has made several investigations of the Tennessee Valley Authority and we have filed our reports in an effort to effect an improvement of conditions. At the last session of Congress a resolution was passed calling for an investigation of the TVA by a congressional committee. We requested permission to introduce evidence concerning discrimination against Negroes before the Committee. This summer Mr. Charles H. Houston and I made another investigation of the TVA, and Mr. Houston testified before the congressional committee, giving them the results of our investigation, including affidavits.

We found a very deplorable situation on the Authority. Separate drinking fountains, separate waiting rooms, separate restaurants and separate convenience for visitors are a part of the general pattern and policy of the TVA.

In answering your questions specifically, we do not believe that the policy of discrimination on TVA is a policy of the Tennessee people. Rather, the Authority has injected a policy of discrimination unknown to the locality.

There are no Negroes working on the Chickamauga Dam, near Chattanooga, in any skilled positions. Negroes are limited to unskilled jobs. The authorities state that Negroes in that locality are not qualified for skilled jobs and that white men will not work under them. Our investigation shows that this is absolutely false. One case in particular tends to explain our conclusion. A Negro by the name of Neil Powell was appointed as foreman after much protest about discrimination against Negroes. He was, however, released without any reason being given. This man, Neil Powell, has been in the construction business all of his life. He has been foreman of several building projects in Tennessee and was chief foreman in the building of a municipal tunnel in Chattanooga only nine miles from Chickamauga Dam. He employed under him white and Negro foremen and white and Negro laborers. There was no friction and no complaint at that time. It seems to us quite clear that TVA is hereby injecting a policy of discrimination unknown to the particular area. There are also Negroes working at skilled trades such as cement finishers, signal men, flag men and others, but they are not classified as such and are paid either unskilled, or semi-skilled salaries. One man in particular is working at cement finishing beside white cement finishers. The white cement finishers are classified as such and receive $1.25 an hour. The colored man is classified as a tunnel worker and receives $.62 ½ an hour.

The Tennessee Valley Authority also includes the model town of Norris near Norris Dam, built by federal funds for use by American citizens. There are absolutely no Negroes in the town of Norris, although the homes there were built by federal funds. The recreational areas maintained by the TVA exclude Negroes. The training program excludes Negroes in the skilled trades and the apprenticeship program maintained to improve ability and to fit men to take their places in other jobs after construction is completed. There are no Negroes employed on the new dams now being prepared for construction.

All of this information and additional information, including the matters mentioned in your letter, were presented to the congressional committee and additional investigations are being made.

We appreciate your interest in this matter and assure you that we are doing all in our power to remedy the conditions. I think it would be very helpful if you would write a letter to Senator Vic Donahey, chairman of the congressional committee investigating the TVA, and set out your observations similar to the way you set them out in your letter to us.

Yours very truly,

Thurgood Marshall

MARSHALL TO RUTH PERRY

Marshall was known as someone who could be gruff and easily dismissive, but here he sends a letter of condolence to a mother whose son, Oscar Perry, had exhausted his legal options for avoiding a death sentence. Perry, 19, and Arthur

Mack, 24, both black, had been convicted of murdering Charles Helton, a white night watchman, on July 31. An NAACP news release about the conviction stated the following:

> *An investigation by A. T. Walden of the Atlanta Branch of the NAACP disclosed that Helton was killed in self-defense by Perry after Perry had been shot three times by the white man. The story is that the Tom Huston Peanut Company of this city [Columbus, Georgia] gave a barbecue and picnic for its employees the night of July 30 and that free refreshments were served. Mack and Perry are said to have returned several times to the beer counter for free beer and the last time they were told not to come back for any more beer.*
>
> *Nevertheless they are said to have come back later to secure some beer which they had drawn out on a previous trip and hidden. Helton is said to have seen them coming and to have turned out the lights and waited for them. When they came within range he opened fire and Mack was shot twice and rendered helpless. Perry was shot three times, but he managed to reach Helton and cut him with a knife. Helton died in the hospital.*

Judge George Monroe, of Columbus, had sought clemency for Mack and Perry, but he lost the case after a series of appeals. In a December 6 letter to Munro, Marshall wrote: "We have received another letter from Mrs. Perry and it will be very hard for us to tell her that there is nothing we can do to save her boy. It is this type of case which tends more and more to bring about a feeling that many of the courts in this country still prefer to permit prejudice to overcome a true sense of justice. However, we are sure that with the ever-growing group of individuals and lawyers in the South like yourself, who are willing to fight for justice, the battle is not lost and we still cling to the hope that eventually we will have in this country justice for all citizens. We fully realize that in this particular case you did all in your power to save these boys [Arthur Mack and Oscar Perry] and I, for one, am certain that it was merely the setup in the court with a jury that was prejudiced which brought about the death of these boys."

DECEMBER 6, 1938

Dear Mrs. Perry:

We have received a letter from Judge Munro telling us that the State

Prison and Parole Commission on November 15 refused to grant clemency in the case of your son.

Judge Munro has done all that he possibly can do in this case. He has not only carried the case through courts and to the appeal courts, but has also gone to the parole commission and the governor. Under our legislative system there is nothing further that can possibly be done in this case. Judge Munro in his letter stated to us that he was more than sorry that the lives of these boys could not be saved, but on the other hand there was nothing further that could be done. The Supreme Court of Georgia in deciding this case paid Judge Munro a fine tribute as to the manner in which he handled the case and his efforts to save the boys.

Although there is nothing that can be done further to save the boys, I think you should face the situation with the feeling that you did all in your power, that Judge Munro did all in his power, and that we did the very best we could to save the boys. If you take this position, I am sure you can face the future with the belief that although justice was not given to your boy, it was something that could not be helped.

We join with you in your sorrow.

Yours sincerely,

Thurgood Marshall

CHAPTER THREE

1939

MARSHALL TO DARTNELL PUBLICATIONS

While Marshall was arguing court cases at the highest levels, it was also his job to follow up on complaints about everyday discrimination and racism, and in the following letter he unleashes a bit of reasonable wrath on Dartnell Publications, a publisher of business magazines, for racist remarks that appeared in the September 1938 issue of American Business. *Marshall's damning postscript refers to a subscription renewal letter titled "Nigger in the Woodpile," in which J. T. Kemp, the comptroller of* American Business, *had written: "[I]f you have just put it off, won't you send along your check for $3.75 now, so we can chase that 'nigger' out."*

JANUARY 4, 1939

Gentlemen:

We have received many complaints from our branches throughout the country and from Negro businessmen in these branches urging us to protest the cover of the *American Business* magazine for September 1938 and the statement entitled "Negroes in Offices." We have read with interest in the press clippings concerning individuals who have also protested against this cover page.

It is to be regretted that a magazine circulated throughout the country should take the position that qualified Negro graduates of northern colleges and high schools should not apply for positions wherever positions are available. It is not a question of Negroes forcing themselves "into situations where they are not welcome and where their opportunity to serve society is necessarily limited." But it is rather the right of every citizen of this country to apply for a position in any type of business and in any place. One of the fundamental principles of democracy is the right to work, and the other fundamental principle is the right not to be discriminated against in the effort to secure employment. The right to seek employment and the right to picket establishments refusing employment to Negroes has been upheld by the Supreme Court of the United States. In the case of the *New Negro Alliance*, et al., *v. Sanitary Grocery Company, Inc.*, the Supreme Court decided on March 28, 1938:

> *. . . the desire for fair and equitable conditions of employment on the part of persons of any race, color, or persuasion, and the removal of discriminations against them by reason of their race or religious beliefs is quite as important to those concerned as fairness and equity in terms and conditions of employment can be to trade or craft unions or any form of labor organization or association. Race discrimination by an employer may reasonably be deemed more unfair and less excusable than discrimination against workers on the ground of union affiliation. There is no justification in the apparent purposes or the express terms of the Act for limiting its definition of labor disputes and cases arising therefrom by excluding those which arise with respect to discrimination in terms and conditions of employment based upon differences of race or color.*

After reading this decision of the Supreme Court of the United States we hope that your publications will follow the theory of our democratic system of government and the Supreme Court of the United States and discontinue the making of such statements as appear on the cover of your magazine of September 1938.

Very truly yours,

Thurgood Marshall

P.S. We have also had called to our attention a letterhead sent out by *American Business* in December 1938, which bears the picture of a woodpile and a human head sticking out of the woodpile, to the right of which is the inscription, "Nigger in the Woodpile." In view of this letterhead, circulated after receiving the protests from other individuals to your cover page of September 1938, on behalf of the twelve million Negro American citizens and others, we urge you to discontinue what seems to be an established policy of attempting to influence public opinion against equality of rights and privileges of American citizens.

MARSHALL TO GOVERNOR W. LEE O'DANIEL

Marshall saw more than a few cases of police brutality against African Americans in Southern jails, and here he sends a letter of protest to Governor Lee O'Daniel of Florida about the beating and death of Cherry Conley in the Ellis County jail.

FEBRUARY 27, 1939

Dear Governor O'Daniel:

There has been called to our attention the shooting and killing of one Cherry Connally at Waxahachie. According to our information Cherry Connally was a prisoner in the Ellis County jail and is alleged to have escaped on or about Tuesday, February 21. Although he and his alleged accomplice are reported to have taken guns when they escaped, Connally was captured by two unarmed youths and returned to the jail.

According to our information, Sheriff Roy went into the cell of Connally after he was returned and severely beat him until he was unconscious. Sheriff Roy is then alleged to have shot Connally thru the chest, causing his death.

According to Sheriff Roy's statement, Connally was about to attack him and Sheriff Roy turned and shot Connally. This statement does not seem to be true in view of the fact that people who viewed Connally's body stated that they saw signs of excessive beatings as well as the gunshot wound. Sheriff Roy has a reputation of being very brutal to Negroes in that vicinity.

We are calling this matter to your attention in the hope that you will have this killing investigated by state officers.

Very truly yours,

Thurgood Marshall

Reuben Williams, the secretary to the governor, replied in a March 29 letter that the local sheriff, Joe Roy, "shot Cherry Conley in defense of his own life." It was an explanation that Marshall heard numerous times when seeking information from local authorities about the deaths of African American inmates, and sometimes there was little he could do to fight the matter from his office in New York.

MARSHALL TO STEPHEN F. WHITMAN & SON, INC.

Perhaps most characteristic about Marshall's NAACP letters is the restraint he used when registering protests in response to blatant racism. In the letter below, Marshall criticizes the manufacturers of Whitman's Candy for calling one of its products a name offensive to Negroes. The picture on the candy box included caricatures of African American children with wild hair, buglike eyes, and a taste for large slices of watermelon.

APRIL 5, 1939

Dear Gentlemen:

A member of our Association has sent to us a package which had contained peppermint candy prepared by your company. The trade name on this package is "Whitman's Pickaninny Peppermints—Chocolate Covered."

On behalf of the members of this Association, we protest the use of the term "pickaninny" as applied to young Negro children whose pictures appear on your package. This term is extremely distasteful to Negroes.

We are calling this matter to your attention in the hope that you will discontinue the use of this term on packages of candy manufactured and distributed by you. We have not taken this matter up with our branches as yet, pending a reply from you. We will therefore appreciate an early reply.

Very truly yours,

Thurgood Marshall

Charles Norris, Jr., an attorney for Whitman, sent Marshall a reply on April 22. "In the first place," Norris wrote, "I should like to emphasize the fact that the Whitman company has not the slightest desire to offend the Negro race, and we are quite surprised that the word 'Pickaninny' is distasteful. Quite to the contrary, we feel that the term connotes a cute Negro child." Norris further reported that Whitman had been using the Pickaninny box since February 1899, and that because the company retained a great number of the boxes, "to discontinue their use would be quite a hardship." But, perhaps in response to Marshall's thinly veiled threat at the end of his letter, Norris also requested a meeting with an NAACP representative to discuss the matter further. "Please do not construe this letter as a refusal to accede to your request," Norris concluded, "because if you are correct, the Whitman company would go to any reasonable extent in removing any objectionable statements." After a long exchange of letters, as well as attention from African American newspapers, Whitman dropped the offensive name.

MARSHALL TO ATTORNEY GENERAL FRANK MURPHY

Marshall asks U.S. Attorney General Frank Murphy to investigate the lynching of Wilder McGowan in Mississippi. The NAACP frequently relied on its own members, or on sympathetic individuals, to investigate local crimes throughout the country, and this letter, like many others in the NAACP Papers, indicates Marshall's use of local supporters.

APRIL 15, 1939

My Dear Sir:

We are calling to your attention the lynching of Wilder McGowan at Wiggins, Mississippi, on November 22, 1938.

McGowan, a 24-year-old Negro, was lynched by a mob of about 200 white men who had trailed him for several hours with bloodhounds after a 74-year-old white woman allegedly was criminally attacked and robbed. The facts, as revealed by an investigation made by a Southerner who is exceptionally able and careful, are as follows:

Mrs. Murray, an elderly white woman who lives alone between Wiggins and Perkinston, Mississippi, reported on Sunday night, November 20, that she had been attacked and robbed by a "light-colored Negro with slick hair at around eight o'clock in the evening."

McGowan was dark brown and not light-colored; at the time of the alleged assault, according to a careful checking of his movements on November 20, he was some distance from the home of Mrs. Murray, where the crime is alleged to have been committed, with friends who can testify as to his whereabouts. He is known to have gone to bed for the night at nine o'clock and to have slept through the night. The next morning he was calmly going about the servicing of his passenger truck to take some men to work at Ten-Mile, and his fiancée, a schoolteacher, to her school about six miles from McHenry, Mississippi. He had planned leaving that night to return to his employment at Gulfport.

Completely unsuspecting that he was being sought or that a crime had been committed, McGowan was dumbfounded when members of the mob with drawn guns commanded him to get out of his truck. Still in the dark, he reluctantly obeyed and asked why they wanted him. Members of the mob cursed him and with shotguns thrust against his back forced him into a car and made him sit on the front seat between two of their number. The automobile was then driven by the mob, followed by other cars to a wooded section where McGowan was lynched.

When McGowan's body was returned in the truck of a white merchant we are informed that white curiosity seekers laughed loudly and gaily as the man's relatives manifested their grief.

It is generally known that McGowan was completely innocent of the crime for which he was put to death and that the alleged crime was merely used as an excuse to lynch McGowan because he was a Negro who "did not know his place." McGowan was manly and refused to be intimidated by the ruffianly whites of Wiggins and had on several occasions been engaged in altercations when they sought to abuse and mistreat him; that on one occasion when a mob of armed drunken whites in an automobile ordered all the Negroes to run McGowan refused to do so and was attacked by the mob. He fought back and took a revolver from one of the white men, whereupon the mob let him alone. However, they bitterly resented his refusal to let them treat him as they wished.

On another occasion McGowan was one of several young colored men who repelled an attempt of a group of white men to invade a Negro dance hall "looking for some good looking nigger women." McGowan was suspected of having cut one of the white men.

Our investigator reports that all these incidents caused this type of Mississippi white to be on the lookout for an excuse to charge McGowan with a crime for which they could try to justify lynching him. To return to the alleged attack on Mrs. Murray:

Bloodhounds belonging to a man by the name of Gantt at Meridian, Mississippi, which were brought to Wiggins to trace the alleged assailant, at no time led the sheriff and mob to McGowan. When no suspect was found the mob determined to wreck vengeance upon any unfortunate suspect on whom might be pinned even the flimsiest sort of circumstantial evidence. A reign of terror was begun with the order that "not a damned Negro leave their quarters." One colored woman, Catherine Fairley by name, thinking that the order was not meant for women, attempted to pass through a cordon thrown around the Negro section of Wiggins to go to her work as a house servant. She was struck a heavy blow on the forehead with the butt of a pistol and told to "git back." The blow cut a long and bloody gash in her head.

Some of the law enforcement officers, several of the merchants of Wiggins, a WPA employee, and other whites joined in the mistreatment of all Negroes. One young Negro was taken to the woods, beaten almost to death and then freed and ordered to get back to town as fast as he could, as an example to others.

The names and addresses of seventeen persons who either participated in or were present at the lynching were submitted to us by our investigator. If you desire, upon your request we will be pleased to send you this list.

We have also received several letters from a resident of Wiggins, Mississippi, concerning the lynching, stating that he can identify at least twenty members of the mob. We are enclosing copies of these letters.

Although this lynching occurred in 1938, we are calling it to your attention in the hope that the Department of Justice will investigate this lynching along with the others of 1939.

Very truly yours,

Thurgood Marshall

On May 31, Welly Hopkins, the acting assistant attorney general, offered a familiar reply to Marshall's request: "The present law as applied to the facts set out in your letter prohibit the intervention of the federal government at this time. Whether the jurisdiction of the federal government should be extended is a matter for consideration by the Congress. Anti-lynching legislation is now pending before that body and the suggestion is offered that you make known your grievances to your representatives with a view to its enactment into law."

MARSHALL TO ROY WILKINS

Marshall solicits Wilkins's help after learning about a textbook that traced cases of gonorrhea to "colored maids." Marshall sent Wilkins information about the text along with the following note. However brief, the note reveals a remarkable willingness on Marshall's part to direct his attention to whatever form of racism and discrimination came his way.

MAY 4, 1939

This type of protest is right down your street. I am wondering if you would write the letter of protest and build the press release around it. If you want to wait until I come back, I will be glad to do it.

Wilkins accepted Marshall's challenge, and his May 5 letter to William Champion, the editor of the book in question, follows here.

We have noted in your new book, *Medical Information for Social Workers*, a statement on page 336, regarding gonorrhea in little children, "the infection is most commonly received from toilet seats soiled by infected members of the household, such as colored maids."

The National Association for the Advancement of Colored People wishes to enter emphatic protest against such statement, which accuses all colored maids of having gonorrhea. This statement is patently unfair and untrue and tends to besmirch the whole Negro race and restrict its chances for employment.

We submit that no statistics can be obtained which would indicate that gonorrhea is more prevalent among colored maids than among white maids. The venereal statistics for this country do not indicate that white persons are free from venereal diseases, and therefore we protest the statement in your book and ask that it be withdrawn immediately.

The United States Census figures for 1930 show that slightly more than one million Negroes are engaged in domestic service, and considerably less than this number is composed of female servants. There are many millions of white domestic servants, and we feel that your insertion of the world "colored" has deliberately slandered Negro servants and the whole Negro race.

MARSHALL TO MRS. E. W. GRANT

In this short letter to the secretary of the Nashville NAACP, Marshall expresses frustration at President Roosevelt upon the nomination of Elmer Davies as judge for the Middle District of Tennessee. Davies testified during his Senate confirmation hearings that he had once been a member of the Ku Klux Klan, and the NAACP waged a furious but unsuccessful campaign to derail his nomination. Roosevelt supported his nominee throughout the NAACP protest and opposed the Senate's request that he return the nomination for further consideration after the Senate had already confirmed it.

JULY 25, 1939

Dear Mrs. Grant:

Mr. White referred to me your letter of July 15 before leaving for Washington.

You will notice from our press releases the position we have taken on the Davies nomination. We believe that it is one of the dirtiest tricks ever pulled on Negroes and labor groups in this country. We congratulate you on your firm stand in the matter, and assure you that although we were unsuccessful, we feel satisfied in having put up a good fight. And, after all, that is our job.

. . .

With all best wishes, I am

Sincerely yours,

Thurgood Marshall

MARSHALL TO CHARLES HOUSTON

Houston, a brilliant tactician in the battle for desegregated education, had enlisted Lloyd Gaines, a graduate of Lincoln University, to apply to the law school of the University of Missouri. Predictably, Missouri denied Gaines's application because he was black. Houston argued the case through the courts, and on December 12, 1938, the U.S. Supreme Court ruled that Gaines "was entitled to be admitted to the law school of the State University in the absence of other and proper provision for his legal training within the State." In response to the ruling, Missouri set out to build a segregated law school at Lincoln, and Houston returned to court, this time arguing that the new law school was not prepared to open on a separate but equal basis. The Missouri State Supreme Court agreed, and below is Marshall's colorful note to Houston. Marshall refers to the boxing champion Joe Louis.

AUGUST 4, 1939

Dear Charlie:

Congratulations, etc. on reversal in University of Missouri case.

I agree with you and suggest that you immediately write Sidney to get in touch with Gaines at once and get him in the mood of going through with this thing. If one person has asked me, at least a hundred have, about whether or not Gaines himself is going to push this thing through. This is a most important item. . . .

I also agree that it will be necessary to send either you or Andy to Jefferson City to begin checking on the separate law school sometime during the early part of September.

Regardless of what happens, and regardless of what type of school is set up at Lincoln University, will it not be necessary for Gaines to present himself as a matter of record to the Law School of the University of Missouri on the opening day? It seems to me that this is absolutely necessary for the record.

I turned the opinion over to Leader Wilkins, who promises a rip-roaring press release which can be summed up in the words of the master, Joe Louis: "I glad I winned."

. . .

Sincerely yours,

Thurgood Marshall

Missouri did not give up, however, and plowed ahead with plans to open a segregated law school—a persistence that required additional legal action by the NAACP. Despite the NAACP's urgings for Gaines to stay the course, he went missing and what happened to him remains unclear to this day, although Walter White believed that Gaines had left the country with a bribe in his back pocket. With their plaintiff missing, the NAACP pulled out of the case, and Marshall became ever vigilant in his selection of which individuals he would represent in important cases.

CHARLES CARTER TO MARSHALL

Charles Carter, an NAACP-affiliated attorney from Jersey City, New Jersey, solicits Marshall's assistance in preventing the extradition of Sam Buchanan back to a chain gang in Georgia. Marshall was very interested in preventing the extradition of African American prisoners to chain gangs in the South, where they would often meet abuse and even death, and he received more than a few letters about the gangs. Just a year earlier, for instance, the following letter from James Blackwell, an inmate at a New York City jail, ended up on Marshall's desk:

> *I am call upon you to keep me I am bout to bee sent back to a chian gang I wont some body to help me now I ran a way in 1936 I had two years on the gang the have got me now they will beat me to death when the get me Will some body help me I need a lauer to keep me Will you give me one plese I don't wont to go back the will kill me shaw Sen some body to talk with me I will bee glad Sen some one let me hear from you at younce*

While it is unclear what became of Blackwell—Marshall asked the local NAACP to handle the case—Charles Carter led the legal fight for Buchanan. The details of Buchanan's case remain (almost) unbelievable.

OCTOBER 25, 1939

Dear Thurgood:

I am sending to you a statement of the facts in the case of which I spoke to you about over the phone.

In September 1925, one Sam Buckhannon, 16 years of age of 141

Chestnut Avenue, Atlanta, Georgia, was asked by another, Julius Brown, also of Atlanta, Georgia, age 27 years, to go into a restaurant in Atlanta and take 2 packages of cigarettes for which he would give him (25) twenty-five cents. The following day Buckhannon was arrested for the larceny of said cigarettes. He was told by the prosecutor at that time that if he pleaded guilty, they would let him go. Upon this advice and because of the fact that his people were in poor circumstances, he was convicted of larceny and sentenced to the chain gang for a term of 22 to 45 years. He had no previous record of any criminal matters whatsoever and was in fact at the time a juvenile. However, he has been on chain gangs from 1925 until some time in June of this year. He hoboed on freight cars to Jersey City, where he was apprehended and sentenced to 6 months in the county penitentiary on a charge of vagrancy. His term will be up on November 16th and the authorities of Georgia are asking that he be extradited to serve the rest of his time.

These facts clearly indicate that it is a grave miscarriage of justice and I would appreciate it if you will arrange to ask for the record in Georgia so that it might be presented to Governor Moore at the proper time so that this man will not be subject to any further punishment.

Thanking you for your cooperation in this matter.

Yours very truly,

Charles W. Carter

Carter won an extraordinary reversal of the extradition warrant on December 11, and Buchanan secured his freedom.

MARSHALL TO B. M. AMOLE

Long before the Montgomery bus boycott started in 1955, Marshall was combating segregation on buses throughout the country. Indeed, if Harry Byrd, the president of the University of Maryland, was the one individual Marshall seemed to detest more than any other during his early years with the NAACP, the Greyhound Bus Company was the one business that evoked Marshall's wrath more than any other during this same era. Marshall simply could not stand Greyhound, and it is easy to guess that the feeling was mutual. His frustration with Greyhound is partially evident in a September 23, 1938, letter he wrote to Maude Tollefson, a resident of Tucson, Arizona, who was the victim of racial discrimination on a Greyhound bus: "We have had many complaints against the Greyhound Bus Company and upon making complaint to them, almost invariably received no redress from them. We are planning an attack on the Jim Crow laws in the South surrounding the trains and bus transportation, but have not as yet been able to put our plans into effect because of our very limited budget."

Below is Marshall's scorching letter to B. M. Amole, the assistant traffic manager of the Atlantic Greyhound Corporation, about his reply to Marshall's protest of yet another case of racial discrimination. Marshall had written Greyhound about a bus driver who had told an African American man to "take the back seat, boy," and about a driver who had transferred African Americans to a taxi so that whites could take their seats on the bus.

OCTOBER 26, 1939

Dear Sir:

This will acknowledge your letter of October 13 in reply to our letter of September 23 being a complaint against the treatment of Negroes on your bus lines.

You state in your letter, "there are certain laws of the various states in which we operate that necessitate the moving of passengers at various times." Although there are certain laws on the statute books, the constitutionality of which we do not concede, providing for the separation of the races, there is no law which either authorizes or permits the removal of Negroes from regular buses and the placing of them in inferior vehicles, causing loss of time and inconvenience.

Under the Fourteenth Amendment and under the decisions of the United States Supreme Court, whenever separation of the races is required by state statute, equal provisions must be made for the separated races. One of the commonest cases interpreting the Fourteenth Amendment as applied to interstate commerce is the case of *McCabe vs. Atchison, Topeka and Santa Fe Railroad* 235 U.S. 151. In this case the defendant railway company defended its refusal to give Negroes equal accommodations on the ground that there were not enough Negroes applying for the service to justify the furnishing of equal facilities to them. The United States Supreme Court, however, held that:

Whether or not particular facilities shall be provided may doubtless be conditioned upon there being a reasonable demand therefor, but, if facilities are provided, substantial equality of treatment of persons traveling under like conditions cannot be refused. It is the individual who is entitled to the equal protection of the laws, and if he is denied by a common carrier, acting in the matter under the authority of a state law, a facility or convenience in the course of his journey which under substantially the same circumstances is furnished to another traveler, he may properly complain that his constitutional privilege has been invaded.

Applying this United States Supreme Court decision to our complaint, it seems clear to us that it is unlawful for your company, acting through its agents, to require Negroes to leave a thru bus and to wait for either a later bus or for a taxicab in order that the Negroes' seats may be occupied by white passengers. There is no semblance of equality in such a system, and it is a flagrant violation of the United States Constitution.

We therefore again call upon you to instruct your drivers and agents to discontinue this practice. Otherwise, it will be necessary for us to make a complaint to the Interstate Commerce Commission.

We will appreciate hearing from you further in this matter.

Yours very truly,

Thurgood Marshall

MARSHALL TO GRACE CORRIGAN

Marshall gives Corrigan, the superintendent of public instruction for the Department of Education in New Mexico, a pointed lesson in the constitutional rights of African American children in public schools.

NOVEMBER 22, 1939

Dear Mrs. Corrigan:

Members of this Association in Alamogordo, New Mexico, have called to our attention the refusal of the school authorities to provide equal educational opportunities for Negro citizens. It seems that the one school for Negroes in Alamogordo is taught by one teacher who teaches grades from the first grade through the junior high school. It is almost unbelievable that in this modern system of education one teacher can be expected to be proficient in teaching all grades from the first grade to the junior high school at the same time and in the same small building.

The citizens of Alamogordo have sent us the letter from your office of August 31, 1939, signed by Mr. L. W. Clark, director of secondary education. It seems that your department is taking the position that (1) under the laws of New Mexico local school authorities can segregate white and Negro pupils if they feel disposed to do so, and (2) that there are not enough Negro children to justify fully equipped laboratories equal to those in the white high school. There are definite answers by the United States Supreme Court to both of these conditions.

It does seem that under the present laws a state may segregate white and colored pupils. However, this permission to segregate is definitely limited by the equal protection clause of the Fourteenth Amendment. The United States Supreme Court, on December 12, 1938, in the case of *Gaines v. Canada, et al.*, passed on the question as to whether or not a qualified Negro applicant could be refused admission to the University of Missouri Law School in the absence of separate and equal provisions for his training elsewhere. This question has been finally determined by the United States Supreme Court in the following language by Mr. Chief Justice Hughes:

> *The basic consideration is not as to what sort of opportunities other states provide, or whether they are as good as those in Missouri, but as to what opportunities Missouri itself furnishes to white students and denies to Negroes solely upon the ground of color. The admissibility of laws separating the races in the enjoyment of privileges afforded by the state rests wholly upon the equality of the privileges which the laws give to the separated groups within the state.*

Applying the rule of the United States Supreme Court to the situation in Alamogordo, the only way the school authorities can deprive Negro children of the right to attend the fully equipped white high school is to establish a high school for Negro children on a basis of equality. I notice that not even the school authorities attempt to justify their action on the ground that equal facilities are offered. So this is clearly a violation of the Fourteenth Amendment as interpreted by the United States Supreme Court.

Now as to the second question concerning the fact that there are very few Negroes qualified for high school training: The United States Supreme Court has also passed on this point in the case of *McCabe v. Atchison, Topeka and Santa Fe Railroad.* In that case, the question was raised as to whether or not equal railroad accommodations in Pullmans have to be provided for a relatively few Negroes. Mr. Associate Justice Hughes in that case held:

> *This argument with respect to volume of traffic seems to us to be without merit. It makes the constitutional right depend upon the number of persons who may be discriminated against, whereas the essence of the constitutional right is that it is a personal one. It is the individual who is entitled to the equal protection of the laws and if he is denied by a common carrier, acting in the matter under the authority of a state law, a facility or convenience in the course of his journey which under substantially the same circumstances is furnished to another traveler, he may properly complain that his constitutional privilege has been invaded.*

Applying these two cases to the situation in Alamogordo, it seems clear that the school authorities must either admit these Negro children to the white high school or establish separate high schools for them equal in all particulars to the existing white high school.

We will appreciate reconsideration of the complaint of these citizens in the hope that their constitutional rights will be protected.

Very truly yours,

Thurgood Marshall

Corrigan sent her reply six days later: "I am sending copies of your letter of November 22 to the President of the Alamogordo Board of Education and the City School Superintendent, with the request that every effort be made to give equal educational opportunities to all children, whether white or colored."

CHAPTER FOUR

1940

MARSHALL TO MORRIS GLICKFELD

The advent of World War II saw Marshall relentlessly attacking discrimination and racism in the U.S. military, and in this letter he sends a pointed reply to Morris Glickfeld, the chair of a welfare council at the University of California at Berkeley, who dared to suggest that there was no discrimination in the U.S. Army.

JANUARY 3, 1940

Dear Mr. Glickfeld:

The suggestion that although there is segregation in the Army there is no discrimination is certainly untrue. In the first place, Negroes are not only segregated but are prevented from enlisting in certain divisions of the Army. No Negroes are enlisted in the Air Corps either as pilots or flying cadets. There are no Negroes in the Signal Corps or the Adjutant General's office. There are several other branches of service from which Negroes are excluded solely because of their race.

No serious effort is being made by the War Department to remedy the situation. The system of segregation has also brought about the question of "quotas" for Negroes so that in the present draft it is expected that approximately ten percent of the enrollees are to be Negroes. This also leads to difficulties of administration as well as an extension of the gap between races, which should be narrowed rather than extended.

It should also be noted that no Negroes are permitted to enlist in the Navy except as messmen with absolutely no opportunity of advancement. No Negroes have ever been permitted in the Marine Corps.

The above brief statements are sufficient to show clearly that there is discrimination in the armed forces.

We are sending you, under separate cover, a copy of Mr. White's article on this subject and copies of recent articles appearing in the *Crisis* on this matter.

Sincerely yours,

Thurgood Marshall

MARSHALL TO GENERAL FRANK HINES

The following is the draft of a letter that Marshall wrote to the administrator of Veteran Affairs in Washington, D.C. It includes some of the strongest language found in Marshall's letters on the relationship between democracy and racial justice. Marshall's name in the signature line is crossed out in the draft, suggesting that he wrote it for White's signature.

NO DATE [JANUARY 1940]

Dear General Hines:

We are enclosing a copy of a complaint from Mr. Joseph Hunter of the Veterans Administration Facility at Sunmount, New York. In this letter Mr. Hunter charges that a system of segregation has been set up in the hospitals of the Veterans Administration whereby separate wards are maintained for Negro and white veterans.

It is to be regretted that this type of discrimination should exist in any project using federal funds exclusively, and the setting up of segregated systems in the state of New York is not only unjust but is against the public policy of the state of New York as set out in the New York state civil rights laws.

With the present unsettled conditions throughout Europe, the United States is itself on trial as the last proving ground for democracy.

The setting up of segregated, discriminatory facilities within an agency of the federal government certainly tends to completely destroy the very foundations of democracy. The defense of the United States depends upon the willingness of its citizens to take up arms. We believe that any discrimination against Negro veterans of the last world war will be taken into consideration in the future whenever citizens are again urged to take up arms in the defense of democracy.

We will, therefore, appreciate a prompt investigation of the complaint of Mr. Hunter and urge that the Veterans Administration establish a policy of prohibiting segregation in the facilities under its jurisdiction.

Very truly yours,

Thurgood Marshall

MARSHALL TO ROY WILKINS

Marshall protests the NAACP's budget lines for legal defense. In following years, the media followed Marshall's lead and criticized the NAACP for devoting little of its formal budget to legal battles.

JANUARY 26, 1940

Dear Roy:

. . .

As to the budget, first of all I understand the condition we are in, *but* someday we will have to realize that we cannot justify our existence unless we do a good amount of legal work. When we compare the money spent for legal defense, we can see that we are getting away with murder. Outside of branch and youth work, which is organization work, *what do we do*? Anti-lynching and legal defense and education. What do we justify our existence upon? These items. Our members and Negroes in general want *action*. To get action we must spend money.

The item of $5,496 for legal defense for a whole year is a *disgrace*. It is getting to be more and more difficult to answer appeal after appeal with the disgraceful statement "no funds," etc. One of these days our reputation will catch up with us—that we just cannot fight for the things we were organized to fight for.

All the above is beside the immediate point of this budget but must be kept in mind. Personally, I do not see how we can cut further. Where can you cut another $1,000? The entire legal defense budget (exclusive of education) is now only *$750* and the general budget *$650* for a total of $1,400. Clearly we cannot operate on $400 because we already owe several hundreds on cases. We can't close out our legal defense work altogether.

How can we cut the U. of Tenn. and the U. of Mo. cases? They are started and the only thing we can do is abandon them. This cannot be done.

The only thing I see to do is to deduct the amount of $250 in Tennessee and $750 in Missouri, which we expect to raise for the cases. This will give you your $1,000 additional saving on the budget.

I am not *altogether* a sourpuss on this whole question, but I am sure you understand my position.

See you Tuesday, I hope.

Regards to the office,

Thurgood

P.S. Sandy and Bill Hastie have terrible colds and mine has about caught up with me. We have had a tough time working on the Norfolk brief, but I guess we will get it in on time. . . .

TM

MARSHALL TO JEROME BRITCHEY

Jerome Britchey of the ACLU had asked whether Marshall would help in answering questions about the decision of the Daughters of the American Revolution (DAR) to refuse Marian Anderson permission to perform at Constitution Hall in Washington, D.C. Ralph Shrader, the minister of Bethany Church in Montpelier, Vermont, had written Britchey that some members of his congregation had told him that the real reason for the Anderson incident was not the color of her skin but the color of her politics—red. Britchey wanted to know specific facts for his reply to Shrader, and below is Marshall's take on the incident.

MARCH 28, 1940

Dear Jerry:

. . .

. . . As to the question of Miss Anderson being a "radical" or the tool, knowingly or unknowingly, of the subversive groups in this country, the answer is positively No! Her proposed concert at Constitution Hall was sponsored by Howard University. Her concert at Lincoln Memorial was sponsored by a group which included, as sponsors, the following persons:

Mrs. Franklin D. Roosevelt
The Chief Justice and Mrs. Hughes
Mr. Justice and Mrs. Black
Mr. Justice and Mrs. Reed
The Secretary of the Treasury and Mrs. Morgenthau
The Attorney General
. . .

It seems clear that the charge made by some members of the DAR that Miss Anderson is a radical is merely an effort to escape full responsibility for excluding Negro artistes from Constitution Hall.

The reason for refusing to permit a concert by Miss Anderson in Constitution Hall is not because of any charge that she is a "radical" but because the DAR has refused to remove its ban against all Negro artists applying for use of Constitution Hall.

Sincerely yours,

Thurgood Marshall

Two months after writing this letter, Marshall, always the antagonist, encouraged the Baltimore NAACP to apply to Constitution Hall for a date for an Anderson concert in the 1940–1941 season.

MARSHALL TO CARTER WESLEY

African Americans were excluded from membership in the Democratic Party in Texas, and they were also denied the right to vote in primaries. Because Democrats controlled Texas politics at this time, African Americans had virtu-

ally no political power in choosing their elected political leaders. With this in mind, Marshall believed that eliminating the white primary was foundational for achieving integration in Texas, and he toured the state in 1940 to build support among African Americans, especially NAACP members, to launch an all-out assault on the white primary. Here he tells Carter Wesley, the editor and publisher of the Informer, *the black newspaper of Houston, that the NAACP will be "militant" in legal efforts to dismantle the all-white primary.*

APRIL 2, 1940

Dear Mr. Wesley:

Thanks for both of your letters, which came this morning, concerning the primary situation in Texas. We certainly appreciate your attitude in this whole matter, and our sorrow at the fact that you were attacked physically is tempered by the fact that you were successful in defending yourself. We intend to stick to our position in attempting to get a case filed and in fighting this thing out in a militant manner thru court procedure rather than with an idea of "negotiation" with the Democratic Party or any other party, or with the idea of pleading with them for "mercy." There is only one way to handle that bunch, and that is to take them into court. This we must do.

. . .

Sincerely yours,

Thurgood Marshall

MARSHALL TO WILLIAM HASTIE

This hard-hitting letter on the question of the right of African Americans to work gives some indication of the fullness of Marshall's legal plate. As he was fighting for the equalization of teachers' salaries in different parts of the country, leading the battle against the white primary in Texas, and gearing up in his battle for desegregation of the armed forces, Marshall was also tending to many other everyday duties at the NAACP. Perhaps most remarkable is that he was the one and only attorney leading the NAACP's legal battles at this point—and doing so without a law library in his office at the NAACP headquarters. It would take three more years—and the unmanageability of legal complaints from African American soldiers—before he would hire Milton Konvitz and Edward Dudley to join the legal team, and then another year before he would bring aboard Robert Carter, who would become Marshall's main assistant. Marshall would have felt comfortable sharing the following request with his good friend William Hastie, now the dean of Howard Law after a stint as the U.S. district judge in the Virgin Islands.

APRIL 19, 1940

Dear Mr. Hastie:

We have several cases in the office of discrimination within labor unions here in New York City which should be attacked. The discrimination extends from the most conservative A.F. of L. unions to the most radical C.I.O. unions. For example, the National Maritime Union (C.I.O.) discriminates against Negroes in the following manner:

All hiring is done from a central hiring hall, but when Negroes are sent to certain ships they are returned with the statement on their card that no Negroes can work on this particular ship, and the interesting point is that the man signing these cards is a member of the same union as the Negroes.

. . .

The most recent complaint and by far the most vicious one concerns the International Longshoremen's Association. The heads of this union have made it clear that their policy is to "run the niggers off the waterfront as far as possible." The Negro members of the union are suffering at the present time and are being pushed further and further away from their good jobs. On the Jersey side, it has reached the point that if a Negro union man applies for work, he is beaten up by members of his own union.

This is a most important phase of our work and one which we should do something about, but the answer is that I simply cannot do anything about it until after the primary cases and the teachers' salary cases are out of the way. We can do just so much and no more. I have told the Longshoremen that I will be able to have a conference with them the latter part of May when I come back from Texas and will make plans for action.

What I would like to know is whether or not we can get help from whoever is teaching labor law in the law school. I do not know who is teaching it this year, and I am wondering if you would talk it over with whoever is the teacher to see if he will help in the preparation of the legal procedure for attacking this problem. The procedure will have to be just about perfect because the Longshoremen's Association is not only powerful but is very "rough," and they do not mind using brute force along with their other tactics. It should make a marvelous scrap, and I think we are all in favor of having a good scrap on this question of the right of Negroes to work.

Sincerely yours,

Thurgood Marshall

MARSHALL TO WILLIAM HASTIE

Legal activists like Marshall saw Booker T. Washington, the founder of the Tuskegee Normal and Industrial Institute in Tuskegee, Alabama, as an accommodationist on issues related to civil rights. Washington had suggested that African Americans in the South could best pursue their rights not by seeking redress through the courts but by working hard, becoming educated, and strengthening personal character within the existing system of segregation. Although brief and lacking in detail, the letter below clearly reveals Marshall's distaste not only for Washington but also for Robert Moton, the president of Tuskegee from 1915 to 1935, and Frederick Patterson, the president of Tuskegee from 1935 to 1953. It was not only Tuskegee that evoked Marshall's displeasure in his early career with the NAACP—the Urban League did, too. As an advocate of direct legal action, Marshall no doubt believed that the Urban League was neither aggressive nor direct enough in its efforts to combat civil rights problems.

Marshall's letter below was in response to an April 18 letter that Clennon King, Jr., had sent Walter White: "I'm just another Negro trying to get an education," King had written, "and in my attempts I have tried to apply for admission to my own state (Georgia) university and have been politely refused. I wish to be a lawyer, but if they will not permit me to study at the University of Georgia there is no other school I can attend of equal or better instructional opportunities."

Marshall's closing point in this letter is noteworthy; he was very selective in choosing his school cases, and more than a few black students were disappointed to learn that he refused their cases because the credentials of their undergraduate colleges did not meet the requirements of the graduate schools to which they applied.

APRIL 23, 1940

Dear Bill:

Enclosed are copies of three letters concerning an applicant to the Law School of the University of Georgia. Personally I think this boy deserves about five medals for having this much courage despite his training at Tuskegee in the atmosphere of Booker T. Washington, Moton, and Patterson. Will you please check with Registrar Wilkinson as to the qualifications of Tuskegee Institute? I am writing King that we will let him know of our decision in this matter as soon as possible.

. . .

Yours truly,

Thurgood Marshall

CHARLES HOUSTON TO MARSHALL

Charles Houston, formerly special counsel of the NAACP, and Marshall normally saw issues eye to eye, but the two disagreed on the question of accepting segregated units in the armed forces. Houston favored moving African American soldiers into all available positions in the armed forces (pilot training camps, for example), even if that meant accepting segregated units; Marshall and the NAACP did not want to accept any segregation at all. In the following letter, Houston, now in private practice, gently charges Marshall with being a heady idealist who might not be able to win tangible benefits for African Americans serving in the military.

APRIL 24, 1940

Dear Thurgood:

Regarding your letter of April 19 concerning the Army, it seems to me the NAACP finds itself in the dilemma it faced in 1917 regarding a separate training camp, Fort Des Moines. I frankly do not think that any one is going to get very far at the present time agitating for Negro integration in the Army unless he will accept the principle of segregated units. I do not think the situation is critical enough at the present time for the NAACP to abandon its traditional fight against segregation in order to advance the status of Negroes in the Army. Therefore, it is my suggestion that the NAACP continue its present line of asking for integration of Negroes in the Army without segregation, realizing that for the present it is accomplishing little more than pointing out the ideal.

On the other hand, I believe it is absolutely necessary for us to move to get Negroes incorporated into all branches of the armed forces, whether we have to accept segregated units or not. I call to your attention that in 1917 the late president of the NAACP, Joel Spingarn, was the first person to agitate for a separate camp and the hardest plugger for the same before the Negro college men took up the issue themselves. As in 1917 we are faced with a condition and not a theory.

Therefore, on this issue I am leaving the NAACP and going over to fight with the *Courier* for the incorporation of Negroes into the armed service, because I believe that we are pointing toward war and that Negroes are going to be inducted any way and I am anxious to get them in the armed forces on the most favorable terms and avoid the tragedies of the last war.

I wish to say that I have complete sympathy for the NAACP's point of view and believe its standing is a necessary counter-weight to what we are going to do. I wish to make it clear that in my action I am not acting at all for the NAACP and I shall do my best to state the position of the NAACP and my complete agreement with it in theory.

Yours very sincerely,

Charlie

MARSHALL TO HIS WIFE VIVIAN MARSHALL

Marshall traveled through the Deep South in May to meet with local NAACP leaders about voting rights, teachers' salaries, state politics, and other matters. Marshall found himself making a number of action plans, and in a May 5 letter to Walter White, he even counseled direct political action to unseat Senator Albert "Happy" Chandler, Jr., of Kentucky, yet another Southern segregationist.

After the stop in Louisville, Maceo Smith, the head of the Texas NAACP, drove Marshall all around the state, seeking to build support for the NAACP campaign to wipe out the all-white Texas primary, and in the letter below Mar-

shall sends handwritten news of the trip to Vivian Marshall. It is one of the few extant letters to his first wife, and its tenderness is rarer still.

NO DATE [MAY 1940]

Dearest Shooksie:

This is really beautiful country down here. A. Maceo Smith drove us over 400 miles yesterday in eight and a half hours. The trip was fine and the scenery was swell. Maceo's wife came along with us so we will be good.

I have been eating so much that I am sure I have gained more weight. The trip as a whole is more than interesting.

Thanks so much for your letter. Don't worry because one of these days I will be able to stop traveling so much and we will be together.

Be good, shooksie—I'll see you soon.

All my love,

Thurgood

The trip energized Marshall, and in a May 14 letter to White, he wrote: "Despite any views to the contrary about Negroes in the South, the Negroes in Texas are not afraid to fight for their rights, are willing to put up their money and are looking to the NAACP for leadership." (In later years, Marshall stated that it was easier for him to build support among African Americans in the South rather than those in the North. "Yes," he stated, "I think that we had more trouble in the North than in the South. We never had any trouble with support in the South. Never. In Texas alone, on the Texas primary case, I raised over half a million dollars down there—right in the state of Texas.")

At the NAACP annual conference a month after this tour, Marshall gave a rousing speech on his plans to attack the white primary. "Take Texas, where there are a million Negroes," he stated. "If we get a million Negroes voting in a bloc we are going to have some fun."

MARSHALL TO WALTER WHITE

Marshall's trip also confirmed his sense that African Americans were eager to gear up for an active campaign even in one of the most dangerous places for blacks at this point in history—Birmingham, Alabama.

MAY 22, 1940

Dear Walter:

Been going so fast have not had time to make report sooner.

. . .

Birmingham: . . .

Birmingham is as expected. The Negroes in Birmingham and other spots I have touched are *not* afraid. They still have courage and are *anxious* to attack the problems confronting Negroes.

. . .

This trip has been the most encouraging yet and I am sure that this voting problem is the problem for us. This is the *only* point that all Negroes will rally around. The NAACP can really go to town in the South now. Everyone is watching for "Fifth Column" movements, and while they are watching for communists, we can go to town.

. . .

I am convinced more than ever of a real program to get the right to vote in the South. Would be good if press release this week would carry story to this effect and the type of cases we have planned in each city as set out in this note. This program will sell itself. Hope to get back by Sunday morning. This trip has been mighty hard but has really been worth it. I am all for these Negroes down here. They want to fight.

Regards to office—see you

Thurgood

REQUESTS FOR HELP TO THE NAACP

The NAACP received countless letters about racial discrimination and violence from anonymous sources, and many of these letters ended up on Marshall's desk. He would often forward them, along with a request for an investigation, to local NAACP leaders, and if he received a credible report in reply, he would sometimes forward the material to the Department of Justice. Immediately below is an anonymous letter that Marshall forwarded to M. M. Flynn, the president of the Shreveport NAACP, with a request for a grassroots investigation. Dated June 10, 1940, the letter is striking in its characterization of the individuals involved in the violence.

I was told of an incident a few weeks ago which I would like to outline to you here.

A Bank which failed in this Town is being liquidated and the operation of the land held under mortgage is being supervised by Mr. Murray Calhoun, a leading citizen of this place. While tending his duties on one of the plantations near here, a discussion with a negro foreman under him resulted in the negro using what Mr. Calhoun considered disrespectful language toward him, where upon Mr. Calhoun struck the negro, and began search for a club to continue the assault. Reports say the negro then informed Mr. Calhoun if he struck him again, he would kill him. Mr. Calhoun then left the scene, and when the negro had time to reflect on what had passed, fled his job and went into hiding. This happened about one month ago.

This morning I learned the negro had been beaten to death about a mile outside the limits of Lansfield a few nights ago by a mob. When the mob had left the scene of the flogging, members of his own race timidly came and took the body to a little town Pleasant Hill, Louisiana, near here and buried it. I suppose these same members were huddled in their homes and with the fear of death running through them, as they listened to the despicable sounds of this cowardly thing.

This was not committed by a band of thugs. The participants are the cream of this society and pillars in the church. In the light they sing love of liberty, and discourse expertly on the Constitution of this Country, then under cover of darkness they do this repulsive thing which violates every fibre of the Constitution, and with immunity unless you can do something about it. . . .

At other times, Marshall would forward anonymous letters not only to law enforcement officials but also to the national media, with the hope of drawing attention to the problems he dealt with every day. A year earlier, for example, he forwarded the following anonymous letter to Time *magazine, which elected not to report on the incident:*

I am herewith informing you that on 8th of this month at Canton, Miss., a Negro named Joe Rodgers was lynched.

It is said that this Negro was a workman at Dinkman Lbr. Co. and was notified by his foreman that he had to live in the mill quarters and he refused to obey these orders. However the Company deducted from his week wages the sum of $5.50 for rent just as if he was living in the mill quarters, this however, the negro protested and asked for his full payment and his foreman struck him with a shovel and the negro struck him back with one upon which he was captured, tied hand and feet, shot, tortured with red hot irons and cut and the body was thrown into Peral River. The body was recovered from the river three days later and was held in the Funeral Parlors of People's Funeral Home at Canton, Miss., and was buried at Forest, Miss. This man was a deacon of Mt. Zion Baptist Church at Canton, Miss., President of the Church Choir and had a splendid record in every way. The News papers of Canton, Miss., have not written a word and there have been no arrests made and the negroes have been told not to discuss the incident. I am asking that you investigate at once. . . .

At the other end of the spectrum, NAACP activists would sometimes bring victims of racial discrimination and violence directly to the NAACP offices in New York. In the case below, George Foster, a resident of New York City, showed up at the NAACP offices with a young man, Robert Booker, who had fled to New York after escaping from peonage, or forced labor, on a farm in rural Georgia. Marshall understood all too well that slavery did not end with the Emancipation Proclamation, and he forwarded Booker's June 5 affidavit below, along with a request for an investigation, to T. M. Alexander, an NAACP activist in the Atlanta area.

I do not know who my parents were. My twin brother, George Booker, who is still on the Laster Farm, and myself were orphans and lived in an orphanage in Atlanta. A white man, Mr. Bibby Laster, took us from the orphan home to his farm. I don't know how old I was, but I carried in wood and carried water into the fields for the workers. Until about five or six months ago I lived on Mr. Laster's farm in Georgia, near Atlanta, within sight of the Federal Prison. One road on the farm leads to the prison, and the other we used to take when going to town to sell watermelons. I do not know exactly where the farm is located. This information may be obtained from a Mr. Lovely, a colored man who brought ice to the farm every day from Atlanta.

Mr. Laster is a heavy-set man, with light brown hair, gray eyes, about 6' in height, and about 250 pounds; with a rough scar on the right cheek from ear to lips.

Mr. Laster used to beat any of the Negro workers whenever they did not move fast enough for him. When working in the fields, he used white men as guards to keep the Negroes from running away, and to keep them at work. We had to get up about 3 o'clock in the morning and get the mules into the field and work all day until dark, when we were made to shell peas. About ten o'clock at night we were given our only meal of the day of cornbread and peas and a piece of meat about the size of your thumb. Before coming to New York I never ate with a fork and knife before. Some of us ate out of tin plates, and some of us ate out of the big pans which they used to mix the bread in. Three of us had to eat out of one of the big pans.

Mr. Laster used the "rabbit-box" when a Negro didn't do what he said to do. Heavy irons were put on the heads of those who were put in the "rabbit-box." Mr. Laster would strike you with a rubber hose or anything.

One Sunday, in about November or December of 1939, Mr. Laster asked me to scrub floors and beat up some peas. I was tired and told him that I had "given out" and did not feel like working. Mr. Laster told me I had to work anyhow whether I felt like it or not, and then he cut me with his pocket knife from back of my left ear to the middle of my throat, and the colored people there had to plead with him not to kill me. After the cut healed, I began plowing again. One day while plowing, I went to the edge of the field to get some water, and hearing the B&O freight train in the gulley, I slide down the hill and caught the train. The "conductor" told me that I could ride between the cars. He told me how to get to New York.

I am about 23 years old, 5′5″, have black hair and brown eyes, and dark brown complexion. I would like to get my brother, George Booker, off that farm too.

I understand everything in this statement and every bit of it is true to the best of my knowledge.

MARSHALL TO PRESIDENT FRANKLIN ROOSEVELT

Restrictive covenants were used by real estate companies to ensure that certain neighborhoods remained all white, and in 1940 the Federal Housing Administration (FHA) proposed that the following covenant be used in its real estate contracts in Dover, Massachusetts: "No person of any race other than ______ [to be filled in by real estate companies] shall use or occupy any building or any lot, except that this covenant shall not prevent occupancy by domestic servants of a different race domiciled with an owner or tenant." Marshall protested this covenant, along with the FHA's practice of refusing to insure loans to African Americans seeking to buy homes in white areas, in a July 23 letter to FHA Director Stewart McDonald: "This type of racial discrimination and segregation is not only unreasonable and unjust but is also unlawful. The use of federal funds for the establishment of segregation in violation of the spirit of the United States Constitution is not only unreasonable to the Negro applicants in Dover, Mass., and white applicants, who are likewise discriminated against, but is a direct insult to the entire Negro population of this country, which insult can be attributed directly to the Federal Housing Administration, a federal agency." With no satisfying answers from the FHA, Marshall feels the need to turn to McDonald's boss—President Roosevelt.

JULY 23, 1940

My Dear Mr. President:

We are enclosing a copy of our letter of this date to Mr. Stewart McDonald, Administrator of the Federal Housing Administration, concerning the problem of segregation being required by the FHA in the issuance of its insurance.

The Jamaica, LI situation, which was considered by you in January, 1939, and the present situation in Dover, Massachusetts, are but examples of other complaints we have received in this office.

The officials of the Federal Housing Administration contend that the maintenance of certain racial restrictions is necessary to maintain property. This, we believe, is untrue. It is clear, however, that the FHA, administrating federal funds, cannot set up these racial restrictions or require them as a prerequisite to the securing of FHA protection. Such a policy amounts to the establishment and preservation of segregation in certain areas and the introduction of racial segregation into states like Massachusetts where segregation is against the public policy of the state.

The Federal Housing Administration has refused to take a firm stand in this matter and, as a result, the practice is continuing and is being extended.

Respectfully,

Thurgood Marshall

Although the president did not respond directly to Marshall's letter, less than a month later FHA Director McDonald sent Marshall news of a landmark vic-

tory for the NAACP. "I am today ordering the restrictive covenant about which you protested removed from our 'Outline of Protective Covenants,'" McDonald wrote. But Marshall was ever wary, and in a November 26, 1940, letter to Ray Guild, the president of the Boston NAACP, he wrote: "Although the matter seems to be cleared up in Dover, we must watch Stewart McDonald, who is Administrator of the FHA. He is definitely anti-Negro in his attitude and cannot be trusted. We will continue to keep after him until all discrimination in the FHA is removed."

MARSHALL TO SECRETARY FRANK KNOX

On June 14, the NAACP sent Franklin Roosevelt a letter asking him "to rescind a recent War Department order designating the New York 369th Infantry as 'colored,' and to order immediate abolition of the 'color line' in the armed forces of the government." Marshall follows up this request with a letter to the secretary of the navy.

JULY 26, 1940

Dear Sir:

One of the problems confronting Negro citizens of this country at the present time is the question of their treatment in the armed forces of the nation. The present program of expansion of the Navy requires the enlistment of large numbers of American citizens and also the reorganization of the present forces. For years Negroes have been refused the right to serve in any but certain separate units of the Navy. They are refused enlistment in any branch of the service with the exception of the mess corps.

The success of the new defense program depends entirely upon the establishment of more "unity" among the American citizens of this country. The refusal to fully integrate Negroes, who constitute the largest minority group in this country, tends to destroy that "unity" which is necessary to the success of the new defense program.

The will of the American people, both Negro and white, is expressed in the platforms of both major political parties, which call for the removal of discrimination against Negroes in the Army and Navy. Although Negroes as American citizens are willing and anxious to do their part in the present national defense program, they insist on the same rights as all other American citizens to serve in all branches of the armed forces without discrimination because of their race or color.

We, therefore, urge you as Secretary of the Navy to take the necessary steps to prevent any discrimination against Negroes in the new defense program and to remove the old types of discrimination now existing in the present armed forces to the end that Negroes will be integrated into the armed forces without any discrimination because of race or color.

Respectfully yours,

Thurgood Marshall

MARSHALL TO SECRETARY HENRY STIMSON

Marshall had sent Henry Stimson, the secretary of war, a letter similar to the July 26 letter to Frank Knox.

AUGUST 7, 1940

Dear Sir:

This will acknowledge your letter of August 2 relative to the use of Negro citizens in the present National Defense Program.

We agree with you that the National Defense Program can best be established by united support of the War Department plans. However, Negro citizens in this country, forming approximately one-tenth of the total population, cannot enter enthusiastically into any program of national defense which is based upon a policy of racial discrimination.

We fully appreciate the fact that under the present rules of the War Department there would be some difficulty in abolishing the existing policy of racial discrimination. At the same time, we believe that the War Department can discontinue this policy and enforce by its rigid discipline a policy of non-discrimination.

The present defense program is being pushed forward for the avowed purpose of protecting democracy in the United States. It is impossible to maintain such a program if the program itself is based upon undemocratic policies such as racial discrimination.

Negroes are willing to take their part in this defense program along with all other American citizens, but at the same time insist that they be given the right to serve in every branch of the armed forces for which they may be qualified without distinction because of race or color. The policy of establishing a few segregated units for Negroes, which do not give the same training as other units, and the refusal to permit Negroes to enlist in the Air Corps and other branches of specialized training, is opposed to both the spirit and letter of the United States Constitution and especially the Fifth Amendment thereto.

In your letter, you mention that "Unity can be destroyed by attempting to establish a program which is contrary to the War Department's plans, by those who are not familiar either with the principles involved or the requirements of such plans." We are thoroughly familiar with the evils of segregation and racial discrimination. From experience in the last war and the period from 1918 to date, we are aware of the disastrous effects of racial discrimination in the armed forces.

The present defense program is supposed to be aimed at obtaining the best qualified men to defend our country. This can never be accomplished as long as approximately one-tenth of the population is excluded from the right to serve in the armed forces solely because of race or color. We do not believe that the full integration of Negro citizens into the armed forces will destroy the unity you mention in your letter but, rather, that it will tend to establish the very unity which is needed.

Much emphasis at the present time is being placed on the necessity of an adequate air force with competent pilots. Mr. James L.N. Peck, author of "Armies With Wings" and several articles on aviation, one of which appeared recently in *The New York Times*, is a Negro trained pilot with much experience. Under the present rules, this man would be ineligible for use in the Army Air Corps simply because of his race or color. There are many other cases similar to this whereby the War Department is not only denying to qualified Negroes the opportunity to serve in that branch of the armed forces for which they are qualified, but also deprives the United States of the services of these men.

We again urge you as Secretary of War to take steps to abolish the policy of racial discrimination which now exists throughout the Army and to establish a policy of non-discrimination because of race or color in keeping with the United States Constitution.

Very truly yours,

Thurgood Marshall

In a remarkably condescending reply, Stimson wrote: "The success of the National Defense Program can best be established by united support of the War Department plans, which have been worked out after several years of study by those who have devoted their lives to these questions. Unity can be destroyed by attempting to establish a program which is contrary to the War Department's plans, by those who are not familiar with the principles involved or the requirements of such plans."

SECRETARY HENRY STIMSON TO MARSHALL

In an August 1 letter to Stimson, Marshall wrote that "the present program of expansion of the armed forces, and the enlisting of new men, has been made without any consideration for Negro citizens. In New York City several Negroes have applied at the regular recruiting offices pursuant to notices in the daily press and radio announcements. They have all been told that applications of Negroes are not being accepted. This type of discrimination against Negro citizens tends to destroy all hopes for complete unity among American citizens at a time when unity is needed more than ever." Marshall enclosed affidavits with his letter and concluded by urging Stimson to "take the necessary steps to abolish this type of discrimination against American citizens to the end that all qualified Negroes may have the right to enlist in the Army on the exact same basis as any other American citizen."

AUGUST 20, 1940

Dear Mr. Marshall:

I have been handed your letter of August 1, 1940, with enclosures, relative to the American negro youth and his right to volunteer to serve his country.

With respect to the Army, negroes are given opportunities for military training, and negro units of the Regular Army, National Guard, Reserve Officers' Training Corps, and the Citizens' Military Training Camps in the augmentation of the Army are now underway. Additional colored units have been authorized. These include one field artillery regiment, two coast artillery anti-aircraft battalions, one engineer regiment for general service, twelve quartermaster truck companies, and one chemical decontamination company. Enlistment of the men to fill up these units will be conducted by the United States Army Recruiting Service.

In accordance with the well-established policy which is endorsed by colored people, the races have never been mixed within the units of the United States Army.

Sincerely yours,

Henry Stimson

ROBERT PATTERSON TO MARSHALL

Patterson, the first U.S. undersecretary of war, replies to Marshall's August 7 letter to Stimson. Although Patterson tries to pass along good news, Marshall would not have considered the following reply as any sort of real victory in light of the NAACP's stance against segregation in the military.

AUGUST 29, 1940

Dear Mr. Marshall:

Reference is made to your letter of August 7, 1940, in further regard to the participation of negro citizens in the National Defense program.

In the Regular Army there are colored persons in all arms and services except the Air Corps, Signal Corps and Finance Department. In the recent augmentation of the Regular Army, colored tactical units have been activated in the Field Artillery, Coast Artillery, Corps of Engineers, Chemical Warfare Service, and Quartermaster Corps. Due to the time required to assemble and organize a trained nucleus for those units, recruiting was not authorized until August 15, 1940. Recruits are now being accepted to fill and maintain all units.

Experience has proved the undesirability of mixing white and colored personnel in the same unit, and the War Department is convinced of the undesirability of changing this policy at the present time.

With respect to aviation, there has been no development of colored personnel in this field. Therefore, the War Department arranged with the Civil Aeronautics Authority to organize an aviation school at Glenview, Illinois.

If selective service is approved, colored personnel will be inducted and trained in the Army of the United States in the ratio the available negro manpower bears to the available white manpower.

Yours very truly,

Robert P. Patterson

MARSHALL TO A. F. WHITNEY

Below is Marshall's letter to A. F. Whitney, the president of the Brotherhood of Railroad Trainmen, who had written a letter protesting the removal of Elizabeth Gurley Flynn, a founding member of the ACLU in 1920, from the ACLU board. The board (which Marshall was a member of) had removed Flynn because of her membership in the Communist Party. As an avowed anticommunist, Marshall did not protest the board's decision, and here he takes Whitney to task, not for defending Flynn, but for presiding over a racist organization—a classic case of switching terms and diverting focus.

SEPTEMBER 5, 1940

Dear Mr. Whitney:

I have just received a copy of your letter to Mr. Roger Baldwin, director of the American Civil Liberties Union, which has been sent to all of the members of the board of directors of the ACLU.

Your letter concerning the removal of Miss Elizabeth Gurley Flynn from the board of directors has presented many points which deserve the careful consideration of all of us.

The tone of your letter seems to stress repeatedly the question of the rights of individuals in this country and, especially, their civil rights. The question of Miss Flynn and the board of directors has been answered by Dr. Holmes, and I have no intention of attempting to add to Dr. Holmes' letter.

While reading your letter, written on the stationery of the Brotherhood of Railroad Trainmen, concerning the rights of individuals in a democracy and the "principle of qualifying liberty," I could not help from being reminded of the fact that the Brotherhood of Railroad

Trainmen by its constitution limits membership in its union to "any white male between the ages of 18 and 65." Thus, all qualified Negroes, solely because of their race, are excluded from membership in the Brotherhood of Railroad Trainmen.

I believe that any of us in speaking or writing on the question of liberty or the question of "qualifying liberty" should take into consideration all of the phases involved, including our own attitude on questions of liberty as applied to all individuals.

Very truly yours,

Thurgood Marshall

MARSHALL TO REPRESENTATIVE MARTIN DIES

Marshall kept close watch over the special investigative committee that would become known as the House Un-American Activities Committee (HUAC). At this point, HUAC—which turned its sights on communists, Nazis, fascists, and anything resembling un-Americanism—was known as the Dies Committee because its cochairman was Representative Martin Dies, Jr., of Texas, a pro-segregationist. Although the following letter to Dies drips with professionally worded sarcasm, it goes without saying that Marshall was deeply troubled by what he took to be a resurgence of the Ku Klux Klan. Indeed, in early 1940, Marshall held a conference with O. John Rogge, the assistant attorney general, about the possibility of prosecuting KKK members under federal statutes. Marshall also encouraged the ACLU to lobby the attorney general so that the Department of Justice would prosecute KKK members "in each instance where the activities of the Klan are aimed at a denial of rights guaranteed by the United States Constitution such as intimidation of voters at federal elections, intimidation of organizers for labor unions, intimidation of individuals seeking to hold public meetings and otherwise making use of the freedom of speech."

SEPTEMBER 27, 1940

Dear Sir:

It is reported in the Dallas, Texas *Morning News* of September 19 that you propose to hold hearings in that city in October on the question of subversive activities among Negroes in Dallas by communists, fascists, and other agents. We are very glad to know that you contemplate investigating subversive activities in Texas and that you will hold hearings in Dallas. We strongly urge that this investigation include the activities of the Ku Klux Klan and other groups active in Dallas County. These latter have been very active against Negro citizens.

On Wednesday, September 22, 1938, Dr. George F. Porter, a Negro juryman, was seized in the county courthouse in Dallas, Texas, by one Walter Miller and an accomplice, dragged from the courthouse in the early afternoon and thrown head first down the front steps. This was done for the sole purpose of intimidating Dr. Porter, who was exercising his right as an American citizen to serve on a jury for which he was called. This act of total disrespect for not only the rights of Dr. Porter, but also for the courthouse itself, is clearly the type of lawlessness prevalent in Dallas, Texas, as a result of the open activities of the Ku Klux Klan in that area.

Within the past few months, many Negroes were forced to move from their homes to make way for a housing project in Dallas. They were unable to find homes in the so-called "Negro" areas, but some were offered homes in the 3500 and 3600 blocks on Howell Street. Despite the guarantees of the federal Constitution and laws providing for the right of an American citizen to occupy property, members of the Ku Klux Klan and other organizations have been throwing rocks into these homes, starting fights and doing all in their power to force the occupants to move from the homes they have purchased. Last week the residence of Logan Jones in South Dallas was damaged by a bomb thrown from a passing automobile. This type of lawlessness is still continuing in Dallas.

If your committee proposes to hold hearings in Dallas and is sincere in its efforts to investigate "subversive" activities, it seems that it should investigate the brazen invasion of the constitutional rights of Negro citizens by certain groups in Dallas.

These acts, rather than the action of Negroes in purchasing property pursuant to their constitutional right and their attempt to live on their property, are the real un-American activities.

The failure of the local police department and sheriff's office to protect Negroes in the exercise of their constitutional right in Dallas is also a denial of the due process and equal protection of the laws by the state of Texas.

The Negroes of Dallas, Texas, will welcome such an investigation, and the members of our branch there are anxious to cooperate with any hearing which is aimed at investigating the un-American activities of the Ku Klux Klan and other subversive groups.

Very truly yours,

Thurgood Marshall

MARSHALL TO ASSISTANT ATTORNEY GENERAL O. JOHN ROGGE

In the summer of 1940, the body of Elbert Williams was retrieved from the Hatchie River in Tennessee. Williams, an organizing member of the Brownsville NAACP, had been lynched because of his efforts to register himself and other African American voters in Haywood County. After the lynching, white mobs expelled other leaders of the local NAACP effort to register voters for the 1940 presidential election, and the NAACP sent telegrams of protest to President Roosevelt. In the letter below, Marshall criticizes Rogge, the assistant U.S. attorney general, for failing to act in response to the Williams lynching.

OCTOBER 9, 1940

My Dear Mr. Rogge:

Please find enclosed copy of a letter we have received from our representative in Jackson, Tennessee, concerning the Brownsville situation, which is self-explanatory. If you desire the name of our representative for the purpose of having him identify the members of the mob, we will be happy to send it to you, provided he is guaranteed the protection to which he is entitled.

In view of the enclosed letter and the facts contained therein, we once again strongly urge the Department of Justice to act effectively in this particular case. You realize, we are sure, that the failure of the Department of Justice and the state of Tennessee to act in the case of Elbert Williams, who was lynched because he attempted to exercise his constitutional right to register to vote in a presidential election, permits the members of the mob to circulate in the community and this in itself is a deterrent to Negro citizens in Brownsville who wish to exercise their constitutional right to vote on next Tuesday in the presidential election. The failure of the Department of Justice and the state of Tennessee to take effective action in a case that is clearly a violation of both the laws of the state of Tennessee and of the United States deprives Negro citizens of Brownsville, Tennessee, of the right of protection in the exercise of the rights guaranteed them by the United States Constitution.

Very truly yours,

Thurgood Marshall

No charges were ever filed, and the local NAACP branch was successfully suppressed for years to come.

MARSHALL TO WILLIAM HASTIE

Marshall, always suspicious of the motives of U.S. military leaders, offers his friend Hastie blunt counsel about accepting an appointment with the Department of War. Although Marshall had lobbied hard for greater racial justice in the military, he seems to have been taken aback when the military sought to hire Hastie to handle race relations. Marshall, no doubt, did not relish the possibility of having to wage a public battle against a personal friend working on the inside for racial justice in the military.

OCTOBER 21, 1940

Dear Bill:

Walter left with me this morning your letter and proposed memorandum, which I have gone over carefully.

The first thing that struck me is that this whole question must be considered in relation to the time when the position is to be created. If this position had been considered months or weeks ago, it would be one thing. We must, however, at this time consider all of the surrounding circumstances.

I have no doubt concerning the integrity of Mr. Patterson, or of others associated with him, who are so well recommended by many people as being fair and just. At the present time, there is a "young war" going on between the Negroes and the War Department and White House. This appointment at this time will be viewed by the public in one or two ways: either as (a) a victory for Negroes in their fight for full integration into the armed forces without discrimination or segregation, or (b) as an act of appeasement, as an effort to fool the Negroes and to use a Negro leader for this purpose. At this stage of the fight, the odds are that such an appointment will be considered as an effort toward appeasement on the part of the War Department without their actually giving up anything.

Of course we are all opposed to the question of appeasement. The point is, however, what will the reaction of the Negro public be? What will be the reaction of the membership of the NAACP? I am convinced that the Negroes believe that this fight against the program of the War Department is one of the most important fights they have ever waged, and they are anxious to maintain a good fight rather than to consent to any method of appeasement.

If the above statements are true, you start off with the odds against you and the only way to counteract this is by actually showing concrete gain for Negroes. With this in mind, here are my suggestions on the memorandum:

Title:

Any title other than that of assistant secretary of war and no less than assistant to the secretary of war is "appeasement." On one hand, Negroes are convinced that *all* of the titles suggested in your memorandum, with the notable exception of Bob Weaver's, mean nothing. On the other hand, the War Department is so peculiarly set up that actually rank and title mean more than anything else under the sun. I cannot imagine a brigadier-general giving any respect to an administrative assistant to the secretary of war. This goes for the other departments as well.

Responsibilities:

I think your responsibility should be limited to the secretary of war only.

There is no serious objection to the other propositions of the memorandum with the exception of the proposed statement to accompany the appointment. This statement should set forth that the appointment is for the express purpose of working out a program for the elimination of discrimination *and* segregation. This, I think, is most important, and unless such a statement is made, I believe you will be "on the spot."

The suggestions given above are all I can think of at this time. If I get any additional ideas, I will telephone you. All of these suggestions are made in complete frankness because we need that at this time.

Sincerely yours,

Thurgood Marshall

Hastie served as civilian aide to the secretary of war from 1940 to 1942, with his primary responsibility lying in race relations within the military, and Marshall frequently called upon his friend to investigate incidents of racial injustice.

MARSHALL TO CARTER WESLEY

Marshall explains the fine nuances of his strategy in the Texas primary case. Wesley, the publisher of Houston's major black newspaper, favored taking on the Democratic Party directly, but Marshall thought that doing so would allow the courts simply to follow precedent set by Grovey v. Townsend *(1935), in which the Supreme Court decided that because the Democratic Party was a private entity and therefore "not subject to limitations imposed on state action," the party did not violate the constitutional rights of R. R. Grovey when he was denied the right to register to vote. Marshall thought the Grovey decision was the biggest setback to the NAACP campaign to enfranchise blacks throughout the South, and he was determined to build a case that would depict the primary as a state, not private, action.*

NOVEMBER 9, 1940

Dear Carter:

. . .

Let me try to explain my theory of the case. If we bring in the Democratic Party as such in the complaint, we will have a case *directly* in point with *Grovey vs Townsend.* If we take the position that the primary is a part of the election machinery as such without mentioning the Democratic Party as such, we will be nearer to *Lane vs Wilson.*

In the second place, this theory is that the primary election judges are *state* officers and not private individuals. They are state officers performing essential governmental functions, i.e., in charge of the primary election which in turn is a part of the regular election *machinery* of the state. We take the position that he acts *solely* under the statutes as a state officer in the exact same status as a judge of the regular election. Unless we can establish this, the whole theory falls and, as a matter of fact, any theory must work on having the primary judges as state officers. I think we are all agreed on the point that they must be state officers.

The question of dispute is on the question of whether we take the position that (a) the Democratic Party under the law in Texas is so constituted as to be acting for the state in holding primaries so as to be within the 14th Amendment, or (b) the primary and the Democratic Party are two separate things and that the primary *itself* is state action, that the judges act under the state and not under the Democratic Party. I lean to the latter on the theory that the primary is a part of the election machinery like the paying of poll tax, listing of qualified voters and the general election itself. The theory is also based on the fact that the statutes regulating elections have always set up the same requirements for primary and general elections. The primary is not something by itself but is a part of the whole thing, i.e., the qualifying procedure for voters, the selection of candidates and the general election itself. The state has taken over this entire job and *each* step is a part of the process of "voting" and is within the term "election."

This we are trying to make clear in the complaint. I think that I am now in a position, with the suggestions from all of the lawyers, to make it clear. If I could get about a week to myself without a million other items, I believe I could make it clear in the complaint. We will all work Monday and Tuesday and we will see what comes out.

Thanks again for your cooperation.

Thurgood

MARSHALL TO SECRETARY CORDELL HULL

Only rarely did Marshall deal with racism beyond the United States, but this letter to the secretary of the navy is an example of his entering the field of international relations as a result of a complaint made by a member of the NAACP. Marshall sent a copy of this letter to President Roosevelt on December 12.

DECEMBER 11, 1940

My Dear Mr. Secretary:

A member of our Association, who is a citizen of the United States and a resident of Philadelphia, Pennsylvania, has sent us copy of a notice posted on an American ship, the "M. S. Gulfhawk," as follows:

. . .

> The Venezuelan Government has issued instructions to all masters of vessels arriving in Venezuelan ports through its immigration boarding officers at port of arrival that the following members of the vessel's crew are not permitted at Venezuelan ports.
>
> 1. Any member of the crew belonging to belligerent nation.
>
> 2. Any person of Negro race.
>
> 3. Any person of the Yellow race (Chinamen).
>
> No passes will be issued to the above-mentioned persons by order of the Venezuelan government. Any person disobeying the above instructions does so at his own risk. What the punishment is for disobeying these instructions, I don't know, but whatever it is, persons disobeying them must be ready to accept the consequences for their actions. So that there shall be no misunderstanding about these instructions you may call at the Venezuelan Consulate for verification through your union agent at Philadelphia.
>
> *(signed) John F. Charlton (Captain)*

This rule by the Venezuelan government demonstrates a case of clear discrimination against Americans of both the Negro and the Oriental races. We fully realize that this is a matter within the jurisdiction of the Venezuelan government. At the same time, we believe it is the duty of our State Department to take the necessary steps to persuade the Venezuelan government to discontinue this policy of discrimination against American citizens. . . .

The United States has protested discrimination against other races by foreign countries in Europe, even to the extent of protesting discrimination against people who are not citizens of the United States. This type of condemnation is to be commended, but at the same time we believe that the State Department should be just as vigorous in protesting discrimination against its own citizens by foreign countries. It is difficult to understand how unity is to be built up in this hemisphere if other nations are permitted to discriminate against American citizens because of their race or color.

Very truly yours,

Thurgood Marshall

A little more than a month later, Harold Finley of the State Department informed Marshall that "a report has been received from our Embassy in Caracas stating that landing privileges have been accorded by the Venezuelan Government to members of the crews of the Grace Line who are American citizens and who are of the Chinese or Negro race. While this permission was granted in connection with the Grace Line, it is not believed any difficulty will be encountered by the crews of other American vessels."

CHAPTER FIVE

1941

MARSHALL TO WILLIAM HASTIE

In this letter to Hastie, formerly at Howard Law and now civilian aide to the secretary of war, Marshall expresses his hope that Hastie and Truman Gibson, who also worked on civil rights issues for the secretary, would hear the concerns of James Peck, a young journalist and an all-around political radical, about the establishment of a segregated air corps at Tuskegee.

JANUARY 17, 1941

Dear Bill:

Jimmie Peck was in the office a few minutes ago and very worried about the newspaper accounts of the Jim Crow air corps to be set up at Tuskegee. He says that it will be impossible to set up a separate unit that will be equal to the regular unit. This is based upon many facts concerning the regular army set up for air corps. He is familiar with all of these facts.

What about our sending him to Washington for an *off the record* conference with you and Gibson to give you the material to attack this set up on a basis of inequality as well as the question of the evil of segregated units? This fellow really has the dope and could act as an expert advisor. We will pay his transportation.

If this is agreeable he can come down the first part of next week. He has several free days. What about it? Let me know by Monday morning because Peck is to call early Monday morning.

Sincerely,

Thurgood

Marshall was incensed by the possibility of a segregated air squadron, and less than a month after he wrote this letter, the NAACP publicly released a formal letter of protest sent to Hastie. The letter characterized the War Department's plans as yet another example of "the undemocratic and un-American practice of segregation of the Negro." The protest fell on deaf ears, however, and African American pilots were trained as a segregated unit at the Tuskegee Army Air Field in Tuskegee, Alabama.

MARSHALL TO ATTORNEY GENERAL ROBERT JACKSON

Marshall sent numerous letters to the Department of Justice during his years with the NAACP, and not all of them had the same urgency. Three days before sending the following letter, for instance, Marshall had asked the attorney general to investigate bombings of the homes of African Americans who had protested restrictive covenants in Dallas, Texas. While the contents of this letter may seem mild by comparison, Marshall always considered the infringement of constitutional rights to be sufficient reason for a direct appeal to the attorney general.

JANUARY 20, 1941

Dear Sir:

. . .

We have just received a letter from our branch in Memphis, a paragraph of which states as follows:

> *The process of intimidating Negroes goes on unabated in Memphis. The incidents are small in themselves but their totality is startling. Police enter any Negro cafe or poolroom at any time, force the patrons to raise their hands, then proceed to paw over them, male and female,*

searching for God-knows-what! They use vulgar and abusive language and any retort brings arrest. So also any Negro on the street at any time, day or night, is liable to search and insult and in many, many cases physical injury. A single illustrative case: a Negro sitting on the last seat in a Jim Crow bus was ordered to get up for a white person who was standing. The Negro pointed out that he was sitting in the last seat of the car. He was arrested. A colored woman, standing nearby, exclaimed, "Lord, what are we coming to!" For that she too was arrested.

We therefore urge that an investigation be made of both sides of this question to the end that the civil rights of Negroes in Memphis be protected.

Very truly yours,

Thurgood Marshall

MARSHALL TO WALTER WHITE

Forced confession was a standard practice of many white law enforcement officials when dealing with African American suspects throughout the country, and Roscoe Dunjee, a national figure in the NAACP and the editor of Oklahoma City's Black Dispatch, *had written the NAACP about a sensational case of forced confession in Hugo, Oklahoma. Dunjee eventually persuaded Marshall to travel to Hugo to help defend W. D. Lyons, an African American sharecropper, from charges that he had killed three members of a white family.*

FEBRUARY 2, 1941

Dear Walter:

Well, we are back from Hugo. Looking back at last week gives much food for thought. When Lyons was arraigned last year there were state troopers, etc. present. When I arrived in Hugo last Sunday night I was not quite sure what was going to happen. Stanley Belden, the white lawyer who was in the case with us, and Dr. Williamston of Idabell, one of Dunjee's regional directors, met me at the bus depot after a seven-hour ride on the back seat of the bus. We went over the case as best we could that night and talked to as many people as possible. Word got around town that "a New York lawyer" was in town for the case.

Monday morning we were in the court at nine a.m., after having talked to Lyons since eight. Both of us were convinced he was innocent. When we walked in court, word went around that "a nigger lawyer from New York" was on the case. Court attaches were very nice and explained that this was their first such an animal. About 9:15 the court opened with several motions about other cases. The chief of police and several officials had just been put in jail for conspiracy to sell whiskey—a model law enforcement community. While these motions were going on I noticed that the judge was smokin' a big cigar and maybe a little informal. We still did not know what the reaction would be to the two factors of a Negro lawyer and a New York lawyer in this case.

Well, our case was called. I was introduced to the court and took a seat at the counsel table—the building did not fall and the world did not come to an end. The courtroom and courthouse were jammed and I mean jammed. The judge announced that "two nationalities" were involved and he did not want any disorder in the courthouse. We started picking a jury. Every juror denied he had any prejudice against Negroes. Each one said he could give a Negro as fair a trial as a white man. Several, however, refused to sit because they had fixed opinions concerning the case—others were opposed to capital punishment. By this time the chief counsel, Roscoe Dunjee, had arrived from Dallas and took his place at the counsel table. By the time we had struck three jurors off and others had been excused, the panel was exhausted and the state's attorney was getting ready to call additional talisman from the streets when we decided it was best to take what we had than to let him go out and get his friends, relatives, etc. The governor had sent down Sam Latimore, assistant attorney general, who also took part in the case.

After the noon recess the crowd had about doubled. During the first part of the state's case we agreed that Belden would do the work and leave me for the confession so that I could keep the record straight on that point. After closing that day word got around that "that nigger lawyer hasn't said anything, etc." That night we looked for a law library or law books or anything similar thereto. No could find. The next day the state put on the warden of the pen to testify about the confession and the fireworks started. We asked the jury be excused while we made objections to the confession. This was done and we put on testimony to show that Lyons was beaten and forced to sign the confession here in Hugo the same day he was taken to the pen where he signed another. After much argument and the citing of our Supreme Court cases—letting him know that we had taken these cases up there—he ruled that the first confession was excluded but that the other could stay in. We took exceptions and the record is ready at that point for the Supreme Court. During this part of the case the county prosecutor became so angry that he admitted he stopped the officers from beating Lyons and also admitted he had seen the state investigator strike Lyons with a strap. That is in the record.

After this particular session many white people stopped us in the halls and on the streets to tell us they enjoyed the way the case was going and that they didn't believe Lyons was guilty. 90% of the white people by this time were with Lyons. One thing this trial accomplished—the good citizens of that area have been given a lesson in constitutional law and the rights of Negroes which they won't forget for some time. Law enforcement officers now know that when they beat a Negro up they might have to answer for it on the witness stand. All of the white people in the courtroom passed some mighty nasty comments after the officers lied on the stand. Several told the officers what they thought of them out in the halls. I did all of the cross-examining of the officers because we figured they would resent being questioned by a Negro and would get angry and this would help us out. It worked perfect. They all became angry at the idea of a Negro pushing them into tight corners and making their lies so obvious. Boy, did I like that—and did the Negroes in the courtroom like it. You can't imagine what it means to these people down there who have been pushed around for years to know that there is an organization that will help them. They are really ready to do their part now. They are ready for anything.

On Tuesday, Wednesday and Thursday there were several classes from the local white schools in court. The judge announced from the bench that they were there and that this was a "gala day"—can you imagine a Negro on trial for his life being considered a gala day? However, these children were also given a lesson in constitutional law and rights of Negroes that they wouldn't get in their schools. I bet they have more respect for Negroes now.

Verni Cheatwood, state investigator, sent down by the governor after two prisoners from the state road gang (criminals) had been arrested for the crime and confessed, admitted all this on the stand. He said he questioned Lyons for six or seven hours but never raised his voice, never cursed him, and positively never struck him with anything. He said he never had a black jack in his life. He did admit that they went out to the house where the deceased man, wife and child were burned and took some of the bones, including the jaw of the woman, and put these bones in Lyons's lap and put them on his arms and hands. That moved everyone in the courtroom. There were from seven to ten officers in the room during the questioning and beating—including the county prosecutor and his assistant. He made the confession early in the morning.

We put on the clerk (white) in the hotel where Cheatwood was staying, who testified that Cheatwood came in the hotel the day after the confession and told the porter to go upstairs and get his "nigger beater," which he showed to people in the lobby of the hotel telling that he had beat Lyons for six or seven hours and made him confess. The father and sister-in-law of the deceased woman both testified that Cheatwood had told them he beat Lyons for seven hours from his head to his feet. There are some good white people in the world.

Last Thursday the county prosecutor and assistant attorney general both asked for the death penalty for such a heinous crime, etc. The jury stayed out five hours and a half and brought in life imprisonment. You know that life for such a crime as that—three people killed, shot with a shotgun and cut up with an axe and then burned—shows clearly that they believed him innocent.

I think we are in a perfect position to appeal. We will prepare a motion for a new trial and file on Monday the tenth. The case has enough angles to raise a real defense fund over the country if handled properly. Think we should aim at $10,000. We have already raised around $275 in that small community down there. We can raise more than a thousand in this state. We could use another good defense fund and this case has more appeal than any up to this time. The beating plus the use of the bones of dead people will raise money. I think we should issue a story this week on the start of the defense fund and when I get back on the tenth we can lay plans for a real drive for funds.

. . .

Regards to the office.

Thurgood

An all-white jury found Lyons guilty, he was sentenced to life in prison, and Marshall appealed. The case eventually landed in the Supreme Court, where a

6–3 ruling sustained the earlier decision, marking Marshall's first loss at the high court.

MARSHALL TO GODFREY CABOT

At Walter White's urging, Marshall frequently corresponded with Godfrey Cabot, one of America's leading philanthropists of the era. Although this is a subtle fund-raising letter, it is an excellent source for understanding Marshall's thinking about the Texas primary case.

APRIL 25, 1941

Dear Mr. Cabot:

Mr. Walter White has referred to me your letter of April 17th and his reply. I returned to the office yesterday from Texas where we had the trial of the case of Sidney Hasgett on behalf of himself and all other qualified Negro voters in an effort to secure the right to vote in primary elections in Texas.

In Texas, and the other states of the Deep South, although Negroes are permitted to vote in the general elections, they are prohibited from voting in the Democratic primary elections. Since nomination at a Democratic primary is tantamount to election in these states, Negroes are effectively disbarred under this system. As long as Negroes are disfranchised in the South, our problems will continue.

The Supreme Court has repeatedly held that Negroes cannot be prevented from registering and qualifying to vote. The United States Supreme Court has also repeatedly held that Negroes cannot be prevented from voting in the general elections. It is our belief that if Negroes cannot be prevented from qualifying to vote and cannot be prevented from voting in the general elections, the same rule should apply in the intermediary step, namely, the selection of candidates when done pursuant to state statutes.

The entire election machinery in Texas was set up in 1905 and included three specific steps: (1) payment of poll tax in order to qualify as an elector, (2) primary elections pursuant to statutes, (3) general elections. The primary in Texas is governed solely by statutes which govern every step in the primary with minute detail. We believe that the primary in Texas is a vital part of the election machinery, and when a Negro is refused the right to vote in one of these elections, he is denied the right to vote within the meaning of the 15th Amendment.

The case was tried on last Friday and we are now awaiting the decision of the local judge. There is no doubt in our mind that the judge will rule against us and we will be faced with the necessity of appealing to the State Court of Appeals, and in the event of an unfavorable decision, to apply for certiorari to the United States Supreme Court.

When we started on this case last year, we estimated the total cost of eight thousand dollars to include a hearing in the United States Supreme Court. Our members in Texas have raised about two thousand dollars and will be able to raise at least a thousand more. The money is being raised by mass meetings, by smaller house meetings, by church socials, taffy-pulls and other means. Although the people in Texas are quite poor, they are bending every effort to finance this case with the full realization that their salvation depends upon the securing of the right to vote. I have made at least five trips to Texas in the last year in the interest of this case, and I am convinced that we must follow this case through and also that the Negroes in Texas are 100 per cent behind the case.

We will be very grateful for whatever assistance you can give toward this end.

Sincerely yours,

Thurgood Marshall

MARSHALL TO ATTORNEY GENERAL ROBERT JACKSON

Long before the Voting Rights Act of 1965, Marshall was protesting discriminatory voting practices in Texas, North Carolina, South Carolina, and all other states in the Deep South.

APRIL 28, 1941

Dear Sir:

Enclosed please find photostats of three affidavits from Negro citizens of Asheville, North Carolina. These citizens met all of the lawful requirements for registration and voting in the state of North Carolina but were refused the right to register in order to qualify for voting in the elections of November 1942 for the President of the United States and other federal officers.

You will notice from the affidavits that although white citizens were permitted to register without examination as to educational fitness, Negroes were required to perform impossible tests in order to qualify for registration. The requirement that Negroes read a paragraph of a book and then write it from memory is quite impossible.

The fact that Negroes were required to meet tests not required of white citizens effectively denied to Negro Americans in Asheville, North Carolina, their constitutional rights and is a violation of the 14th and 15th Amendments to the United States Constitution. We therefore urge an immediate investigation of the facts stated in the affidavits to the end that the guilty parties will be prosecuted under the laws of the United States.

Sincerely,

Thurgood Marshall

In his May 19 reply, Wendell Berge, the assistant attorney general, wrote: "A preliminary investigation has satisfied the United States Attorney that the state registrars used permissive discretion under the state statutes. Since it appears that the registrars complied with the North Carolina law in this respect, it is his opinion that an investigation is not necessary." Marshall responded to Berge's disappointing news partly by citing Guinn v. U.S., *a case in which the Supreme Court struck down educational requirements used by the state of Oklahoma to deny African Americans the right to vote. "Since the decision in* Guinn vs. U.S. *came as a result of a prosecution instigated in 1913 by the U.S. Department of Justice," Marshall wrote Berge, "we believe that it is no more than a reasonable request to urge the U.S. Department of Justice, in 1941, to be no less vigilant in attacking that provision in the Constitution and laws of the state of North Carolina when it is used to deprive Negro Americans of their right to vote in congressional elections."*

A little more than a year later, Marshall wrote James Hinton, the major activist of the South Carolina NAACP, to enlist him in the cause of dismantling the state's white primary. "[T]here is nothing more important at the present time than the fight to secure full suffrage for Negro citizens throughout the country,"

Marshall wrote. Showing considerable political sagacity, he also encouraged Hinton to "have as many soldiers as possible to enroll in the Democratic primary and also attempt to vote in the primary and point out in the affidavits for them that they are United States soldiers or sailors."

MARSHALL TO CAROLINE CUNINGHAME

In his March 25 letter to Caroline Cuninghame, a case consultant for Alabama's Department of Public Welfare, Marshall protested the department's refusal to grant assistance to Mary Woods, of Pell City, Alabama. Cuninghame responded to Marshall's letter on May 16: "Mary has two daughters living in the home with her. Both of these women are employed as cooks and average $2.50 each week for their services. The income of these two daughters is thought to be sufficient to support their mother in the manner in which she has been accustomed to all her life." The following letter is especially important because it is such a clear example of Marshall's nuanced understanding of the relationship between race and class.

JUNE 17, 1941

Dear Miss Cuninghame:

I regret that your letter of May 16 has not been answered sooner. I have been on the road continuously for many weeks working on cases throughout the South and have just returned to the office.

The fact that because the family of Mrs. Mary Woods, Pell City, Alabama, received a total of five dollars a week prevents them from getting assistance is certainly deplorable. However, we realize that it is not the fault of the Department of Public Welfare; it is rather the fault of the authorities charged with the duty of providing sufficient funds to prevent citizens of this country from being in need. It is for this reason that our organization has always urged Congress and local legislatures to increase rather than decrease appropriations to aid needy American citizens.

Negroes as a race are generally in the majority of the group requiring assistance. The reason for this is that Negroes are always the last to be hired and the first to be fired. We still believe that under our democratic system of government the time will come when all American citizens will live as human beings.

We thank you for your continued interest in this case.

Sincerely,

Thurgood Marshall

MARSHALL TO THE AMERICAN CIVIL LIBERTIES UNION

Marshall sought to form alliances with organizations that he felt would benefit his work with the NAACP, and here he lobbies one of his favorites, the ACLU, to support his efforts to desegregate housing in Dallas, Texas. Marshall's memo describes the extremely hostile environment of Dallas for African Americans seeking to reside in traditionally white neighborhoods, and he asks the ACLU to post rewards for tips that would lead to the conviction of individuals responsible for violence against blacks.

JULY 28, 1941

Background

For quite some time now there has been a growing housing shortage among Negroes in Dallas, Texas. When the United States housing project was proposed, it was necessary to purchase or condemn much of the Negro property. Negroes living on this property found themselves without homes, and because of the housing shortage, they were unable to secure suitable homes in the so-called "Negro" area. These Negroes purchased property on the outskirts of this so-called "Negro" area and proceeded to occupy their homes after they were purchased. All of this began during the latter part of the summer of 1940. When Negroes began to move into the thirty-four-hundred block of Howell Street, white residents in the thirty-five to thirty-nine hundred blocks of Howell Street organized themselves into mobs and began threatening the Negro homeowners. Negroes immediately requested protection from the local police force. While a squadron of police was patrolling the neighborhood September 4, 1940, the members of the mob stoned the home of Mr. O. L. Walker, and the former owner of the house, a white man, was knocked down by some of the members of the mob. The members of the police force finally "persuaded" the members of the mob to disperse.

Acts of Violence

Since that time there have been continuing threats of violence against these homeowners. There have been at least nineteen actual acts of violence, most of them bombings. All of these have come as a result of the purchase of property by Negroes in certain areas. A list of these bombings is attached hereto.

The Negroes in Dallas, Texas, through the local branch of the NAACP, have repeatedly requested assistance from the police department of the city of Dallas. Although investigations have been promised, not one arrest has been made. The Negroes have also applied to the governor of the state of Texas, and the governor has refused to take any action in this matter. The Negroes have also applied to the United States Department of Justice and to President Roosevelt. They have been advised that the federal government has no jurisdiction. As soon as the matter was brought to the attention of the federal government, Congressman Dies immediately instituted an investigation of the local branch of the NAACP on the ground that it was a "communistic" organization. The members of the branch notified Congressman Dies and his representatives that they were ready at all times to testify before the Committee and to explain the un-American activities being carried on in Dallas, Texas, by the members of the mob with the protection of the local police force.

In view of the fact that the Negro homeowners in these areas in Dallas, Texas, have been denied protection from the municipal, state and federal governments, they are forced to rely upon the basic principle of the right of a man to protect his home. Unless some action is taken, the owners of these homes will be forced to defend themselves by any means they may see fit to employ, which will unfortunately result in bloodshed. It is difficult to believe that American citizens in this country can find no protection for their own homes, which they have purchased.

The mayor and city councilman of Dallas, Texas, appointed an "interracial committee," composed solely of white men, for the purpose of investigating conditions. As a result of the recommendation of this committee, an ordinance was passed by the city of Dallas compelling segregation, in violation of the decisions of the United States Supreme Court.

On December 24 a case was filed in the local federal court to enjoin the enforcement of this ordinance, and on January 11, 1941, the case was dismissed "without prejudice" on the assurance of the city council that the ordinance had previously been rescinded. Judge Atwell, however, pointed out that such an ordinance was clearly unconstitutional.

At the present time local groups in the area are insisting that the Negro high school, built with PWA [Public Works Administration] funds, be turned over to white children. These groups have threatened physical violence against Negro children unless this is done.

I think that the above information is sufficient to form a basis for a letter to the acting attorney general and also for the posting of a reward. One word of caution should be made, however. In view of the fact that the police system in Dallas is extremely corrupt, the reward notice should be carefully worded so that it will apply only upon *arrest and conviction.* Otherwise, efforts might be made to collect the reward without any affirmative action being taken.

MARSHALL TO J. E. ANDREWS

Marshall tells the regional director of the Atlantic and Pacific Stores that one of their products is "repulsive."

AUGUST 8, 1941

My Dear Mr. Andrews:

Several weeks ago, one of our members brought to our office a can of stove polish purchased at one of the A. and P. stores in Jamaica, L. I. The top of the can contained the following words: "Nigger Head Stove Polish." A representative of this office immediately telephoned the district purchasing agent for the A. and P. stores, and was assured that this product was not on the list of products purchased by the A. and P. stores. An investigation, however, was promised.

This week, when we received additional complaints, another representative of this office on August 2 went to the A. and P. self-service store at 171-11 Linden Boulevard, Jamaica, L. I., and purchased a can of "Nigger Head Stove Polish." There was a full supply of this stove polish in this store. We are enclosing a reproduction of the top on the can of stove polish purchased.

No argument is needed to explain that the top of this can is not only repulsive to all Negroes, including the many Negro customers of A. and P. stores, but is purposely drawn up to ridicule the entire Negro race. In view of the fact that this matter was called to the attention of the purchasing agent for the A. and P. stores sometime ago, and in view of the fact that there has been no effort to correct the continuation of the sale of this product by A. and P. stores, we are calling upon you to immediately discontinue the sale of this product in your stores. We are confident that the Atlantic and Pacific stores will not continue to use this method of holding up the Negro race to ridicule, and to insult the many Negro customers of their stores.

We will appreciate your immediate attention to this matter.

Very sincerely yours,

Thurgood Marshall

MARSHALL TO THE NAACP OFFICE

*Along with W. J. Durham, an NAACP attorney in Texas, Marshall argued the first Texas primary case in federal court in April 1941, and his efforts were quickly undermined when the judge discovered that Marshall's client, Sidney Hasgett, had tried to vote only in the August 1940 runoff election, not in the primary itself. With this surprising information in hand, the judge ruled that the NAACP case had no standing, and as a result, local NAACP leaders in Texas, as well as the black media, grew sharply critical of Marshall's handling of the case. In the memorandum below, Marshall gives glimpses of a new primary case—*Smith v. Allwright. *This time, the plaintiff, Lonnie Smith, had tried to vote in a straight primary election, and Houston election judge S. E. Allwright had denied Smith the right to vote.*

Writing in a sarcastic mood, Marshall refers to Arthur Mitchell, the first African American Democrat to win a seat in the House of Representatives. Earlier in 1941, Mitchell, a graduate of Tuskegee Institute, had appeared before the Supreme Court and successfully argued his own case against the Chicago and Rock Island Railroad, which Mitchell brought after the railroad had forced him to sit in the Jim Crow section of the train. The humor reflected in the closing line is vintage Marshall, and so is the signature he used when writing in a good mood. Incidentally, the NAACP staff frequently called Marshall "TM" in their communications with him.

NOVEMBER 17, 1941

Background

Left New York October 31 for two days in Washington with enough clothes for one day and a toothbrush—still on the road.

Old Texas Primary Case

Only way to get to Dallas in time for the meeting on Wednesday, November 5th, was to fly by way of New Orleans to Houston and then to Dallas. On Tuesday night before I arrived in Dallas, Charlie Brackins and some other members of the local committee made some rather bad statements about "messing up" the case, etc. Had to take most of the time Wednesday pointing out to Brackins and others the true difficulties in the case and the benefits of filing another case. All agreed that if we did not get another case started all of us would have to leave the U.S. and go live with Hitler or some other peace-loving individual who would be less difficult than the Negroes in Texas who had put up the money for the case.

New Case????

The gang in Dallas swore that they had a good plaintiff for a new case. We immediately started drafting a new complaint to fit this situation. By the time the man returned to town we discovered that he was not sure when he tried to vote. On checking the dailies we found that he had attempted to vote in the "run-off" primary in 1940 and we were right where we started—out in the street. Checked again and could find no cases in Dallas. Next stop Houston—still not anxious to go live with Hitler. This was on November 8th.

In Houston talked with Dr. L. E. Smith, who is alleged to have attempted to vote at the right time. Checked his story as best I could. Started drafting complaint. Davis' stenographer can't type worth a dime. Tried for a day to get a stenographer who specialized in typing—no such animal available. Called Carter Wesley and drafted his secretary, who really can type.

Had to go to courthouse to find names of officials involved in case. . . . Went to file the case on Saturday. Court clerk said: "What, you here again." Discovered that I needed another copy for the court. Telephoned Carter again and drafted his secretary once more. Well, that case is in the fire. Departure from the United States was thereby delayed at least.

Came to New Orleans again yesterday and I arrived on the same day as the most illustrious leader of the Negro race, the Hon. Arthur W. Mitchell, who is to speak here tonight. Feel very bad because the people met Mitchell and gave him a sweet bouquet of roses (quite appropriate), and did not give me any. Speaking about giving Mitchell roses, I know a whole lot of things about him but never suspected that—did you?

Please note attached letters about Virginia and Minneapolis cases.

Our case is to be argued here on Wednesday and I will prepare the brief today and tomorrow. One of our leaders here was told by a leader of the other race Saturday that the powers that be here cannot afford to let a "northern nigger" win a case against them so they want to settle. Will you please respect the fact that I am now a *northern* nigger.

. . .

Regards to the office.

TM

Not quite three years later, Marshall and Hastie offered winning arguments when Smith v. Allwright *appeared before the Supreme Court.*

MARSHALL TO E. NORMAN LACEY

Lacey, the secretary of the Tampa NAACP, suggested that Marshall was negligent in a Tampa voting case, and here Marshall sends a blistering reply, coming across as an elitist attorney who sniffs at laypeople and their lack of familiarity with legal proceedings.

DECEMBER 16, 1941

Dear Mr. Lacey:

This will acknowledge receipt of copy of your letter, which you sent to Mr. LeFlore.

. . .

. . . No doubt you, as a layman, might believe as other laymen do that the only thing necessary to file and win a case is to draw up a pleading and put it in court. To give you an idea of what is necessary in these cases: We did research for *four years* before filing our cases to break down discrimination in state universities; we did research for more than *three years*, and are still doing research, on the cases to equalize teachers' salaries; we have been working on the question of primaries *since 1925*, and the first real break is at hand as a result of the recent decision of the United States Supreme Court in a case involving a primary in Louisiana. . . .

. . .

It seems to me that your entire complaint is that we do not understand the situation in your branch and other small branches, especially in the South. I think you should also realize that it is quite evident you do not understand the situation here in this office. There is one fulltime lawyer on the staff of the NAACP. There are 409 other active branches of the Association throughout the country. There are from fifty to one hundred branches which are semi-active. All of these branches consider this office as the headquarters and quite naturally consider me as their lawyer. In addition to these branches, there are hundreds of individuals who are members of the Association who are constantly writing to us for advice. . . .

. . .

Sincerely yours,

Thurgood Marshall

MARSHALL TO SECRETARIES OF WAR AND NAVY

Below is Marshall's draft of a letter mailed under Walter White's signature on December 30. The letter argues that the U.S. government is wrong to support the Red Cross's refusal to accept blood plasma donated by African Americans.

DECEMBER 30, 1941

Dear Sir:

The Blood Donor Service of the American Red Cross is now busily engaged in securing blood plasma from volunteers throughout the United States. According to the New York *Herald-Tribune* of yesterday, the Red Cross must now collect millions of blood plasma units instead of the 200,000 units previously sought. Despite this greatly increased need for blood plasma units in order to adequately protect our military forces, the Red Cross refuses to accept the blood plasma of Negro donors. The

Director of the Blood Donor Service of the American Red Cross states that in doing this, "the American Red Cross is acting pursuant to the requests and instructions of the Army and Navy."

The policy of refusing to take blood from Negro donors is against the prevailing practice in civil life. In New York City the prevailing practice, as we have been advised, has been to take blood regardless of the racial identity of the donor. In one particular hospital in New York City that has a large average of Negro patients, blood has always been accepted from all donors regardless of race. In this hospital there are performed at least 1,400 transfusions each year, with many instances of one patient receiving more than one transfusion. Thus, in civil life, transfusions are made without regard to race or color.

Dr. Charles R. Drew, who was medical supervisor of the Blood for Britain project, accepted blood from all racial groups without question. Dr. Drew has advised us that there is absolutely no basis in medical science for refusing the blood of Negro donors, and that there is absolutely no difference between the plasma obtained from the blood of a white and a Negro individual.

There can be no argument or belief that a white man who is given a transfusion of blood plasma from a Negro thereby becomes a Negro any more so than the injection of horse serum would make a human being become a horse or the injection of snake serum would change a human being into a water moccasin. Surely a transfusion of German or Italian blood plasma would not change an American into a German or Italian. We are sure there are no rules which will permit a member of an Irish-American racial group to insist on blood from an Irish-American rather than blood from a German-American.

During the present emergency, which is made clear by the increase in the requests for blood plasma from 200,000 units to millions of units, we believe that our government should not exclude more than ten percent of its population from the opportunity to join in giving their blood to save our way of life. We therefore appeal to you to discontinue the present policy and to instruct the Red Cross to accept the blood of all donors, regardless of race providing all other requirements are met.

Respectfully yours,

Thurgood Marshall

In his January 15, 1942, reply to Walter White, Ross McIntyre, a rear admiral in the navy's Bureau of Medicine and Surgery, wrote a rather weak defense: "So far as the Navy is concerned I wish to tell you that it has never requested the American Red Cross to refuse to take blood from negro donors." In 1942, when the Red Cross did accept blood from African American donors, the organization separated the blood of white and black donors; it continued the practice of blood segregation throughout the war years.

CHAPTER SIX

1942–1943

MARSHALL TO ASSISTANT ATTORNEY GENERAL WENDELL BERGE

Marshall details his criticism of the department's decision to "drop the case" against Tip Hunter, the sheriff of Haywood County, Tennessee, whose tenure was marked by intimidation and violence against local African Americans, especially those who sought to exercise their right to vote. Marshall also sent a copy of this letter to the attorney general, adding: "The denial of the right to vote, along with the prevalence of the spirit of mob violence, is doing more to destroy democracy in this country than anything else."

JANUARY 30, 1942

Dear Mr. Berge:

This will acknowledge your letter of January 24 confirming the conference held recently with Messrs. Rotnem and O'Donnell, at which conference I was advised that the Department had decided to close the files on the case involving Tip Hunter of Brownsville, Tennessee. At that conference I objected to dropping this case and wish to again express our extreme dissatisfaction at the decision.

The reason given for dropping the case is that there is not sufficient evidence to warrant prosecution. There does not seem to be any question of the quality of the evidence, but rather its quantity. The reason there is no more evidence is because of the type of investigation made by the Federal Bureau of Investigation. This case was reported to the Department in June of 1940. The FBI agents sent to investigate the charges against Tip Hunter talked to Tip Hunter as soon as they reached Brownsville and took him with them on their rounds to question witnesses. Quite naturally, the Negroes would not "talk" in front of Tip Hunter, who had already killed at least one Negro and run several others out of town.

The charges against Tip Hunter involve the use of force and intimidation to prevent the Negroes of Brownsville, Tennessee, from exercising their right to register and vote. All of the Negroes in Brownsville know that Tip Hunter killed one man and ran several other Negroes out of town who had attempted to register. If no action is taken against him by the Department, the intimidation of other Negroes who want to register and vote will be complete.

On May 6, 1940, several Negroes attempted to register but were told that the books would not be open until August. Tip Hunter and several others began to question Negroes as to whether or not they were going to register. Trouble began. Later in May, a Negro attorney of Jackson was run out of the courthouse in Brownsville. On the night of June 12, 1940, Tip Hunter and other members of a mob went to the home of Elbert Williams and took him from his home without even giving him time to dress. The next day Elbert Williams's body was found in the river. Tip Hunter and members of the mob also seized Elisha Davis, a responsible businessman of the town, and took him down to the river where they questioned him about his leadership in getting Negroes to register and vote. Davis was threatened with death and ordered to leave the county. Mrs. Elisha Davis can also identify several members of the mob who seized her husband. Another witness can testify as to having seen Davis down at the river being held by a mob, although he cannot identify any members of the mob.

Although the FBI investigation has not produced sufficient evidence, we have sent affidavits from both Mr. and Mrs. Elisha Davis to the Department. The affidavits of both give the names of the members of the mob, including Tip Hunter, who seized Davis. Davis's affidavit gives in detail what happened, including the questions asked him by the mob, showing the purpose of the threats made and also the actual threats made. In addition, we furnished the Department the name and address of another person who saw Davis down at the river in the hands of the mob. Further corroborating evidence is the fact that Davis, a businessman, left his home, his business, his property and his family and now is living in Michigan.

We agree that this is not a clear-cut case with a dozen eyewitnesses, but it is a case with two eyewitnesses as to a part of the act and an eyewitness to the entire transaction who was also the victim. There have been convictions on circumstantial evidence alone without any eyewitnesses.

We therefore urge that this matter be reconsidered to the end that it be presented to the grand jury.

Very truly yours,

Thurgood Marshall

Berge replied on February 11. "Careful consideration," he wrote, "has been given to the investigative materials collected in connection with the Brownsville matter and it was the studied opinion of the Department that the facts developed did not justify prosecutive action by the Department. Your comments relative to the conduct of the Department's investigation have been carefully noted and will receive appropriate attention."

MARSHALL TO GOVERNOR KEEN JOHNSON

In the following letter to Governor Keen Johnson of Kentucky, Marshall sounds a theme that recurred in many of his letters during the war years—the dissonance between the fight for democracy abroad and the struggle for constitutional rights at home.

MAY 29, 1942

My Dear Governor Johnson:

I am enclosing herewith a copy of a letter which we have today received from a member of our Association which explains a disgraceful situation now existing around Hazard, Kentucky.

On May 16, a prominent white young lady was found dead, and all of the Negroes in the town were immediately threatened, questioned, and many of them arrested. It is alleged that a confession has been secured from one Negro, who was carried to Jackson as a precaution against mob violence. However, on last Monday a mob from Hazard went to Jackson in an effort to return the Negro and lynch him in Hazard. The report points out that the mob was thwarted by again moving this Negro.

In the meantime, the spirit of mob violence prevails throughout Hazard, and several instances of this are set out in the enclosed report.

We therefore request you, as the governor of the state of Kentucky, to take the necessary steps to protect not only this particular Negro from a possible lynching, but to take sufficient precautions to prevent the recurrence of the mob action around Hazard against innocent Negroes and citizens of the state of Kentucky. During these times when democracy is facing a supreme test, there is only one answer to the question as to whether democracy will work; and that answer is forthright action by officials of the states and the federal government. Negro Americans who are being drafted every day for service in the armed forces and other Negroes who are paying taxes every day to support the war effort quite naturally expect from officials of the government complete protection in the exercise of their rights.

Sincerely yours,

Thurgood Marshall

Johnson replied on June 6, and Marshall wrote a rare note of appreciation on June 12. "We have received no word subsequent to our letter to you of May 29 as to any additional mob action on the scene, and it is assumed that precautionary measures taken against such action have proved efficacious. We appreciate your courtesy in the matter."

MARSHALL TO NORMAN HOLMES

Marshall did not look kindly upon African American soldiers who protested racial injustice in the military by going AWOL, and here he advises an angry soldier to return to the army. In June of 1940, Holmes wrote that his application for officers' candidate school had been rejected because he was black and that he had since been "subjected to some terrible things." "Now," he added, "I am being sent away from [Fort Belvoir in Virginia] to a combat outfit just starting run by incompetent Lts. and made up of men who have only been in the army two-to-six weeks. . . . I'm not asking why all of these things happened, I'm only asking that something be done about them. I'm loyal to a certain extent when I am treated as an American and not as a member of a minority group. For this reason I've left. I wouldn't call it desertion only a fight for justice and rights for Negro soldiers and until some thing is done I'm not going back."

Marshall's letter is especially significant because it foreshadows his negative reaction to civil disobedience practiced by Martin Luther King, Jr., and his followers in the modern civil rights movement. Marshall was a firm believer in the rule of law and had little tolerance for people who broke any law without submitting to lawful penalties. But it is also important to note here that four years after writing the following letter, Marshall agreed to accept an invitation from A. J. Muste, the leading American pacifist during World War II, to become a member of the Committee for Amnesty, an organization that sought amnesty for all conscientious objectors to war and conscription in the United States.

JULY 2, 1942

Dear Mr. Holmes:

This will acknowledge your letter of June 23, which has been called to my attention upon my return to the office.

In the first place, if you are AWOL, I would suggest that you report to the nearest Army post, or you will be in danger of being considered a deserter. You cannot fight the discrimination in the Army against Negroes by going AWOL, because it will merely mean that you will be court-martialed. I cannot too strongly urge that you either report back to your post or to the nearest Army post to your present location.

In the meantime, I am sending a copy of your letter to Judge William H. Hastie, civilian aide to the secretary of war, with the request that the matter be investigated.

Sincerely yours,

Thurgood Marshall

MARSHALL TO HARRY BUTLER

Partly because he did not want to attract attention to himself and thus away from the NAACP's cause, Marshall willingly played the role of the segregated black man when he traveled throughout the South—he sat in the backs of buses, ate in segregated restaurants, and stayed in hotels just for African Americans. But Marshall did not tolerate those who discriminated against him outside the South, and here he writes Harry Butler, the manager of the dining car, restau-

rant, and news service department of the Southern Pacific Company, about discrimination that he and other NAACP executives faced when traveling aboard a train operated by the Rock Island & Southern Pacific Railroad.

JULY 27, 1942

Dear Mr. Butler:

This will acknowledge your telegram of July 21, which was received at Ogden, and also your letter of the same date, which has been called to my attention upon my return to the office this morning.

In reply to your letter, here are the facts concerning the actions of Mr. Meredith:

We went to our conference in Los Angeles by way of the Rock Island & Southern Pacific Railroad. We were treated with extreme courtesy throughout the trip by the members of the train crew and dining car crew.

A portion of the staff of the national office of this Association was returning from our conference on the Challenger. The party consisted of nine members of the staff, including three ladies. On the morning of July 21, while we were preparing to go into the dining car for breakfast, Mr. Meredith came through the car announcing the last call for breakfast. I told Mr. Meredith that there were nine members of our party and we would appreciate having two 4-seat tables and a single seat, if possible. Mr. Meredith, in a very gruff voice, replied by asking whether we were "deadhead porters." I told him that we were not "deadhead porters," that it was none of his business, and that we resented his efforts to classify us as "deadhead porters" simply because we were Negroes. Mr. Meredith then stated that he still wanted to know whether we were "deadhead porters," and continued to refer to us as porters. While we were in the dining car trying to eat our breakfast, Mr. Meredith continually interrupted our meal, stating that "Whenever I see a gang of you *boys* traveling together, I naturally consider them porters." Once again I told Mr. Meredith that we resented his insults, and he replied that we were merely passengers and he had a right to ask us any questions he wished. At this point, I told Mr. Meredith that we had already decided to report the matter, and that in order that there might be no further difficulties I would suggest that he leave our table and stop talking to us at all. Whereupon Mr. Meredith, with much ceremony, reached into his pocket, took out a personal card, tossed it on our table, and told us to write whatever we pleased, that he did not care. He then left our table and went down to the table where the three ladies of our party were eating breakfast with Mr. Roy Wilkins, our assistant secretary, and took up where he had left off with his insults.

I am sure you realize that the term "boy," when used in connection with Negro men, is offensive, to say the least. Use of this term and several others has done as much to destroy unity in this country as any other factor. We doubt that it is the custom of the Southern Pacific Railroad to consider all Negro passengers as "deadhead porters" simply because they happen to be Negro Americans. It is quite obvious that Mr. Meredith knew better when he made the statement, and further evidence of this is his continued use of the word "porter" even after full explanation was made.

The attitude of Mr. Meredith toward our party is not an isolated instance because we checked with members of the crew on the Challenger on this point, and all of the members were unanimous in their condemnation of Mr. Meredith's attitude toward Negro passengers and crew members.

The conduct of this man is not only thoroughly objectionable to us, but has certainly destroyed any good will that members of our staff or our Association may have had toward the Southern Pacific Railroad. We have a convention once a year, and it is the duty of this office to advise our delegates throughout the country as to the best routes to travel to and from these conventions. Unless definitive action is taken against Mr. Meredith, we will be unable to again recommend the Southern Pacific for use by our delegates.

Very truly yours,

Thurgood Marshall

Butler replied two days later, assuring Marshall that Stewart Meredith "did not conduct himself in accordance with Company rules and regulations."

MARSHALL TO WALTER WHITE AND WILLIAM HASTIE

In September 1942, Marshall argued a teachers' salary case in Little Rock, Arkansas, and the memorandum below is an excellent example of the outrageous conditions that he faced in his fight for equality in salaries.

SEPTEMBER 30, 1942

Case started on Monday morning in local federal courts under Judge Trimble. So far we have examined the members of the school board as hostile witnesses and the superintendent of schools. They all deny that there has been any discrimination on account of race or color. They, however, admit that the plaintiff, Susie Morris, and twenty-four other Negro teachers in the Dunbar High School get less salary than any white teacher in either the elementary or high school.

The plaintiff testified that she has an AB degree from Talladega College (admitted to be an accredited school) and that she has done graduate work at Atlanta U and U of Chicago. That all of her grades in graduate work have been "A," with one exception, and that was a "B." She testified that she was either a member or chairman of some five committees of Dunbar, including the committee on curricular revision. She has been teaching more than seven years in Little Rock High School and has been head of the English department during all of that time save one year. She is a regular member of the local Baptist church and is a member of the YWCA and on two of its committees. She is president of the local Delta Sigma Theta sorority and is a national officer of the same. This summer she took work at the U of Chicago graduate school and got an "A" in teaching methods. The principal of the local Negro high school, Prof. J. H. Lewis, testified that he has an MA degree from U of Chicago, a BD from Yale, and has done further graduate work at U of Southern California. He is a former president of Morris Brown College and qualified as an expert on rating teachers. He testified Susie Morris was a "superior teacher," a superb teacher, a teacher in the upper brackets, one of the best teachers he has come across.

However, the superintendent of schools, T. R. Scobee, testified she was a very poor teacher. He admitted on cross that he had only seen her teach 10 minutes, and that was after the case was filed. He said, however, he consulted with the supervisor of the colored high schools, who is a white principal of an elementary school with only an AB degree, and they concluded Susie Morris was not a good teacher. They also admitted that this conclusion was reached after the salaries had been fixed and after the case was filed.

We have prepared and are now using in evidence sheets which compare teachers by race, salary, qualifications and experience. In all comparable levels, Negroes get less. We have just reached the point after a day and a half of testimony by the local superintendent where he cannot explain the difference in certain salaries on any ground other than race.

He has also admitted that a bonus payment was made to all teachers in 1941 and again this year. It was worked out on a basis of experience, degree and salary, and then a certain number of points was arrived at for each teacher. The same yardstick was used for both white and Negro teachers. When the number of units per teacher was worked out, each white teacher was given $3.00 per point and each Negro teacher $1.50 a point. It was admitted that this plan was submitted by a committee of white teachers without consultation with any Negro teachers. Each of the board members admitted all of these facts but denied that race was used as the basis. However, the superintendent, after a few hours of questioning on this point, found himself obliged to admit that race was used.

The minutes of the board show that all Negroes new to the system get from $615 to $630 and all white teachers new to the system get from $810 and up. However, they deny that race is involved. It "just so happens that salaries are fixed at that level."

This morning they offered into evidence a composite rating sheet which gave all the ratings for all teachers. Guess what? All the Negroes are rated lower than the white ones. It was admitted that this was prepared after the salaries were fixed for the year, was not prepared for the purpose of fixing salaries, was produced by persons who were not produced as witnesses, was not accurate . . . However, the judge admitted it in evidence over our objection.

. . .

Thurgood

The Little Rock judge ruled against the teachers' claim, but Marshall won the case on appeal.

WALTER WHITE TO MORRIS ERNST

Along with several other prominent attorneys, Ernst, a white member of the NAACP's legal committee, had encouraged the Department of Justice to hire Marshall. Having heard that Walter White was blocking the department from recruiting Marshall, Ernst protested. "For God's sake," he wrote White, "lay hands off. You can pick up a dozen Thurgoods and you can tell him so, but

Justice cannot get a guy as good as Thurgood." It does not seem that the department extended a formal job offer to Marshall at this point.

OCTOBER 31, 1942

Dear Morris:

Who told you I was blocking Thurgood's appointment to the Department of Justice staff? I don't want to lose him, but I told Rotnem that I would not stand in the way of any member of the NAACP staff doing a necessary job or advancing himself.

Now that that's off my chest I'd be ever so grateful to you if you would let me know the place where I "can pick up a dozen Thurgoods"!

All the best.

Cordially,

Walter

MARSHALL TO ASSISTANT ATTORNEY GENERAL WENDELL BERGE

The war years saw Marshall visiting with and pleading the cases of African American soldiers who faced racial discrimination and violence at military bases in the South, and in the letter below he writes the assistant attorney general about a young soldier, Private Raymond Carr, who had been killed by a state police officer in Louisiana. In an earlier letter to Attorney General Biddle, Marshall had pleaded for prosecution in the case: "It seems to us that the United States Department of Justice should be more than anxious to protect the rights of members of our armed forces. It is difficult to believe that our democracy has a chance of survival as long as it is unable to punish an individual who kills a United States soldier while on duty pursuant to orders of the War Department. We, therefore, once again urge the Department to prosecute in this case."

APRIL 26, 1943

Dear Mr. Berge:

This is to acknowledge receipt of your letter of April 23, advising us that you have recommended to the attorney general that no further action be taken concerning the killing of Private Raymond Carr in Alexandria, Louisiana. This decision on your part comes as a distinct shock to us.

No one has ever questioned the facts in this case that Private Carr, while in the uniform of the United States Army, and while on duty pursuant to orders of his superior officers, was murdered in cold blood by an officer of the state police department of Louisiana because Private Carr refused to leave the post assigned him by his superior officers. There likewise seems to be no dispute that this act is a violation, not only of the laws of the state of Louisiana, but also of the laws of the United States.

. . .

It is the sworn duty of the officials of the United States Department of Justice to prosecute all persons guilty of violations of the federal criminal code. Because of the importance to our government of prosecutions of persons committing any of the crimes under chapter 3, being the chapter dealing with crimes against the election franchise and civil rights of citizens, Congress has passed certain special provisions for the purpose of ensuring protections for these crimes.

Title 8, Section 49, of the United States Code provides specifically for the prosecution of persons violating chapter 3 of title 18 (offenses against civil rights).

Title 8, Section 54, of the United States Code provides that wherever the President has reasons to believe that offenses under Chapter 3 are about to be committed, he may direct the local federal judge, marshal, and district attorney to proceed to the places for whatever time he so designates.

These statutes were passed for the express purpose of ensuring the protection of the civil rights of American citizens. In view of the fact that this case involves the killing of an American citizen in uniform and on duty, there is even more reason to expect prosecution. The state policeman in this case, in killing an American soldier, has shown his complete disregard for our government. While the United States is prosecuting individuals for so-called seditious statements against the government, it refuses to take action against a man who has demonstrated his contempt for the federal government by killing a uniformed soldier.

Several months ago, the War Department issued a statement that there were more than 500,000 Negro troops. This number has been steadily increasing. The majority of Negro troops are stationed in the Deep South in places similar to Louisiana. These troops are placed there by order of the United States government. It is only reasonable that they expect the

United States government to protect them. Numerous assaults on Negro troops have occurred on buses, trains, and on the streets in most of the cities of the South. No affirmative action has been taken by the federal government to protect these soldiers. The more extreme cases have been referred to the Department of Justice and the War Department.

On August 14, 1941, near Gurden, Arkansas, Negro troops and their white officer, while engaged in army maneuvers, were assaulted by a mob composed of state policemen and citizens.

A thorough investigation was made and affidavits forwarded to the department. It was also investigated by the Office of the Inspector General and the Federal Bureau of Investigation. Despite the fact that there was no question of the factual situation and no question of the violation of federal laws, no prosecutions were instituted. In this case we pointed out that "failure to act in this instance will encourage further disrespect for the United States uniform, which will lead to additional unprovoked assault and further disrespect to the United States government." We were then advised that the department's files in this matter have been closed.

A short time thereafter, on March 22, 1942, Sergeant Thomas B. Foster of the United States Army was shot to death by a city policeman at the doorsteps of the Allison Presbyterian Church in Little Rock, Arkansas. Prosecution in this case was halted by the induction of the city policeman into the United States Army.

On July 28, 1942, Private Charles J. Rico, of the United States Army, was murdered by a policeman of Beaumont, Texas. On August 14, 1942, Attorney General Biddle announced the filing of an information against this policeman for the killing of Private Rico. On January 16, a press release from the local United States attorney pointed out that the case would not be prosecuted because "it is lacking in those elements promising a successful prosecution." We urged the attorney general to reconsider the matter, and by letter of February 3, were advised that the case "would not be opened or reinvestigated."

There are numerous other cases which are not outlined here. The cases as set out in this letter are sufficient to demonstrate that action by the Department of Justice is imperative if we are to expect a high type of morale among our Negro troops, which is necessary to win the war.

. . .

At the present time there are tens of thousands of Negro troops in Louisiana, and all of these troops who visit Alexandria and who are assigned to Alexandria are at the mercy of the city policeman who killed Raymond Carr and whose total punishment for this crime has been suspension from duty for one day. Such "punishment" is neither a deterrent to him nor to any other individual with similar criminal tendencies.

Respectfully yours,

Thurgood Marshall

After he learned that the assistant attorney general did not favor prosecution, Marshall then fired off this item for the NAACP's Bulletin*:*

> *Private Raymond Carr, a Negro soldier on duty as a military policeman in Alexandria, Louisiana, was murdered in cold blood by an officer of the state police department because he refused to leave his post.*
>
> *The state of Louisiana "punished" the state policeman by suspending him from duty for one day. The state grand jury refused to indict. The United States Department of Justice advised us that the federal government will not prosecute.*
>
> *At least two other Negro soldiers have been murdered by local policemen in the South and nothing has been done. We are therefore suggesting that you telephone or write Attorney General Francis M. Biddle in Washington, urging him to order the prosecution of these policemen who have murdered these Negro soldiers.*

At this point, few things irritated Marshall more than the indignities suffered by African American soldiers at the hands of racist Southerners. When writing about the situation in October 1943, Marshall would state: "Maybe one of these days the South will stop fighting the Civil War."

As Marshall fought for the civil rights of African American soldiers in early 1943, Walter White expressed deep concern about the possibility of losing Marshall to the military draft. NAACP executives had strategized about whether Marshall should enlist and seek promotion in the military, but the idea of enlistment was scuttled because White did not want to lose Marshall's invaluable legal work. Marshall was not especially interested in military service, either, and while he made his own efforts to avoid being drafted, most notably by pleading directly with the New York draft board, White asked William Hastie, now back at Howard Law after a frustrating stint as civilian aide to the secretary of war, to write him a letter "stating the uniqueness of Thurgood's talents based on ability and experience with Association in arguing various Association cases now pending and showing no other lawyer can argue them except Thurgood." Hastie wrote the letter, and White apparently forwarded it to the draft board. White then mailed an update to Hastie, telling him that he had had a long talk with Rev. E. E. Hall, the chair of the local draft board, who assured him that Marshall "is worth a million times more to the war effort continuing his work than he would be in the Army."

FBI FIELD REPORT

The following is a field report filed in Savannah, Georgia, where the regional FBI office had tracked Marshall's recent appearance in Florence, South Carolina. The content of the report, which gives evidence of the conservative side of Marshall's patriotism, should have endeared him to the anticommunist FBI director—J. Edgar Hoover.

SEPTEMBER 9, 1943

. . .

MARSHALL mentioned the recent riots in Detroit, Michigan and attributed them to subversive groups. He also discussed treatment of colored people by the United States Army and was very praiseworthy of the way the Army and the entire federal government treats colored people. However, he stated this is not true of many local agencies and cited examples of mistreatment of colored soldiers by local police officials.

MARSHALL said the war was being fought for the benefit of all and that colored people had more to gain than white persons, for white persons already had all rights that could be desired, whereas victory could also open the door for the black man. He said colored persons also had more to lose, for they would be punished more, should Axis nations be victorious. In general he condemned subversive organizations of all kinds, and warned negroes against allying themselves with any such organizations. He said they should be ever alert to advancing the cause of colored people, but they should be Americans first and strive for their own betterment secondly. He said that communists were not as active among the colored people today as they were fifteen years ago, for the colored people have found that communism does not give them what they expect to get.

These latter statements were made by MARSHALL in a principal speech in the Trinity Baptist Church on the first day of the meeting. He was also active in other meetings, which were devoted to the question of teachers' salaries in South Carolina and the question of enfranchising negroes in the South.

[Deleted material.]

— CLOSED —

MARSHALL TO WALTER WHITE

Marshall's economics (a topic he rarely commented on) favored a progressive income tax plan, and here he asks White to give his attention to the possibility of approving the NAACP as a public sponsor of a tax plan set forth by the National Lawyers Guild. In an earlier letter, Marshall wrote: "We all hope that this will meet with your approval because, incidentally, the tax plan of the Guild will certainly meet with the approval of all of us since it provides for increased exemptions and lowering of taxes as to those of us in the lower brackets, and lays it on those making more than $25,000."

OCTOBER 15, 1943

. . .

I think it very wise that at some time when Hastie is in town, we sit down together and discuss this same plan. I, for one, am in favor of our cooperating in an affirmative tax plan since the lowering of the base for income tax purposes is hitting more and more Negroes, so that we should become more interested in seeing that a fair plan is inaugurated.

White supported giving the Association's formal approval to the plan, but NAACP President Arthur Spingarn, who was most likely making more than $25,000 a year, opposed it.

MARSHALL TO GEORGE L. P. WEAVER

As Martin Luther King, Jr., would do more than a decade later, Marshall calls for an alliance between labor and African Americans in a coordinated effort to defeat "reactionaries in Congress." In a memorandum Marshall wrote two days earlier, he described the 1944 elections as "the most important elections yet held in the United States. . . . Most of the progressive legislation in Congress has either been killed or is in the process of being destroyed by a reactionary block which must be removed." George Weaver served on the National C.I.O. Committee to Abolish Racial Discrimination.

NOVEMBER 30, 1943

Dear George:

We have been following with great interest the program of the C.I.O. on the question of preparing a program to defeat the reactionaries in Congress. In areas of the Deep South, Negroes are denied the right to vote either by poll tax, white primary, discriminatory registration practices, and in some instances, all three of these devices.

The NAACP has a test case now pending in the United States District Court of Birmingham, Alabama, to test the discriminatory registration practices in that state.

The case of *Smith vs. Allwright* is now pending in the United States Supreme Court, testing the white primary.

We are now collecting from our lawyers and our branches in the South information on the particular method of disfranchise at present in their particular areas. We expect to attack all forms of discrimination against Negroes in voting by bringing several cases in several of the states of the Deep South. We will, of course, concentrate on those areas where the reactionary Congressmen have been elected. This will be a tremendous task and if it is to be properly handled will require more funds than we now have available in the NAACP.

We expect to have our program prepared by the first of the year, and I am calling this matter to your attention at this time so that you may bear it in mind and bring it to the attention of the other officials of the C.I.O. because it seems to us that the only possible means of defeating reactionaries in Congress is by the combined intelligent vote of Negroes and members of labor unions.

Sincerely yours,

Thurgood Marshall

MARSHALL TO THE NAACP OFFICE

This excerpt of a memorandum penned in San Francisco, where he was fighting to integrate a union of marine ship workers, shows that Marshall sometimes became involved in, if not altogether enjoyed, the rough-and-tumble of local NAACP politics. Although he seems tolerant of the presence of communists in local NAACP leadership positions at this point, he would grow quite intolerant in the following years.

DECEMBER 7, 1943

. . .

Confidential

The branch is in a hell of a fix. They tried to hold an election two weeks ago and because of disorder—bordering on a riot—the election was postponed until last Sunday. Within fifteen minutes there was the same disorder. Hitler Marshall took over with a baseball bat and held an election. The insurgent group won by eleven votes. Both sides satisfied with fairness of election—I hope.

The real fight involves personalities. Regular officers accused of being "intellectuals," "selfish," no connection with common man, social-minded, not doing anything. Insurgent group charged with being "*communists*," etc., not heretofore interested in NAACP.

There is no doubt in my mind that *some* of the insurgents are communists or fellow travelers. No doubt that former officers were not doing much.

. . .

MARSHALL TO WALTER WHITE

Attorney General Biddle had announced that he intended to resign from the Federal Bar Association because it refused to admit Louis Mehlinger, an African American serving in the claims division of the Department of Justice. No doubt hoping to thank his boss, Mehlinger then pressed the NAACP to acknowledge Biddle's good deed, and Bill Hastie agreed to the request, suggesting "a sentence that although we have been greatly disappointed at the unwill-

ingness of the Department of Justice to act in many matters of violence against Negro soldiers and primary election cases, we hope that his personal statement in the Federal Bar Association matter will be followed by a bolder and more aggressive policy in the Department." Walter White found this to be a good idea and asked Marshall to draft, sign, and send the letter. Ever the good foot soldier, Marshall agreed to draft the letter, but in the handwritten note below, he bristles at the suggestion that he sign it.

NO DATE [DECEMBER 1943]

I simply cannot sign such a letter to Biddle—I still think he is a *skunk*. All right if Roy will sign it.

TM

MARSHALL TO MACEO SMITH

Marshall writes Maceo Smith, the secretary of the Texas NAACP, an angry note about an internal dispute related to the question of which NAACP officials should be present when arguing the Texas primary case, which sought to wipe out the all-white primary, before the Supreme Court. Marshall clarifies that he is willing to pay expenses for William Durham, perhaps the most influential African American attorney in Texas, to travel to Washington and help prepare for the argument.

DECEMBER 31, 1943

Dear Maceo:

Carter has sent me a letter in which he points out that he is leaving for Mexico City and for that reason I am sending this letter directly to you. In the first place, I think we should make it clear that the primary case is one of the most important cases to Negroes that has ever been before the courts. For that reason alone we should not take any chances. It will be disastrous if after the argument we say that a point which was presented by the Court could have been answered better if we had discussed the matter with Durham before argument.

. . .

It is to be regretted that after fighting this case for over three years and now at a time when we all feel we are about to win it, there has to be a lot of "running off at the mouth." We can always stick together when we are losing, but tend to find means of breaking up when we are winning. Incidentally, one of the best ways to lose a case is to create dissension, and I only hope that we will not be met with this along with the state of Texas, the Democratic Party and the other forces opposed to us, who are now united more than ever before.

Sincerely yours,

Thurgood Marshall

CHAPTER SEVEN

1944–1945

MARSHALL TO SENATOR CLAUDE PEPPER

Marshall kicks off the New Year by asking Senator Claude Pepper of Florida for assistance in bringing about an investigation of the lynching of William James Howard, Jr. Governor Spessard Holland had ordered an investigation, but a grand jury of Suwannee County failed to return an indictment in the case. In the letter he sent to a white girl, referenced below, Howard had written: "I know you don't think much of our kind of people but we don't hate you all we want to be all your friends but you want let us please dont let any body see this . . . I wish this was a northern state I guess you call me fresh. Write an tell me what you think of me good or bad. . . . I love your name. I love your voice, for a S.H. you are my choice."

JANUARY 28, 1944

Dear Senator Pepper:

Yesterday the War Department released stories of Japanese torture and inhumane treatment of American boys in prison camps after the fall of Corregidor. At the same time, numerous letters reached our office concerning a vicious crime committed in Live Oaks, Florida.

During the first week in January a fourteen-year-old Negro boy living in Live Oaks, Florida, was taken from his home by three men, tied hand

and foot, and drowned in the Swanee River. The only offense committed by this boy was the alleged passing of a note to a white girl in the store where they worked. The body was turned over to the local colored undertaker.

The boy's father, William James Howell, Sr., has been threatened not to talk under penalty of similar treatment and it is our understanding that he has sold his property and left town.

This is the type of material that Radio Tokyo is constantly on the alert for and will use effectively in attempting to offset our very legitimate protest in respect to the handling of American citizens who unfortunately are prisoners of war.

We respectfully request that you use your very good offices and influence to urge an investigation of this matter through the appropriate officers for the purpose of bringing to trial the perpetrators of this uncivilized act.

We have also written to Governor Holland and enclose a copy of our letter to him for your information.

With best wishes.

Respectfully yours,

Thurgood Marshall

MARSHALL TO ATTORNEY GENERAL FRANCIS BIDDLE

Marshall reargued the Texas primary case before the Supreme Court on January 12, and the Court ruled in his favor on April 3. Marshall celebrated the ruling with a few stiff drinks and did not hesitate in taking the occasion to criticize the attorney general for failing to support the NAACP's attack on the all-white primary. Because he also believed that Biddle would drag his feet in response to the Court's landmark ruling, Marshall encouraged the attorney general to execute a speedy implementation of the decision.

APRIL 3, 1944

Dear Mr. Biddle:

We have just been advised that the United States Supreme Court has reversed the judgment of the Circuit Court of Appeals in the case of *Smith v. Allwright* (Texas primary case). Although the Department of Justice did not deem it wise to intervene in this case as amicus curiae, we are sure that the department will now recognize that criminal jurisdiction over interference with the right to vote because of color extends to primary elections.

The decision in this case, along with the decision in *United States v. Classic*, clearly establishes the illegality of the practice in most of the states of the Deep South of refusing to permit qualified Negro electors to participate in party primary elections. Immediately after the 1942 primaries, the NAACP sent to the department a large number of affidavits from Negro citizens in Texas, Arkansas and South Carolina, concerning the refusal to permit them to vote in primary elections. All of these complaints have been investigated by the FBI, but no further action has been taken.

Now that there can be no doubt that such exclusion is a federal crime, we urge you to issue definite instructions to all United States attorneys, pointing out to them the effect of these decisions and further instructing them to take definitive action in each instance of the refusal to permit qualified Negro electors to vote in primary elections in states coming within the purview of the two decisions. We also suggest that this fact be made known, by the Department of Justice directly or through the several United States attorneys, to the party officials in the several states now practicing the policy of refusing to permit qualified Negroes to vote in primary elections.

The present Texas primary litigation lasted for a period of more than three years and was financed by voluntary contributions of the citizens of Texas and other fair-minded Americans. The precedent having been established, we now urge the United States Department of Justice to enforce the criminal statutes of the United States and to prosecute vigorously persons who deny to others rights guaranteed under the Constitution and laws of the United States, especially the right to vote.

Sincerely yours,

Thurgood Marshall

Biddle replied on April 10. "At present," he wrote, "the Department is giving careful consideration to the opinion of the Court in that case in order to determine its full scope. I hope that when you are in Washington you will come to see Mr. Rotnem of the Civil Rights Section to discuss the situation with him." Marshall considered the Texas primary case to be the greatest one he took part in during his years with the NAACP. As he put it, Smith v. Allwright *was the "case that started the whole voting of the Negroes in the South."*

MARSHALL TO THE NAACP OFFICE

Shortly after his victory in the Texas primary case, Marshall toured the state, strategizing with African Americans about ways to make their votes count most effectively. Marshall was especially interested in unseating a vocal opponent of the NAACP, Representative Martin Dies.

APRIL 15, 1944

. . .

Houston, 11th to 14th:

Mass meeting on the night of the 11th was the largest I have seen in Texas. Church was packed at seven for an eight o'clock meeting. They had loudspeakers outside and the crowd outside was as large as the crowd inside. The only way the plaintiff in the case could get in the church was by climbing through the window in the back of the church. White people driving by, including policemen, stopped their cars to hear the "nigger lawyer from New York." Traffic was thereby blocked. More than a thousand dollars in memberships were reported that night, which should help the drive.

Galveston:

Went over to Galveston the following night for a mass meeting. Crowd was fair but not as large as expected because of shortness of time to organize the meeting. Met with the Negro politicians after the meeting. All night on road returning to Houston.

On Thursday met with local Negro politicians to see what was going on. The factions are terrific. However, looks as though Carter Wesley will come out on top. Spent the afternoon with Arthur Mandell, lawyer, who represents the CIO in this area. He says that Martin Dies can be defeated this time. Asked him whether a campaign by us among the Negroes would help Dies to get white votes and he says no because the man running against him is of such high caliber and is above reproach. He also thinks we should go out after Hatton Sumners in Dallas. He is to arrange a conference for me in Dallas on Monday with the state leaders of the CIO.

San Antonio:

Damn Hitler . . . no space available in Pullmans on train yesterday. Stood up from Houston to San Antonio (six hours). Dirty, hot, smelly train. White people also standing—if anything their coaches were more crowded. Negroes were assigned 1½ of the 8 coaches on the train.

Huge crowd at the meeting last night. All the local white political office holders were there to give speeches of welcome—doubt that they enjoyed my talk.

. . .

Glad I came down to Texas. The white press . . . had them worried. Don't know about the other states but bet even money the Negroes in Texas are going to vote.

Will be in Dallas Monday and Little Rock Tuesday. New York on Friday.

Two weeks later Marshall wrote the following to Maceo Smith: "I have just returned to the office and am still interested in the question of defeating Martin Dies. Please check and let me know the number of Negroes who have paid the poll tax in his district and also let me know the name of the person you suggested to help us."

While it is unclear whether Marshall did anything substantive in the run-up to the 1944 congressional campaign, Dies retired from the House when the CIO, one of his favorite targets, organized voter registration efforts in his home district and recruited an opposing candidate.

MARSHALL TO GODFREY CABOT

Using a moving personal anecdote, Marshall defends the NAACP's efforts to eliminate the poll tax and keeps the NAACP benefactor Godfrey Cabot posted about other developments. Cabot had expressed interest in cases related to the right to vote, and Marshall sent him more than a few substantive letters about discrimination in voting practices. Just a year earlier, for instance, Marshall wrote: "As to the question of placing educational requirements on the right to vote, it seems to me that if educational requirements are fairly administered, there would be no discrimination involved. However, our experience has been that the educational tests are not fairly administered. For example: The Regis-

trar in Asheville, N.C. had a system whereby white applicants were asked simple questions while Negro applicants were asked such questions as 'Do you know what Article 2 of the Constitution provides?' The Negro applicants were then requested to write down Article 2 from memory."

Marshall refers below to Representative John Rankin of Mississippi, a segregationist who frequently touted the "states' rights" argument.

MAY 1, 1944

Dear Mr. Cabot:

Your letter of April 22nd has been called to my attention on my return to the office. The reason the NAACP and other organizations are tempted to remove the poll tax as a requisite for voting is that in the Deep South there are thousands of Negro and white underprivileged American citizens who are unable to pay even the one dollar tax per year.

I have seen Negro sharecroppers in Mississippi who have never seen a dollar bill in their lives. There are many others in this same position, and as long as the poll tax is on the books, we will continue to have such congressmen as Mr. Rankin disgracing our government almost daily.

. . .

I am taking the liberty of sending you a copy of the decision in the Texas primary case, which you were interested in. We are now busily engaged in having our branches work diligently in seeing to it that the decision is enforced. We are preparing a campaign which will see to it that Negroes will actually vote in the primary elections. We are at the same time trying to raise sufficient funds to insure them protection as well as to guarantee them the protection in the courts if they are refused the right to vote despite the decision of the United States Supreme Court.

With all best wishes.

Sincerely yours,

Thurgood Marshall

MARSHALL TO ASSISTANT ATTORNEY GENERAL TOM CLARK

Marshall writes Tom Clark, the assistant attorney general, and expresses his disappointment that the Department of Justice had decided not to take action in the case of the murder of Private Edward Green. On March 14, Green was riding a bus in Alexandria, Louisiana, when the driver told him that he was sitting in a section reserved for whites. Green did not move out of the white section and instead told the driver that he would rather leave the bus. "The facts in the case show that Private Green was deliberately shot and killed by a bus driver after he had alighted from the bus and the driver had followed him to the road," according to an NAACP press release. "After the driver came out of the bus into the road where Private Green stood, he shot and killed him in cold blood."

MAY 5, 1944

Dear Mr. Clark:

This will acknowledge receipt of your letter of May 4, 1944, advising us that no investigation will be made of the killing of Private Edward Green on March 14, 1944, by a bus driver at Alexandria, La.

The bus driver is still working in Alexandria, and we are repeatedly receiving requests from Negro soldiers in that area as to what, if anything, is going to be done about this man. I hope you can realize the effect on the morale of the Negro soldiers who realize that although one of their members is killed without provocation, the same government for which they are fighting refuses to take any action whatsoever to prosecute the guilty party.

Needless to say, the refusal of the government to take action in the killing of Private Raymond Carr, which killing was an admitted violation of Section 52 of Title 18, is also to be taken into consideration by these men and by Negroes in general throughout the country. When the department refuses to take action in a case where there is a clear violation of a federal statute, it is difficult to expect prosecution in other cases.

There have been numerous killings of Negro soldiers by civilians and civilian police. There have been many more instances of severe beatings of Negro soldiers in certain areas in the South. We are not aware of a single instance of prosecution or of any steps being taken by the federal government to either punish the guilty parties or to prevent the recurrence of those crimes against the uniform of the United States Army.

You advise us that a bill is now pending to amend Section 255 of Title 18. We are familiar with this bill, yet we do not know of any section by the Department of Justice in favor of this bill. Will you please advise us as to whether or not the Department of Justice has in any manner urged the passage of this bill?

Very truly yours,

Thurgood Marshall

MARSHALL TO SAM WINTER

Sounding a rare note of cheery optimism, Marshall spells out the implications of Smith v. Allwright, *the Texas primary case, for Sam Winter, a resident of Austin, Texas.*

MAY 10, 1944

Dear Mr. Winter:

. . .

In answering your question as to our attitude concerning the case, I would prefer to divide it into two sections: the legal effect and social effect.

As to the legal effect, it seems to me that this opinion settles once and for all the question of the right of Negroes to participate in primary elections similar to those in Texas, i.e., where the primary election is an integral part of the election machinery of the state. . . .

As to the social effect of the decision, it is our belief that it will become a landmark. . . . I doubt seriously that any thinking election official will be willing to take the risk of criminal penalty by refusing a qualified Negro elector the right to vote. I cannot imagine any thinking American citizen objecting to the enforcement of the Constitution and laws of the United States. For these reasons it is our belief that the decision will be of tremendous benefit to the cause of the Negro voter in the South as well as to the cause of democracy in general.

I hope I have succeeded in giving you our impressions concerning the decision. If there is anything not quite clear, please let us know at once. Thank you for your interest.

Sincerely yours,

Thurgood Marshall

MARSHALL TO GEORGE SCHUYLER

Marshall sends George Schuyler, the editor of the NAACP's Bulletin, *a column that takes a swipe at Biddle's reaction to the white primary case.*

MAY 25, 1944

After a series of cases beginning in 1925, the precedent is now established which effectively destroys the "white primary" in Texas and other states of the Deep South. The decision of the United States Supreme Court on April 3 and the denial of the petition for rehearing in May removes all doubt as to the illegality of the white primary. The opinion in this case, filed by Mr. Justice Reed of the Supreme Court, is perfectly clear and leaves no doubt as to the interpretation of the United States Constitution on the question of the right to vote in primary elections which are a part of the election machinery of the state.

. . .

On the day of the decision in the Texas primary case, we requested Attorney General Francis Biddle "to enforce the criminal statutes of the United States and to prosecute vigorously persons who deny to others rights guaranteed under the Constitution and laws of the United States, especially the right to vote." We also urged Attorney General Biddle to issue definite instructions to all United States attorneys concerning the effect of the decision and to have this fact made known to the party officials in the several states now practicing the policy of refusing to permit qualified Negroes to vote in primary elections.

Although the Texas primary case involved the question of the enforcement of the United States Constitution and the protection of the rights of hundreds of thousands of Negro citizens of this country, the Department of Justice did not even see fit to file a brief amicus curiae while the case was pending. Despite the fact that Negro voters were denied the right to vote in the recent primary elections in several places in Florida and Alabama and despite the fact that the other Southern states will be holding primary elections within the next two months, the only reply we have received from the Department of Justice concerning our letter of April 3 is their letter . . . advising us that "At present the Department is giving careful consideration to the opinion of the Court in that case in order to determine its full scope." There is no ambiguity in that opinion. There is no question of the "scope" of it. Affidavits on the refusal to permit qualified Negroes to vote in the primaries in Alabama have been forwarded to the Department of Justice, and affidavits from Florida will be forwarded as soon as they are completed. Failure of the Department of Justice to prosecute election judges who refuse to permit qualified Negroes to vote in the Democratic primaries in states covered by the decision in the Texas case will be for political rather than legal reasons. There is no legal reason for the United States Department of Justice to refuse to enforce the United States Constitution as interpreted by the United States Supreme Court.

. . .

MARSHALL TO ROGER BALDWIN

Shortly after his Supreme Court victory, Marshall criticizes the head of the ACLU and announces his plans to take on the pernicious root of "all of the evils of segregations"—residential segregation.

JUNE 9, 1944

Dear Roger:

Thanks for your letter of June 6 and enclosures concerning the proposed study to be made by Mr. Robinson on the question of residential segregation.

. . .

I do not at all agree with the belief that residential segregation is not one of the most important questions of friction in this country today. As to New York, the reason that Negro occupancy of the Harlem area has spread toward Washington Heights and into the Bronx is that the white population has moved from those areas. The question of increased employment for Negroes is not the answer because the rents in Harlem are much higher than in any other area of comparable buildings in New York today. If we had not had the residential segregation over this long period of years, we would not now be faced with all of the evils of segregation which exist today. It should also be pointed out that we are receiving more and more requests for assistance in fighting residential segregation. Just as an example, in Detroit, residential segregation has brought about the situation where, according to the latest reports, there are no more white families so poorly housed as to be eligible for the government housing projects; and yet there are an estimated 45,000 Negroes without proper housing. Other large cities suffer from the same type of discrimination. The pattern of residential segregation by restrictive covenants is also being used by governmental offices as the basis for their rule to segregate people in public housing projects. Here is an excerpt from a letter we received only yesterday on this problem:

> *I am a colored man operating a tailoring and cleaning business in a lily white neighborhood. Have been in the township for 9 years successfully. Although I had a white partner when I started, I've bought him out, purchased the property and now the troubles begin. I can't move my family in the building.*

Both Judge Hastie and I believe that residential segregation should be attacked at the earliest possible moment. We also agree that it can only be attacked after careful planning.

Sincerely yours,

Thurgood Marshall

Just four days after writing this letter, Marshall invited members of his national legal committee to strategize about how best to attack restrictive covenants. "The problem of restrictive covenants," he wrote, "is becoming increasingly important. The question of housing now and in the postwar period is the foremost problem confronting Negroes today. As you know, restrictive covenants are increasing in number and we are constantly being requested to work out some procedure for invalidating them."

MARSHALL TO ATTORNEY GENERAL FRANCIS BIDDLE

In his May 10 letter to Sam Winter, Marshall had sounded optimistic when he expressed doubt that "any thinking election official will be willing to take the risk of criminal penalty by refusing a qualified Negro elector the right to vote." Tempered by Southern intransigence, however, Marshall now calls for the attorney general to prosecute election officials who openly disobeyed the decision in the Texas primary case. Needless to say, the possibility of African Americans voting throughout the South did not sit well with local segregationists, and some of them told local blacks as much through threatening flyers. One such flyer, with "NO NEGRO VOTES" handwritten at the top, delivered the following warning: "YOU WILL BE HELD RESPONSIBLE FOR ACTION. DON'T SEEK ADVICE FROM NORTHERN LEAGUES. THEY ENDANGER THE DEMOCRATIC PARTY. ADVISE OTHERS. ALL NEGROES VOTING WILL BE DELT WITH LATER. THE KLAN."

JULY 5, 1944

Dear Attorney General Biddle:

On yesterday, July 4th, qualified Negro electors were denied the right to vote in the Democratic primary throughout Georgia. Mr. A. T. Walden, a member of our national legal committee, Mr. C. A. Scott, the editor of the *Atlanta Daily World*, and several other Negro educators, insurance executives, and others were denied the right to vote in Atlanta. Attorney Walden is forwarding to you affidavits of several of the persons who were denied the right to vote in the Georgia primary yesterday solely because of their race or color.

We have previously sent to you affidavits of the refusal to permit Negroes to vote in primary elections in Alabama and Florida. We have not as yet been advised as to what, if any, action has been taken on these cases other than the notice that they are being investigated. There is no doubt that the fact that no action has been taken in these other cases influences to some degree the actions of the officials in Georgia.

The decision of the United States Supreme Court, rendered on April 3rd, clarifying once and for all the law as to voting in primary elections, will mean nothing to the millions of Negroes in the South who have been denied the right to vote unless the United States Department of Justice vigorously enforces the statutes construed by the United States Supreme Court in this decision.

Negro soldiers fighting throughout the world today are constantly inquiring as to whether or not their families are permitted to vote in the Democratic primaries in the Deep South, and whether or not they will be permitted to vote in these primaries if they are fortunate enough to return.

The question as to whether or not Negroes will have the right to vote in primary elections throughout the South can only be decided by the vigor with which the United States Department of Justice prosecutes these cases.

We, therefore, strongly urge you to bring about the prosecution, not only of the election officials in Georgia, but also those in Alabama and Florida, who have deliberately flaunted the Constitution and laws of the United States, even after the opinion of the United States Supreme Court.

Very truly yours,

Thurgood Marshall

MARSHALL TO CAROLYN MOORE

In this letter to Carolyn Moore, the executive secretary of the Philadelphia NAACP, an angry Marshall lights into African Americans in North Carolina who resisted the NAACP's participation in the case of Booker Spicely. On July 8, 1944, Spicely, an African American private in the U.S. Army, refused a driver's demand that he move to the back of a bus after white soldiers had boarded. Spicely argued with the driver, and the driver followed him off the bus and shot him twice in the chest. Although the driver was indicted on second-degree murder charges, a jury acquitted him on the grounds that he was acting in self-defense.

SEPTEMBER 7, 1944

Dear Carolyn:

Thanks for sending me your letter on the Spicely case. We had received the letter from Mr. Robert Spicely of Tuskegee and also much of the other material.

. . .

The whole trouble around the Spicely case is the same trouble we have around all cases in North Carolina. You will remember that the case to get a Negro admitted to the University of North Carolina was killed through the cooperation of certain Negroes. It is also true that although Virginia and Maryland took an active stand on the question of equalization of teachers' salaries, and although we had been requested by teachers in North Carolina to file suit, all of these efforts were stopped by certain Negro groups in North Carolina who believe that the only way to handle the problem is to handle it in North Carolina "without outside influence." One thing is certain and that is that the NAACP will not itself be intimidated by anyone, whether he be white or Negro.

One of these days, North Carolina will realize that none of us can handle our problems alone.

As to the Spicely case, as long as the family wants us to remain in the case, we will remain in it, and it does not matter who attempts to get us out.

Sincerely yours,

Thurgood Marshall

MARSHALL TO THE NAACP OFFICE

In this remarkable memorandum from Nashville, Marshall reports on a case to equalize teachers' salaries in Jackson, Tennessee. In the fall of 1943, the average weekly pay for teachers in Tennessee's white high schools was $139.63, while the average pay for teachers in the state's black high schools was $80.00.

SEPTEMBER 20, 1944

The case to equalize teachers' salaries ended yesterday by a consent decree. . . .

. . .

Superintendent of Schools C.B. Ijame, examined by us as a hostile witness, testified as to the method of operating the schools in Jackson. The entire administration of the public school system was in his hands. His word was final. He admitted that his only college training was as follows: B.S. degree in 1895 and an A.M. in 1898 from a small college in Henderson, Tennessee, which closed shortly thereafter and reopened as a junior college; he also went to summer school at Columbia in 1910 and 1911. No college training since that time. No training in either school administration or the methods of fixing teachers' salaries. Testified that he did read several books and periodicals on school administration but was unable to name any of them other than one magazine.

He admitted that the same courses of study were followed in both white and colored schools and that the schools all remained open the same length of time and that instruction was the same. However, Negro teachers received less salary than white teachers but it was not because of racial discrimination. He testified that "Negroes just didn't measure up" and that this was true as a group. He said that in the fixing of salaries he offered the teachers what he thought they should get and they could take it or leave it.

He testified that he did not put much weight on college degrees and that he did not know just what accreditation the several colleges in Tennessee had. He also did not put much weight on the question of experience. He kept no records as to teachers' ability to teach except that he kept everything in his head and made up his own mind. He testified that if he had more money he "might" pay the Negro teachers more salary.

Yesterday after the defense had put on one witness, counsel entered into negotiations for a settlement. A decree was agreed upon which provided "That in the future no distinction shall be made in the fixing of salaries of teachers and principals in the public schools of Jackson, Tennessee on the basis of race or color.". . .

TM

MARSHALL TO SECRETARY JAMES FORRESTAL

O*n October 3, Joe James, the president of the San Francisco NAACP, called Walter White with an urgent request that he or Marshall travel to San Francisco to offer civilian counsel to fifty African American sailors on trial for mutiny. The sailors were accused of refusing to obey an order to load a ship in need of ammunition at the naval depot at Mare Island—an incident that occurred shortly after improper ammunition handling and loading had resulted in the explosion of two ships and the deaths of 327 individuals at Port Chicago. Six days before he sent this damning request to the secretary of the navy, Marshall was quoted in an NAACP news release as saying that the fifty sailors were being tried only because of their race. According to the release, Marshall also maintained that the men did not ever believe that they were disobeying a direct order to load ammunition and that they did not act with collective intent. Marshall's conclusions—"There is no sufficient evidence of mutiny or conspiracy. There is no evidence of refusal to obey a* direct *order. These men are being tried for* mutiny *solely because of their race or color"—clearly suggested that the navy was guilty of racism. After their indictments, Marshall became civilian counsel for the men.*

OCTOBER 19, 1944

Dear Mr. Forrestal:

I have just returned from San Francisco, where for the past twelve days I have been investigating the circumstances leading to the court martial of the fifty Negro seamen charged with mutiny, which is now being conducted on Yerba Buena Island.

As to the trial itself, I am convinced that the accused were advised of their rights to civilian counsel prior to the trial and that they had signified their willingness to accept naval counsel. While attending the trial for several days, I was convinced that defense counsel . . . is doing a splendid job in defending these men and, within the limitations of Navy rules, is doing everything possible toward protecting their rights at the trial as well as the development of the case itself.

In addition to attending the trial, I made an investigation as far as possible into the incidents leading up to the Port Chicago explosion and conditions immediately prior to the alleged refusal to obey orders, resulting in the present trial. I, of course, realize it would be impossible to make a thorough investigation since I am a civilian. There are many factors involved in the working conditions in the Twelfth Naval District which could not be brought out in the court martial. I am convinced that there are sufficient facts involved to warrant a thorough and complete investigation by your office as to the following conditions, which existed in the Twelfth Naval District:

1. Why is it that the only naval personnel loading ammunition regularly were Negroes with the exception of their officers and petty officers?
2. Why is it that Negro seamen, many of whom have had special training in such schools as gunnery schools, were nevertheless relegated to the duty of loading ammunition?
3. Why is it that these men were not given any training whatsoever in the dangers to be found in loading ammunition or the proper methods to be used in loading ammunition?
4. Why is it that men with no prior experience whatsoever were given the duty of handling winches in the loading of ammunition when civilian longshoremen were not permitted to handle winches or ammunition unless they had had several years' experience in winch-handling?

5. Why is it that Negro seamen with no prior experience in ammunition were given the job of hatch tender in the loading of ammunition?
6. Why is it that officers "raced" their gangs in contests in the loading of ammunition?
7. Why is it that one of the accused, Seaman Green, while suffering with a broken wrist, despite the fact that the Navy doctors ordered him on the sick list, was not placed on the sick list, but was ordered to load ammunition?
8. Why is it that the Negro seamen who had been loading ammunition and who were at Port Chicago at the time of the explosion were not given any leave whatsoever as a result of this explosion, but were forced to return to the duty of loading ammunition? A psychiatrist from the United States Navy testified at the court martial proceedings that such an explosion as occurred at Port Chicago would have a lasting effect upon the minds of the men who were near the explosion.

Practically all of the Negroes at Port Chicago were trained at great length and were led to believe that they were being trained to serve as regular seamen. This they are anxious to do. When these men were assigned to Port Chicago instead of being given an opportunity to serve in whatever branch of the service they might find themselves fitted, they were, solely because of their race or color, restricted to the task of loading ammunition and other menial tasks.

As a result of the action of the Twelfth Naval District in releasing some of the men who allegedly refused to obey orders, shipping 150 of the men to the Pacific around the middle of August, the giving of summary courts to some of the men and the singling out of an even 50 to be charged with mutiny, Negro members of the armed forces, as well as Negro and white civilians, believe that a thorough, complete and impartial investigation by your office is essential at this time.

We have been receiving reports in this office for several months, and my investigation in the Bay area seems to justify all of the complaints we have received concerning the discriminatory policies being practiced by the Twelfth Naval District.

In this request for an impartial investigation, we by no means wish to reflect at all upon the manner in which the actual court martial proceedings are being conducted. It is for that reason we believe the investigation is necessary.

Sincerely yours,

Thurgood Marshall

MARSHALL TO ROY WILKINS

Echoing the criticism that Houston directed his way at the beginning of the war, Marshall now lambastes the NAACP's "Sunday school idealistic theories" and calls for the organization to become more calculating in its politics. Marshall's criticism refers to Governor Thomas Dewey of New York, who had just signed legislation creating a Fair Employment Practices Committee (FEPC) in New York. Interestingly, shortly after Dewey had killed a similar bill in 1944, Marshall and Hastie held a news conference in which they predicted that, because of Dewey's actions, African Americans would vote for Franklin Roosevelt over Dewey in the presidential campaign. Marshall's letter here also refers to Theodore Bilbo, the infamous segregationist senator from Mississippi.

MARCH 12, 1945

Dear Roy:

. . .

As to the Dewey meeting I still think we should have held it. Let us grant that Dewey was wrong last year. And I for one still say he was. However, he did a good job for us this time and one of these days the NAACP will reward people for what they do. If Bilbo would support a federal FEPC, I for one would thank him. Of course it is not always fair to compare people, but as things now stand Dewey has done more for us than Lehman (I know it is treason for me to say that). It is time that we became hard, cold and practical. The meeting would not endorse Dewey for anything. We all praised Roosevelt for his FEPC which he established *after* we threw everything, including the kitchen stove, at him to compel him to do it. Even if we grant that Dewey did a good job on this bill after he learned his lesson, the answer is that he did it and he could have given us lip service and then stood by and let the bill be killed. He put everything behind the bill and got it through. One of these days we will get our heads up out of the political sands. We are still dealing with cold, practical politicians and still using Sunday school idealistic theories.

Will be in Birmingham from Tuesday night on for the teachers' case.

Thurgood

Incidentally, none of the talk about Dewey is aimed at you. I think we agree on most of what I said.

MARSHALL TO SECRETARY HENRY STIMSON

In this letter to the secretary of war, Marshall denounces a brigadier general's unqualified claim that African American soldiers preferred warm climates.

MAY 24, 1945

Dear Mr. Stimson:

We have received copy of memorandum dated 15 May 1945 from Brigadier General Ray L. Owens, deputy chief of air staff for the commanding general, to Mr. Truman H. Gibson, Jr., civilian aide to the secretary of war. A copy of this memorandum is herewith enclosed. The memorandum is the result of a complaint on behalf of two Negro soldiers who were assigned to Plattsburg Hospital and then transferred to the convalescent hospital at Bowman Field, Louisville, Kentucky. The memorandum points out that:

> During the early part of February of this year, four (4) of the Negro patients were interviewed and it was found that the Negro personnel assigned there were very unhappy in their situation due largely to the severe winter climate and to the fact that there is a negligible Negro population in that vicinity. The total civilian Negro population in the vicinity consisted of one family.
>
> As a result of the above findings the Plattsburg Convalescent Hospital recommended to the Personnel Distribution Command on 10 February 1945 that no more Negro patients be sent to that hospital. This recommendation was accepted and adopted as policy by the Personnel Distribution Command and put into practice.

The establishment of this policy by the air staff is in keeping with its policy of segregation prevalent throughout the Air Corps so that now the policy of segregation is extended even after the time of actual combat. It is to be remembered that the Air Corps refused to permit any Negro pilots to be trained until after the filing of a suit in 1941 to compel their admission. It was not until March 1941 that applications of Negroes were accepted for aviation cadet training, and it was not until several months later that training of Negroes actually began. The Air Corps, however, insisted on maintaining a policy of segregation even after being forced to admit Negroes to this training. I am sure you are aware of the many complaints concerning the rules of promotion in the Army Air Corps which discriminate directly against Negroes as well as the refusal to permit Negroes to qualify as pilots in the Air Transport Command.

As a result of this most recent statement of policy of the Army Air Corps, all Negroes are excluded from Plattsburg solely because of their race or color. The explanation for this policy is another example of the fallacious reasoning of the Air Corps. All Negroes in the Air Corps eligible for convalescent treatment are excluded because of the alleged opinions of four Negroes to the effect that they were "unhappy" in the northern climate.

It is unbelievable that the Air command in charge of air bases with Negro personnel in northern sections of the United States as well as in areas of other countries with severely cold climates should suddenly assume that Negroes are "unhappy" because of the winter climate at Plattsburg. There is no doubt that many of the white patients from homes in lower Florida, Louisiana, Texas and California might be "unhappy" in the winter climate of Plattsburg. This is the same type of reasoning used in an unsuccessful effort to justify segregation.

The policy of the Army Air Corps in excluding Negroes from convalescent hospitals used by white servicemen is without justification. The determination of the Army Air Corps to perpetuate and extend its policy of segregation will increase friction between the races and is destructive of our efforts to win a just and lasting peace. We therefore urge you as secretary of war to issue an order countermanding the action of the air staff in excluding Negroes from Plattsburg and other convalescent hospitals solely on the ground of race.

Sincerely yours,

Thurgood Marshall

MARSHALL TO SECRETARY HENRY STIMSON

African American soldiers faced court-martials in disproportionate numbers compared to their white counterparts, and here Marshall criticizes General Dwight Eisenhower for failing to respond to repeated inquiries about many of the cases. The NAACP Papers contain numerous legal petitions related to court-martial cases.

JULY 6, 1945

Dear Mr. Secretary:

This office receives numerous requests from interested servicemen and their families to give legal assistance in cases where Negro soldiers have been condemned to death by sentences of court-martials in the European theater of operations. Since such aid can only be rendered after a careful study of the court-martial record involved, we have followed the procedure of sending cablegrams to General Eisenhower, requesting a stay of execution to afford our staff an opportunity to study the record and, where such action is warranted, to file a brief with appropriate military authorities. In most instances, we receive neither an acknowledgment of our cablegram, a copy of the court-martial record, nor any information as to the final disposition of these cases.

We feel certain that some formula can be worked out in those instances which would afford our staff an opportunity to study the record where requested and to file a brief in the deserving cases. The adoption of an acceptable formula on this score would certainly be in the interest of justice and should not run counter to either military necessity or requirements now that the European phase of the present war has ended. If we were afforded the opportunity requested, it would greatly improve the morale of Negro soldiers and civilians alike and would certainly help to lay at rest current rumors that Negro servicemen are being sentenced to death on insufficient and fabricated evidence.

This letter is being sent to you since we have been unable to determine General Eisenhower's present address and feel that the matter warrants immediate attention.

Respectfully yours,

Thurgood Marshall

MARSHALL TO SECRETARY JAMES FORRESTAL

Once again, Marshall appeals, this time angrily, to the secretary of the navy for a review of the Yerba Buena Island case in which fifty soldiers were convicted of mutiny.

JULY 13, 1945

Dear Mr. Forrestal:

I have formally represented the fifty Negro seamen tried in joinder at Yerba Buena Island on a charge of mutiny since their conviction. I advised you and the Navy Department of this immediately. I made repeated requests for a personal conference with you and was denied this conference because you believed that it would be improper to hold such a conference before the case was officially presented to you for review.

I filed a memorandum on March 2 on behalf of these men and appeared personally on April 3 before the assistant judge advocate general and his staff. Since that time I have made repeated requests of your office for information as to the status of this case and have been given no information as to the action of the judge advocate general. I was repeatedly assured that I would be advised of the decision in this case and would be given an opportunity to appear on behalf of these men at each stage of the review of their case.

However, in a routine form letter to Mr. William Brooks, of Columbus, Ohio, Mr. Ralph A. Bard advised that "The trials were conducted fairly and impartially. Racial discrimination was guarded against" and that "A person who is a prominent official of a national Negro organization has expressed his satisfaction with the conduct of the proceedings." I immediately wrote you requesting advice as to whether or not the judge advocate general had made any decision in the case and yesterday received a letter from Rear Admiral Fechteler that the judge advocate general of the Navy has held the trial to have been legal.

It is only reasonable for us to have expected that the attorney for these men, duly recognized by the Navy Department, would have been informed of the decision in this case at least before it was made public in letters to people throughout the country. As a matter of fact, I now wonder if we would have ever been officially advised if it had not been for the fact that Mr. Brooks sent us a copy of the letter to him.

. . .

It is shocking, to say the least, that the judge advocate general of the United States Navy could reach the conclusion that the conviction was legal and that "the trials were conducted fairly and impartially and racial discrimination was guarded against." The latter statement, quoting from Mr. Bard's letter to Mr. Brooks, is unbelievable. In my experience in similar cases and in the review of court-martial records in both the Army and the Navy and in the trial of cases in civilian courts in the Deep South, I have never run across a prosecutor with a more definite racial bias than that exemplified by Lieutenant Commander William Coakley in the instant case. The board sustained Lieutenant Commander Coakley throughout the trial. I made this clear in the memorandum filed before the judge advocate general, copy of which was furnished you, and in my statement before the assistant judge advocate general and his staff, which was transcribed and, I assume, copy referred to you.

Rear Admiral Fechteler, in his letter of July 11, says that "The statement 'A person who is a prominent official of a national Negro organization has expressed his satisfaction with the conduct of the proceedings' was based on the second and closing paragraphs of our letter to Honorable James V. Forrestal on October 19, 1944." . . . I have never, at any time, used any language which by the widest interpretation could possibly have been viewed as an expression of "satisfaction" with the conduct of the proceedings by either the Twelfth Naval District, the court martial board, or the trial judge advocate. As a matter of fact, at the time this letter was written, the Navy Department was aware of my statements published in the daily press of San Francisco condemning Lieutenant Commander Coakley, trial judge advocate, as showing evidence of distinct racial prejudice in his presentation of the same. Prior to the sending out of these letters by your office stating that I expressed satisfaction with the conduct of the proceedings, you were aware of the position taken by me in the memorandum, as well as the statement to the judge advocate general and my many letters to you. Therefore, any statement that I expressed satisfaction with the conduct of the proceedings is not only untrue, but is a deliberate attempt to discredit these men by discrediting their attorney and an attempt to discredit this organization.

We therefore believe that because of the importance of this case to the morale of the members of our armed forces, you should (1) grant to us the right to file additional memoranda and to appear before you personally on behalf of these men, and (2) take the necessary steps to correct the erroneous impression given by your office in the letters being sent to persons writing on this case that we have at any time expressed satisfaction with the conduct of the proceedings in this case.

Sincerely yours,

Thurgood Marshall

Forrestal replied on October 29: "I should be happy to confer with you about this case if I felt that any purpose would be served. In my consideration of the case I have had the advantage of having before me the substance of the extended oral presentation and the text of the written presentation that has been made to the Judge Advocate General on behalf of these men and I do not feel that any purpose would be served by a further presentation."

Nevertheless, after a navy review board later suggested a second trial because of problems it found with submitted evidence, Forrestal ordered the release of the men and allowed them to return to duty.

WALTER WHITE TO MARSHALL

White offers blunt criticism of Marshall's office.

JULY 17, 1945

I have hesitated for a long time about mentioning to you the standards of work and some patterns of behavior in the Inc. Fund offices, but certain recent developments make it desirable that I do so.

I hope it is necessary for me only to refer to the fact that as executive secretary, I have never insisted on any patterns of behavior in the office which are stilted or routine. But there are certain standards of relationship which are necessary to maintain office standards. I do not feel that this is always done in the Inc. Fund office. I gain the impression that a good deal of wasted motion is indulged in and that the volume of work which could be turned out has not been maintained.

I feel, also, that there is over-familiarity and casualness to which no opprobrium whatever is attached, but which might be misunderstood by visitors to the office. The use of first names, for example, between executives and secretaries or stenographers during office hours does not seem to me good office practice. I have heard comments which are not as favorable as an association like ours, dependent as it is on public support, requires.

On the part of at least one member of the Inc. Fund staff there becomes increasingly apparent an indication that she does not consider herself responsible to the office manager and that she considers herself as occupying a role apart from other members of the Inc. Fund staff or the Association staff.

I know that the work of the Inc. Fund has increased, particularly in briefs and other emergency work which has to be done. But there is pressure on the NAACP staff, also. The Inc. Fund clerical staff should be responsible for getting out receipts for Inc. Fund contributions. More sustained work with fewer absences from the office and a tightened-up discipline in the Inc. Fund office should enable it to take care of these receipts as well as the normal work of the Inc. Fund. I am asking that you see that this is done.

MARSHALL TO ATTORNEY GENERAL TOM CLARK

Marshall's brief letter to the attorney general included the following statement that Ida McCoy Lee made to the Houston NAACP on October 9. Lee's remarkable case is helpful for showing not only the abuse of power by local white authorities but also the sheer courage of an everyday black woman and the importance of the national office of the NAACP.

> *I, Ida McCoy Lee, was born in Rusk County near Henderson, Texas and have spent the most of my life there. I am a public school teacher and have taught for more than twenty years, although I am not teaching now. . . . I take part in all the civic activities for the uplift of my people and community. I am a member of the Henderson branch of the NAACP, serving as chairman of the Education Committee. I am a member of the State Progressive Voter's League of Texas, being secretary of the Rusk County League, and have served on various committees of the League at the state meetings. I attend all the meetings of these two organizations and try with utmost to get every Negro in my County to become members of them because I believe that in the end, these two progressive organizations will win the rightful place for Negroes in Texas and he will finally enjoy full Democracy.*
>
> *For the past five years, with my mother and father, Salem and Hattie D. McCoy, who are 88 and 78 years old respectively, I have lived on the farm of Mr. Bynun Strong, about two and one half*

miles from town of Henderson, Texas on the Tatum Highway. When it became impossible to get someone to do the plowing for our truck patches, I did days-work for several white people, some of whom are the most outstanding people of Rusk County. . . .

On Monday, Sept. 17, 1945, I had an argument with Mr. Selah Bassett who lives a short distance from me, about 100 yards or more, about a cow of his that he pastured in the same pasture with mine. Before the argument about the cow, I had never had a word with Mr. Bassett. I had been friendly enough with him and his family to go in and out of their home and work for them. We were neighborly enough for me to stay in their house, sleep in their bed and take care of their little boy until they returned. On the morning of September 17, I went to the home of Mr. Bassett to get a setting of eggs, and to use the phone to call Mrs. C. A. Doerge whom I was working for. After asking Mrs. Bassett how she felt, for she is the mother of a very young baby, she preceded to tell me, also she told me that Lovie, who had cooked for her during her illness, had not shown up, neither the wash woman, Pearline. In the meantime, little Bobbye who is about four years old, kept kicking me and saying, "Get out of here nigger, Daddy don't want you here, Nigger." I said to Mrs. Bassett, if they do not come I will be glad to help you out as usual. I have washed, cooked and cleaned house for her off and on for the past five years, and had never had a cross word with her. After the child kept kicking me, I said to him, "stop kicking me Bobbye, don't do that, maybe that is the reason Lovie is not here cooking for your mother." That seemingly made Mrs. Bassett angry and she said, "Don't talk to him that way, Selah doesn't want you here, so you go home." I said "why, I don't know what this is all about, thank you, I don't have to stay where I am not wanted. If you think you need me, let me know." I left.

Later that afternoon as I started to the pasture to let my cows out, Mr. Bassett was coming down the road in his car and swerved it around in front of me as if he would run over me and said, "Ida, don't open your mouth or I will get out of this car and beat your brains out." As I opened my mouth to speak, he acted as if he was opening the door of the car and yelled, "Don't open your mouth God-dammit, didn't I tell you to keep your cows out of the pasture with mine?" (We both had permission from the owner to put our stock in the pasture. It didn't belong to me nor him.) I asked him, "What is this all about? What have I done to you all?" He kept telling me to shut up and cursing me for everything, and saying he was going to beat me. So I finally said to him, "Like Hell you'll beat me. I have not done anything to you and you are not going to beat me. I am damn sure of that and if you get out of that car I am going to beat you down to the ground." He drove off a piece and stopped. I opened the gate and let my cows out of the pasture. He turned around then and came back to the gate and wired it up. The next morning, Mrs. T. T. Harrison let me put my cows in her pasture, which was next to the one I had had them in. Mr. Bassett talked to the Harrisons who are also neighbors of ours and that night, Mr. Harrison told me not to put the cows in his pasture.

That same night after the argument about the cows, Mr. Bassett came to our house with a bunch of white men. (He is white) . . . The car was driven by Selah Bassett. [Policeman] Tatum Brown seemed to have been the spokesman for the crowd, who said to me, "You all niggers move. I came out here to tell you and Ida, don't open your mouth. The less you say will be the better for you, because we don't want to come out here and kill up a bunch of you niggers. Get out of this white man's house right now." I said, "Yes Sir, we are going to move as soon as we can." "Shut up," he said, "Move, and don't say a word."

Wednesday morning as we were packing our belongings to have ready to load on my Brother-in-the-law's wagon, who was on his way to move us to his house up in Henderson, the sheriff, Mr. William Whitehead, with his Deputy came and arrested me, saying that he had come to take me up to the Court house. After being placed in jail, that same afternoon the sheriff came over and took me over to the Court House, before the Justice of the Peace, Mr. J. J. Velvin, who said to me, "Ida, we have two charges against you, one for disturbing the Peace and one for using abusive language. Are you guilty or not?" I said I am not guilty. He then called for the Prosecuting Attorney, Mr. Matt Barton and told him that I had pleaded not guilty, to which Mr. Barton replied, "Whether she pleads guilty or not, we are going to place her in jail, and fine her two hundred dollars on each count. Round here cursing a white man." The justice then asked me if I had any money with which to pay my fine and I told him no. Mr. Barton told the sheriff to take me back to jail. Sherriff Whitehead, stopped me at his desk, took out a pencil and pad, and asked me what kinds of organizations were these that I belonged to, that I had going on secretly around here. Teaching niggers not to work for white folks unless they were paid seventy-five dollars a month? I said to him, I have not heard of a secret organization teaching Negroes anything. Why do you think I would teach them to not work for less than seventy-five dollars and I, myself make less than thirty? Well, said he that is what they got you for. I said to him, I am the secretary of the Rusk County Voter's League, which is part of the Negro Voters League of Texas. I am the chairman of the National Association for the Advancement of Colored People for the Henderson Branch, and I sure know that neither of these organizations are a secret. They are state and Nationally known. I know what they stand for and will prove to you people in Henderson what they stand for.

I was kept in jail thirteen days, irregardless to an approved Bond, which my brother secured for me by having influencial people sign it. He also paid an attorney, Mr. Robert Allen, twenty five dollars to get me out of Jail. Mr. Allen told my sister that the sherriff was holding me, and would not let me out unless I get out of town. On Monday, October 1, my sister, Mrs. Florence Menefee came to the jail and asked the sheriff to let me out. He told her if he let me out I would have to leave town. She asked him how much money was needed to get me out and he told her to get as much as she could. When my sister returned after she went to get the money to get me out he asked her how much did she get and she told him. He said well I will get her. He did. I hold the receipts for two fines, for fourteen dollars and thirty cents each, signed by Mr. Velvin.

In the meantime while my sister was gone to get the money, the sheriff, Mr. Whitehead came to the jail cell where I was. He had with him a man whom I took to be the father of Mr. Bassett, and told me, "Your sister has gone to get some money for us to let you out of here. I am going to let you out with this understanding, I am not even giving you time to get your clothes, I am going to take you to the Bus station and see to it that you get out of town, if she brings enough money. Will you promise to get out this town without any further trouble, because we don't want to mob and kill up a bunch of you niggers. A nigger like you is a dangerous nigger to be left loose with all these organizations you are fostering and if I let you stay, we will have to kill up a mess of you niggers. You niggers got to work for these white folks as long as you are here. You be sure and get the first Bus coming through here and stay out. If I am not here, be sure you tell the man who is here to escort you to the Bus so I will know that you are gone. Before I caught the Bus, I went by the Jail and showed my ticket to the Jailer and told him to tell the Sheriff that I was gone. I came on to Houston where I have relatives and where I may report this trouble and secure help and advice from you and National body in New York.

I have never been arrested before in all my life. I have told my story to you with the hope that you will be able to help me to make it possible for me to go back to the place of my birth, where I have lived almost all of my life, so that I can continue to care for my very aged parents, who still are there.

Thanks for any help or advice.

OCTOBER 15, 1945

Dear Mr. Clark:

Enclosed is copy of a statement by Mrs. Ida McCoy Lee, of Rusk County near Henderson, Texas.

From this statement, it is apparent that a group of citizens near the place where Mrs. Lee lives has conspired together to intimidate Mrs. Lee in exercising her rights including the right to occupy a home and other rights incidental thereto. It is obvious that this conspiracy also includes the Justice of the Peace, the Prosecuting Attorney and other law enforcement officers.

We would appreciate an immediate investigation of this complaint, and if the facts are substantiated, we would appreciate procedure being started for the prosecution of the guilty parties.

Sincerely yours,

Thurgood Marshall

MARSHALL TO THE NAACP BRANCHES

Marshall expressed his patriotism in a variety of ways in 1945. In August, for instance, he sent a chain letter that, if successful, would have resulted in "an astronomical amount of war stamps sold, and that, after all is our patriotic duty." As the letter below shows, Marshall also understood his patriotic duty to be ensuring that African American veterans would be able to take full advantage of their right to attend graduate and professional schools.

NOVEMBER 14, 1945

The importance of equal educational opportunities is too obvious to need discussion especially with NAACP branches. The NAACP has established court precedents guaranteeing the right of absolute equality in education from all levels from the highest graduate school to the lowest elementary school. However, we have not been diligent in enforcing these principles in any areas of the country. We do not have a "separate but equal" school system in any place in the United States. The proposed postwar program of cities, counties and states throughout the South propose to give Negroes an even smaller percentage of public funds than before. Unless we can act fast there will be decades before we will have schools equalized.

. . .

Returning veterans are denied the right to attend graduate and professional schools throughout the South. No other public education is offered them within their states. This is a flagrant violation of the principle established in the Gaines case, and it is the duty of the NAACP to see to it that our returning veterans are not denied their constitutional rights. The least we can do is to protect the rights of these veterans. We would, therefore, appreciate a report from you at the earliest possible time on what progress is being made in your branch on this program which we are sure will be one of the most important items of your yearly program, if not the most important point.

Yours very truly,

Thurgood Marshall

MARSHALL TO PRESIDENT HARRY TRUMAN

Marshall lobbies Truman to support a bill that would establish comprehensive, universal health care coverage. Such coverage, of course, would have begun to rectify the gross racial inequalities of the health care system suffered by African American citizens.

NOVEMBER 14, 1945

Your message to Congress September 6th included statement that you at a later date would send special message on medical care. We respectfully urge that you send to Congress message requesting immediate action on the nationwide health insurance program provided in Wagner-Murray-Dingell bill. Deplorable health conditions of our country brought to light by Selective Service examinations during past war make such action imperative.

Thurgood Marshall

Truman did not reply to the telegram, but William Hassett, the president's secretary, sent Marshall the following note on November 24: "This is to acknowledge the receipt of your telegram of November fourteenth and to assure you that your interest in wiring is appreciated. As you know, the President on November nineteenth sent a Message to Congress regarding the matter to which you refer. I am enclosing a copy of it herewith." Truman backed the bill.

CHAPTER EIGHT

1946

MARSHALL TO AMOS HALL

On January 14, 1946, Ada Sipuel, an honors graduate of Langston University in Oklahoma, applied to the University of Oklahoma College of Law with encouragement and coaching from Roscoe Dunjee, the president of the Oklahoma NAACP, the editor of the Black Dispatch *of Oklahoma City, and an NAACP board member. Oklahoma laws prohibited integrated education, and George Cross, the president of the university, denied Sipuel admission because of her race, even though he conceded that there was no academic reason for refusing her application. Amos Hall, an attorney from Tulsa, acted as Sipuel's local counsel, and in the following letter, Marshall draws upon his years of experience to introduce Hall to the procedural details of moving the case properly.*

JANUARY 24, 1946

Dear Amos:

We have received from Roscoe Dunjee the material concerning the refusal to admit Miss Ada Sipuel to the law school of the University of Oklahoma. I talked to Roscoe over the telephone from New Orleans last Sunday and told him that I would be happy to handle the case and we agreed that we would both appreciate your being associated in the case.

I also told him that it was impossible for me to get to Oklahoma for at least the next 2½ weeks, but I thought that we could get most of the preliminaries organized by correspondence between the two of us.

From the information I have it appears that Miss Sipuel was refused admission by the president in a very clearly worded letter. Although the Board of Regents has previously passed a resolution refusing to admit Negroes, I am still of the opinion that you should make a direct appeal to the Board of Regents for the refusal to admit Miss Sipuel. To my mind there is no need for taking the chance of having the case thrown out on the question of our having failed to exhaust our administrative remedies. I am sure you will remember the first University of Tennessee cases were lost on that point, and since we have such a clear case from all other angles, I would not like to see it go off on such a technicality. I am wondering if you agree.

As to the actual court action, we are still of the opinion that in these university cases we should proceed by mandamus in the state courts rather than action in the federal courts. One of the reasons for this is that the mandamus procedure has such clear precedents in the University of Missouri and the University of Maryland cases.

If you agree with me about being required to appeal to the Board of Regents, I suggest that you send the letter on Miss Sipuel's behalf and in the letter point out that you request immediate consideration in order that her legal rights may not be jeopardized by delay. This should give us an opportunity to get moving in the actual court case as soon as possible.

With all best wishes.

Sincerely,

Thurgood Marshall

Marshall and Hall joined forces on the case and became lead counsels in Sipuel v. Board of Regents of University of Oklahoma. *A district court dismissed the case, stating the separate but equal law did not require her admission to the University of Oklahoma, and Marshall and Hall appealed to the Oklahoma Supreme Court in April 1947, when they lost yet again, and later to the U.S. Supreme Court.*

MARSHALL TO ASSISTANT SECRETARY OF WAR
HOWARD PETERSEN

Marshall thought of his ongoing protests to the secretary of war, most of them very specific in content, as a way of helping the military avoid racial resentment and even race riots. On January 11, for instance, he wrote the following to Robert Patterson: "Enclosed please find photostat copy of a letter written by a private in the United States Army who on November 17th was stationed at Ft. Meade, Maryland. The name of the soldier is not clear from the letter or envelope. However, the serial number is perfectly clear and it appears to be 43012762. In this letter, the soldier, apparently writing to a girlfriend of his, points out that he had been on K.P. duty serving 'nigers' and that 'we spit on the food. The food is really what I would cal slop. I tell you about it when I get home, if I do.'" Marshall further stated that this type of behavior "is an admitted violation of the Articles of War and demonstrates the type of human being which most certainly will do more to destroy morale in the Army than to benefit anyone." He also requested an immediate investigation into the matter, and below is his reply to Howard Petersen, the assistant secretary of war, who responded to the January 11 letter.

JANUARY 30, 1946

Dear Mr. Petersen:

This will acknowledge your letter of January 25th, in reply to our letter of January 11th, concerning the letter of the soldier.

You mentioned in your letter that there are several reasons for not going into this complaint. In the first place, you mention the difficulty in establishing the identity of the author. I assumed that that could be easily established from the soldier's serial number, which appeared on the envelope we sent to you. I also assumed that with this serial number it would not be too difficult to locate the party involved.

The reason that we are tremendously interested in this particular incident is that such action has the possibility of not only destroying morale but of bringing about open friction between races in the Army, leading to possible violence. If soldiers spit in the food of other soldiers, I do not think there is any doubt that if this fact is known, there will be resentment. If it is true that this soldier and other soldiers did spit into food they were preparing, and if these same soldiers are still in the Army and still follow that routine, we have before us the possibilities of a riot.

Therefore, it seems clear to me that it is the duty of the War

Department to find out whether or not the statements in the letter are true and whether or not the particular soldier is still in the Army. We therefore strongly urge that you reconsider this complaint and order an investigation be made.

Very truly yours,

Thurgood Marshall

MARSHALL TO THE TRIAL COMMITTEE OF THE NEW YORK CITY BOARD OF EDUCATION

On February 27, 1946, the New York City Board of Education voted on the bizarre case of May Quinn, a civics teacher in Brooklyn, who had been suspended four months earlier on charges stemming from an incident in which she required her students to copy six sentences that she had written on the blackboard. The factually false sentences—which included statements such as "The first American soldier to kill a Jap was Michael Murphy" and "The first American flyer to bag a Jap plane was Captain John O'Hara"—were taken verbatim from a political leaflet that praised Irish Americans and ridiculed Jewish Americans. The trial was too delicious for Marshall not to pass comment on, and below is a memorandum he authored with Marian Perry, his special assistant, and sent to the board's trial committee. The memorandum here is especially important for showing that Marshall's legal work at the NAACP extended beyond cases in which African Americans were directly involved.

NO DATE [FEBRUARY 1946]

The National Association for the Advancement of Colored People is concerned with the maintenance of an educational system in America which will make possible the better integration of Negroes as well as all other minority groups into the life of the country. It is for this reason that the Association has followed carefully the trial of Miss Quinn before your committee and presents this memorandum for the consideration of the committee.

. . .

First, the evidence establishes that the six sentences entitled "First Americans," which Miss Quinn caused her class to copy, were the same six sentences which were the basis of a series of anti-Semitic leaflets flooding the city at that time. The identity of names and incidents, including errors, between Miss Quinn's statements and those in the subversive leaflets leaves no doubt on this point. We submit that at the very least, interpreting conflicting evidence in her favor, Miss Quinn was guilty of teaching to her class untruths which she was under a duty to check and the falsity of which she could have established. She made no effort to check the accuracy of these statements, which she received from a friend on the bus and proceeded posthaste to transmit as a lesson to her pupils.

Secondly, the evidence indicates that Miss Quinn has testified falsely under oath. . . .

Thirdly, the testimony of an overwhelming number of Miss Quinn's students and fellow teachers indicates that she used the classroom to spread un-American and undemocratic bigoted ideas.

. . .

Conclusion

We call the attention of the committee to the dangerous increase in tension in the field of race relations in our country. This trend, temporarily arrested during the war, will be one of the greatest dangers to American democracy. The teachings of Miss Quinn as proved before your committee can add fuel to the dangerous fires already smoldering in our city. We respectfully urge your committee to recommend to the Board of Education the immediate dismissal of Miss Quinn from the public school system.

Respectfully submitted,

Thurgood Marshall

Marian Wynn Perry

By a vote of 5 to 1, the board acquitted Quinn of all charges save one (neglect of duty); the lone dissenting vote was from the famed jurist John Marshall.

MARSHALL TO J. EDGAR HOOVER

On Monday, February 25, William Fleming, a white radio repairman, assaulted Gladys Stephenson, an African American woman, in Columbia, Tennessee, after she had dared to suggest that he did not fix her radio properly. Her son, James Stephenson, responded to the assault by slugging Fleming and pushing him through a plate-glass window. The Stephensons landed in the city jail, and later that evening, after a white mob had gathered in front of the jail, two prominent African American residents of Columbia, with assistance from the sheriff, met the Stephensons at the back door and drove them out of town.

African American residents of Columbia learned of the gathering mob and began to arm themselves, and when four city police officers went to the black section of Columbia known as Mink Slide, all were shot. Governor Jim McCord then ordered five hundred state troopers and members of the state guard to conduct a house-to-house search for weapons, and the troopers and guard members cordoned off Mink Slide and reportedly fired their weapons. An infuriated Marshall responded by stating that "the action of the Tennessee state troopers in roping off the Negro section of Columbia, Tennessee, and firing at will and indiscriminately was closer to the action of the German storm troopers than any recent police action in the country, the South not excepted." In the following letter to the director of the FBI, Marshall complains about the investigation into the racial violence and calls for internal changes to the FBI.

MAY 10, 1946

Dear Mr. Hoover:

I am sure that you are familiar with the recent happenings in Columbia, Tennessee. Immediately after the occurrence, the NAACP and other organizations requested action by the United States Department of Justice. Subsequent thereto, an investigation was made by the Federal Bureau of Investigation.

I have talked to most of the Negroes whose rights were violated by state highway policemen of the State National Guard of Tennessee. It is apparent that the Negroes in Columbia were subjected to the deprivation of many of their federal rights by these state officers. All of the Negroes complained of the action of the FBI agents in making their investigation. The procedure in all instances was for the agents to immediately antagonize the Negroes and to ask them such questions as, "What were you doing with a gun?," "You knew it was unlawful to carry a gun," and other similar questions, giving a clear impression to the Negroes whose rights had been violated that they were being investigated rather than the state officers.

We have had other complaints concerning the attitude of FBI agents in questioning Negroes in other places, and we believe that it is necessary for you to take affirmative action to: (1) employ qualified Negro FBI agents with full status and (2) instruct all FBI agents to make their investigations on a fair and impartial basis without regard to race or color. The present attitude of most of the FBI agents prevents Negroes from cooperating with their government in these investigations and enables guilty parties to escape punishment.

I would appreciate an opportunity to discuss this entire matter with you at your convenience.

Very truly yours,

Thurgood Marshall

J. EDGAR HOOVER TO MARSHALL

MAY 14, 1946

Dear Mr. Marshall:

I have received your letter of May 10, 1946, referring to the bureau's investigation of the recent disorder in Columbia, Tennessee. I have observed with the greatest concern your statement that Negroes interviewed by you complained "of the action of the FBI agents in making their investigation." I note in your letter that bureau agents are alleged to have antagonized the Negroes by asking them such questions as "What were you doing with a gun?," "You knew it was unlawful to carry a gun," and other similar questions. You state that this action gave "a clear impression to the Negroes whose rights had been violated that they were being investigated rather than the state officers."

In an effort to afford the bureau's investigation of this case the most expeditious and efficient attention, a number of special agents were assigned to this investigation to the exclusion of all other assignments. In order that I may conduct an immediate administrative inquiry into the charges which you have made, I would greatly appreciate it if you would furnish me with the names of the persons whom you interviewed and who made charges against the bureau agents who interviewed them. All special agents of the Federal Bureau of Investigation are required to refrain at all times from any statements, conduct, or actions which are prejudicial in any way to the rights of any person under investigation or being interviewed. Stringent disciplinary action is taken against any special agent who by any act prejudices the bureau's program of conducting thorough, impartial, and entirely ethical and legal investigations of all cases. You will appreciate, therefore, my desire to receive from you immediately the basic facts relative to the identity of persons complaining regarding the conduct of bureau agents, in order that I may initiate an administrative inquiry immediately into this situation.

I note further from your letter your statement that you have had "other complaints concerning the attitude of FBI agents in questioning Negroes in other places." I request that you furnish to me immediately specific details concerning these complaints, indicating the persons making the complaint and such other identifying data as will enable me to determine the identity of any bureau agent who may be engaged in any unethical conduct. Concerning your belief that it is necessary for the Federal Bureau of Investigation to "employ qualified Negro FBI agents with full status," I desire to advise you that the bureau has a number of FBI Negro agents with the same status as other agents.

Relative to your statement that I should "instruct all FBI agents to make their investigations on a fair and impartial basis without regard to race or color," I desire to reiterate, as I have pointed out above, that all bureau agents operate under strict instructions at all times to conduct their investigations upon a non-partisan, non-prejudiced, fair, and impartial basis. I request that you furnish me with specific details concerning any situation in which you have evidence to the contrary. I must make the same observation concerning your statement that "the present attitude of most of the FBI agents prevents Negroes from cooperating with their government in these investigations and enables guilty parties to escape punishment." I request that in an effort to assist the bureau in its efforts to carry out the responsibilities imposed upon it by Congress, you furnish to me specific data concerning any situation in which you have reason to believe that the attitude of FBI agents has prevented Negroes, or anyone else, from cooperating with their government. I feel that each and every citizen has a patriotic duty to furnish to me such information as will assist me in operating and maintaining the bureau as a government agency, operating on a high plane of efficiency with due regard both to the rights of all Americans and its obligations to the American people.

I would suggest that any discussion of this matter be deferred until such time as you have furnished me with the facts which I have requested above, and I have had an opportunity to initiate an appropriate inquiry into these facts.

Very truly yours,

J. Edgar Hoover

Marshall did not mail a reply.

MARSHALL TO ATTORNEY GENERAL TOM CLARK

On May 18, Clark delivered a speech that addressed the resurgence of the Ku Klux Klan, citing in particular recent cross burnings in Georgia and California. "In my capacity as Attorney General of the United States," he said, "I wish to state here and now that all the federal laws at my command and all that Congress deems fit to give me in the future, will be enforced to the very limit in stamping out any organization or group which aims at extermination of our priceless liberties. No quarter will be given."

MAY 28, 1946

Dear Mr. Clark:

I have been out of the office for quite some time on cases in the Middle West and have been unable to write you sooner concerning your speech in Philadelphia on May 18th to the National Conference on Citizenship.

Your forthright statement concerning the position of the Department of Justice in regard to the Klan was most encouraging. Please accept our sincere appreciation for this statement. I hope that it will be possible to stamp out the Klan and all that it stands for to the end that we will have an opportunity to see our government moving forward rather than falling backward to the evils of the last century.

We stand ready to cooperate in all lawful endeavors to prevent the resurgence of the Klan or other similar organizations. If there is need for more specific federal legislation to enable you to act, we will cooperate in every possible way to get such legislation before Congress.

Very truly yours,

Thurgood Marshall

WALTER WHITE TO MARSHALL

In July 1944, Irene Morgan was traveling to Baltimore by Greyhound after visiting her mother in Virginia. When the bus became crowded, the driver insisted that Morgan surrender her seat to a white person. Morgan refused, and when a deputy sheriff sought to arrest her, she resisted again. "He put his hand on me to arrest me," Morgan later recounted, "so I took my foot and kicked him. He was blue and purple and turned all colors. I started to bite him, but he looked dirty, so I couldn't bite him. So all I could do was claw and tear his clothes." Although she later pleaded guilty to resisting arrest, Morgan refused to pay a fine for violating Virginia's segregation laws.

The NAACP represented her when she appealed the sentence, and her case, Morgan v. Commonwealth of Virginia, *eventually landed in the U.S. Supreme Court, where Marshall and the Howard Law professor Spottswood Robinson argued on March 29 that segregated seating prohibited free movement from state to state. Marshall also took the occasion to set the case in historical context: "Today we are just emerging from a war in which all of the people of the United States were united in a death struggle against the apostles of racism. How much clearer must it be today . . . that the national business of interstate commerce is not to be disfigured by disruptive local practices bred of racial notions alien to our national ideals."*

Walter White was yet again deeply impressed with the man who led his legal team, and in the following month he applauded Marshall's selection as the 1946 recipient of the NAACP's Spingarn Award, an annual award for distinguished achievement. "No more suitable choice could possibly have been made," he wrote Marshall.

On June 3, the Supreme Court ruled in favor of Irene Morgan, and Marshall issued the following statement from Columbia, Tennessee: "The opinion of the United States Supreme Court in Irene Morgan versus Virginia, *declaring that state statutes requiring the segregation of races cannot be applied to interstate passengers, is one of the most momentous decisions in the history of the country. It is a decisive blow to the evil of segregation and all that it stands for. We earnestly hope that the states will abide by the decision with good faith. Now is the time to push for the end of all forms of segregation throughout the country."*

JUNE 5, 1946

You deserve far more credit than I or anyone else have words to express for victory in the Irene Morgan case.

Walter White

MARSHALL TO THE NAACP OFFICE

Marshall acted as chief counsel for twenty-five African American men charged with attempt to commit murder during the racial violence in Columbia, and in the memorandum below he details his creative efforts to combat an all-white jury. Marshall realized that trying the case there would be dangerous, and when he was asked whether he had police protection, he stated: "They destroyed the Negro community. They slapped the Negroes around. They killed the two Negroes who were in jail. And I most certainly don't want them to protect me." Marshall added that Maurice Weaver, an NAACP-affiliated attorney who had gone to Columbia right after the initial arrests, had received threats that "his body would be found at the bottom of Duck River."

JUNE 12, 1946

The defense closed its testimony on the pleas in abatement yesterday afternoon. We had called 217 Negroes who testified that they were adult male Negro householders and otherwise qualified for jury service but who had not been called for jury service at any time during their residence in Maury County. They also testified that they had never heard of a Negro being called for jury service or serving on a jury in Maury County. The reason we stopped this line of the testimony is that we announced at the beginning of the hearing that we were going to call Negroes to the stand until the state would agree that there were qualified Negroes for jury service who had not been called. They refused to stipulate to this so we continued to call witnesses until yesterday morning when they gave up and stipulated that there were numerous other Negroes in Maury County whom we could and would call to the stand who would testify substantially as the 217 already called. With this stipulation we closed that portion of the testimony.

We then called to the stand (Miss) Dabney Anderson, clerk of the Maury County Court, who testified that she had been clerk of the court for seven years and had never seen a Negro on a jury in Maury County. She did not know whether or not any Negroes had been summoned but said that she had noticed one Negro who had been called for jury service but who was excused by the judge in open court. . . .

. . .

One of the most interesting features of the trial to date was the examination of Sheriff Underwood. I asked that he be called as a hostile witness, and when he took the stand he had a terrific loss of memory. He testified that he had never seen a Negro serve on a jury in Maury County. However, when we began on the question of whether they had ever been subpoenaed, he said that he knew that Negroes had been subpoenaed and that he had excused some of them, even though he did not have the authority to do this. I questioned him for some time, and he could not give a single name or any idea or whether it was one year or five years ago. He could not give any particulars at all but said he might be able to remember later. I recalled him in the afternoon, and he could only name one person, the white woman who called him to ask him to excuse an 80-year-old Negro who had been subpoenaed.

The state asked for a recess until afternoon of Thursday to start their evidence.

MARSHALL TO THE EDITOR OF *THE NEW YORK TIMES*

This is a rough draft of Marshall's scathing reply to a Times *article that gave a glowing report on white people in Columbia, Tennessee, including their view that Marshall and other NAACP attorneys were outsiders who stirred up negative racial feelings that otherwise would not have existed. Marshall's concluding words—"I bitterly resent"—reveal just how angry he was with Harold Hinton's article.*

JULY 2, 1946

Dear Sir:

I have read the article written for you by Harold B. Hinton from Columbia, Tennessee, under date of June 30th, which appeared in *The New York Times* on July 1, 1946, under the heading "Trial Vexes Pride in Columbia, Tennessee."

I feel that the readers of *The New York Times* are entitled to know some of the facts concerning Columbia, Tennessee, and some of the background of the trial about which Mr. Hinton wrote but which does not appear in Mr. Hinton's article. All of us who work in the field of race relations are constantly confronted with the statement that things would be better for the Negro in the South if Northerners would stay out. This seems to be the main thesis contained in Mr. Hinton's article. Mr. Hinton, however, carries this thesis even further since he devotes some space to pointing out that Mr. Maurice Weaver, one of the attorneys representing the case, came from as far away as Chattanooga, Tennessee, to interfere in the purely local matter which happened ____ miles away in Columbia, Tennessee. This would seem to be a narrowing of the freedom of individuals beyond that sought by most Southerners, who would seek merely to exclude Northerners from defending their Negro victims. Apparently now the white lawyer from ____ miles away is considered an outsider if he comes to the defense of Negroes in a Southern community. A point is made in Mr. Hinton's article that I, a Negro lawyer from New York, have displaced Mr. Weaver as chief counsel. I gathered that I too am regarded as an outsider. I, therefore, feel that it is necessary for me to point out that I spend the greater part of my time in and was brought up in the South. I have a broad Southern accent. While my office is in the North, I feel myself an integral part of any Negro community in the South. I have devoted ____ years to working in the defense of the basic human and constitutional rights of Negroes in the South, and I know that the dangers which face the Negro do not vary from one Southern community to another. It is time that intelligent people stop lending credence to the conception that any person who does not live full time in the South can have no right to an opinion of any sort about basic American principles and their lack of application in the South. As a lawyer, I know that the United States Constitution and the decisions of the Supreme Court are supposed to have the same force and effect in Tennessee as they have in New York and as a citizen I know that I have a duty to aid in upholding the Constitution and the laws of this nation everywhere in this country.

Proceeding further in Mr. Hinton's description of Maury County as a prosperous, proud, and cultural community of 43,000 people, I would like to point out that in this citadel of American democracy there have been ____ lynchings in the last 20 years, the last of which occurred in 19__.

On July 1, 1926, a mob of 200 persons killed a white man who had killed a deputy sheriff in Kenton, Tennessee. On October 8, 1926, R. Bell, a Negro, was taken from jail by a mob of 75 men and hanged. *The New York Times* of June 18, 1927, reports the lynching of one James Upchurch in Paris, Tennessee, on June 17th, and on September 28th a lynching took place two miles outside of Memphis, Tennessee. On November 13, 1927, an 18-year-old Negro boy was taken from the jail in Columbia, Tennessee, by a band of 250 men and hanged from a second story window of the courthouse building. *The New York Times* of May 30, 1929, reports the lynching of Joe Boxley, a 19-year-old boy in Alamoe, Tennessee. The Nashville *Banner*, published in Tennessee in March 1931, reported the lynching of Eli Johnson, a 25-year-old Negro, on March 29th by a mob. On June 10, 1933, the New York *Herald-Tribune* reported the lynching of two white men in Huntsville, Tennessee. These men were removed from jail by a group of 25 armed white men. On December 16, 1933, it was recorded in *The New York Times* that the body of Cordie Cheek, a 20-year-old Negro whom the grand jury had refused to indict after his arrest for attempted attack upon an 11-year-old white girl, was found hanging from the limb of a tree. *The Evening Tennessean*, published in Nashville on June 16th, reported the lynching of a Negro in Manchester, Tennessee, on the 24th of June 1934. The New York *World Telegram* of August 14, 1937, reported the lynching of Albert Goodman of Covington, Tennessee. The account of this lynching indicates that this was the second attempt of a mob to get at Goodman. On June 27, 1940, the Knoxville *News Sentinel* reported the lynching of Albert Williams on June 20th, who had dared to register to vote in a presidential election in Brownsville, Tennessee.

In the face of this factual record, it is shocking to find a reporter for *The New York Times* setting forth ejaculately the statement, "We haven't lynched anybody here in twenty years."

In this fine community, from which Mr. Hinton implies that outside lawyers should be excluded, the overwhelming weight of evidence presented in this trial indicated that no Negro sat upon any jury, grand or petty, in the past 40 years or in fact in the memory of any witness. The evidence which was elicited in the questioning of Mr. Weaver, the white foreign lawyer from Chattanooga, indicated that the vicious system of segregation would have made it impossible for Negroes to sit in the same jury box with white citizens. In fact, this very situation, in which the pattern of segregation has made it impossible for a Southern community to respect the right of Negroes to sit on jury, was foreseen by Mr. Justice Harlan in a decision which he wrote in an opinion in New York in the case of *Plessy vs. Ferguson*. In that case, the Supreme Court upheld a statute requiring segregation of the races in railroad coaches. Mr. Justice Harlan in his dissenting opinion pointed out, "It is clear that there has been a great deal of feeling among some of the great minds of our country, including Abe Lincoln, that what goes on in the South and what is done to our Negro fellow citizens in the South is the business of every citizen of the country."

More fundamental than anything else in Mr. Hinton's story, however, is his complete failure to present an objective account of the incident leading up to the arrest of the 25 defendants whom I have the honor to call my clients. It is fundamental, and it is known to every white person and Negro who has bothered to inform himself of the facts, that the Negro community feared another lynching. The federal grand jury report issued recently concerning the incident has established the fact that a group of white persons, some of whom were armed, crowded around the jail in which they believed Mrs. Stephenson and her son were confined and demanded to know where they were. There is no Negro in the country, and there are not many white people in the South, who do not know that that is the established preliminary to lynching. To read Mr. Hinton's story, one would believe that the Negroes presently on trial (or one of them) calmly and deliberately fired upon unarmed policemen without the slightest provocation. In fact, reading the story, I am sure the question must come to the minds of any person who did not know the facts as to why any shots were fired and whether my clients or the people who fired the shots upon the policemen were insane or habitual criminals. Particularly is this true in light of Mr. Hinton's touching description of his "Walk in the Sun" through the community where the shooting took place in February. The Negroes in Mr. Hinton's story are a happy, carefree, well-adjusted lot who joked with their white neighbors.

As the attorney representing the 25 defendants who are on trial in Columbia, Tennessee, I bitterly resent the wholly biased, unfair, and unjustified attack upon my clients and upon my right as a lawyer to defend my clients. But most bitterly do I resent the publication of false statements concerning the lynch record of the state of Tennessee and the background of the incident which gave rise to the arrest of my clients.

Thurgood Marshall

It seems that Marshall did not mail the letter.

WALTER WHITE TO THE NAACP BOARD

Marshall was never the picture of health during his NAACP years—he was a chain-smoker, a serious whiskey drinker, and a lover of fatty foods—and he landed in the hospital with pneumonia in August 1946. Although he often ignored his health concerns, the trip to the hospital made him a bit more sober than usual. "Boy, I have had the works and how," he wrote upon leaving the hospital after a monthlong stay. "I never believed I could be completely knocked off my feet."

His clients in the Columbia riots case sent him "a great big, twenty-pound, country-cured ham" during his hospital stay, and the NAACP board approved the expenditure White requests below. With Marshall absent, the local Nashville attorney Z. Alexander Looby, the Howard law professor Leon Ransom, and the white labor lawyer Maurice Weaver took the reins of the Columbia trial.

The following letter also shows just how close Marshall and Hastie were not only professionally but also personally. The two loved to joke around together, and Marshall once asked the new father Hastie to let him know "when the christening of Thurgooda will take place."

SEPTEMBER 9, 1946

I talked at length yesterday with Dr. Louis T. Wright regarding the examination he had just made of Mr. Thurgood Marshall, our special counsel. Dr. Wright informs me that Mr. Marshall has responded excellently to hospital and other treatment which he has been undergoing since June. But Dr. Wright further states that Mr. Marshall's condition is such that it will be at least six weeks before he can return to work, and if he is able to return then, he can do so to work not more than three hours a day every other day.

Governor Hastie has invited Mr. and Mrs. Marshall to come to the Virgin Islands for a visit and I have strongly urged upon Mr. Marshall that he accept that invitation because the change of scene and the excellent climate at this time of year will undoubtedly hasten Mr. Marshall's recovery.

Mr. Marshall's condition is due solely to the fact that he has worked himself almost to death without any thought of self. I think it would be a most gracious act on the part of the NAACP Legal Defense and Educational Fund, Inc. to contribute $500 towards Mr. Marshall's expenses in regaining his health. I am, therefore, writing to ask if you, as a member of the board, would be good enough to indicate on the enclosed slip if you would favor such a contribution.

Ever sincerely,

Walter White

MARSHALL TO CARTER WESLEY

By this point, Marshall's relationship with Wesley had soured, and here he sharply criticizes the publisher and editor of the Houston Informer *for supporting an organization that sought better education for African Americans within the segregated school system of Texas. The relationship had soured primarily because Wesley, like others in Texas, was concerned that a pure push for integration would jeopardize staff, funds, and programs at already existing black schools. Marshall was no longer interested at this point in making the legal case for equalizing segregated facilities, and during strategy sessions on desegregating education in 1946, he and his legal colleagues agreed that they would push for cases in which African American students directly sought to be integrated into all-white schools. This represented a monumental shift in legal strategy for Marshall; no longer was he pursuing the indirect strategy that Margold had suggested years earlier. According to Marshall's later reminiscences, he and his legal team "found [Margold] wasn't working, so then we shifted to hitting [segregation] straight on."*

Marshall refers below to Heman Sweatt, a thirty-three-year-old African American letter carrier from Texas who, with support from the NAACP and coaching from Marshall, had applied for admission to the University of Texas Law School earlier in the year. The university registrar had rejected Sweatt's application because of his race, and Sweatt sued with the help of Marshall as his lead attorney. Marshall pleaded for integration at the law school, arguing that because the state did not have a law school for African Americans, it had a legal obligation to admit Sweatt to the all-white law school. The state court decided to give the state time to set up a law school just for African Americans, but with Marshall's encouragement, Sweatt refused to attend the school and continued his suit.

OCTOBER 25, 1946

Dear Carter:

This letter is not only marked "personal" but is considered "personal," and for once, I am serious.

The thing I am worried about at the present time is the program of the Texas Conference for the Equalization of Educational Opportunities. I have been out of the office since the first of July because of illness and have just returned this week. I spent yesterday checking through the files on the information we have, and it appears that this organization is set up as a coordinating body and is also set up for the purpose of doing research and raising funds for the prosecution of such cases as do not come within the NAACP's non-segregation field. You can readily imagine the anxiety on our part regarding the functioning of such an organization.

In the first place, not only as a staff member of the NAACP, but as an individual, I have always taken the position that duplicating organizations duplicate effort and bring about additional expenses as well as effort. Of course your obvious answer to this is that the organization does not duplicate the NAACP. Well, it seems to me that if it does not duplicate the work of the NAACP, then it can only be considered as a competing organization, and I base this on the point that the Texas organization is set up to work on cases in the segregated field of education. I say quite frankly on this that any organization that works toward the establishment of segregated educational facilities is an organization competing with the principles of the NAACP.

I do not have to cite to you the instances of the evils of segregation because you are opposed to segregation. The problem of temporary segregation or a little segregation is much like a woman being "a little pregnant." You just simply cannot have a little segregation; you cannot rationalize on the necessity of segregation at all. The NAACP has banged its head up against the brick wall on segregation enough times to understand this.

The NAACP's state conference in Texas is opposed to segregation in any form. Now we have another organization that, despite fine-sounding language, is going to try to get as much as possible under the segregated system. The Negroes in Texas will most certainly end up in two divided camps, and I do not believe it is possible to be in both camps at the same time. You and I can both cite numerous people, as a matter of fact hundreds of people, who have tried to carry water on both shoulders and have ended up with both buckets and water parked on the middle of their skulls. On the question of Negroes' rights, the skull will not be the individual's skull, but will be the skull of the Negro people in general, not only in Texas but throughout the country.

You know as well as I do that progress is being made in the fight against segregation. You and I both know that the fight can eventually be won. We both know that the only way it can be won is to get as many people as possible to fight the common cause without other interests. It was inevitable when we started to make inroads into segregation and other inequalities in educational facilities and inroads into segregation in transportation and inroads in voting and registration inequalities that there were going to be moves and countermoves. I am afraid that despite the good intentions of this organization in Texas, it can be viewed by the opposition as a countermove and as a compromise answer to the problem.

You will be interested to know that an editorial appeared in a Tulsa newspaper after the adverse decision in the Sipuel case against the University of Oklahoma, congratulating Texas on the decision of the court in the Sweatt case and deploring the opinion of the Oklahoma judge dismissing the case against the University of Oklahoma. One of the editorials had this to say: "It will not be surprising if a good many of us change our minds about Negro higher education in the next few years and arrive at the opinion that the best interests of the state may be served if Negroes are admitted to the O. U. Law School at Norman and the O. U. Medical School at Oklahoma City. These are postgraduate schools in a sense. The students in them are supposed to be matured. They are there for a serious, not a social, purpose. There may be no patience on the part of the public when the alternatives are admitting a few Negroes to these upper-branch schools or spending thousands of dollars per pupil per year setting up and maintaining separate law and medical schools for them." Certainly, we as Negroes cannot be in position to demand less for our people than whites do. In view of the successful decision in the Sweatt case, it certainly seems most inadvisable for us now to retreat from the victory we have won in that case and begin clamoring for a segregated school. We have gained the advantage, and now is the time for us to press forward in an attempt to get the states to admit Negroes into the law school, medical school, school of journalism, graduate school, and every other school at the University of Texas which has no counterpart in the Negro colleges maintained in the state.

Every segregated elementary school, every segregated high school and every segregated college unit is a monument to the perpetuation of segregation. It is one thing to "take" segregation that is forced upon you, and it is another thing to ask for segregation. I still believe that if the opposition finds that there are *representative* and *respectable* Negroes who cannot be bought, who have standing and who are in favor of segregation, then they will consider that as a much better victory than any legal case that they can win against us.

For all of these reasons and many others which I can discuss with you at length, I am wondering if you could take time and consider them in the light of all of our past work.

Sincerely yours,

Thurgood Marshall

MARSHALL TO ELEANOR ROOSEVELT

In this letter to Roosevelt, a longtime advocate of African American causes, Marshall once again criticizes the FBI and the Department of Justice. He also writes about Robert Bomar, the state safety commissioner who supervised the highway patrol officers as they ransacked the homes of African Americans during the racial violence in Columbia. Marshall also sent a detailed critique of Bomar to Ed Sullivan, at this point a popular columnist for the New York Daily News.

OCTOBER 28, 1946

Dear Mrs. Roosevelt:

I returned to the office a few days ago and have gone over the correspondence between you and Attorney General Tom Clark concerning the grand jury investigation of the Columbia, Tennessee case.

In the first place, Mr. Clark takes the position throughout the letter that there is no positive identification of any of the state officials responsible for the destruction of property and other items. I have always been surprised at these statements because the United States Department of Justice never seems to have any hesitancy in admitting its inability to perform its functions in regard to Negroes' rights. The FBI has one of the finest records of any investigating organization that we know of. They have been able to ferret out spies and other espionage agents, saboteurs, well-known gangsters such as Dillinger, etc., and I know of no instance where they have been unable to get positive identification of criminals or to build up cases where there has been a violation of federal law—except where the victims are Negroes. A huge National Guard unit was present on the scene when this property was destroyed. There was also a tremendous number of highway patrolmen. There were large numbers of white former mob members standing around, and now the Department of Justice says they cannot get a single person to identify at least one person guilty of what can only be termed as "wholesale destruction of people's property."

Either the Department of Justice, including the FBI, fell down on the job of investigating the case or they deliberately closed their eyes. However, I would not be completely frank unless I admitted that I did not expect a wholehearted attempt by the Department of Justice to bring about any convictions of any state officers in Senator McKellar's home state. I am always aware of at least one other very important case where a sheriff killed at least one Negro without cause, and the Department of Justice found itself unable to prosecute because it was, I imagine, too close to Boss Crump's territory. This was, of course, before Attorney General Clark's term of office.

As to the grand jury investigation itself, there are several questions which Attorney General Clark has ignored, one of which is that the Negro witnesses who were the victims were placed before the grand jury without any consultation whatsoever with any lawyer of the United States Department of Justice. In all of my years of practice, I have never heard of a prosecuting attorney presenting a complaining witness, or witnesses, to a grand jury without first talking with him. It has also never been satisfactorily explained to me why the federal government permitted one of its witnesses, while waiting to testify before the grand jury, to be carried away by state officers to be questioned for a long time and otherwise threatened. It is also an anomaly to consider the all-white jury investigating an occurrence between white and colored people where the whole question was as to whether the Negro or the white group was responsible.

Last, but not least, it has never been satisfactorily explained to me why the attorney general, while conversant with the conditions in Nashville, and especially in view of the fact that the United States district attorney was a resident of Columbia, Tennessee, who had already issued a statement that no federal rights had been violated, did not proceed by the filing of an information rather than by having a grand jury investigation. I do not think there is any doubt that the grand jury investigation turned out to be an investigation not of a violation of the civil rights of Negroes, but an investigation of organizations and other matters foreign to the subject.

As to the grand jury report, I think we can gather from the admissions of Mr. Bomar at the Columbia trials that there can be no question that federal civil rights were violated. If the Department of Justice would only go after Mr. Bomar as they should, I have no doubt, after observing him at the earlier portions of the Columbia trial, that he would "tell it all."

Sincerely yours,

Thurgood Marshall

Bomar was never punished for his role in the riots and, perhaps predictably, even went on to become head of the Texas state prison system.

MARSHALL TO LULU WHITE

Lulu White, the executive secretary for the Houston NAACP, publicly opposed gradualists within her local NAACP who did not favor running African American candidates in 1946 as part of a coordinated effort to increase black participation in Texas politics. She also differed with Carter Wesley and other individuals who supported the Texas Conference for the Equalization of Educational Opportunities and who favored the state's plans to build a segregated law school over Marshall's work in the Sweatt case.

NOVEMBER 6, 1946

Dear Lulu:

Roy has shared with me your letter of November 1st.

As to the candidacy of Reverend Simpson, I think Negroes are clearly right in running a Negro candidate, and if he is as qualified as the other candidates, I believe that Negroes should most certainly support him. As for people who say "The time is not ripe," my reply to them has always been the time will never be "ripe," and there is no better time than the present to enforce your rights. I believe that the right to run for public office is just as important as the right to vote. I am not worried about the other side using this factor to attempt to disenfranchise Negroes in the future. They do not need any help in their campaign to try to disenfranchise us. You know, young lady, there is only one way to go in our business, and that is down the straight road. As soon as you begin to curve and go around corners, you get off balance and you end up on that invariable merry-go-round known as a "rat race."

As to the new organization set up for educational opportunities, I agree with everything in your letter. However, I believe that it is a matter to be settled in Texas by Texans, and unless and until that organization directly interferes with NAACP work, I merely stand in a position to comment on it, but not publicly unless called on to do so. All I can say is that you did right, and I am not kidding. The time to fight against segregation in Texas is not a time in the future, nor, as a matter of fact, should it be the present time. It should have been 1866. It is certainly good to know that there are some people in Texas and in the South and Southwest who are willing to stick to their guns. You know, Negroes as a group stick together as a group until they win something and then they tend to split apart. Maybe we shouldn't win cases, or maybe we shouldn't split up. At any rate, stick to your guns.

Sincerely yours,

Thurgood Marshall

MARSHALL TO ATTORNEY GENERAL TOM CLARK

In a surprise decision, the all-white jury in the Columbia riot case found that twenty-three of the twenty-five accused black men were not guilty. After the acquittals, William Pillow and Lloyd Kennedy still faced attempted murder charges, and Marshall returned to Columbia on November 16 to defend the two men. Marshall secured an acquittal for Pillow but failed to do the same for Kennedy. Shortly after the landmark trial, Marshall found himself under arrest, as sketched in this telegram to the attorney general.

NOVEMBER 19, 1946

Last night after leaving Columbia, Tennessee, where we secured acquittal of one of two Negroes charged with crimes growing out of February disturbances, three lawyers, including myself, were stopped outside of Columbia in the night by three carloads of officers, including deputy sheriff, constables, and highway patrolmen. Alleged purpose was to search car for whiskey. When no whiskey found, we were stopped by same officials two more times, and on last occasion I was placed under arrest for driving while drunk and returned to Columbia. Magistrate refused to place me in jail after examining me and finding I was extremely sober. This type of intimidation of defense lawyers charged with duty of defending persons charged with crime cannot go unnoticed. Therefore demand immediate investigation and criminal charges against officers participating in last night's outrage. Three lawyers were Z. Alexander Looby, Maurice M. Weaver, and myself.

Thurgood Marshall

The NAACP publicized the incident, and NAACP supporters sent countless telegrams of protest to the White House.

MARSHALL TO ATTORNEY GENERAL TOM CLARK

On August 9, 1946, local fishermen discovered the body of John C. Jones, a twenty-eight-year-old African American, floating in Dorcheat Bayou, near Minden, Louisiana. An NAACP investigation revealed that Jones had been lynched, and NAACP news releases reported that he had been hacked by a meat cleaver and burned with a blowtorch. "The excessive heat and beatings caused the victim's eyes to pop from their sockets," according to the news release. The NAACP investigation led to a formal FBI investigation, and after locals failed to convict the guilty parties, Clark instructed Malcolm Lafargue, the U.S. attorney for the Western District of Louisiana, to begin federal proceedings against the lynchers. A federal grand jury indicted six men, including Benjamin Gantt, the chief of police in Minden, and below Marshall expresses his bitter disappointment upon learning that Clark approved dropping charges against Gantt. Clark offered his approval most likely because Gantt had cooperated with the federal government in the case.

DECEMBER 3, 1946

According to AP dispatch of 27th, charges against police chief Benjamin Gantt, Minden, La., dismissed on recommendation of United States Attorney Lafargue with consent of United States attorney general. This apparent authentic report is unbelievable. Action by the United States attorney with your apparent approval to drop indictment returned by a federal grand jury demonstrates the opposite type of law enforcement expected of representatives of the U.S. Department of Justice. Procedure of obtaining indictments and giving publicity to obtaining of indictments and then dismissing charges subsequent thereto tends to destroy respect for our government and at same time gives impression to criminals prone to injure Negroes the belief that although indictments might be returned against them, they can expect that these indictments will be later dismissed.

Thurgood Marshall

MARSHALL TO MACEO HUBBARD

Marshall protested his November 18 arrest to the attorney general in an earlier telegram, but in the letter below—which he mailed to Assistant Attorney General Theron Caudle and marked to the attention of Maceo Hubbard, the first African American staff attorney in the civil rights division of the Department of Justice—Marshall offers the details surrounding his arrest.

Marshall found himself not only under arrest for drunken driving but also wondering whether he was about to face his own lynching at Duck River, the site of numerous lynchings in the past. Indeed, he later learned, presumably after sending this letter, that waiting at Duck River was a mob of white men, fully prepared to lynch him, who were thwarted only because his friends were closely following the police car in which he was traveling to the river.

In an interview he gave decades later, Marshall stated that at his appearance before the justice of the peace, the police said: "'We got this Nigger for drunk driving.' And [the justice] says, 'Boy, you wanna take my test? I never had a drink in my life and I can smell a drink a mile off. You want to take a chance?' I said, 'Well, sure, I'll take a chance.' He said, 'Blow your breath on me.' I blew it so hard he rocked. 'That man hasn't had a drink in 24 hours,' he said. 'What the hell are you talking about?'"

DECEMBER 4, 1946

Dear Mr. Hubbard:

The facts concerning the incident in Columbia, Tennessee, on Monday night, November 18th, are as follows:

The trial of William Pillow and Lloyd Kennedy in Columbia, Tennessee, was completed a short time after 7 PM with a verdict of guilty for Kennedy and acquittal for Pillow. The courtroom was almost empty at the time . . . although there were many individuals in the courtroom during the trial and several seated around the table of the district attorney general. When the jury returned, there was only one person at the table of the district attorney general, and that was Mr. Bumpus himself.

We left the courtroom, went down to the area referred to by some as "Mink Slide," went into the drugstore of Mr. Julius Blair, and purchased soft drinks and crackers. We then got into the car of Mr. Z. Alexander Looby and started for Nashville with me driving at, I would say, approximately 7:30. We went over the bridge from Columbia and on, going on a main road to Nashville a very short distance. . . . I noticed what appeared to be a gray automobile standing on the pavement and a state highway patrol car on his right off the pavement. I believe there was a filling station at the same place. A car was coming in the opposite direction, and I slowed down for the car to pass and blew my horn in an effort to have the car parked in front of me move off the highway, and when it did not move, I pulled around it, still headed for Nashville. We had gone on a very short distance down the road when we heard a siren blowing. As I was slowing down to pull off the road, a car with men in civilian clothes pulled up opposite, flashing flashlights and with their doors open, telling me to pull off the road, which I did. This car pulled in front of us, and approximately four men came back and told us they had a warrant to search the car for whiskey and that we should all get out, which we did. When we got out, we noticed a state highway patrol car parked behind our car and another car parked on the right of the car with a spotlight turned on the car, which made three cars in all. A man read the search warrant, and the car was searched. However, Mr. Weaver and myself watched carefully to make certain that no whiskey was placed in the car by the men searching it. Mr. Looby, another of the attorneys, and Mr. Harry Raymond, a reporter for the *Daily Worker*, were also in the car and stood by. After the car was searched and no whiskey found, some question was raised as to whether there was a warrant to search our persons. There didn't appear to be any warrant, and we were not searched. We then asked if we might move on, and we were told to go ahead. I got into the driver's seat. There had been some difficulty in the hydromatic system of Mr. Looby's car, and while I was trying to get it started, the suggestion was made that Looby should drive, and I agreed to this. I got out of the car and changed places with Looby, and as we started off, flashlights were flashed again and there was much yelling to halt and to stop, which we did. Then the group gathered around the car again, flashing lights in everyone's face, stating that this man was not the driver of the car, and who was driving when we drove up. Someone immediately pointed me out, and they asked me for my driver's license. They took my driver's license, examined it and returned it to me, and we were again told we could go ahead to Nashville.

As we started off the third time, the same procedure was followed. Lights flashed, and there was yelling to stop and halt. The rear door opposite where I was seated was opened and someone, I think his name is Lynch, but at any rate in the group, said, "We have got to arrest you for drunken driving." We all, of course, stated that I was not drunk nor had I been drinking, but I was told to get out of the car and did. I was placed in the rear seat of the car reported to be owned by the man named Lynch, and four men got in the car with me. All appeared to be deputy sheriffs or constables. Mr. Looby and the others were told that they were free to go to Nashville. Instead of going back on the main highway to Columbia, the car I was in turned left down the road leading toward the famous Duck River. Mr. Looby, instead of driving toward Nashville, followed the car, whereupon the car turned left twice back to the main road and on to Columbia.

When we reached Columbia, someone got out of the car I was in, and I asked what was next, and they told me to go over to the building across the street to the magistrate's office. I told them that if we went over there, we were all going over there together since I wasn't going by myself inasmuch as I was under arrest.

When we went into Mr. Pough's office, Mr. Weaver came in as my attorney, and Mr. Pough wanted to know what was going on, and he was told that I was arrested for drunken driving, and he should issue a warrant or some other paper. Mr. Pough went over to his desk to fill out the papers, and Mr. Weaver told him that this was a "frame-up" and that he would appreciate it if he, Mr. Pough, would smell my breath. Mr. Pough agreed to do so, and on examining my breath, said, "This man isn't drunk, he hasn't even had a drink," whereupon all of the men left the office except a man by the name of Bars or Butts, who swore out the original warrant to search the car, and Mr. Butts agreed with Mr. Pough that I wasn't anywheres near drunk. Mr. Pough refused to sign any papers and told me I was free to go. When we went out into the street, we noticed that the streets were deserted in the business section of the town with the exception of cars of local police and deputy sheriffs circling around. We returned to "Mink Slide" and left Columbia in another automobile entirely different from Mr. Looby's car and made the trip to Nashville without incident. Some friends of ours brought Mr. Looby's car to Nashville the following day.

The above statements are true to the best of my recollection, and there are many facts in this statement which justify our belief that a thorough and complete investigation must be made with the necessary steps to not only punish the guilty parties but to make it apparent that officers of the law acting with state authority cannot attempt to deprive a citizen of the United States from his right to not only travel on the highways unmolested, but to go about his lawful vocation of practicing law and representing defendants in criminal actions wherever it might be.

Yours very truly,

Thurgood Marshall

Around the time of this near lynching, which no doubt scarred him, Marshall told a youth conference in New Orleans that "a disobedience movement on the part of Negroes and their white allies, if employed in the South, would result in wholesale slaughter with no good achieved." According to Marshall, "well-meaning radical groups in New York" had approached him about the possibility of using Gandhi's nonviolent methods in order to achieve racial justice in the South. "Don't do it that way," Marshall counseled the youths. "In the Deep South, any nonviolence or disobedience movement executed on this pattern would bring violence on the part of local and state police which would result in the imprisonment of hundreds of young people and the death of scores, with nothing achieved except a measure of publicity which we are now getting for our struggles with a minimum of suffering."

MARSHALL TO CARTER WESLEY

By the end of 1946, Marshall and Wesley held each other in contempt, and this is one of the angriest letters Marshall ever wrote during his NAACP years. He was enraged especially by Wesley's public criticisms of the NAACP, some of which are sketched in this letter, and by his personal attacks on Marshall's character. Marshall refers below to hearings on Senator Theodore Bilbo of Mississippi, who was under investigation for inciting racial discrimination during his campaign for the Senate seat. In June 1946, Bilbo had urged the "red-blooded Anglo-Saxon man in Mississippi to resort to any means to keep hundreds of Negroes from the polls in the July 2 primary."

DECEMBER 27, 1946

Dear Carter:

I have just received your letter of December 23rd, and I think I at last have a true picture of what is going on in Texas so far as you are concerned. In the first place, I don't think Lulu White needs me or anyone else to make up her mind for her, and I know darn well I don't need Lulu White or anyone else to make up my mind for me, although at the same time, I am always anxious and willing to get the views of as many people as possible before jumping to conclusions. On reading the first part of your letter, I was of the opinion that I should say to you to continue your plan but that I, of course, could not agree with it. However, on going further into your letter, I find that it is necessary to try to keep the record straight with you, although I find it exceedingly difficult. The reason it is difficult is because you are not only unwilling to see other people's sides of a question, but you are a little careless with the truth.

Your statement as to the NAACP's part in applying for applications to the university and that if the appeal is lost, nothing is to be done about it, is so wrong that I leave it as such. You don't care what we have in the brief in the Oklahoma case, and you don't care what the students of the University of Texas say, promise or do. This is further evidence of a narrowness that is unbelievable. You then point out, "It is you who are concerned with acclaim and the public light, I am concerned with the problem of winning equal educational opportunities." Both portions of that sentence are barefaced lies.

You mention the fact that the NAACP refused to enter the fight against Bilbo because it was not instituted in Jackson by the local chapter—another double-barreled, barefaced lie. The Jackson branch of the NAACP did everything in its power to bring about the hearing against Bilbo. The NAACP circulated all of its branches in Mississippi to get persons to testify. Charlie Houston went down before the hearings and worked with the people during the hearings as the official representative of the NAACP. Charlie Houston and Franklin H. Williams are now preparing a detailed brief on *behalf* of the NAACP to be presented to the members of the committee and every senator.

You mention that the NAACP refused to participate in the Grovey case and "nasty remarks you made about the case when the Supreme Court ruled against Atkins." At this stage, it is unbelievable how far you will go with your lies. I was not even with the NAACP when the Grovey case was decided. If you want to know what I think about it, I think *Grovey vs. Townsend* was not only one of the biggest mistakes made in the fight for Negroes' rights, but it set the fight against primary elections back at least fifteen years. . . .

I know you must feel good all by yourself in your charges that I am selfish and want everything, and I will take for its face value your suggestion that I can go to hell, at least so far as the two of us are concerned. Since you want to get personal, let's get personal. Let us agree that both of us are fighting for the rights of Negroes, and after we both agree that we are fighting for the rights of Negroes, let us at the end of the year add up what each one of us made in cash money while fighting for the right of Negroes—you take your income from the newspapers and I will take my income from the NAACP, and we will compare them and see who is selfish.

Finally, you state that "If you and Lulu want to fight on the issue, I'll send the fight right back to you." Other and bigger and more selfish people have made similar statements before about fighting the NAACP, and we continue to do alright. The reason we have been able to survive these many years is because no one individual, whether he be Carter Wesley or anyone else, can run the NAACP.

. . .

I know that although you have been around this world longer than I have, in my limited experience, I have found that in this type of work you very often get disgusted, etc., and very often when the fight against the common enemy gets hot, you begin to look around for someone else to jump on. I have had this experience before with other people, and it doesn't worry me. However, when it reaches the point that any individual takes the fight and tries to aim it at the NAACP or its work, then I take a different position. We have all won certain victories, legal and otherwise, and the enemies such as the officials of the state of Texas are scurrying for cover to try to find some way out. I can think of no better way out for them than to have a split among the Negroes themselves, and I say quite frankly that you are doing all in your power to bring this about. As a matter of fact, you are doing a finer job than some other Negroes in Texas admittedly working for the powers that be. I had always respected your judgment and you know of many instances where I followed it. I think that you will agree that the few gains we have made in Texas have been made through this type of cooperation. But when it reaches the point where you are afraid to sit down in a meeting with our executive committee and argue this entire thing out on a sane and rational basis, I, for one, cannot continue the respect I had. Obviously, there is more to it than I knew about, and for that reason, the next move is up to you, and you can do or say anything you want to about me personally, but if you want to join the other people in your newspaper profession that are attacking the NAACP, I, for one, will defend the NAACP. If you have anything better to offer than the NAACP in the matter of getting rights for Negroes, I will join you. In the meantime, I will stick to the NAACP and you can go your merry way.

Very truly yours,

Thurgood Marshall

MARSHALL TO ATTORNEY GENERAL TOM CLARK

On February 12, 1946, Isaac Woodard, an African American veteran who had just served fifteen months in the Philippines, was traveling by bus to see his mother in South Carolina. After Woodard caused a delay during a bathroom visit at one of the bus stops, the driver became incensed and arranged for two police officers to meet Woodard at the next stop. Woodard told the officers that he had done nothing to warrant their attention, but the white officers hauled him to jail, beat him with a blackjack, and blinded him in both eyes with the end of a nightstick. The FBI investigated the barbaric incident, but prosecutors were not able to convict the officers, including police chief Linwood Shull, with the evidence turned over by the FBI agents. In response, Marshall grew livid, and below is his letter of protest to the attorney general.

In the postscript to this tough letter, Marshall refers to a New York Times *editorial that commented on a 1946 lynching near Moore's Ford Bridge, about fifty miles east of Atlanta, Georgia, when twenty unmasked white men beat and shot to death two African American couples—George Dorsey and his wife, Mae Murray Dorsey, and his sister and her husband, Dorothy Dorsey Malcom and Roger Malcom. President Truman had ordered a federal investigation of this vicious lynching, but no one was convicted. Shortly after the federal grand jury returned no indictments, a* Times *editorial stated: "The death cries of the Negroes will not cease to ring in the ears of decent people of South and North with the jury's finding of no true bill. For this jury brings in also, through its very failure to find the guilty, a scathing indictment: of cowardly human nature that declined to name the guilty, either through bigoted hatred of the Negro race or from fear of reprisal or self-incrimination; of Georgia law enforcement agencies that may or may not have proceeded too timidly or too tardily to gather and preserve the essential evidence, so that even the FBI, with its almost fabulous record of success in other difficult cases, is now forced to confess in this case that with all its science of detection it cannot find the criminals, although it has not yet given up the hunt."*

DECEMBER 27, 1946

Dear Mr. Clark:

You will remember that sometime ago I agreed to bring to your personal attention matters which affect Negroes in connection with the Department of Justice. The Federal Bureau of Investigation has done a good job on peonage in the South. With the exception of peonage, the record of the FBI in investigating cases involving Negroes has been notably one-sided. The inability of the FBI to identify any members of the lynch mob in the Monroe, Georgia, lynchings is the latest example of this. In the disturbance at Columbia, Tennessee, on February 25th and 26th of this year, it is reported that FBI agents were sent in almost immediately and were supposed to have made a thorough and complete investigation, yet they were unable to produce the name of a single individual responsible for the acts of violence and the destruction of the property of the Negroes in that town.

In the past, the NAACP and other organizations have used inexperienced investigators who have usually been able to produce the names of the members of the mobs. In the recent Minden, Louisiana, lynching, the president of our New Orleans branch, with no experience as an investigator, was able to produce the names of members of that mob. In the beating of Isaac Woodard by Officer Shull in Batesburg, S.C., we were able to produce eyewitnesses and the name of the police officer.

The FBI has established for itself an incomparable record for ferreting out persons violating our federal laws. This great record extends from the persecution of vicious spies and saboteurs who are trained in the methods of evading identification and arrest to nondescript hoodlums who steal cheap automobiles and drive them across state lines. On the other hand, the FBI has been unable to identify or bring to trial persons charged with violations of federal statutes where Negroes are the victims. Such a record demonstrates the uneven administration of federal criminal statutes, which should not be tolerated.

You have called for a strengthening of the federal civil rights statutes, yet I am sure it is apparent that there would be very little use to strengthen these civil rights statutes if the FBI continues its policy of being unable to produce the names of persons guilty of such crimes.

You will remember that Section 40 of Title C provides that you and other officials of the federal government are specifically required, at the expense of the United States, "to institute prosecution against all persons violating any of the provisions of Chapter 3 and Title 16 . . . and to cause such persons to be arrested and imprisoned, or bailed, for trial before the Court of the United States or the territorial court having cognizance of the offense." This statute places an additional burden upon you and other law enforcement officials of the federal government over and above other duties included in the oath of office. For this reason, I believe that you, as attorney general of the United States, have the clear duty and responsibility of making a complete investigation of one of your departments, namely, the FBI, to determine why it is impossible for this department to maintain a record as to crimes in which Negroes are victims comparable to its record as to other crimes.

This letter is being sent to you without being released to the press, and no publicity whatsoever is being given to it other than possible discussion with members of our staff. I expect to be in Washington during the early part of January and would appreciate an opportunity to discuss this matter further with you if you so desire.

Very truly yours,

Thurgood Marshall

P.S. In connection with the failure to identify members of the mob in the Monroe, Ga., lynchings, I imagine you have noticed the editorial in *The New York Times* for Saturday, December 21st, captioned "The Silent Indictment."

CHAPTER NINE

1947

ATTORNEY GENERAL TOM CLARK TO MARSHALL

The attorney general offers a detailed—and spirited—defense of the civil rights work in the Department of Justice. The content of the letter follows a written suggestion that Hoover had sent to Clark: "To refute Marshall's charge that the FBI has racial bias and prejudice I believe that a few cases where successful prosecutions have been had in civil rights cases should be cited and that Marshall should be informed in no uncertain terms that all investigations conducted by the Bureau are conducted impartially and without regard to the race or color of any persons involved." The Clark letter is especially important for inclusion here, in its full form, because it provides strong evidence of the deep respect that the attorney general had for Marshall. It also reveals the high level of legal debates between Clark and Marshall.

JANUARY 13, 1947

Dear Mr. Marshall:

This will acknowledge receipt of your letter dated December 27, 1946, primarily concerning investigations conducted by the FBI in cases involving Negroes. You make reference to four specific cases concerning which I wish to make a few pertinent comments.

The first case referred to by you is that involving the killing of the four Negroes near Monroe, Georgia. I wish to point out that as soon as the report of that crime was received, an investigation was immediately instituted by the FBI on specific instructions from me. A thorough and exhaustive investigation, an investigation confronted with many obstacles, has continued over a period of several months, and to date nearly 2,600 individuals in the vicinity of Monroe, Georgia, have been interviewed. I recently instructed that the facts and evidence developed be presented to a federal grand jury for consideration, and such a grand jury sitting at Athens, Georgia, recently heard the testimony of approximately 106 witnesses. At the conclusion of this testimony, the jury did not see fit to return an indictment against any of the individuals suspected of complicity in this crime because the facts did not, in the opinion of the grand jury, constitute a violation of a federal statute.

It is to be noted that shortly after the grand jury hearing on January 1, 1947, one of the Negro witnesses who had testified was allegedly beaten by two white men. An investigation was immediately instituted, and the FBI took into custody the two men believed responsible. From the information obtained, there can be no doubt that the FBI has been carefully and thoroughly investigating every phase of this case.

You referred in your letter to the disturbance at Columbia, Tennessee, on February 25 and 26, 1946, concerning which an investigation was conducted by the FBI. I wish to point out in this connection that after a most thorough and complete investigation had been conducted, all of the facts and evidence developed were considered by a federal grand jury. All individuals who were in any way connected with the disturbance or who had any information concerning the matter were called to testify before the jury, and after hearing the complete testimony of all witnesses, the jury concluded that there had been no violation of a federal statute. With reference to this case, I might point out that the grand jury commended the law enforcement officers for their handling of this case.

You pointed out in your letter that I have recently called for a strengthening of the federal civil rights statute. I believe that the developments in the cases referred to above show not a weakness in the investigations conducted by the FBI, but rather the need for more specific statutes in this field. The statutes under which we are presently forced to operate are clearly too general to adequately protect private individuals in those rights which the federal courts have held to be federally protected rights. When a grand jury, after considering all available evidence in a particular case, feels that because of the controversial nature of the particular statute involved, there has been no clear-cut violation and refuses to hand down an indictment, the FBI and the Department of Justice are powerless to proceed further. I believe it is most unfair to place on the investigating agency the responsibility for the failure of a grand jury to return an indictment, or of a petit jury to return a verdict of guilty, when all available evidence has been completely and impartially obtained and carefully presented.

You also stated that in the recent Minden, Louisiana, case inexperienced investigators of your organization were able to produce the names of members of the mob. I wish to comment that it is the duty of every person, as a citizen of these United States, to furnish to proper authorities any information in his possession concerning the commission of a crime. An inexperienced investigator, or any private individual, can, in many cases, furnish the names of individuals suspected of having committed a particular crime, and such information is frequently of great assistance in the investigation of that crime. The mere naming of suspects, however, does not constitute a solution to the crime. As an attorney, you are certainly aware that the real investigative problem arises in any case in obtaining positive, concrete evidence admissible in court which will prove without any doubt that the suspected party is, in fact, the party responsible. Indictments as a result of the FBI's investigation of this case have been returned against Deputy Sheriff Haynes, Deputy Sheriff Edwards, and three private individuals who were members of the mob.

With reference to the Isaac Woodard case, it appears from your comments that you are not in possession of the complete facts. It was originally reported by your organization and by Isaac Woodard himself that the alleged beating occurred at Aiken, South Carolina, at the hands of the chief of police of that city. The subsequent investigation conducted by the FBI disclosed that the incident occurred not at Aiken but at Batesburg, South Carolina, and that the chief of police at Batesburg was the man involved. Your organization did furnish the names of certain individuals who were riding on the same bus with Isaac Woodard, and FBI agents interviewed these persons and furnished complete reports of the facts in their possession to the government attorney for his use in presenting this case to the grand jury and the trial court.

In your letter you have referred to cases which have, as yet, not resulted in actual convictions and penitentiary sentences. You infer that this is due to bias and prejudice on the part of the FBI in conducting investigations of cases involving Negroes. In order to indicate the lack of foundation for such an accusation, I should like to refer you to a few of the recent cases involving the civil rights of Negroes which have been investigated by the FBI and which have resulted in convictions and sentences.

A short time ago an investigation was conducted of the alleged beating and subsequent death of a Negro, Sam McFadden, resulting from the acts of Tom A. Crews, former city marshal of Branford, Florida. The evidence developed reflected that on September 21, 1945, Crews forced McFadden to jump from a bridge over the Swanee River to his death in the river below. On October 3, 1946, Crews was found guilty in federal court for violating one of the civil rights statutes, Section 52, title 18, U.S. Code, and received the maximum sentence under that statute.

In another case nine defendants, including one former sheriff and three former deputy sheriffs, were convicted in the United States district court at Danville, Illinois, on December 9, 1946, for violations of the civil rights statutes which arose out of the killing of James E. Person, a Negro who was en route to Chicago from Tennessee at the time he was shot.

On November 19, 1945, William McMillan, a registrar of voters in Ashe County, North Carolina, was convicted in federal court for violation of the civil rights statutes for depriving a Negro of his right to vote in a federal election solely because of the Negro's color.

Similarly, on April 1, 1946, Robert W. Lewis and John S. Brown, registrars of voters in Washington County, North Carolina, were convicted of violations of the civil rights statutes for their refusal to register as voters several Negroes because of their color.

I know that Director Hoover of the FBI has made vigorous efforts to conduct thorough, complete, and impartial investigations in every case in which there has been an allegation of a violation of civil rights. Unfortunately, he has not always received complete cooperation, particularly from your organization, in his efforts to carry out these investigations. I recall that Mr. Hoover advised me of the letter which you addressed to him on May 10, 1946, in which you made charges of improper conduct on the part of the special agents of the FBI. Mr. Hoover has advised me that by a letter dated May 14, 1946, he outlined to you his policy of requiring bureau agents to refrain at all times from any "statement, conduct or actions which are prejudicial in any way to the rights of any person under investigation or being interviewed." In his letter of May 14th, Mr. Hoover advised you that "stringent disciplinary action is taken against any special agent who, by any act, prejudices the bureau's program of conducting thorough, impartial and entirely ethical and legal investigation of all cases." In that letter Mr. Hoover requested you to furnish him with specific data concerning the basis of your complaints which were of a general nature relative to the conduct of bureau agents in order that he might initiate an immediate administrative investigation. By his letter he assured you that, if facts were developed which would substantiate your charges, he would take prompt disciplinary action. Mr. Hoover has expressed to me his regret that you never saw fit to answer his letter of May 14, 1946, or to furnish any information upon which he could predicate an inquiry into the charges which you made.

Further indicative of the unwillingness of your associates to cooperate with the FBI, I desire to invite your attention to the investigation conducted some months ago into the charges that the chief of police at Batesburg, South Carolina, assaulted and caused the blindness of Isaac Woodard. This case is referred to heretofore in this letter, but you will recall that when FBI agents who were attempting to ascertain the full facts in this case interviewed Isaac Woodard, he informed the agents that upon the instructions of Franklin H. Williams, counsel of the National Association for the Advancement of Colored People, he was not to furnish information to FBI agents or to be interviewed without the approval of Mr. Williams. Mr. Woodard quoted Mr. Williams as stating that the FBI agents "are not on your side—they are on the side of the government." Although Isaac Woodard was not a defendant in this case but was actually a key witness upon whose cooperation the FBI was required to depend, the restrictions imposed upon his discussion of the facts in his case with the bureau agents caused considerable unnecessary delay in the investigation of this case.

Permit me to assure you that it is and always has been the policy of the FBI to conduct all investigations of violations of federal law in a completely unbiased manner without regard to the race, color, or religious belief of any persons involved. I know of no instance in the history of the FBI in which any statements to the contrary have any basis in fact. To this end I solicit your aid and assistance and that of your associates in bringing to my attention and to that of Mr. Hoover any specific facts which you believe justify our consideration.

Sincerely yours,

Tom Clark

Rather than sending a detailed reply to Clark's vigorous defense, Marshall sent him an uncharacteristically tame letter a week later, thanking him for his frankness and requesting a meeting. Clark obliged, and during the meeting the attorney general expressed support for Marshall's own convictions that the federal government could do more in fighting race-based crimes and that there was an urgent need for strong antilynching laws. But sensitive to the importance of personal politics, Clark also encouraged Marshall not to alienate Hoover. The NAACP, after all, would need the bureau's support when dealing with local police authorities.

J. EDGAR HOOVER TO WALTER WHITE

Hoover appeals directly to the head of the NAACP.

JANUARY 13, 1947

DEAR MR. WHITE:

In accord with our understanding, I wanted to bring to your attention a situation which is causing me increasing concern. It relates to the repeated efforts upon the part of Mr. Thurgood Marshall, special counsel of your Association, to embarrass the Federal Bureau of Investigation and to discredit its investigation, particularly of cases involving the civil rights of Negroes. This situation is of particular concern to me at this time because Attorney General Clark has brought to my attention a letter addressed to him by Mr. Marshall on December 27, 1946, in which Mr. Marshall is unfairly critical of the work of the bureau in investigating cases involving the civil rights of Negroes.

As you know, I have endeavored through the years to so administer the work of the Federal Bureau of Investigation that all of its work would be carried out on a judicial, impartial, nonpartisan basis. Whenever information has been brought to my attention alleging that an individual agent has not conducted himself in an entirely ethical, fair and impartial manner, I have immediately initiated an administrative inquiry, and where the circumstances justified it, I have not hesitated to take drastic administrative action. Despite these efforts, however, it does not appear that Mr. Marshall has accepted the fact that the Bureau endeavors to do a thorough job in its investigative work, regardless of the identity of the persons involved in the investigation.

I, of course, recognize the right of Mr. Marshall to have a personal opinion about the bureau and I recognize his right to express that opinion. I do think, however, that when Mr. Marshall, in his official capacity, addresses a letter to the attorney general of the United States relating to the work of the Federal Bureau of Investigation, he might reasonably be expected to be truthful as to the facts in the situation about which he complains.

It is an unfortunate fact that the federal statutes penalizing violations of civil rights are not as broad or comprehensive as they could be. It is a further fact that these federal statutes do not embrace all of the situations in which the bureau has conducted investigation and, through the United States attorneys, presented the results of its investigation to a grand jury. As you realize, however, the Federal Bureau of Investigation has nothing whatsoever to do with the nature or context of federal statutes which are initiated, approved and placed on the statute books by the Congress of the United States. If these statutes are defective or inadequate, the responsibility is that of Congress. I do not believe it is ethical or fair of Mr. Marshall to charge the bureau with dereliction of duty when a grand jury finds that a federal statute has not been violated or a petit jury finds a defendant not guilty of a violation of a federal statute, despite the fact that the bureau has conducted a complete and thorough investigation of the facts in a particular case.

It is a fact, as you know, that Mr. Thurgood Marshall and his associates in the legal branch of your Association have not rendered full and complete cooperation to the Federal Bureau of Investigation, and this lack of cooperation has not served to facilitate or improve the work of the bureau. As a matter of fact, I don't think that the attitude and actions of Mr. Marshall and some of his legal associates measure up to the standards of cooperation which have been set by you in your very efficient administration of the affairs of the National Association for the Advancement of Colored People. I, frankly, am trying, personally and officially, to do everything possible in connection with the civil rights cases, and I know that you and I share similar views as to the problems involved in these cases. I do not believe that the attaining of the ideal objectives of our mutual responsibilities in this field is rendered more feasible or certain by the attitude repeatedly displayed by Mr. Marshall.

I have written you at some length about my views in this situation because of our understanding that you and I would frankly bring to each other's attention any situations which we believed required discussion and clarification.

With best wishes and kind regards,

Sincerely yours,

J. Edgar Hoover

Seven days later, White wrote Marshall the following short memorandum: "Attached is a self-explanatory letter from J. Edgar Hoover received today. Will you give me a reply which I suggest be temperate and documented? I would also like to see a copy of the letter you wrote to him on December 27, 1946."

MARSHALL TO WALTER WHITE

Marshall does not address the charge that he neglected to follow up on Hoover's letter of May 14, 1946.

JANUARY 23, 1947

The letter to Tom Clark was sent as a result of the Monroe, Ga., lynching case. I am attaching hereto a copy of my letter to Tom Clark and a copy of his reply, along with a copy of my request for a personal conference with him.

You will note that in my letter to Tom Clark, I pointed out in the first paragraph that this was being done because of my promise to him to bring to his personal attention matters which affect Negroes in connection with the Justice Department. In the last paragraph, I pointed out, "This letter is being sent to you without being released to the press, and no publicity whatsoever is being given to it other than the possible discussion with members of our staff." Of course, I didn't doubt that Clark would turn the letter over to Hoover.

The only thing about Hoover's letter that to my mind is bad is that he charges me with not cooperating with the FBI. Any charge that I have not cooperated with the FBI is just not true. You will notice in the letter from Tom Clark that he points out that Franklin H. Williams insisted on being present when they interviewed Isaac Woodard. I don't see anything wrong in that, and I can see no harm in having Williams present when Woodard was being interviewed by the FBI.

The basis of our letter concerning the Monroe, Ga., case was the written report of the grand jury which stated that "Ending a three-week investigation, during which about 100 witnesses were questioned, a federal grand jury today reported inability 'to establish the identity of any persons guilty of violating the civil rights statute in the shotgun lynching of four Negroes near Monroe, Ga., in Walton County, last July 25." You will note that both Clark and Hoover dodged that point.

I will talk to Clark personally about it, and I am more than anxious to have him do something. I, however, have no faith in Mr. Hoover or his investigators, and there is no use in my saying I do. I fail to see anything in my letter to Tom Clark which is untrue.

I might also point out that in your letter to Mr. Hoover, you should point out to him that editorial comment throughout the country, after the Monroe, Ga. lynchings, seemed to give the same impression that I gave as to the failure of the FBI. Unfortunately, I do not have these clippings in the office, but we do have the one from *The New York Times.*

J. EDGAR HOOVER TO WALTER WHITE

JANUARY 28, 1947

Dear Mr. White:

I want to thank you for your letter of January 24th in response to my letter of the 13th instant in which I took exception to the misstatements made by Mr. Thurgood Marshall, special counsel for the National Association for the Advancement of Colored People. I note that you suggest that much good might come if Mr. Marshall and I sat down and talked frankly with each other. I think that this would have been indeed the proper procedure to follow in the original instance, before Mr. Marshall resorted to gross misstatements and unfounded accusations against the Federal Bureau of Investigation and my administration of it. I have always found that when one sincerely desires to advance a cause of a worthwhile character, he first endeavors to inform himself fully upon all aspects and difficulties of that problem, and then makes a fair and sincere effort to reach a meeting of the minds with those having mutual interests or responsibilities in the handling of that problem. That, Mr. Marshall did not do in this instance.

As for you, I think it is not necessary for me to say that I always welcome your visits and believe that they have been productive of much good and better understanding of those things for which you and I stand.

Sincerely,

J. Edgar Hoover

In spite of what he wrote, Hoover agreed to meet Marshall in October. During the cordial meeting, Hoover told Marshall that the FBI would welcome him as an ally, and Marshall pressed for more effective investigations of race-based crimes.

MARSHALL TO RUBY HURLEY

At the end of 1946, the youth council of the NAACP in Lumberton, North Carolina, organized a strike against local school authorities because of poor facilities in black schools. Marshall wrote that the strike "is one of the finest things ever pulled in the NAACP and needs our cooperation rather than our condemnation." Marshall then enlisted the attorneys Curtiss Todd and Herman Taylor to work on the case, and local NAACP leaders secured affidavits and raised money for the case. But local activists, including the youths who had staged the strike, grew impatient and asked one of their leaders to call the NAACP staffer Ruby Hurley to let her know that they felt the national office was "letting them down." Below is Marshall's furious reply to the charge.

FEBRUARY 6, 1947

Will you please tell Dr. Smith, and everybody else in Lumberton who may be interested, that you don't run into court with a legal case overnight and that, believe it or not, it takes time to prepare the case. Both Todd and Taylor are working on it.

I, personally, get sick and tired of people in our branches who wait 81 years to get to the point of bringing legal action to secure their rights and then want the lawyers to prepare the case, file it, have it decided and have everything straightened out in fifteen minutes.

MARSHALL TO HOWARD JOHNSON RESTAURANTS

This was not the first time Marshall contacted Howard Johnson about discrimination against African Americans, but in this particular incident he enlisted an attorney, J. LeRoy Jordan of Elizabeth, New Jersey, to file suit against the Roadside Corporation, the company that operated the Howard Johnson where Marshall encountered the discrimination he describes below.

FEBRUARY 7, 1947

Dear Sir:

On Friday, January 24th, Mr. Andrew Weinberger and I were en route to Washington, D.C., for a conference of lawyers to discuss the enforcement of civil rights legislation. We stopped at the Howard Johnson's restaurant in Elizabeth, New Jersey, at the corner of Spring and East Jersey Streets, at a short time after 2 p.m., for the purpose of having lunch. When we went into the restaurant, we went immediately to the dining room where we were stopped by the hostess, who asked if we had "reservations." I think you can imagine our surprise at being asked for reservations in a restaurant catering to tourist trade. We, of course, stated that we did not have reservations and were told that we could not be served in the dining room proper but could be served at one of the small tables over in the section beside the soda fountain. We did not go in for either sodas, ice cream, or frankfurters, but for a full lunch. We noted that the main dining room was in two sections with a connecting alcove and that people were eating there. We also noted that two military officers had just been seated in the main dining room, having come in just ahead of us, and I didn't notice that they were stopped at all concerning reservations or anything else.

The hostess was positive that we could not be served in the main portion of the dining room without reservations. The manager, who stated that his name was Hannos, told us that the rule had been established that after 2 p.m. no one can be served in the main dining room without a reservation. I looked at my watch and at the time I was talking to the manager, after having talked with the hostess, it was between one and two minutes after two. He pointed out that there were "reserved" cards on the tables, and we noted that there were "reserved" cards on *some* of the tables. He also explained that at 2 p.m. several of the waitresses were off duty and that he had a shortage of waitresses after 2 p.m. We explained to him that it seemed odd that such a rule would be made to meet a situation caused by a shortage of waitresses in that part of the people would be in one section of the dining room and we would be at the far end of the soda fountain section, requiring the waitresses to cover a large section of the building, going from one group of tables to our isolated table. He then took the position that he reserved the right to seat patrons in his own way.

When I asked for his name and took down notes on a piece of paper in my pocket, he then came around from where he was seated at the cash register and immediately set about creating a disturbance by calling to people in the dining room in a quite disturbed voice, "You are witnesses that I have offered to serve these men and they have refused." I do not know what prompted his efforts to create a disturbance in his own place of business because it is my understanding that the proper procedure is to prevent disturbances. I did not deem it wise, advisable or necessary to argue the point out with either Mr. Hannos or any of the other patrons, none of whom I was acquainted with, so we left the premises in complete disgust, fully realizing the differences in the treatment accorded us and the statements of policy set out by Mr. A. E. Miller, former general manager of Howard Johnson's, in letters to me concerning another incident in 1941.

I should also mention that when we left the place we particularly noticed that among the cars parked on the outside were cars from several states, and it is obvious that the patrons from those cars did not make "reservations."

I do not believe that Howard Johnson's will tolerate this asinine effort to circumvent the policy of Howard Johnson's Restaurants, as well as the civil rights law of the state of New Jersey. You are, therefore, requested that immediate steps be taken to correct this situation. I told Mr. Hannos that I would take this matter up with Howard Johnson's Restaurants, Inc., and as we left, he was busily engaged in trying to persuade the other Howard Johnson's restaurant patrons to give him their names and addresses and to say that he had offered us service and we had refused. I have no doubt that you have a report from him already in anticipation of this letter.

Very truly yours,

Thurgood Marshall

MARSHALL TO WILLIAM HASTIE

Marshall describes a potentially explosive development in the Sweatt case (which sought to desegregate the University of Texas School of Law), expresses his new desire for a direct attack on segregation itself, and sketches the type of tactics that he would later adopt when arguing Brown, *especially the use of anthropological, sociological, and economic arguments to attack the separate but equal doctrine.*

APRIL 3, 1947

Dear Bill:

When we argued the appeal in the University of Texas case (*Heman Marion Sweatt v. Theophilus Shickel Painter, et al.)*, the attorney general filed a motion to remand, requesting the court to rule on the question of segregation and to remand the case for further evidence showing the establishment of a separate but equal law school. The hearing was on both the motion and the appeal. Durham and I argued for a short time and concluded by stating that we did not oppose the motion excepting the portion requesting the court to rule on segregation being invalid. The court thereupon denied the motion to remand, found error in the lower court's decision and remanded the case.

The interesting thing is that the court refused to rule as a matter of law that segregation was invalid and the chief justice made the statement from the bench that it was the appellant's position that segregation and discrimination were tied up together and could not be separated and that he was not willing to rule that that point was precluded from the case. We then went to the lower court judge on the question of a hearing date, and Judge Archer said that he understood the case was "wide open" and that we should have a full hearing on the merits, which we will have beginning April 28th.

So, whether we want it or not, we are now faced with the proposition of going into the question of segregation as such. I think we should do so because even if we don't take the case far, we at least should experiment on the type of evidence which we may be able to produce on this question. For example, we want to produce experts such as Charlie Thompson to testify as to the inevitable effects of segregation in per capita expenditures, etc. We are also contemplating putting up Otto Kleinberg to testify as to the racial characteristics not being present and other evils of segregation.

We are also contemplating putting on anthropologists to show that there is no difference between folks.

I am leaving for Washington today to meet with Charlie Houston, Charlie Thompson, George Johnson, Jim Nabrit, Ruth Weyand, et al. Time is short and I would appreciate your suggestions as to how far we can go and should go on this in view of the fact that all of the Negroes in the state of Texas, with the exception of Carter Wesley, are determined to hit segregation and we already have a college chapter of the NAACP at the University of Texas with more than 200 members. There are several faculty members at the University of Texas on our side. Please jot down your suggestions and let me know what they are because we would like to get this thing really mapped out so that we can have a real trial.

I am enclosing a copy of this for Dudley. Please give my very best to Beryl, Karen, the latest heir and the Lockharts.

Sincerely yours,

Thurgood Marshall

Six days later, Marshall hinted at his new strategy to longtime friend Donald Murray, the plaintiff in the NAACP's successful case against the University of Maryland more than a decade earlier. "In this particular case," Marshall wrote, "we expect to try out the entire issue of segregation and we will go into all the phases thereof. As matters now shape up, it would be very helpful if we could produce you as a witness to show that when you entered the University of Maryland, you were not ostracized or in any manner interfered with because of race, or, in other words, that you were accepted as a student the same as other students, etc." Marshall also clarified his new direction in a press conference he held on June 27. "There can be no equality as long as there is segregation, regardless of the so-called 'dollar-and-cent equality argument' that any persons have raised in the past," he said. "The only way to attack racial segregation is to attack racial segregation."

MARSHALL TO FRANK DECOSTA

DeCosta, the acting head of the graduate division of the State Agricultural and Mechanical College in Orangeburg, South Carolina, wrote Marshall about potential candidates for a segregated law school in the state. Marshall simply detested makeshift schools established by states hoping to hold off on integration at their white universities, but his answer below is characteristically civil in tone. He refers to a case in which John Wrighten, of Charleston, South Carolina, had petitioned for a federal court order to enjoin the University of South Carolina from refusing applicants to its law school because of race.

JULY 1, 1947

Dear Frank:

Your letter of June 19th was called to my attention on my return to the office. You ought to be careful throwing your bouquets around and hold them at least until after the decision in the case. At any rate, I do think we had quite a time on the case itself and I believe that much was accomplished.

I hope you will also tell your president that we were more than impressed with his frank testimony on the witness stand, which testimony certainly required courage. You know, at times you have to make up your mind as to whether you are going to be a man or a mouse, and more and more, we are getting tremendous respect for certain educators in the South.

As to the dean of the law school, the story is simple. I do not know of anyone who is qualified and who would be interested in the job. I say this in all frankness and with all sincerity. There is a horrible shortage of qualified Negro law school professors. Of course, I think I should be completely fair with you and say that I don't believe that a Negro lawyer should be interested in being dean of a Jim Crow law school. I, for one, am opposed to the extension of segregation, and the setting up of these small law schools certainly can only be labeled as extensions of segregation.

With all best wishes, I am

Sincerely yours,

Thurgood Marshall

On July 12, Judge J. Waties Waring refused the Wrigthen petition but also ruled that Wrighten would be permitted to enter USC the following year unless the state offered a similar course of study at the State Agricultural and Mechanical College.

MARSHALL TO GLOSTER CURRENT

This letter to Gloster Current, who moved from Detroit to New York in 1946 to become the NAACP's director of branch services and field administration, should dispel any notion that Marshall was focused on lawsuits to the exclusion of the wider work of the NAACP. Marshall had a finely nuanced understanding of the dangers posed by legal action running too far in front of the opinions of everyday African Americans. Especially noteworthy here is his comment on the value of strikes in relation to legal action.

JULY 8, 1947

I have repeatedly stated that the legal work of the NAACP should be closely coordinated with our branches and branch department. For years, the legal department has been included in the report of the secretary to the board of directors and has been sent to all members of the staff so that the staff has been kept abreast of the important legal cases. Sometime ago at one of the staff conferences, a suggestion was made that the several departments exchange reports of their work so that each department would be familiar with the work of the other departments. In keeping with this suggestion, the legal department has prepared bimonthly reports which have been sent to each department, in addition to the regular monthly reports.

The members of the legal department, while preparing and trying cases in the field, have always worked closely with the local branches and state conferences where they exist. However, it is clear that there must be additional work with these branches and state conferences in areas where important cases are being tried. It is therefore again suggested that the branch department, in planning its fieldwork during the fall and winter months, should give as much consideration as possible to doing fieldwork in areas where important legal precedents are being established.

For example, the cases against state universities, which are brand new types of legal action striking at segregation per se, are now pending in Oklahoma, Texas, Louisiana, and South Carolina. In Texas, as a result of the intensive work by the state conference and others, there is hardly a Negro in Texas today who is not convinced that segregation is not only bad, but cannot be tolerated. It is likewise evident that this sentiment does not exist in any other Southern state where we are operating. I remember, for example, that several months ago we had a meeting in Austin, Texas;

I made the statement that the NAACP was sick and tired of "separate but equal" and would fight to the last ditch to remove all segregation, and the applause of the white and Negro people in the audience was terrific. A week thereafter I made the same statement in Charleston, S.C., at a regional meeting, on three different occasions, including twice in the working session and once at the mass meeting, and there was absolutely no applause, but rather a look of apprehension on the faces of most of our delegates.

These cases establishing new precedents can only be adequately tried when we have the complete support of all of the Negroes in these states on the correctness of our position. This has been done in Texas and has not been done in any other state. This is a clear example of the urgent need for intensive fieldwork from branch to branch and person to person to sell them on NAACP policy. This is necessary to the legal case, but more important than that, it is necessary to the continued survival of the Association.

. . .

It would be a dangerous undertaking if our legal work outruns the branches. What I mean by that is that it would be dangerous if we reached the point where we are filing legal cases on matters such as segregation in public schools in areas where our branch people are not whole-heartedly opposed to segregation. It seems, therefore, to be apparent that we must use additional effort to get our branches sold on the problem, anxious to work on it and determined to fight the matter out.

. . .

STATEMENT OF POLICY CONCERNING THE NAACP'S EDUCATION CASES

Marshall sent this memorandum to NAACP branches and members partly as a counterforce to local traditions that accepted "separate but equal" education. It is the clearest written expression of his take on both Plessy v. Ferguson *and the ways in which segregation statutes violated the Fourteenth Amendment.*

SEPTEMBER 1947

Illegality of Separate School System

Some courts, lawyers and laymen assume that "separate but equal" facilities existing in seventeen states and the District of Columbia are legal and do not violate the Fourteenth Amendment to the United States Constitution. This fiction in the law has grown up as a result of certain statements appearing in decisions of courts, including the United States Supreme Court. An examination of these decisions reveals that the United States Supreme Court has never specifically passed upon the validity or invalidity of segregation statutes in public schools but has merely restated the "separate but equal" doctrine first advanced in the case of *Plessy v. Ferguson* involving transportation. In other cases following this decision, the point has never been raised as such. In the Plessy case, there was no evidence or other data challenging the validity of segregation statutes.

All of these issues have been clearly raised and supported by expert testimony in the University of Texas case, and this test case will do much to determine the future course of litigation on this point.

The NAACP is convinced that segregation statutes violate the Fourteenth Amendment for several reasons, among which are:

1. There is no scientific basis for racial classification by the states.
2. That experience has demonstrated that segregation statutes have brought about discrimination against Negroes and were never intended to provide equal facilities but rather to set up a system of dual citizenship.
3. That it is impossible to have equality in a segregated school system.

Policy

All cases on the professional, graduate and college levels shall be carried through on the basis of the Texas and other university cases by means of mandamus or injunctive actions seeking the admission of the Negro to the existing facilities.

On the high school and elementary level, two types of cases are proposed, one type similar to the university cases directly asking for admission to the existing facilities previously reserved for white students only. The other type of action proposed will set forth the existing inequalities resulting in direct discrimination against Negroes and with a request that the court issue an order requiring the school officials to cease discriminating against Negroes.

In the high school and elementary cases, the types of action set out above 1) do not ask for segregation and 2) do not recognize the validity of separate school statutes. This is necessary if we are to keep our position clear, which is that we do not consider segregation statutes legal, do not recognize them as being legal and will continue to challenge them in legal proceedings.

Finally, it must be pointed out that because of the reasons set out above, the NAACP cannot take part in any legal proceeding which seeks to enforce segregation statutes, which condones segregation in public schools, or which admits the validity of these statutes.

Of course, all of the procedure set out above is for cases proposed to be filed in the interim until the Texas case reaches the United States Supreme Court.

Thurgood Marshall

MARSHALL TO THE NEW YORK *HERALD TRIBUNE*

Harriet Beecher Stowe created the character "Topsy" for her book Uncle Tom's Cabin *as a way to draw attention to the pernicious effects of slavery on children. In Stowe's description, Topsy "was one of the blackest of her race; and her round, shining eyes, glittering as glass beads, moved with quick and relentless glances over everything in the room. Her mouth half open with astonishment at the wonders of the new Mas'r's parlor, displayed a white and brilliant set of teeth. Her woolly hair was braided in sundry little tails, which stuck out in every direction. The expression of her face was an odd mixture of shrewdness and cunning, over which was oddly drawn, like a veil, an expression of the most doleful gravity and solemnity. She was dressed in a single filthy, ragged garment, made of bagging; and stood with her hands demurely folded in front of her." In spite of Stowe's intentions, Topsy began to appear in arts and the media as the perfect object for ridicule—a stupid, poor, dirty black girl who could barely speak English. In the cartoon that Marshall indicts below, Topsy appeared as an especially hideous-looking girl of gargantuan proportion.*

SEPTEMBER 18, 1947

Your cartoon appearing in this morning's *Herald Tribune* entitled "Topsy Didn't Just Grow" is insulting to Negroes and mischievous in its every implication and probable consequence. It is entirely unworthy of a major national newspaper and goes far toward undoing in one shocking and inexplicable transgression the reputation for fairness and decency which the *Herald Tribune* has been building.

In the first place, "Topsy" is a fictional character which has, over a period of years, become a symbol of a disgraceful portion of the history of this country in which slavery was practiced. "Topsy" is not only a symbol of all the evils of slavery but has come to represent the remaining incidents of slavery in the form of discriminatory practices against Negroes now in practice. The character of "Topsy" in this cartoon, I should mention in passing, is, in addition, the most revolting representation of the mythical character I have yet seen.

The cartoon is silly and meaningless, unless it is interpreted as a slur against Negroes. It can easily be interpreted as an effort to make the Negro the scapegoat for high prices. In the left-hand corner of the cartoon appears "Excessive Demands," represented by a hideous individual intended to represent a Negro woman. Standing beside "Excessive Demands" is "Low Production," depicted by an equally obnoxious figure pictured as a Negro smoking a huge cigar. One conclusion to be drawn from this cartoon is that Negroes are making "Excessive Demands" while being guilty of "Low Production." This vicious libel on 10 percent of the population of this country cannot be minimized.

Thurgood Marshall

MARSHALL TO JOHN WRIGHTEN

Marshall pens a letter to John Wrighten, the NAACP's client in its legal efforts to seek integration at the University of South Carolina School of Law. Marshall sent copies of the following letter to his legal team, and in an accompanying memorandum he wrote about his frustration with local blacks who allegedly favored a segregated law school at the State Agricultural and Mechanical College over an integrated USC: "For the life of me, I can't see why, if the Negroes in Texas refuse to accept a $100,000 law school in a three and a half million dollar university that the Negroes in South Carolina would accept a $10,000 dollar law school in a $1.50 university."

SEPTEMBER 29, 1947

Dear Mr. Wrighten:

I have received your letter of September 29th in which you point out that when you returned to South Carolina and told the people there that I had advised you not to go to the Jim Crow law school, which has been set up in one room in the administration building in Orangeburg with practically no library and three teachers without any previous law school teaching experience and all the other inequalities, "they almost cursed me out, and that is the opinion of some of the members and officials of the NAACP here."

I do not understand how any official of the NAACP can take the stand that an individual who refused to take a stand in favor of Jim Crow education should be cursed out. The NAACP has always been opposed to segregation and all officials of the NAACP are required to follow these principles, and if I ever hear of any NAACP official speaking in favor of segregation or in saying that we cannot fight segregation "because of the ill feeling that might be developed among the whites," I will personally file charges against that member or officer. I have never heard of such actions before or during my work with the NAACP. I would therefore appreciate your advising me as to which NAACP officials told you that.

You also point out that you gave up your job at Avery Institute because you had been advised to go to the Jim Crow law school, and for that reason you are out of work, as I advised you not to go to the law school. It is of course difficult for me at this end to suggest as to what procedure you should go through to get employment, and I did not know that that was a problem involved in this case. However, I am certain that among the people in South Carolina there must be numerous Negroes with businesses such as insurance companies and banks and other businesses who would be willing to employ you. In the meantime, I would therefore suggest that you apply to these businesses, insurance companies and banks and let me know what results you have. I also assure you that this office and the South Carolina conference of branches will stand behind you.

Sincerely,

Thurgood Marshall

The whole case, including Wrighten, frustrated Marshall, and six months later he wrote Harold Boulware, the NAACP attorney in Columbia, South Carolina, with the request that he take as minimal action as possible on the case, primarily because Wrighten was proving to be an unreliable plaintiff.

MARSHALL TO THE EDITOR OF *LIFE*

Texas established a separate law school for African American students, and Life *magazine's coverage of the school irritated Marshall. In this diplomatic reply to the magazine, Marshall sketches both the historic importance of the* Sweatt *case and his evolving legal strategy.*

SEPTEMBER 29, 1947

Dear Sir:

I was very interested in the article in last week's *Life* and the very splendid pictures concerning the new school for Negroes in Texas. I realize that *Life* is always burdened with the problem of lack of space, and I am sure that that is the reason that many important features of the case were not carried.

For example, the case of *Heman Marion Sweatt vs. The University of Texas* is being appealed to the Court of Civil Appeals, and the brief will be filed this Wednesday. The brief in this case points out:

> The record in the instant case for the first time presents testimony and documentary evidence clearly establishing that:
>
> 1. There is no rational basis for racial classification for school purposes.
>
> 2. Public schools, "separate but equal" in theory, are in fact and in practical administration consistently unequal and discriminatory.
>
> 3. It is impossible to have the equality required by the Fourteenth Amendment in a public school system which relegates citizens of a disadvantaged racial minority group to separate schools.

In this brief there is full legal and scientific material to back up these statements. This case is the first case of this kind in which there is a direct attack made on the segregation laws in public education, and we believe that it will be a most important one.

As to the story in *Life* itself, the picture of the building of the so-called Negro university should have included the statement that the building was not only built for the Houston College for Negroes but was built by voluntary subscriptions solicited from both white and Negro citizens of Texas and was not built by the state of Texas.

It should also be pointed out that the school is not offering all of the courses offered at the University of Texas and is not furnishing equality of education in either quality or quantity. Had there been more space in *Life*, I am sure you would have included the additional facts that the facilities were not only inadequate as to quality but were much too small for the number of students who were unable to find living quarters any place in the near area.

I think it should also be pointed out that up to last week there is only one Negro student in the law school in Austin mentioned in the article. . . .

I hope that at sometime in the near future the entire story can be told and the facts surrounding this case such as the expert testimony of such witnesses as Dean Karl G. Harrison of the University of Pennsylvania; Dr. Robert Redfield, head of the department of anthropology at the University of Chicago; Dr. Malcolm F. Sharp of the University of Chicago School of Law; and Dr. Charles Thompson, dean of the graduate school of Howard University. All of these witnesses at the trial of the Sweatt case gave to the court for the first time in any court record scientific data demonstrating that there is no difference between the ability to learn of the white and Negro student and that there is no scientific basis for segregation of the races in public education. They also gave expert opinions that even to follow the so-called gradual method to remove segregation makes it possible to start in a professional school such as the law school and that there would be no repercussions.

We thank you for your coverage of the *Sweatt* case and only wish that there had been space for a fuller story with the information set out above.

Yours very truly,

Thurgood Marshall

MARSHALL TO THE EDITOR OF THE DALLAS *MORNING NEWS*

A prolific Marshall takes on one more media outlet for the day, this time declaring that separate but equal schools simply do not exist. The angry tone of Marshall's letter stemmed from the newspaper's accusation that the NAACP was stirring up trouble that otherwise would not have existed.

SEPTEMBER 29, 1947

Dear Sir:

. . .

The case of *Plessy v. Ferguson* was decided by the United States Supreme Court in 1896, who made it clear fifty-one years ago that segregation could only be upheld on the basis of equality. Almost twenty years ago, the United States Supreme Court in the *University of Missouri* case established the principle that in the absence of completely equal facilities in public education, Negroes were entitled to admission into so-called white institutions. Despite this decision, which was given the widest of publicity and was the subject of much discussion by school officials and the conference of governors in many special meetings, inequality in educational facilities in those furnished for white and Negro Americans has increased rather than decreased. In almost twenty years, the South has made no effort to follow either of these decisions. The state of Texas, while placing in its Constitution a requirement that separate schools be maintained, included the requirement for "impartial provision" for these schools. The state has only concentrated on following the first portion of this section.

In your editorial you say that the National Association for the Advancement of Colored People is only interested in these cases in order "to stir up trouble." Do you consider an effort to enforce the Constitution of the United States as interpreted by the United States Supreme Court an effort to "stir up trouble"? Do you believe that Negroes and other interested Americans in this country have just as much right to enforce the Fourteenth Amendment against racial discrimination as the newspapers have to enforce the First Amendment as to freedom of speech? Or do you believe that you are obliged only to believe in certain provisions of the Constitution? Getting back to the Hearne situation, are you aware of the fact that the Negro population of Hearne is larger than the white population and that more than sixty percent of the taxpayers of that town are Negroes? Despite the facts, Negro schools are so far below white schools in facilities afforded and training available as to make it impossible to give the appearance of even the semblance of equality, and that as a matter of fact, in view of the population the Negro schools should be larger.

In view of this situation, the Negro student denied the equal facilities has applied to the white school in direct compliance with the decisions of the United States Supreme Court in the case of *Gaines v. Canada et al.,* cited above. By simply following the law of the land and the specific ruling of the Supreme Court, we are charged with "stirring up trouble." I think that before this country takes up the position that it must demand complete equality of right of citizens of all other countries throughout the world, we must first demonstrate our good faith by showing that in this country our Negro Americans are recognized as full citizens with complete equality. If in seeking to do this, we must be charged with attempting to "stir up trouble," please be assured that such charges, although keenly resented, will not under any circumstances deter us in our determination to use every *lawful means* to enforce our Constitution in the courts of the land. And it is our only hope that at some time in the future newspapers, such as the Dallas *Morning News,* will use their editorial space in an effort to compel enforcement of our Constitution rather than to look around for a scapegoat to excuse non-compliance.

Yours very truly,

Thurgood Marshall

In reply to Marshall's letter, the editor William Ruggles wrote: "The association's tendency to stir up trouble is far more conspicuous in our view than its contribution to the advancement of interracial relations in this section."

MARSHALL TO HEMAN SWEATT

More than any other letter, this one reveals the importance Marshall ascribed to the character of his clients, as well as the way in which he sought to mingle the professional and personal in order to strengthen his clients' resolve in the face of hostile detractors. At this point, Marshall was also sending the Sweatt *brief to influential individuals, including Ed Sullivan at the New York* Daily News.

SEPTEMBER 30, 1947

Dear Sweatt:

Thanks so much for your two recent letters concerning our case and the clippings and your articles, which I have gone over hurriedly and will go over again in the near future.

You are continuing in the manner in which all of us were certain you would. We learned one thing from our earlier university cases. Donald Murray, whom you met in Austin, was well-known to me because we both lived in Baltimore and I knew his entire family. I knew his background, and for these reasons, I knew that we could rely upon him and that he would stick it out regardless of the consequences. This he did. None of us knew Lloyd Gaines in the Missouri case very well and we took a chance. At the time we needed Gaines most, he disappeared and we have not found him until this day. As a result, although we had spent much over $25,000 on that case, it could not be concluded. The lesson from these two cases is simple. It is more important to have the proper type of plaintiff than anything else in these cases, other than the community support, which we, of course, must have in order to operate.

Donald Murray had the full, complete and unqualified support, financial and otherwise, from our Negro newspaper in Maryland, the *Afro-American.* In your case, we have no support at all that can be relied upon from the *Informer* newspapers, yet we are perfectly willing to proceed and we are just as sure of victory as in the University of Maryland case because we are assured that you will stick it out. The similarity between the two instances is that Durham knows you as well as I knew Donald, and since I have the utmost respect for Durham's judgment, I have no question in my mind at all of the outcome in this case. This has been our position all along. I am sure you have been aware of it, but I believe that at times it is important to put things down on paper. We can lick this case if we all stick together. When "the turf gets tough," there will be people who will scurry to cover, but as long as we stick together we can lick it. Whenever there is any question whatsoever in your mind, will you please go to Dallas at our expense and discuss it with Durham, and if at any time you deem it necessary, call me collect. But under no circumstances let anything get in your way without discussing it with us. We are not only your lawyers, but we are your friends, and I mean this in every sense of the word.

I am enclosing a copy of the brief which Durham is filing in your case tomorrow, and I would like for you to go over it carefully. The purpose of this brief is to put practically everything in it in order that we may, between now and the time the case reaches the Supreme Court of Texas, rewrite it in such a manner as to make it the best possible brief we can put in. Texas procedure in this case is very involved, and it is just as complicated to me as it is simple and clear to Durham. However, by working closely together, we have been able to get the job done. We, of course, have had the assistance of all of the other lawyers and research people on our staff here and other places.

Sincerely yours,

Thurgood Marshall

P.S. I wonder if you heard of the statement quoted in the Austin paper made by Doyle when he applied to the "Uncle Tom's Cabin" law school in Austin. His statement was "It's just like having a steaming plate of chicken on a box in the backyard. I'd rather have it in the house, but chicken is chicken and it's better in the backyard than not at all." He should have added to this statement that while the white people will be eating the breast, the thigh and the other good portions of the chicken in the house, he is not only eating in the backyard, but his eating is limited to the neck and the feet. This makes the issue quite clear to young Negroes and others in Texas that on one side we have you standing up like a man and fighting for your rights, and on the other hand we have Doyle. On one side we have a Negro American and on the other side we have the remnants of a Negro slave. . . .

Marshall ridiculed Doyle in several letters during this time period, and alluded to him once again in a February 5, 1948, letter to the editor of the Dallas Morning News *(see page 230). The Supreme Court would deliver a ruling on Sweatt in June 1950 (see page 273).*

MARSHALL TO GEOFFREY PARSONS

In this letter to Geoffrey Parsons, an editorial writer for the New York Herald Tribune, *Marshall refers to a July 12 ruling by Judge J. Waties Waring of South Carolina. Waring had ruled in a case argued by Marshall and brought by George Elmore, an African American resident of Columbia, South Carolina, who claimed that officials of the state's Democratic Party had prevented him from voting in the 1946 primary because of his color. Disagreeing with the argument that the party was a private organization with full authority to determine its membership, Waring wrote that "Negroes are entitled to be enrolled to vote" in the Democratic primaries. The decision represented a huge victory for Marshall and the NAACP, let alone the African American voters of South Carolina.*

SEPTEMBER 30, 1947

Dear Mr. Parsons:

I have just returned to the office from Chicago and Washington. First of all, I appreciate your carrying my letter in the *Tribune*, and I have gone over your comments. I would like very much at some future time to sit down and discuss with you at length this entire problem surrounding the editorial.

In your issue of Wednesday, September 24th, there is an editorial entitled "Segregating the Voter" in which you discuss the proposed rule to segregate voters in the primaries in Georgia. As you know, the Negro voter in Georgia is the largest of footballs being kicked around by Thompson and Talmadge.

I am sure you are aware of the fact that Georgia did not seriously abandon the white primary move similar to the one in South Carolina until after Judge Waties Waring had issued an order enjoining the Democratic Party of South Carolina from excluding Negroes. In Judge Waring's opinion, which I think will apply in Georgia as well as South Carolina, he states: "I cannot see where the skies will fall if South Carolina is put in the same class with these and other states."

I am also sure you are familiar with the plan in Arkansas inaugurated after the Texas primary case in which they set up two primaries, one for federal officials and one for state officials, in an effort to exclude Negroes from voting for state officials while purporting to permit them to vote for federal officials. I understand that this plan was abandoned in Arkansas because they found it too expensive to run two sets of polling places. I have no doubt that the same will be true in Georgia, and if it is true that there is not enough money to run two, I don't think there is any question in your mind, or my mind, as to which of the polls will not open.

I think the point which you did not emphasize other than to mention in the editorial is the fact that it is obvious to anyone that Negro votes will not be counted and we will be right back in court again. Our representatives in Georgia at the present time are canvassing opinions and will meet in the very near future to decide as to what position they will take, and we will most certainly support them in their position, which has been the policy of this Association for years. We do not try to establish the policy for areas such as Georgia, but prefer to sit down with them and work out joint policy as well as joint strategy, and that is why most of my time is spent in the South and not here in New York.

I certainly hope that you can find time to talk to me about the whole problem,

Yours very truly,

Thurgood Marshall

MARSHALL TO GEOFFREY PARSONS

Marshall loathed the argument that "substantial equality" in educational opportunities was constitutionally legal, and here he challenges Parsons once again, this time to understand that a recent editorial was largely inaccurate in its characterization of educational opportunities for African Americans in the South. Marshall's letter also included a few of his briefs for Parsons's reading pleasure.

OCTOBER 4, 1947

Dear Mr. Parsons:

I have read with interest the article on the editorial page by Henry Lesesne titled "Education Advances in the South." The article on the whole seems to give a picture of the problem. However, I think that there are certain statements which are not quite accurate.

In commenting upon the Missouri case (*Gaines v. Canada et al.*, 305 U.S. 337), the statement is made that in that case "The Supreme Court ruled . . . that substantially the same graduate educational opportunities must be furnished to the minority race." The word "substantial" has grown up in many sections of the country as a qualifying word for "equal," which appears in the Fourteenth Amendment, when as a matter of fact the Supreme Court of the United States has always insisted on equality rather than substantial equality, and I assure you there is quite a difference.

Getting back to the Gaines case itself, the statement in Mr. Lesesne's column is not at all accurate, for in that case it was pointed out that unless the state furnished equal facilities for Negroes *within* the state, the Negro was entitled to admission into the existing facilities (white). That is the gravamen of that decision. . . .

. . .

Realizing the complete inadequacy of education for Negroes in the South and the apparent unwillingness of the South to comply with the Fourteenth Amendment, we now have pending several cases in the states of Texas, Oklahoma, Louisiana, and South Carolina, as well as Virginia, on this problem. I am enclosing copy of a brief filed in the Court of Civil Appeals in Texas, which was filed last Wednesday, and also a copy of a petition for certiorari and the brief in support thereof in the United States Supreme Court on another case from Oklahoma. I know how busy you are, but would appreciate your glancing through these briefs in order to get the other side of the picture.

Very truly yours,

Thurgood Marshall

MARSHALL TO THE NAACP COMMITTEE ON ADMINISTRATION

An exasperated Marshall complains about White's unwillingness to provide more office space to Marshall and his legal team. The detailed memo offers a close look at Marshall's breathtaking schedule of cases.

OCTOBER 27, 1947

I believe that the record of my few years with the Association will show that I, for one, have never gone beyond the secretary or the staff in presenting a matter to the board or the committee on administration without the approval of either the secretary or the staff. However, I am forced to do so at the present time. The question which is ever present before the entire legal staff is the question of being required to do the most careful research in the preparation of the trial and appeal of cases in quarters that are so cramped as to make it impossible to do either.

In the quarters which the legal department has used since I have been here, the space has always been so crowded as to make it impossible to do a good job without being seriously handicapped and/or at the cost of the health of the persons involved. We have, however, been willing to take a chance on the minor items of health, etc., in the interest of getting a job done. We have now reached the place where we cannot even get the job done.

I want to first discuss my own individual position. I believe that I am the only member of the NAACP staff who has never had an office to himself since I have been here, and with the exception of a couple of people, I have been here as long as anybody else. There is a slight exception to this in that prior to the time we appointed our "first legal research assistant" after Charles Houston left, I did have the office to myself for a little while. In addition, I think that as a lawyer I have had more opportunity than any member of the staff to make an outside income but have refused to do so because I believed that the Association needed my entire time. I have not only turned down jobs of my own free will, which paid double what this job paid, but I have, with one exception involving a period of forty-five minutes, refused to do any part-time legal work outside of this Association. I have not only refused to take any strictly legal cases or matters involving the giving of strictly legal advice privately, but have refused to write anything for which I have been paid. I might say, however, that I am very proud of the forty-five minutes I did spend year before last in sitting in on a conference where I gave my legal opinion during the forty-five minutes, which, incidentally, was valued by the client as expressed by his check for $2600.

The legal department has refused to turn down proper legal cases and has taken on cases within the program of the Association time and time again when there did not appear to be sufficient time to do the job but in the interest of the work of the Association has felt obliged to do so. The number and type of cases have increased no end. Where in the beginning of the legal work we had certain set principles to work with, we have now used up these principles and are striking out into new and uncharted territory requiring the most careful research as well as the most careful type of planning of legal strategy.

As matters now stand, we have two offices for the so-called executives of the legal department in which six people are divided as follows: Dudley,

Marshall referred to himself as "an old rebel" when reflecting on his own experiences on the picket line. Although he is not pictured here, he did join this picket line at the National Crime Conference in Washington, D.C., in December 1934, as did his mentor Charles Hamilton Houston *(with camera, on right)* and Roy Wilkins *(far left)*, the future leader of the NAACP. (Library of Congress, Prints & Photographs Division, Visual Materials from the NAACP Records)

Marshall and Houston *(far right)* argued a landmark case in 1935 that led to the admission of Donald Gaines Murray *(center)* to the University of Maryland's all-white law school. The case increased Marshall's stature in both the NAACP and the wider African American community. (Library of Congress, Prints & Photographs Division, Visual Materials from the NAACP Records)

Marshall joined Houston and others in documenting the inferior state of black public schools as early as 1934. This school bus for black children in Louisa County, Virginia, in 1935, symbolizes the type of conditions that served as the groundwork for the historic ruling in *Brown v. Board of Education of Topeka, Kansas,* nearly twenty years later. (Library of Congress, Prints & Photographs Division, Visual Materials from the NAACP Records)

NAACP chief Walter White *(left)* accepted Houston's recommendation that the NAACP hire Thurgood Marshall in 1936, a year before this photo was taken. For the rest of his life, Marshall credited Houston *(right)* with teaching him that the practice of law could and should serve as a tool for creating equality in society. (Library of Congress, Prints & Photographs Division, Visual Materials from the NAACP Records)

The top three NAACP executives, New York City, ca. 1940. Marshall *(right)* considered Roy Wilkins *(left)* a close friend, but clashed with Walter White *(center)* when the NAACP secretary sought to give advice on legal matters, denied Marshall's requests for additional office space, or consulted with the Department of Justice without Marshall's knowledge. (Library of Congress, Prints & Photographs Division, Visual Materials from the NAACP Records)

Thurgood Marshall, ca. 1940. (Library of Congress, Prints & Photographs Division, Visual Materials from the NAACP Records)

After the 1942 burning of Cleo Wright in Sikeston, Missouri, the NAACP implored President Franklin D. Roosevelt to push for anti-lynching legislation. Roosevelt did not back the NAACP campaign, and Marshall, who had lobbied hard for anti-lynching laws, spoke bitterly of Roosevelt for the rest of his life. (Library of Congress, Prints & Photographs Division, Visual Materials from the NAACP Records)

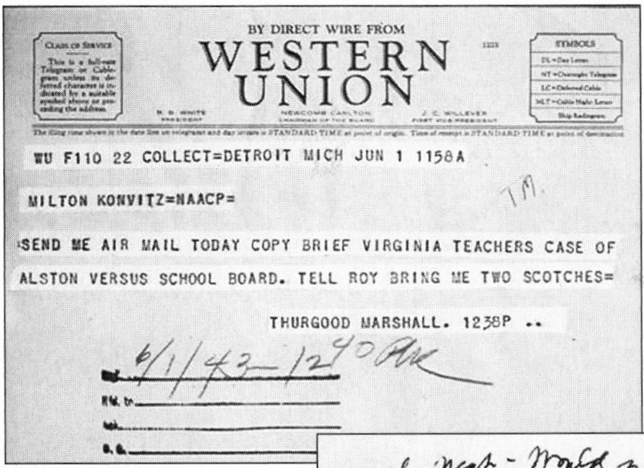

BY DIRECT WIRE FROM

WESTERN UNION

WU F110 22 COLLECT=DETROIT MICH JUN 1 1158A

MILTON KONVITZ=NAACP=

SEND ME AIR MAIL TODAY COPY BRIEF VIRGINIA TEACHERS CASE OF ALSTON VERSUS SCHOOL BOARD. TELL ROY BRING ME TWO SCOTCHES=

THURGOOD MARSHALL. 1238P ..

6/1/43—12⁴⁰ PM

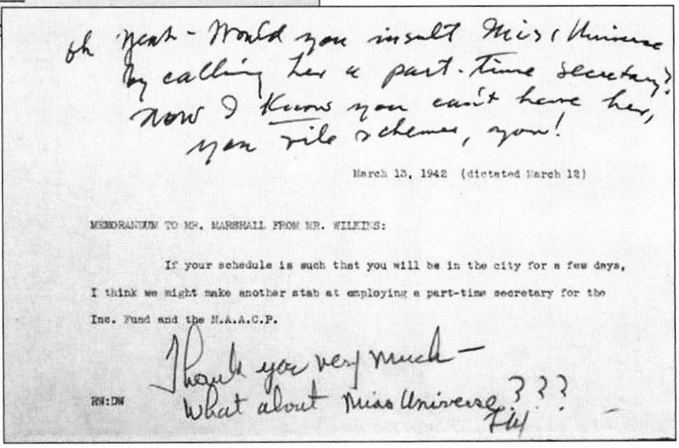

oh yeah—Would you insult Miss Universe by calling her a part-time secretary? Now I know you can't have her, you vile schemer, you!

March 13, 1942 (dictated March 12)

MEMORANDUM TO MR. MARSHALL FROM MR. WILKINS:

If your schedule is such that you will be in the city for a few days, I think we might make another stab at employing a part-time secretary for the Inc. Fund and the N.A.A.C.P.

RW:DW

Thank you very much—
What about Miss Universe???
TM

Marshall's letters and telegrams were normally all business, but when he did venture personal remarks, he often focused on whiskey, cards, and women. (NAACP Papers, Library of Congress, photographed by Michael G. Long)

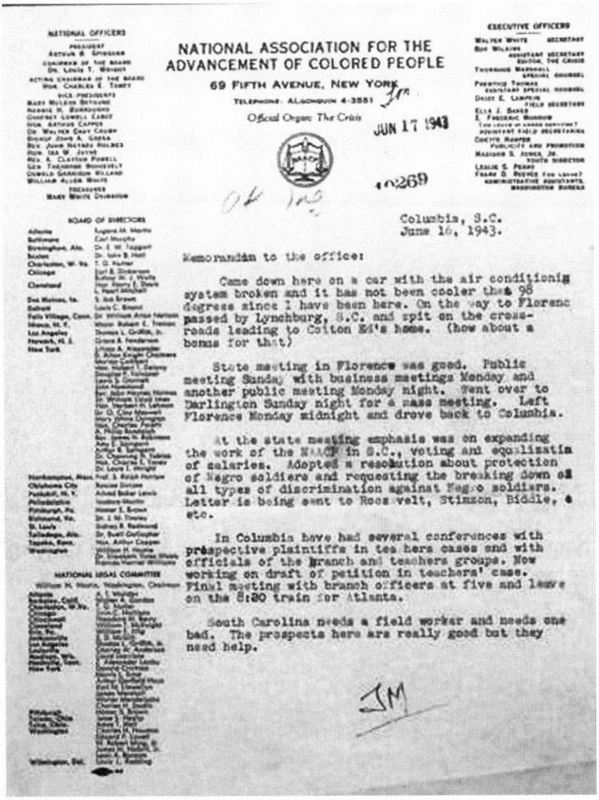

NATIONAL ASSOCIATION FOR THE ADVANCEMENT OF COLORED PEOPLE

69 FIFTH AVENUE, NEW YORK

Official Organ: The Crisis

JUN 17 1943

Columbia, S.C.
June 16, 1943.

Memorandum to the office:

Came down here on a car with the air conditioning system broken and it has not been cooler than 98 degrees since I have been here. On the way to Florence passed by Lynchburg, S.C. and spit on the cross-roads leading to Cotton Ed's home. (how about a bonus for that)

State meeting in Florence was good. Public meeting Sunday with business meetings Monday and another public meeting Monday night. Went over to Darlington Sunday night for a mass meeting. Left Florence Monday midnight and drove back to Columbia.

At the state meeting emphasis was on expanding the work of the NAACP in S.C., voting and equalization of salaries. Adopted a resolution about protection of Negro soldiers and requesting the breaking down of all types of discrimination against Negro soldiers. Letter is being sent to Roosevelt, Stimson, Biddle, & etc.

In Columbia have had several conferences with prospective plaintiffs in teachers cases and with officials of the branch and teachers groups. Now working on draft of petition in teachers' case. Final meeting with branch officers at five and leave on the 8:30 train for Atlanta.

South Carolina needs a field worker and needs one bad. The prospects here are really good but they need help.

TM

Marshall typed and handwrote memoranda for the office while on the road, suggesting ways to improve local organizations, reporting on local cases, and sometimes offering colorful characterizations of local politics. Here he makes an amusing reference to Senator Ellison Smith of South Carolina, who was known for his segregationist politics and his use of a spittoon on the Senate floor. (NAACP Papers, Library of Congress, photographed by Michael G. Long)

During World War II, Marshall defended black munitions soldiers charged with mutiny, protested violence against black soldiers stationed in the South, wrote countless requests for desegregation of the armed forces, and even bought war stamps. (Courtesy of the Afro-American Newspapers Archives and Research Center)

Although he did not personally like George McLaurin, seated here in an anteroom at the University of Oklahoma in 1948, Marshall defended McLaurin's right to attend the university's all-white graduate school and to sit with the rest of the class. (Library of Congress, Prints & Photographs Division, Visual Materials from the NAACP Records)

George E. C. Hayes, Marshall, and James Nabrit celebrate outside the Supreme Court after the historic *Brown* decision in 1954. The celebration turned into disappointment when the Court later decided not to set a deadline for desegregating public schools. (Library of Congress, Prints & Photographs Division, Visual Materials from the NAACP Records)

Emmett Till, a fourteen-year-old boy from Chicago, was lynched in Money, Mississippi, in 1955. The ensuing trial saw an all-white jury acquit the two white defendants, and the verdict, coupled with nationally publicized photos of Till's brutalized face, helped spark the modern civil rights movement. Marshall, pictured a year later with NAACP executives Henry Moon, Roy Wilkins, and Herbert Hill, considered Mississippi to be "the worst hole in the world." (Reproduced from Library of Congress, Prints & Photographs Division; NYWT&S Collection, Al Raveena)

Marshall, pictured at the NAACP office in 1957, was fond of telling colorful stories during breaks from the research that he and his legal team conducted. (Reproduced from Library of Congress, Prints & Photographs Division; U.S. News & World Report Magazine Collection, Thomas O' Halloran, Jr.)

Perry, and Williams are in one room with three desks, one table, one-half of the library, three telephones, and it is more the rule than the exception that the three telephones are working at the same time along with the dictation of letters, briefs, and memoranda concerning the varied types of legal action. The other room I share with Mrs. Motley and Miss Peyser where, incidentally, we only have one phone and the three of us have to share our time on the one phone while the others are working on varied types of legal problems. In both offices, there is a constant stream of visitors never visiting more than one of the individuals in each of the two rooms, Incidentally, 90% of these "visitors" are people with problems unrelated to the Association which are always referred to the legal department.

A few weeks ago, three of us were working on the Texas University case, which involved a brand new principle of law as far removed from the University of Missouri case as the University of Missouri case was removed from the old case of *Plessy v. Ferguson*, and Bob Carter, Marian Perry and I were working on it together with the other members of the staff helping on certain points. There was no place where any one of us could go and think alone so that we ended up with everyone annoying everyone else, which didn't injure anyone of us and I doubt that it injured the case *too much*, but I assure you it did injure the case.

For the ensuing thirty days we have the following program:

The teachers' salary case in Atlanta is set for November 10, which means that Dudley, who is to try this case, must work with at least me during the days prior to that time in preparing that case and also to make preparations for the filing of teachers' salary cases in Mississippi, in order for Dudley to meet with the teachers in Mississippi on November 1st.

The brief in the South Carolina primary case must be filed in the Circuit Court of Appeals for the Fourth Circuit by November 5th and is to be argued on November 18th.

The University of South Carolina case brief must be filed by November 5th and is due to be argued on November 21st.

The case of *Patton v. the State of Mississippi*, involving the question as to whether or not Negroes prevented from registering to vote affects the conviction of a Negro by a jury restricted to registered voters . . . will be argued in the Supreme Court on November 21st. This case will be argued by me but is being prepared by Frank Williams.

The case of *Isaac Woodard v. the Greyhound Bus Company* will start in Charleston, W. Va., on November 10th, to be handled by Messrs. Williams and T. O. Nutter.

The latest case attacking the school system in Louisiana is due to be argued in Baton Rouge sometime during the month of November; the date is not certain.

Kemp v. Rubin, the restrictive covenant case here in New York, is set for argument on November 17th.

The restrictive covenant cases in the Supreme Court are set for argument the week of December 8th and the brief must be printed and filed by November 17th, and our draft of these briefs is due today but obviously cannot be finished before the end of this week. Miss Perry and Miss Peyser are working on those.

Mrs. Motley is working on the South Carolina cases, and Dudley is also working on the South Carolina cases.

I have set all these facts out many times before and have pleaded for space, and it is obvious that there will be no more space allotted to the legal department in this building. If I am expected to supervise the work to be done by the legal department and to produce the type of work you expect . . . I am finally convinced that this cannot be done in the present quarters. I could very well say that if other arrangements are not made I will quit, but this would be an untrue statement because I have had opportunities to quit and go other places before and have refused to do so and will most likely take the same position in the future. But I do say that I will not continue to work under the existing circumstances; and if the NAACP is unable to furnish quarters for us in which we can work better than we are working now, then I will be obliged to recommend to the board of the Inc. Fund that we place in next year's budget a sum sufficient to find quarters elsewhere in New York City for the legal staff, because it is impossible to break the staff up. All of us use the same books, the same research materials and the same files, and it is impossible to put one-half of the group in one place and the other half in another place or to separate any member of the staff from these materials.

MARSHALL TO ROY WILKINS

An angry Marshall expresses irritation that not everyone in the NAACP, especially those in South Carolina, is in line with the Association's written policy on attacking segregation.

OCTOBER 28, 1947

I *had* assumed that the NAACP really meant business about an all-out attack against segregation, especially in the public school system. I *had* assumed that we not only realized that segregation was an evil but had come to the conclusion that *nothing* can be gained under the doctrine of "separate but equal." I *had* assumed that the board of directors, as well as the branches and branch officers, were in agreement on this. I *had* assumed that the resolutions adopted at the annual conference and the beautiful statements made at board and staff meetings meant exactly what they said. On this basis, we have proceeded to develop the legal techniques for this all-out attack on segregation.

Therefore, on our new wave of university cases, we have filed them along this new theory following the decision of the United States Supreme Court that in the absence of facilities equal to the white facilities, the Negro is entitled to admission into the white facilities. The Texas case so developed as to make it possible to try this issue out and this we are doing. As to other cases being filed while the Texas case is on appeal, we propose to file these cases on the theory that facilities are unequal and to request an injunction by the court to enjoin the maintenance of the policy of discrimination. This will bring about either equal facilities or the breaking down of segregation. All of this was explained in the memorandum on policy, which concludes with the following two paragraphs:

> Finally, it must be pointed out that because of the reasons set out above, the NAACP cannot take part in any legal proceeding which seeks to enforce segregation statutes, which condones segregation in public schools, or which admits the validity of these statutes.
>
> Of course, all of the procedure set out above is for cases proposed to be filed in the interim until the Texas case reaches the United States Supreme Court. You will note from this procedure that the real difference is that we do not at any place admit the validity of segregation statutes and we do not call for the enforcement of these illegal statutes.

Because of the action of certain persons in South Carolina and the very confused status of our university case there, I am beginning to doubt that our branch officers are fully indoctrinated on the policy of the NAACP in being opposed to segregation. It is therefore obvious that we need to educate our branch officers and in turn the membership, and finally, the people in the need for complete support in this all-out attack on segregation, because it will be impossible for our branch officers to do a good job unless we first sell them. Along this same line, I think it would be most helpful to have the matter fully discussed in a staff conference so that the staff will be in complete agreement as to what our approach shall be, and, finally, I agree with you that the matter should be thrashed out before the board of directors.

The end is the same as the beginning—I assumed that we were operating completely within the scope of our program and hope that we have not gone beyond the program.

MARSHALL TO ROY WILKINS

At this point, HUAC was conducting hearings on communist infiltration in the U.S. film industry, and a week before Marshall sent this memorandum, Ronald Reagan, then president of the Screen Actors Guild, appeared before the committee and stated that a "very small minority" of the guild's members belonged to the Communist Party and that this small group was unsuccessful in its attempts to control the guild. "I abhor the communist philosophy," Reagan added, "but more than that I detest their tactics which are the tactics of a fifth column. However, as a citizen, I hope that we are never prompted by fear or resentment of communism into compromising any of our democratic principles in order to fight them." As noted below, the NAACP was concerned about the hearings at least partly because of their negative effects on the depictions of African Americans in films.

OCTOBER 30, 1947

I had a long talk over the telephone yesterday with a person who has reliable information concerning the latest repercussions of the investigation of the Committee on Un-American Activities into the Hollywood situation, and here are the definite facts which can be substantiated, if necessary:

1. The producers are scared to death.
2. They are determined to delete from all scripts now in production and all future scripts any type of materials which can be interpreted as "communist propaganda."

3. Their interpretation of "communist propaganda" is anything in opposition to the status quo of the country as demonstrated by the well-known stereotypes.
4. Negro and other minorities will now revert to the old-line treatment by Hollywood producers.

I know that all of this is not surprising. However, there are two particular scripts which give us a basis for a strong letter. One is that in a script (unnamed), there was a line providing for a white actress to call a Negro actress "Mrs. Bigby." This has been changed so that the Negro actress will be called by her first name. In another script, a white actress, in talking to a Negro actor at a race track, asked him to give her the name of a horse to bet on, and he was to reply very politely, "Madam, I do not know anything about horse racing or gambling." This line has been struck out entirely.

Along the lines of the discussion we had the other day, it seems to me that it would be most helpful if a letter by the NAACP was sent to, say, the Speaker of the House, pointing out this additional fact as further grounds for pressure for the abolition of the damn committee.

MARSHALL TO GEOFFREY PARSONS

Marshall sends a warm note to Parsons, of the New York Herald Tribune, *regarding his favorable editorial on the President's Committee on Civil Rights. At the committee's organizational meeting on January 15, 1947, Truman recalled seeing the KKK, which "met on hills and burned crosses and worked behind sheets," during his first run for elective office in 1922. Warning against a resurgence of the KKK, Truman told the committee that he did not "want to see any race discrimination," that the time had come to leave gradualism behind, and that he wanted to know "just how far [the attorney general] can go legally" in protecting civil rights.*

Channing Tobias, an NAACP board member, was a member of Truman's committee, and on January 6 Marshall drafted a letter asking branch officers to forward any information on lynching, police brutality, denial of the right to register and vote, and discrimination in employment, housing, transportation, recreation, education, and health—information that he could pass on to Tobias.

On January 14, Marshall also sent Tobias a preliminary memorandum he had just drafted on the purpose and scope of the committee. "In consideration of the present status of the protection of civil rights of minority groups in this country," Marshall wrote, "we are constantly faced with the lack of a clear statement from Congress opposing discrimination, and this lack of a clear statement of policy has thwarted efforts to protect many basic civil rights. It is therefore necessary that the Committee must recommend legislation which will clearly set forth the public policy of the United States as being opposed to discrimination because of race, creed or national origin. The proposed legislation should contain language such as the following: It is the public policy of the United States that no distinction because of race, creed, color or national origin shall be made or sanctioned by any governmental agency subject to the legislative jurisdiction of the United States."

More remarkable, however, was Marshall's push for comprehensive civil rights legislation. "Federal protection of civil rights," he argued, "must specifically embrace protection against mob violence and police brutality, the right to vote, to travel freely, to earn a decent livelihood, to a decent home, and to health and recreational facilities. Each individual citizen must be fully protected in the enjoyment of these basic rights if our democratic institutions are to survive. Experience has shown that such protection cannot be left to local government agencies. On the contrary, it is now unquestionably clear that the civil rights of minority groups must be effectively protected only by affirmative action of the federal government."

In his own appearance before the committee on April 18, Marshall stated: "It is clear that racism is a scourge. Its spread is viewed with alarm by almost universal respectable opinion. As long as a denial of basic rights to any portion of our people continues, the nation's well-being and security are threatened. This disease must be rooted out of our life; it must be contained and not permitted to spread further. Only the federal government can adequately do this job. It must, therefore, finish the job begun in 1865 to forever wipe out slavery from the United States."

The committee submitted its report to Truman at the end of October 1947, and the report's fifty-four recommendations included nearly all of Marshall's own recommendations.

OCTOBER 30, 1947

Dear Mr. Parsons:

The editorial in this morning's *Tribune*, entitled "To Secure These Rights," is a marvelous one. It not only puts in capsule form the intent, as well as the contents, of the report of the President's Committee on Civil Rights, but calls for the type of action which is most needed to back up this splendid report. We are most grateful for the *Tribune*'s urgent request for action in the conclusion of the editorial, stating the report "is a program for justice and freedom; as such it should command not only the support but the enthusiasm of Americans."

We have no doubt that despite this well-documented report and its recommendation for the enforcement of the rights well grounded in our constitutional form of government, there will be individuals, organizations, and newspapers who will condemn the report and even call for the continuance of the status quo as to racial and religious prejudices.

It is therefore heartening to have the wholehearted support of the *Tribune* and its influence behind this program of action. We will continue to need this type of support throughout the inevitable struggle to have the program on civil rights put into action.

Sincerely yours,

Thurgood Marshall

CHAPTER TEN

1948

MARSHALL TO THE EDITOR OF THE DALLAS *MORNING NEWS*

Marshall complains about an editorial defending the newly established—and segregated—law school for blacks in Texas. The state established this school in response to the NAACP's efforts, through the Sweatt *case, to integrate the University of Texas School of Law.*

FEBRUARY 5, 1948

Dear Sir:

We have just received the Dallas *Morning News* for last Thursday, January 29th, in which there are two editorials, "It Makes a Difference" and "An Honest Effort."

In the editorial "An Honest Effort," you rely upon the statement of one of the two Negro students at the so-called Negro law school that the institution is "generally satisfactory." You also point out that this student compares his instruction favorably with that received at the University of Texas. It is difficult to understand how Mr. Doyle can make this comparison on any first-hand information since he is obviously not aware of the type of education being offered at the University of Texas Law School. It is also obvious that a first-year law school student is not in a position to determine the equality as to either quantity or quality of education. There are, of course, many experts in the field of legal education, and I am sure that you cannot get any one of these experts to agree with Mr. Doyle. I assume also that the Dallas *Morning News* is aware of the fact that when Mr. Doyle speaks concerning this problem, he speaks not as a disinterested individual but rather as an employee of the state of Texas with the position of "secretary-custodian" of the law school.

The basis of your conclusion that Texas has made an honest effort to give equal facilities to the two Negro law students is "That they have far better facilities than the pioneer students of the University of Texas Law School at its inception . . ." Surely you do not take the position that the equality guaranteed by the Fourteenth Amendment is that a Negro at the present time is entitled to no better education than was offered white students when these schools began. You have commented several times on the opinions of the Supreme Court to the effect that the equality required is equality *now*. Then, too, your factual basis is incorrect because the testimony in the Sweatt case of officials of the University of Texas revealed that when the school was first built it was adequate for 400 of the "pioneer students" and was not started in the basement of a small building.

As to your editorial "It Makes a Difference," you again raise the question as to what Negroes actually want. Negroes want no more and no less than is offered to other students in Texas. Undisputed facts several times recognized by the Dallas *Morning News* demonstrate that it is impossible for Negroes to get the same type of education as is offered other citizens in the present segregated system of schools in Texas. In this editorial, you admit that the present facilities offered Negroes for collegiate training are unequal, and it is your suggestion that the Negro people wait until they are made equal. I assume that you recognize that in the meantime Negroes will be receiving inferior education and that the authorities of the state of Texas will continue to violate the Fourteenth Amendment, and it is my understanding that you suggest that nothing be done about it. It is the Negro's position that constitutional rights are individual rights and are entitled to be protected to the same extent as other rights. You point out that neither the NAACP nor the men and women for whom they have taken up the cudgels are interested in going through the processes which have brought forward white higher education. It is not clear what you mean by this statement other than the inference that Negroes have not borne their full share of the responsibilities of government. This Negroes have always done wherever permitted to do so.

However, in Texas they have for years been deprived of this opportunity by being deprived of the right to vote.

I may also suggest to you that the facilities for white education in Texas are not restricted to those who have worked so hard for it but are available to any white citizen regardless of what he might have done for or against the state of Texas. Although Sweatt is denied admission to the Law School of Texas, I know of no regulation that would prevent a former enemy alien from admission to the law school, providing he be white. The truth is not what the individual has done for the educational system in Texas or the state of Texas but is rather the race of the individual involved; and there is no way in which the Dallas *Morning News* can confuse this issue. The facts still remain that the only reason Heman Marion Sweatt is denied admission to the law school of the University of Texas is his race and color. It would make no difference how much he and his family had contributed in Texas; how long they had been resident in the state of Texas; how diligent they had been supporting their government; or how hard they had worked to save their country and state. As long as Sweatt is non-white, he is non-eligible for admission to the law school. The only way he and other Negroes can get an education equal to that offered white students in Texas at the present time is to be admitted to the existing facilities. The only place he can get equal facilities required by the Fourteenth Amendment is in this way.

The responsibility for the collapse of the doctrine of "separate but equal" facilities is on the state of Texas and its officials and no one else, and neither the Dallas *Morning News* nor anyone else can shift responsibility.

Yours very truly,

Thurgood Marshall

In his reply, the editor William Ruggles wrote: "I cannot see that the Negro is receiving an inferior legal education when he is offered the same faculty that the students at the University of Texas are offered and adequate library facilities. Short of equipping him with a brain, I cannot see that the state of Texas can go farther."

MARSHALL TO WALTER WHITE

As part of its efforts to harass the NAACP and other organizations, HUAC, as well as individual legislators, called for the release of the Association's membership and donor lists. So did state legislators and attorneys throughout the South who were intent on suing the NAACP as an outside lobbying organization that unlawfully failed to pay taxes. Marshall refers below to Arthur Garfield Hays, the general counsel for the ACLU, and Morris Ernst, the head of the ACLU.

FEBRUARY 13, 1948

While in Washington on Wednesday, February 11th, Arthur Garfield Hays told me that Morris Ernst, in testifying before the Un-American Activities Committee that day, had stated that you approved his proposal concerning the divulging of membership lists and contributors of organizations similar to ours.

Hays wanted to know whether or not this was the official policy of the NAACP and I told him that I did not know of any official position of the NAACP on this measure, but that I, for one, was opposed to it because it would wreck the NAACP. I thought you would be interested in knowing that Ernst did quote you as being in favor of the proposal as secretary of the NAACP.

MARSHALL TO ROSCOE DUNJEE

In January 1948, the U.S. Supreme Court ruled in favor of Ada Lois Sipuel, who had been denied admission at the University of Oklahoma because of her race, and Marshall and Dunjee fully expected that the school would admit her for the spring term. But the university's board of regents resisted the decision by establishing Langston University Law School, a Jim Crow law school located in the state capitol. When the regents instructed Sipuel to apply to the new law school, Marshall advised her to ignore the instructions and petitioned the U.S. Supreme Court to admit Sipuel to the all-white university. The high court denied the petition, and Marshall then sued once again for her admission to the university. In his April 15 letter, Dunjee informed Marshall that the state was planning to add two new faculty members to the faculty at Langston University Law School just before the new trial in the Sipuel case. Interestingly, Marshall's reply takes two words that whites frequently used when degrading blacks—"boys" and "shuffle"—and turns them on their heads.

APRIL 20, 1948

Dear Roscoe:

Thanks so much for your letter of April 15 with the latest information on the Jim Crow law school. They can do everything they want to try to bolster the Jim Crow law school, but that will not help them at all. We are going to hit segregation head on so they can shuffle around as much as they want to and it won't help them.

On the other hand, it is most helpful to have this interesting dope and I hope that you will continue to send it to us.

Incidentally the other method that is being used by the boys out your way is that they are sending letters to the Negro law schools requesting information as to number of students, white and colored, the number of the faculty, white and colored, etc., for the purpose of showing that (1) all Negro schools are good and (2) that there are schools in which there are only Negroes. With everybody watching out, we'll keep up with the birds.

Sincerely,

Thurgood Marshall

MARSHALL TO THE PRESS

On April 19, James Hinton, the head of the NAACP in South Carolina, sent Marshall the following telegram: "Congratulations on your outstanding victory in opening the Democratic primaries to Negroes in South Carolina. It is the New Emancipation to thousands of Negroes in South Carolina, raising them to first class citizenship." Hinton was referring to a Supreme Court decision, delivered on the same day, which upheld a ruling that the white primary in South Carolina was an infringement on the constitutional rights of African American residents of the state. In his reply to Hinton, Marshall wrote: "It has been a long, hard fight dating back to the first Texas primary case."

Marshall won yet another historic decision, arguably his most important victory yet, when the Supreme Court unanimously ruled on May 3 that racially restrictive covenants—property covenants that prevented African Americans and other racial minorities from owning or occupying real estate in white areas—were legally unenforceable. The Court decided on three cases—includ-

ing the NAACP's Shelley v. Kraemer *and* McGhee v. Sipes*—and in his comments on two of the cases Chief Justice Fred Vinson wrote: "Because of the race or color of these petitioners, they have been denied rights of ownership or occupancy enjoyed as a matter of course by other citizens of different race or color. The Fourteenth Amendment declares that all persons, whether colored or white, shall stand equal before the laws of the states, and, in regard to the colored race, for whose protection the Amendment was primarily designed, that no discrimination shall be made against them by law because of their color. In these cases the states have acted to deny petitioners the equal protection of the laws guaranteed by the Fourteenth Amendment." Given what Marshall felt about residential segregation—that it was the most pernicious form of segregation—he must have been ecstatic, though the following statement to the press is markedly reserved in tone.*

MAY 3, 1948

Today's decision of the Supreme Court of the United States in holding racial restrictive covenants unenforceable is a complete justification of the National Association for the Advancement of Colored People's thirty-one-year fight to outlaw discrimination in housing. This ruling by the court gives thousands of prospective homebuyers throughout the United States new courage and hope in the American form of government.

Since 1917, when the Supreme Court outlawed local ordinances seeking to restrict the occupancy of property by persons because of their race or color, the NAACP has steadily fought the enforcement by the courts of private agreements seeking to achieve the same purpose. It is obvious that no greater blow to date has been made against the pattern of segregation existing within the United States.

MARSHALL TO GEORGE BEAVER, JR.

In this letter to an executive with Golden State Mutual Life Insurance Company, Marshall confesses to having been fearful of the Supreme Court decision on restrictive covenants—an extremely rare confession—and places the decision in its broader context. Marshall also notes his use of sociologists and anthropologists during the trial—a tactic he would replicate when arguing Brown.

MAY 13, 1948

Dear George:

Thanks so much for your letter of congratulations on the restrictive covenants cases. The victory was made possible only through the cooperation of a whole gang of lawyers, both white and Negro, including Loren Miller, whose cooperation was better than marvelous. In addition, we had a whole staff of experts in the field of sociology, anthropology, etc., so that you see we all can claim a share of the credit, and we most certainly recognize the cooperation of our branches and individuals who put their hard-earned cash on the faith that the case could be won, with the full realization that it was a difficult case, to say the least. The favorable decision is therefore most gratifying because, frankly, we were all scared to death!

I assume that your biggest hurdle in Los Angeles will be the question of mortgages, and I am wondering, although knowing you I should not wonder, if you are taking the necessary steps to see to it that mortgages will be forthcoming to Negroes purchasing in heretofore restricted areas. All in all, we have another victory but a tough road to go. For example, we will be starting a new trial in our University of Oklahoma case on May 24th, and we will thereby be grabbing off another large hunk with just as difficult a job ahead as in the covenant cases.

As a matter of fact, believe me, the jobs are getting tougher each time. However, as long as guys like you have faith in guys like us, it is always worth a try. The best of everything to you and the wife.

Sincerely yours,

Thurgood Marshall

MARSHALL TO CHARLES ANDERSON

Marshall offers pointed legal counsel to an African American attorney who was recruited to teach at the segregated law school in Houston. In his May 18 letter to Marshall, Anderson wrote about the reaction he and other recruits had to the opening of the segregated school. "To the extent that legal education will thereby be made available to a larger number of Negro youth," he wrote, "we are pleased. But insofar as such separate institutions tend to perpetuate the traditional pattern of segregation, and conflict with a long-range program to secure more fundamental gains, we feel that they are not entitled to our support. Any advice that you may offer will be appreciated."

JUNE 3, 1948

Dear Mr. Anderson:

. . .

As to the particular question in your letter, I believe it would be a distinct mistake for a person of your caliber to teach in a segregated Jim Crow law school created for the sole purpose of evading the Supreme Court decisions. I believe that more and more people, in and out of the legal profession, will condemn all persons who take part in this subterfuge.

It seems to me that your best bet would be in private practice at this time. I firmly believe that the Jim Crow law school will be the first victim in our fight against segregation in public schools, so that those who take part in these Jim Crow law schools might very possibly have but a short time in the teaching profession, and when it is added up, there will be more harm than good to the individual involved.

This is not based upon any emotion but is rather based upon cold fact and a truthful belief that these Jim Crow law schools will be of short duration. As to Texas itself, I can say that there, more than any place else in the country, the Negroes and good-thinking white people think as one in their condemnation of the Jim Crow law school, regardless of how elaborate it might be, and it would most certainly not be fair for you to share the brunt of this condemnation.

I have tried to give you my best advice in a more or less rambling fashion, and if there is any portion of it which is not clear, please write me and I will try to clear it up for you.

With all best wishes, I am

Sincerely yours,

Thurgood Marshall

MARSHALL TO ERWIN GRISWOLD

Erwin Griswold, the famous dean of Harvard Law School, had encouraged Marshall to proceed with caution in the Sipuel trial (the case to integrate the University of Oklahoma College of Law). Although he did not explain his argument in detail, Griswold had written that the complicated procedural background of the case would make it difficult for Marshall to use the case as a springboard for attacking segregation in education.

JUNE 14, 1948

Dear Dean Griswold:

Thanks so much for your letter of June 10, which was called to my attention upon my return to the office this morning.

I know that we are not apart on our opinions as to the ultimate goal, and I do not believe we are very far apart on our procedure. One thing is certain and that is that we have not made much progress in obtaining even dollars and cents equalization on a segregated level. On the other hand, I do not believe that there is any doubt that we will not break down segregation overnight. Now, in between these two we will find the procedure which can be considered sane from every viewpoint.

Personally, I believe that we have a better chance of breaking down segregation in professional schools and especially law schools than on any other level of public education. I likewise believe that we will have the least amount of friction and opposition on that level. In view of the fact that the student bodies of the law schools of both Texas and Oklahoma are overwhelmingly in favor of the admission of Negroes, our job is made even easier. In addition, there is still the possibility that Oklahoma will overrule the attorney general and admit our plaintiff to the law school.

At any rate, we shall wait and see, and before any decision is made on whatever judgment is issued in the case, we will most certainly get in touch with you and the other people who have worked so well with us on this case.

With all best wishes.

Sincerely,

Thurgood Marshall

Marshall took the occasion of the trial to argue that the segregated education Sipuel would face at the segregated law school would inherently place her at a disadvantage compared to students trained at the all-white law school at the

University of Oklahoma. While Marshall lost the case, the university's president, who was racially progressive, at least relative to the board of regents, engineered Sipuel's admission to the university, with the provision that she sit in the back of the school's classrooms.

MARSHALL TO GOVERNOR M. E. THOMPSON

On September 7, Isiah Nixon, an African American father of six children, went to his local polling place in Alston, Georgia, to vote in the Democratic primary for governor. Election officials in Alston had advised Nixon not to exercise his right to vote, but Nixon insisted and eventually cast his ballot. Later that night, M. A. Johnson, a white logger from Alston, went to Nixon's home and shot him three times in front of his wife and children. Nixon died, and Herman Talmadge, who had praised white supremacy while denouncing President Harry Truman's civil rights agenda during the campaign, won the primary.

SEPTEMBER 13, 1948

On behalf of National Association for Advancement Colored People, its branches in Georgia and other states of union, we urge you as governor of the state of Georgia to use your full authority to intervene in and push vigorously for the prosecution of parties guilty of killing Isiah Nixon of Alston, Georgia, solely because of the fact that he exercised his American right of voting. This type intimidation is aimed at preventing other American citizens from exercising their constitutional rights. If permitted to go unpunished, it will make our Constitution a farce. We therefore earnestly appeal you to use all powers at your command to bring the guilty parties to justice and to prevent further recurrence of such intimidation.

Thurgood Marshall

In his reply to Marshall, Governor Thompson wrote: "It is my understanding that the matter referred to in your telegram is being pushed vigorously by the prosecuting authorities in the judicial circuit where the alleged murder occurred. Meanwhile, you may be assured of my willingness to do everything I can as long as I am Chief Executive to see that those violating the law of this State are brought to justice."

MARSHALL TO THE EDITOR OF THE *DALLAS NEWS*

Marshall excoriates the editor of the Dallas News *for claiming that the election of segregationist politicians—particularly Representative John Rankin of Mississippi, Senator Russell Long of Louisiana, and Governor Herman Talmadge of Georgia—was directly traceable to the presence of the NAACP in the South.*

SEPTEMBER 21, 1948

Dear Sir:

I have received a clipping of an editorial appearing in the *Dallas News* for September 10th, entitled "Who's to Blame at Southern Polls?" I know it is a common practice for the average person who is himself responsible for misconduct to seek to salve his own conscience by putting the blame on someone else. I am, however, surprised that a newspaper with the reputation of the *Dallas News* would seek to blame the perpetuation in office of Congressman Rankin and the election to office of Senator Long and Governor Herman Talmadge on the National Association for the Advancement of Colored People, as you did in your editorial.

The truth of the matter is that in each of the areas responsible for these elections, the good-thinking citizens have either been precluded from voting by poll taxes, threats and intimidation, or have failed to vote for other reasons. The National Association for the Advancement of Colored People cannot be blamed for any of these reasons. You know as well as I do that the reason for these elections is the abandonment of the governmental processes by you and others to the demagogues of the South. You cannot escape your responsibility at this time by attempting to shift the burden to us. Negroes have suffered enough as the result of your inaction in the support of our Constitution, but we will not permit you to shift the additional burden upon us.

In this editorial, as in others, you constantly refer to the National Association for the Advancement of Colored People as "outsiders." As a newspaper, I am sure you are interested in facts. The facts are that this Association is a national association operating in forty-five states, including all of the Southern states and the District of Columbia. More than 60% of our branches are in the South. No action whatsoever is taken concerning any area of the country without consultation with and approval of the area affected. It should also be noted that the membership of this Association in the South, as well as other sections of the country, is interracial.

Finally, despite our disagreements in the past, I am serious when I say that I am shocked at your attempt in this editorial to find a scapegoat upon which to shift the blame for the inaction of yourself and others in the South. By what logic do you differentiate between the National Association for the Advancement of Colored People when it speaks out against patent violations of our Constitution and all good newspapers which feel it their duty to take a stand against lawless and unconstitutional acts? Do you actually mean, as your editorial suggests, that citizens of this country, North and South, are obliged to tolerate, without opposition of any kind, deliberate violations of our Constitution and the federal criminal laws? Are those of us who are Negroes expected to permit individuals and governmental officers to deprive us of the rights guaranteed to us without even a recourse to protect?

Very truly yours,

Thurgood Marshall

MARSHALL TO HENRY MOON

The following memorandum to Moon, the director of public relations for the NAACP, is press material that Marshall wrote about another important case in the desegregation of education—G.W. McLaurin v. Oklahoma State Regents. *The memorandum offers a very helpful description of the case, and, once again, Marshall also draws attention to the importance of branch sentiment. In a letter to his legal team nine days earlier, Marshall had sketched some of his thoughts on using the case to score a direct hit against the separate but equal doctrine: "It seems to me that this case gives us a good opportunity to show that the segregation statutes are not, as believed in* Plessy v. Ferguson, *intended as a burden on either group. In this instance, we have a class of students sitting down studying together, etc. and one student ostracized from the immediate classroom and forced to study in a position of seclusion for the obvious purpose of humiliation, degrading and what have you. McLaurin will testify that it is impossible for him to do his best work under these conditions and, as a matter of fact, he has threatened to withdraw for this reason. I think his testimony will be good. . . . I personally would like to move on the question that there is no legal basis for this type of classification."*

OCTOBER 28, 1948

On Monday, October 25th, in Oklahoma City, a hearing was held before the special three-judge federal court in the case of *G.W. McLaurin vs. University of Oklahoma.* The original case was filed in August 1948, and after two hearings the federal court entered an order on October 6th decreeing that the statutes of Oklahoma prohibiting the Negro and white students from attending the same school, college or university were unconstitutional and unenforceable insofar as they prevented McLaurin from obtaining his desired education at the University of Oklahoma. The Court, however, refused to issue an injunction.

McLaurin was admitted to the Graduate School of the University of Oklahoma on October 13th and was placed in a small anteroom adjoining the classroom behind a desk in the doorway between the two rooms. He was also assigned a table on the top floor of the library back in a corner which had previously been used to store old newspapers. He was also assigned separate eating and separate facilities in one building. NAACP lawyers for McLaurin immediately filed a petition for further relief, seeking to have the court prohibit segregation of McLaurin. At the last hearing, the issue was made clear that an attack was being made on segregation as such, that the officials of the University of Oklahoma were without authority to segregate McLaurin, and that the segregation of this Negro student denied him the equal protection of the laws guaranteed by the Constitution of the United States.

Attorney General Mac Q. Williams, of the state of Oklahoma, claimed that the officials of the University of Oklahoma had the inherent authority to segregate students. The case was taken under advisement by the court, and a ruling is expected immediately after the filing of briefs by both sides.

. . .

It may be well to weave into the story the fact that the officers of our state conference of Oklahoma met in Oklahoma City on Sunday, October 24th, and reaffirmed their stand as being opposed to segregation in any form in public education and voted their full and complete support to the fight against segregation in public education. The vote was unanimous. . . .

MARSHALL TO SETH RICHARDSON

In this letter to the chair of the Loyalty Review Board of the Civil Service Commission, Marshall protests charges of disloyalty being leveled against African Americans in government agencies.

NO DATE [1948]

Dear Mr. Richardson:

The National Association for the Advancement of Colored People is deeply concerned about procedures used by certain government agencies on loyalty matters.

We have before us at this time an illustration in charges filed against Mrs. Bertha W. Lomack, who is employed in the Government Printing Office. There is a long history of discrimination against colored people because of race in the Government Printing Office. Incredible as it may seem, this agency of government segregates Negroes in its cafeteria, requires that they use separate restrooms and generally confines them to low-grade positions.

A remedy for this type of offense on the part of government agencies is provided for by President Truman's recent order against discrimination in the government service. We shall avail ourselves of the machinery of this order in meeting the discrimination outlined. However, it appears that the present charges against Mrs. Lomack are the climax of a series of attacks made by the agency to get rid of her because, as thousands of other Americans, she objected to the undemocratic practices in the Government Printing Office. We feel certain that you do not wish to have the purposes of the Loyalty Review Board prostituted by a number of small-minded individuals in the government service who use it to get rid of employees who will speak out for their rights as citizens of the United States. Therefore, before the hearing is held on this case, we would appreciate a ruling on the following things:

Is it proper to bring charges of disloyalty against an employee who is alleged to have been a member of or contributed to a so-called communist front organization prior to the issuance of executive order 9835?

1. Where an employee is shown to have resigned from a so-called communist front organization prior to the issuance of executive order 9835 and has revealed this to the Federal Bureau of

Investigation, is it proper for the agency's loyalty review board to charge that employee with being disloyal on the basis of such former affiliation?

2. If the employee made contributions or gave support to so-called communist front organizations simply because these organizations were carrying on a fight for civil rights or some other human objective, is it necessary that the employee explain the circumstances under which such contributions and support were given prior to the issuance of executive order 9835?
3. If an employee during his period of college training was active in or made speeches for the so-called communist front organizations, is this sufficient reason to bring charges of disloyalty against him?
4. When the employee's record shows an extensive history of opposition to racial discrimination within an agency or activity in behalf of organized labor, what provision will be made for weighing this evidence against charges of disloyalty?

We raise these questions because there seems to be an increasing tendency on the part of some of the more discriminatory federal agencies to bring charges of disloyalty against colored persons and union members who have been active against discriminatory practices based on race or membership in unions.

We believe that the Loyalty Review Board should make it crystal clear that its functions must not be subverted in this manner. We, therefore, urgently request that the Board pass upon these questions that we have raised at its next meeting. We believe that, if a determination of the Board's position is made, much needless harassment of federal employees will be avoided.

Sincerely yours,

Thurgood Marshall

MARSHALL TO WALTER WHITE

Marshall voices his opposition to the belief that the NAACP LDF (Legal Defense and Educational Fund) should restrict itself "solely to cases in which

Negroes are involved," and below he protests the board's refusal to file a "friend of the court" brief in the case of the Hollywood Ten. On August 5, 1947, a federal grand jury indicted ten Hollywood writers, producers, and directors—Albert Maltz, Dalton Trumbo, Samuel Ornitz, John Howard Lawson, Ring Lardner, Jr., Herbert Biberman, Robert Adrian Scott, Lester Cole, Alvah Bessie, and Edward Dmytryk—for contempt of Congress. During HUAC hearings on the influence of communism in Hollywood, the ten men had refused to state whether they were members of the Communist Party. The ten were convicted, they filed an appeal, and their case landed in the Supreme Court.

DECEMBER 20, 1948

The question was raised in the discussion concerning the Hollywood writers case that there is a possibility of establishing a harmful precedent by our agreeing to go into these cases as amicus curiae. I believe that the action of the board in refusing to permit the staff to file a brief amicus curiae in this case is a dangerous precedent. If we expect to limit our work solely to cases in which Negroes are involved, then our cause is lost because this Association, I have understood, has always been of the opinion that this problem cannot be solved either by Negroes alone or by emphasis on the Negro problem alone. For example, there is a proposal now being considered to change the name of the Association to the International Association for the Advancement of Negroes. We are constantly talking about "broadening" our program. At one time, this Association could not understand that the problem of the Negro was related to the problem of organized labor. Fortunately we have passed that hurdle.

As to the proposed brief amicus curiae, it was to be limited to our position in that the writers involved were those *among the writers* in Hollywood who had been most friendly to Negroes. Of course, there are others in Hollywood, like some actresses, such as Bette Davis, and some producers, such as Walter Wanger, who claim to be friends of the Negro, or something of that sort, but I have yet to see anything that any of them have done for Negroes, and I have yet to see where any of them have made any contributions to the cause, even for the purpose of getting tax exemptions. On the other hand, the writers in this case have taken the position in their actual work in Hollywood in writing scripts of giving the Negro as fair a break as they possibly could do. Mrs. Perry has a full list of the scripts they wrote, which will be submitted.

It is not unworthy of notice that as long as Hollywood was producing the regular run-of-the-mill of anti-Semitic, anti-Negro pictures, led by the *Birth of a Nation*, the Un-American Activities Committee was not interested in investigating "communism in Hollywood." It should also be noted that the greatest impetus to the investigation of communism in Hollywood came about shortly after such pictures as "Gentlemen's Agreement" and the few pictures in which the Negro was given any semblance of decency. Perhaps there is no connection in fact, but there is an undisputed connection in timing. On the question of timing, it should also be noted that immediately after the Hollywood writers were cited for contempt, the Hollywood producers had every script in production and ready for production checked as to references to Negroes, and all decent references to Negroes were stricken from the scripts. This is not hearsay but comes from a confidential report from an investigator from *Time* magazine.

Getting back to the question of precedent and policy, I don't doubt that most of the organizations who filed briefs amicus curiae in our restrictive covenant cases could have declined to do so on the grounds of the case being outside the direct scope of their organization. We are hoping for an even larger group to file briefs in our university cases, and of course the only people *directly* affected by these decisions are Negroes, but I assume that many of these organizations will file briefs because of the incidental effect to their organization and the direct effect to our democratic form of government. As to the Hollywood writers case, I assume that if a member of our organization were examined in Mississippi by a member of the committee and refused to testify as to whether or not he was a member of the NAACP, we could not expect any other organization to intervene in amicus curiae in our defense of that case when the individual was charged with contempt by the Un-American Activities Committee. I do believe that we have a stock in preserving the very basic principles of democracy whether Negroes are involved or not.

MARSHALL TO ROSCOE DUNJEE

While he claims to have "no fear of communists," Marshall writes the following letter to enlist local NAACP leader Dunjee in an effort to squelch communists from taking control of a student NAACP group at the University of Oklahoma.

DECEMBER 29, 1948

Dear Roscoe:

Here is a real difficulty which we are facing, and these two letters will give you an idea of where we stand. I know that you have no fear of communists and I certainly do not have any, yet I am opposed to communists controlling any of our movements. It is not a question of communists being members of the committee but rather of known, committed communists being at the head of the committees. The leadership of these movements surrounding these cases should be ours and should not be given to anyone else, and if the communists are really serious in their protestation of wanting to help Negroes, they should be willing to do so in such a manner as not to wreck the case they claim to be supporting.

I think the present situation concerning the movement at Oklahoma University is at a very dangerously low ebb and can do untold harm to our case. You can do more to prevent this than anyone else, and it is for this reason that I hope you will cooperate, because the case and the whole fight against segregation is more important than any one group. We have a good chance of action in the legislature or action in the United States Supreme Court, both of which will admittedly be seriously handicapped if the red brush is placed on our movements to break down segregation at the University of Oklahoma. I have written you quite frankly because I want you to have our views and at the same time we need your cooperation.

Sincerely yours,

Thurgood Marshall

CHAPTER ELEVEN

1949–1950

MARSHALL TO HERBERT SWOPE

On January 12, a delegation of the National Citizens Council on Civil Rights, cochaired by Herbert Swope, the editor of the New York World, *met with President Truman and urged him to establish a permanent federal commission on civil rights. While he most likely appreciated the recommendation, Marshall registers a major complaint.*

JANUARY 12, 1949

Dear Mr. Swope:

There has been considerable discussion among certain people since Monday of this week concerning the delegation from the council which met with President Truman concerning the permanent commission on civil rights. The discussion has centered around the personnel of the committee and has had nothing at all to do with either the purpose of the committee or the report given to the President. Rather than enter such a discussion, I have decided that it would be best to give you my views in the spirit of constructive criticism. It is perhaps obvious at this point that the question involved is the absence of a Negro representative on the committee.

This is not a matter of special pleading. It is not a matter of being thin-skinned. It is not a matter of racial-consciousness. It does seem to me, however, that when a committee interested in civil rights consisting of seven people fails to include a Negro, then there is grave question as to whether Negroes have been completely integrated into the very group which is advocating their cause. If the committee was chosen because of an interest in civil rights and a civil rights commission, it is even more unexplainable how it is possible to pick such a committee without selecting at least one Negro, not because the individual is a Negro, but because Negroes constitute the largest minority in this country, are the most frequent victims of the denial of civil rights, and therefore have had to fight hardest in the civil rights area.

In short, there are many Negroes who have done their share of fighting for the protection of the civil rights of other minorities, and one of this group could very well have been on your committee.

In conclusion, I believe that the failure to include a Negro in the group was a distinct mistake and a detriment to the program which all of us are supporting. If the purpose was to demonstrate that persons other than Negroes were pushing for legislation that would protect Negroes and other minority groups, it could only be on the basis that it was being done in the spirit of cooperation. However, if the purpose is to be interpreted as a paternalistic interest in the protection of minority groups, then that interpretation will be disastrous to the main cause and to the national council in particular. Fortunately, it cannot be interpreted as meaning that Negroes are not interested in this problem. Then, too, I wonder at the reaction of President Truman to such a delegation, which is different from other delegations which have appeared before him on other civil rights issues, all of which delegations included representatives from all groups in the country.

As I mentioned above, this letter is written in the spirit of constructive criticism, but it does give my opinions on the inevitable result of returning to the days when groups would plead for the rights of minority groups without representation of the groups for which they were pleading. I had hoped that we had reached the position today where Negroes had at least been fully and completely integrated into the forces fighting for equality, civil rights and other measures.

Sincerely yours,

Thurgood Marshall

MARSHALL TO WALTER WHITE

It is not true that Marshall did not ever favor direct political action campaigns. In an August 1949 letter to the head of the Texas NAACP, for instance, Marshall offered enthusiastic support for the idea of picketing the state legislature of Texas. Marshall himself had picketed several times in his life. When he was a student at Howard University, he joined Charles Houston and other members of the law school community as they picketed an anticrime conference, headed by the attorney general, for not including lynching on their agenda. And when he was NAACP counsel in Baltimore, he joined the local branch in picketing both drugstores that would not serve African Americans and a grocery store chain that would not hire African Americans. Years later, as he was reflecting on his picketing experiences, he stated: "I guess I'm an old rebel anyhow." The following letter is additional evidence that Marshall favored direct political action campaigns, and this time his idea is to pressure Congress so that it would begin to pass Truman's civil rights legislation. Both of the senators Marshall refers to—Frances Myers of Pennsylvania and Scott Lucas of Illinois—lost their bids for reelection in 1950.

FEBRUARY 16, 1949

The telegram you proposed seems to me to be all right but this once again raises the question of strategy, and I respectfully suggest that we make a definite change in strategy. It is obvious that something more needs to be done if we are to change the minds of the leaders in the Senate.

In the past, we have operated on lobbying by our national office representatives and telegrams from other organizations as well as our branches. It seems to me that if anything is to be accomplished now, we must "go to the country" and bring the country to Washington. I still believe that we should have a full-blown legislative meeting of as many of our branches as possible in Washington so that they can buttonhole senators personally.

At the same time, I fully agree with Hastie that we should have terrific mass meetings in every state where senators are up for election in 1950. We should most certainly have meetings in Illinois and Pennsylvania to make Myers and Lucas realize what the score is.

MARSHALL TO LEMUEL GRAVES, JR.

In this letter to the Washington correspondent for the Pittsburgh Courier, *Marshall recommends major changes at the federal agency he most despised—the Federal Housing Administration. Marshall's letter here includes recommendations he had sent President Truman in a detailed memorandum on February 1. The pointed memo ran for twenty-one pages and centered on the following argument: "Instead of contributing to the solution of the housing problems of minority groups, the FHA . . . embarked upon a program in which it followed traditional private real estate practice, fostered and spread race restrictive covenants, restricted mortgage insurance for Negroes to occupancy only in areas already occupied by Negroes, and thus further curtailed needed living space and confounded the housing problems of racial minorities. . . . It is the thesis of this memorandum that support by the FHA of residential segregation in any shape or form is contrary and odious to the public policy of the United States as evidenced by the decisions of the United States Supreme Court last May prohibiting judicial enforcement of racial covenants and by the Report of the President's Committee on Civil Rights."*

FEBRUARY 24, 1949

Dear Lem:

Here is some of the material I think you can use as to our reaction to the latest moves being made by the FHA. The NAACP has requested that the FHA cease to insure mortgages on property in which the applicant for insurance has inserted a restrictive covenant or to approve any projects where restrictive covenants are to be inserted. From the latest memoranda and from reports we have received, it appears that FHA feels that it cannot comply with this request because to do so would deny to Negroes an opportunity to secure homes in such projects.

This is a very fallacious piece of reasoning. The NAACP is obviously not suggesting anything that will limit the amount of housing that Negroes can obtain. It is perfectly clear that where a builder such as Levitt, who is building thousands of homes in one community, inserts race restrictions in the deeds and leases of those properties, he is not going to make any property available to Negro purchasers or leasees. The whole purpose of including restrictive covenants in these projects is to make it clear to everyone who goes to live there that it is a "restricted" community where no Negroes are wanted. The propaganda value of such covenant remains great even though they cannot be enforced in court. Every person who is forced to sign a lease containing such a covenant or deed is forced to become a contributor to the walls of the Negro ghetto and becomes committed to a policy of restrictive covenants.

If FHA will adopt an affirmative policy of refusing to approve mortgage insurance projects or mortgages where race restrictions are *newly* inserted by the applicant for mortgage insurance, this would put an end to new race restrictive covenants and would make the policy of FHA clearly in line with the policy of the federal government.

We were very careful not to ask FHA to refuse mortgage insurance on property where there are *old* and established racial covenants. Our suggestions were forward-looking and would, if adopted, eliminate many new restrictive covenants which would be placed on newly developed property.

FHA, since its inception, has been operating under a policy requiring its underwriters to consider the race of the prospective property owner. After years and years of constant protest, FHA deleted these sections from its manual, but over the period of years, the persons operating in FHA have been using race as a factor, and the only way to remove race from their minds is by affirmative action by FHA. The latest instructions are so weakly drawn as to mean little on the factor of removing race as a consideration. As a matter of fact, the word "Negro" is not even used. We still believe that nothing will be accomplished until the FHA takes sufficient affirmative action to counteract the inherent evil brought about by years and years of using race as a consideration.

Finally, this cannot be accomplished by any memoranda but can only be accomplished by a complete overhauling of the entire setup brought about by most careful consideration and put into motion by a top-level directive affirmatively removing race not only from the manual and from the memoranda but also from the official minds of all subordinate officials in FHA.

Sincerely yours,

Thurgood Marshall

Before the end of the year, Truman would ban federal financing for new homes or apartments operating under racial covenants.

MARSHALL TO J. WATIES WARING

Marshall stays in close touch with the judge who ruled favorably in the case of the white primary in South Carolina, celebrates an advance in the government's stance on the KKK, and seems uncharacteristically optimistic in his assessment of the civil rights climate in Georgia.

MAY 4, 1949

My Dear Judge Waring:

I have just returned to the office and find your letters and the clippings. The handbill passed out by the KKK at the parade celebrating "Azalea Festival Week" is in keeping with their plans. However, there are two bright sides to the problem—one is that Attorney General Tom Clark has placed this group on his list of organizations, which I believe is the first time this has been done by a governmental agency. Then, too, I noticed in the *Herald Tribune* yesterday a clipping, which I am enclosing, that the Atlanta, Ga. city council voted to "Unmask Klan."

Mrs. Tilly, of Georgia, who was a member of the President's Committee on Civil Rights, will be in New York this week, and Walter and I will discuss with her the whole Georgia situation. It is most interesting that the white people of Georgia are beginning to move toward the eradication of the Talmadge element, and it seems as though people like Mrs. Tilly are getting more and more support. So it looks as though some progress is being made, even though it is very small.

I argued another case in the Supreme Court on Monday of last week, *Watts vs. State of Indiana*, involving the question of the exclusion of Negroes from jury service in Indianapolis and the question of extorted confessions. Frankly, it is a case that I did not want to get into because the petitioner appears to be a really bad egg. However, it is likewise disgusting to have Negroes excluded from grand jury service in Indianapolis. We are determined that we will not continue to bring such cases in the South and to permit places like Indiana to discriminate. At least we will act with equal fairness below and above the "Smith and Wesson Line."

. . .

Sincerely yours,

Thurgood Marshall

STEPHEN SPINGARN TO CLARK CLIFFORD

The following is an excerpt from a White House memorandum from Stephen Spingarn, the administrative assistant to the president, to Clark Clifford, the special counsel to the president. The memo includes quotes from a letter sent to Spingarn from his uncle, NAACP president Arthur Spingarn, who wanted the president to consider Marshall as a new federal judge for the Southern District of New York.

In his own memo to Clifford, below, Stephen Spingarn argues that Marshall was a "strong supporter of President Truman," and he was more than accurate on this point. When asked years later about Truman, Marshall stated: "Well, you knew you had someone to rely on. Who would go the whole hog, and one you—I almost said, it's a spiritual feeling. It's a warm feeling, you just can't put your hands on. But you know he's there when you need him." This was perhaps the highest praise Marshall ever spoke in reference to any U.S. politician.

MAY 16, 1949

Thurgood Marshall has had a distinguished legal career. For the past ten years he has been Special Counsel for the NAACP and in that capacity in active charge of all legal cases instituted by that Association to serve and protect full citizenship rights for negroes. This has involved trial and appellate work in all categories of federal courts, including the U.S. Supreme Court, and in most of the state courts of the South. The NAACP has won 24 of its 26 appeals to the U.S. Supreme Court. Marshall participated in more than half of these and was chief counsel in 5 of them.

In addition, Marshall (who is only 40 years old) has supervised legal work of all the NAACP branches at its State Conferences. During the war, he participated in a number of court martial cases involving racial discrimination and was instrumental in convincing several negroes who had refused to be drafted to submit to the draft.

A few years ago he won the annual award for the American negro who had made the greatest contribution to American life. With the possible exception of Governor Hastie of the Virgin Islands and Charles Houston, of Washington, Marshall is by far the best and most favorably known lawyer among the negro public.

Marshall is a strong supporter of President Truman. At a negro conference last month in Washington, he was the leader in defeating an attempt by a left-wing group to condemn President Truman as well as the

Southern Democrats and some Northern Republicans for the failure of Congress to approve civil rights measures. *The New York Times* of April 24, 1949, in its story on this conference, quotes Marshall as telling the conference that President Truman has "done more up to date for civil rights than all the other Presidents put together."

Attached is an article from the January 1949 issue of *The Survey* concerning Thurgood Marshall.

I think that Thurgood Marshall would be an outstanding choice for one of the new federal judgeships in the Southern District of New York.

Not long after Spingarn wrote this letter, Marshall also defended Truman before a group of left-wing students at a conference held by college chapters of the NAACP. Truman, Marshall argued, had "done more up to date for civil rights than all the other Presidents put together." Marshall was referring not only to Truman's civil rights proposals before Congress but also to an executive order that the president had signed in 1948. Executive Order 9981 stated: It is hereby declared to be the policy of the President that there shall be equality of treatment and opportunity for all persons in the armed services without regard to race, color, religion, or national origin."

Eleanor Roosevelt wrote a letter supporting Marshall to Paul Fitzpatrick, the chair of the Democratic State Committee of New York. While Roosevelt worked her political connections, Marshall refused to meet with, let alone kowtow to, influential African American politicians associated with New York's famous Tammany Hall political machine. Consequently, they did not back him, and Marshall saw their lack of support as the main reason for his failure to receive the judgeship.

JAMES HINTON TO MARSHALL

Hinton, the president of the South Carolina NAACP, provides a detailed description of an incident of racial violence he suffered a month earlier. It is one of the most courageous—and inspiring—letters in the NAACP Papers.

MAY 26, 1949

Dear Mr. Marshall:

. . .

April 21st (Thursday), I went home to 1499 Wrightsboro Road about

9:00 P.M., and retired immediately. I was the only person in the house. Mrs. Annie E. Ball, the lady with whom I live, came in about 10:00 P.M., and a few minutes afterwards, the bell rang, and a person is alleged to have said to Mrs. Ball, "I want to see the man who has that 1936 Ford parked in the driveway, as it has been in a wreck." He is further alleged to have said, "I am an officer." Mrs. Ball called me, and I arose, and without any thought of anything wrong, put on my house slippers, and went to the door. The man said the same thing to me as stated above, and asked that I step to my car, and he would show me where my car had been in the wreck. I stepped on the porch, and as I turned to go to the car, which was to my left, he grabbed me, and two other men came and bodily took me to a car that was parked in front of the house. I cried out, and a white man who lives across the street, and upstairs, saw the incident. He called the police, who came to 1944 Wrightsboro within 5 minutes. I was taken for about 9 miles out. I was thrown on the floor of the car, and one of the men in the car kept his foot on my neck, and his other foot on the side of my head. When the car reached the place where it stopped, I was dragged out, and blindfolded. On the way out and while I was in the car, a man with an accent spoke to me saying "What is your name?" I did not reply at once, and he then said, "Aren't you James M. Hinton?" I replied "yes." He further said, "You want to place Negroes in the College of Charleston." He said, "Don't you know that cannot be done in South Carolina?" I did not reply to him.

After being dragged from the car, a flashlight was thrown in my face and one man said, "This is not the nigger." They told me to lie down on the ground until they left, and I should not make any attempt to move until they drove away. I waited and it appeared there must have been three or four cars, judging from the sound. I waited until they had driven away, and arose, and listened, and followed the sound of cars, and finally found my way back to the highway. A bus came along and I inquired the way back to Augusta. He told me to turn left. I walked in bare feet at least 5 miles in a downpour of rain. The same bus had gone to "Clark Hill Dam," and was en route back to Augusta. I flagged him down, and asked him to take me to Augusta, I related to the driver what had occurred. He brought me to Augusta. I learned that it was near a place called Martinez.

The City Police had put the thing on the teletype, also the radio. It was all over Augusta and Columbia.

The F.B.I. reached me about 4:00 A.M., after I had reached home about 3:00 A.M. They took all of the information I could give to them. I later learned some car numbers, two of them. A car had been seen to stand nearly all day in front of Harlem Theatre on Gwinnett Street with 6 rough white men inside. This number was given to the F.B.I., as well as another number that was seen near the home in which I live. I telephoned this information to Savannah, Ga., the headquarters of the F.B.I., as I was not able to get the man in Augusta. I have heard nothing from it.

I am living at the same address, and still in Augusta. I have no intention of moving or giving up the fight in South Carolina. I am more fully determined than ever to carry it through.

I received more than 100 calls from white people who left their names to be identified in Columbia, asking for my safety. I had more than 50 calls (long distance) from many places. I had so many local calls, letters and other expressions.

I am thoroughly convinced that Negroes can be organized and do care. They have shown that in that one incident.

I think this is about all of the angles that I know. Trusting this information for the record will suffice.

Very truly yours,

James M. Hinton

MARSHALL TO MACEO SMITH

Marshall uses strong language in pressuring Maceo Smith, the secretary of the Texas NAACP, to line up behind the NAACP's policy on segregated housing. Marshall considered the integration of housing to be an indispensable goal in the postwar era.

JUNE 1, 1949

Dear Maceo:

. . .

As I understand it, your representation on the Texas Council of Negro Organizations is in the official capacity as a representative of the NAACP. As the official representative of the NAACP, you are bound by board policy. While acting in such capacity, you should forget your relationship with private and federal housing agencies. So that it seems clear to me that your position while acting as the NAACP official is directly contrary to the policy of the board of directors, of which you are a member. The arguments you made in your memorandum are substantially the same as those you made at the meeting of the board of directors in January, and you were voted down. You are a good enough organization man to know that your only recourse in such a case is either to have the matter reopened or to consider yourself bound by the policy of the board insofar as your *official* capacity with the NAACP is concerned.

But leaving the official part aside for a moment, I find it very difficult to see how you can maintain your position as to public housing along with your position as to Jim-Crow education. As to Jim-Crow education, I understand your personal position to be that you are opposed to segregation under any circumstances. As to public housing, I understand your position to be that you are opposed to segregated housing, but you are unwilling to go so far as to insist upon non-segregation clauses in the federal legislation. Of course, I recognize the portion of your memorandum about the legal attack on segregation in public housing which we are carrying on at the present time, but I am wondering exactly where your head is on the particular amendments proposed by Bricker and Cain. As I understand it, you would take the position that we should not support such an amendment under any circumstances. . . . You could not do business with Hitler, nor can you now do business with the Dixiecrats. If this problem is going to be solved, it will only be solved by hitting back at them every time we can in every way we can. Every time we cave in, we lose.

One very clear example is in the University of Texas Law School case and the University of Oklahoma Law School case. In Texas, Negroes went to the Jim Crow law school and it is running full bloom despite the lawsuit which is now pending. In Oklahoma, they refused to go to the law school and Ada Lois Sipuel is now going to be admitted to the existing law school.

. . .

All of the above I have written because you and I have never hesitated to tell each other what we think without any recriminations. I have also written this because I know your basic philosophy on our problem is correct. I believe that all of us go off the deep end at times, and I frankly believe that you are in the water up to your ears. I believe that your tremendous interest in housing and public housing has temporarily blotted out your basic philosophy so that you cannot apply this philosophy to public housing. If you will go back and pick up your basic philosophy where you dropped it in the mud and apply it to public housing for just a moment, you cannot help from coming out the right way. You, of course, have to make up your own mind, but I am going to do my damnedest to make it up for you.

Sincerely yours,

Thurgood Marshall

MARSHALL TO ASSISTANT ATTORNEY GENERAL ALEXANDER CAMPBELL

On March 25, three houses owned by African Americans in Birmingham were dynamited. The shocking incidence of racial violence resulted from the recent purchase of homes in a white area of the city by African Americans. Marshall's office received numerous complaints about the violence, and he became especially concerned when he learned that the local police chief, Eugene "Bull" Connor, who would later become famous for facing off against Martin Luther King, Jr., was in collusion with the white perpetrators. Below is an urgent appeal Marshall sent to the assistant attorney general.

JUNE 1, 1949

Dear Mr. Campbell:

On April 5th, Attorney Arthur D. Shores, of Birmingham, Alabama, filed a complaint with the United States District Attorney, John D. Hill, of Birmingham, concerning the bombings of property owned by Negroes in Birmingham on March 25th and at later dates. . . .

We cannot too strongly urge action by the Department of Justice in this type of case because it involves the use of extreme force and violence for the sole purpose of depriving American citizens of their right to occupy property owned by them. There is also evidence of both action and inaction on the part of officials of the city of Birmingham. All in all, it is the type of case which deserves prompt and vigorous action.

I assume that the Department has made an investigation of this complaint, and if so, would appreciate information as to the present status.

Very truly yours,

Thurgood Marshall

Campbell replied to Marshall's letter two weeks later, writing that it was "inadvisable for us to furnish additional information at this time." Birmingham racists, of course, would continue to bomb black residents for years to come, and the most tragic violence occurred when four little girls died in a church bombing shortly after Martin Luther King, Jr., delivered his "I have a dream" speech.

MARSHALL TO HORACE BOND

Marshall sends a sharply worded letter to the president of Lincoln University, his alma mater, about integration and education.

JUNE 13, 1949

Dear Doctor Bond:

. . .

In the first place, when I talked Monday night at the dinner, I was not "rabbling." I have never been more serious in my life about anything. . . .

. . .

I am still willing to credit you with being truly interested in making Lincoln an interracial school, in fact as well as theory. But let's get a few facts straight. When you talk about a few students making Lincoln an interracial school, you know as well as I do that that is not true. Maybe a few Negroes in an otherwise white school make it interracial, but that depends solely on whether or not the Negroes there are mere tokens or are really integrated into the school system. But you cannot, under any circumstances, claim that Lincoln is now or ever has been an interracial school. Maybe it is much like the experiment that most children have made of putting one drop of ink in a glass of milk and watching the milk turn black and then putting several quarts of milk in a glass of ink in an effort to make the ink turn white. You can't do it.

Lincoln University has been in existence for ninety-five years. In the past, it has had a reasonably good faculty with bright and dark spots. In the past few years and at the present time, it has had an extremely good faculty. It has a great tradition. Although it does not have enough money, it has some money to operate on. Now, will you please tell me why does it not attract white students? The answer to my mind is very simple. Despite all of the things I just mentioned, it is still in the eyes of the public, educators and others a Negro school. That is the sole reason it does not attract white students.

You quite rightfully are proud that the trustee board and the faculty at Lincoln are now interracial. We are all proud of this accomplishment. But that no more makes Lincoln an interracial school than a mixed faculty and a mixed trustee board would make an otherwise white school an interracial school. Lincoln has made progress, but for some reason we do not have a truly interracial student body.

You heard me explain at the meeting the uncontradicted testimony of expert witnesses that education by the best faculty in the world in the best equipped school in the world would not afford equal educational advantages unless the student body was a truly representative student body with people of all races, creeds and colors in attendance.

As a result of the vicious theory of segregation in public and private institutions throughout the country, the label "Negro" in connection with *any* institution has branded that institution as inferior and no one wants to go to an inferior school. You can do everything you want to and carry out every plan you have in mind, but as long as Lincoln is labeled a Negro school in the eyes of the public, it will be considered to be inferior.

As mentioned above, I had assumed that you were in full accord with this premise and I considered myself as helping you and Lincoln. If I am in error, then we disagree. My whole life has been devoted to the belief that segregation was wrong and it had to be removed from American life. I am most certainly not alone in this determination. When I express this belief, whether it be before Congress, in the courts of the deepest South, in the United States Supreme Court, in a social gathering or at Lincoln University, I am not rabbling, but dead serious. If we don't agree, I do hope that we now understand each other.

Sincerely yours,

Thurgood Marshall

In his equally pointed reply, Bond wrote: "To be frank, it seems to me that what you . . . mean by interracial is WHITE."

MARSHALL TO WILLIAM WINSTON

Winston, the president of the Bridgeport (Connecticut) NAACP, had inquired about the NAACP's policy on labor issues, and Marshall takes the occasion to criticize quota systems in labor practices.

JULY 27, 1949

Dear Mr. Winston:

The purpose of this letter is to advise you of the official policy of the National Association for the Advancement of Colored People regarding the concept of separate quota systems for colored workers in hiring and firing, and also our official policy with regard to so-called "super seniority."

It has long been a cardinal point in the program of the Association to strongly oppose any idea that would distinguish colored citizens as a unique or separate group apart from the rest of the American people. The essence of the proposed plan for a separate quota system is segregation; therefore, we are forced to vigorously oppose this concept.

The NAACP cannot countenance any such labor philosophy that indicates segregation. Once a union establishes separate seniority lists for colored members, it can then logically proceed to establish separate job classifications, separate departments, separate membership lists, meetings, cafeterias, and eventually separate unions based on color.

If there are members of the Association who are at present proposing this idea, then it is your responsibility to inform them that they are violating the official and established program upon which the national Association has been successfully operating for over forty years.

The Association has been fighting against those trade unions which have been guilty of Jim Crow practices, that is, maintaining separate seniority lists of colored workers, among other things. It is entirely out of the question for a local branch of the Association to call upon the trade union movement to institute a Jim Crow quota system.

Sincerely yours,

Thurgood Marshall

MARSHALL TO ROBERT SILBERSTEIN

Although Marshall sometimes clashed with Tom Clark during his tenure at the Department of Justice, Marshall found Clark to be the best attorney general among those with whom he had worked. Clark had given Marshall helpful counsel in dealing with Hoover, he had given public speeches about protecting African Americans, and his leadership at Justice had backed Marshall's courtroom victories. Marshall credited Clark especially with advancing the right of African Americans to vote in the South. As Marshall put it, after the victory in the Texas primary case, Clark "told the other states they'd better fall in line or he'd whack them one." Interestingly, the following note to the executive secretary of the National Lawyers Guild can now be found in the FBI files.

AUGUST 2, 1949

Dear Bob:

I have received your memorandum of July 29, 1949, concerning the appointment of Tom Clark to the United States Supreme Court.

I am opposed to the intensive Guild campaign to reject the nomination of Tom Clark. On July 29, I sent the following telegram to Attorney General Clark: "Our sincerest congratulations, etc."

Thurgood Marshall

A. P. TUREAUD TO MARSHALL

Tureaud, the leading NAACP attorney in Louisiana, pleads for help in response to the intimidation of African American activists by local authorities. Especially noteworthy in this letter is Tureaud's report that law enforcement officials used imprisoned African Americans to assist them with their brutal tactics. Of course, plaintiffs were not the only ones to face brutality and threats. As the attorney in several important civil rights cases, Tureaud himself was subject to numerous threats, including the one in this note:

> *WELL OLD BUZZARD TUREAUD. YOU ARE AT IT AGAIN. YOU KEPT QUIET FOR AWHILE AND THEN YOU CAME ALIVE. BETTER GET BACK IN YOUR SHELL. THERE IS A NICE ALLIGATOR IN A SWAMP THAT WOULD MAKE*

A GOOD MEAL OUT OF YOU. I LOOKED RIGHT INTO YOUR FACE THE OTHER DAY. I CAN PUT MY HANDS ON YOUR SHOULDER ANY HOUR OF THE DAY OR NIGHT. YOU WILL NOT BE HARD TO PICK UP. ALSO TELL YOUR FRIEND KANGAROO THURGOOD MARSHALL TO GO BACK HOME BEFORE OUR TEXAS BRANCH GETS ANGRY AND DUMPS HIM IN A SHARK HOLE. BEWARE!!! LAST WARNING. STAY QUIET AND STAY OUT OF THE LIMELIGHT IF YOU BOTH WANT TO LIVE. WE ARE WELL ORGANIZED IN NEW ORLEANS AND THE HOUR IS NOT FAR FOR US TO STRIKE. SOME WHITE TRASH WILL BE PICKED UP WHO HAVE BEEN STURRING THINGS UP.

KKK

AUGUST 4, 1949

Dear Thurgood:

Recently I filed suit against the St. Andrew Parish School Board to equalize facilities and provide bus transportation on behalf of Negro citizens. A motion was filed to extend the time to answer. More recently, Louis Thierry, . . . one of the plaintiffs in this suit, was arrested and jailed on July 28 on charge of gambling and/or operating a place of business on Sunday in violation of the Sunday closing law. When placed in jail, Thierry was beaten by Negro cellmates, presumably on orders. Without his solicitation, one August Fontenot, Sr., father of the district attorney of St. Andrew Parish, also named August Fontenot, came to the jail and offered his assistance, suggesting meanwhile that Thierry sign certain documents, withdrawing from the case. Thierry at first refused to sign and was returned to his cell with the admonition that any harm which may come to him will be due to his own folly. He subsequently agreed to sign the documents whereupon he was immediately released and taken back to his home in the car of August Fontenot, Sr., who in the course of conversation advised Thierry not to reveal what had transpired. Thierry was further told by Fontenot that he merely did what he did for him for a favor and to avoid more serious consequences.

I have been informed that two other plaintiffs in this same case have been induced to sign some form of document for the same purpose.

Thierry is fearful that harm may come to him. He doesn't feel secure and constantly lives in fear of his own safety. It would be appreciated if you would take this matter up direct with the United States Department of Justice.

This is the same parish in which three Negroes . . . were driven from the registration office on June 28.

Sincerely yours,

A. P. Tureaud

WALTER WHITE TO MARSHALL

The board of the NAACP LDF had earlier prevented Marshall from filing a "friend of the court" brief in the case of the Hollywood Ten (see December 20, 1948, letter), and White can barely hide his irritation here as he asks for an update.

NOVEMBER 16, 1949

Dear Thurgood:

Is it true that the NAACP filed a brief amicus in the Hollywood Ten case? The communists are ballyhooing the statement that we did file such a brief along with the Civil Rights Congress, the Council on African Affairs and the American Slav Congress. Since all three of those groups are classified as communist, our reported joining in with them, along with the alarming taking over or infiltration of our branches out here by the communists or their total eclipse of our branches as at Richmond, has done us no good. Last year Richmond had 600 members; today it hasn't one, Noah tells me.

What hurts us most so far as Hollywood is concerned is that a great many people who are neither communist nor anti-communist and have been fighting for more decent picturization of the Negro on the screen are annoyed at the quotation of the NAACP saying that the Hollywood Ten are the only ones who have worked on this issue. They point out that except for a few speeches like that of Dalton Trumbo at the world writers' conference in 1941 or 1942, all the accused have rendered only lip service while non-communists have made pictures like *Home of the*

Brave, *Lost Boundaries*, *Intruders in the Dust*, *Pinky* and other pictures and documentaries already made or to be made. They resent the communists or alleged communists being given credit for something which they had nothing whatever to do with. Mind you, these are not reactionaries but people who have been battling for years for us and whose efforts are just now showing results.

If pro-Negro pictures make money, our filing a brief amicus isn't going to stop more pictures from being made. But the brief has materially lessened the influence of the NAACP in Hollywood. As I pointed out when the filing of a brief was discussed at a meeting of the Inc. Fund Board last spring, we have enough issues of free speech to fight without becoming involved in the very tangled Hollywood Ten case.

Ever sincerely,

Walter

In his reply, Marshall did not answer the implied charge that his filing of the brief ran counter to the earlier board vote.

MARSHALL TO COMMISSIONER FRANKLIN RICHARDS

This letter to the FHA commissioner is a perfect example of Marshall's civil—and yet relentlessly aggressive—efforts to change the racist attitudes and actions of powerful leaders in government.

DECEMBER 7, 1949

Dear Commissioner Richards:

Thanks for sending me a copy of the statement of Solicitor General Philip B. Perlman which was made last Friday. Since that time we have watched with interest varied newspaper comments and alleged statements of yours. The story in the New York *Herald Tribune* yesterday was particularly vicious and at first blush gave the appearance that you were making statements in direct conflict with the spirit of Solicitor General Perlman's statement.

The *Herald Tribune* story reported that one of your top field associates said, "You can't change economics, and there is no doubt that in most cases the entrance of a Negro into a white section will adversely affect values." This statement, taken in connection with earlier statements in the article that FHA will continue to consider the "compatibility among neighborhood occupants," gives the impression that FHA intends to operate as before. Of course there are some of us who know this is not correct and that earlier this year efforts were made to change that policy by means of a memorandum of February 18, 1949.

In the meantime, we have refused to make any specific statements requested by the press because we are more interested in getting the job done than in contributing to the confusion being brought about by interests which are contrary to our principles.

It is obvious, however, that you as commissioner of FHA should make it clear to the public that your interest is in carrying through on this new policy and is not, as reported in the press, to make narrow constructions in order to give aid and comfort to those in this country who are determined to continue and to expand racial segregation in public as well as private housing. In other words, we believe that you should follow the pattern as set down by President Truman, who, in addressing our annual convention in 1947, stated:

> Our case for democracy should be as strong as we can make it. It should rest on practical evidence that we have been able to put our own house in order.
>
> For these compelling reasons, we can no longer afford the luxury of a leisurely attack upon prejudice and discrimination. There is much that state and local governments can do in providing positive safeguards for civil rights. But we cannot, any longer, await the growth of a will to action in the slowest state or the most backward community.
>
> Our national government must show the way.

Sincerely yours,

Thurgood Marshall

MARSHALL TO JOHN MCCRAY

Marshall pens an angry letter to the editor of The Lighthouse and Informer, *a black newspaper in Columbia, South Carolina. A recent editorial in the paper had accused lawyers on the NAACP's national staff of enjoying comfortable salaries and national exposure while underpaying attorneys in local NAACP cases.*

DECEMBER 12, 1949

Dear John:

I have just received the copy of an editorial from *The Lighthouse and Informer* captioned "Lawyers Sabotaging the NAACP?"

To be perfectly frank, this editorial in your newspaper shocked me. We have always considered you and the newspaper you represent as friends who would at least give us an opportunity to clarify the facts involved before publishing such an editorial. Here are a few of these facts:

1. In the first place, I do not believe that you have been at all fair to the majority of the lawyers who have worked for the Association. With the exception of the time that Charlie Houston was on the payroll of this Association (incidentally, at a smaller salary than he was getting as dean of the Howard Law School, which job he left to come to the NAACP), Houston has not collected on any NAACP cases that I know of.
2. Governor Hastie has never received more than expenses and in many instances has not received expenses on NAACP cases.
3. Colonel Walden, for almost as many years as you and I have lived, has worked for the NAACP for nothing, and it is only in recent years that he has insisted on being paid small amounts. . . .

. . .

I have taken the position since I have been special counsel that lawyers working for the NAACP should be paid something for their services. The doctors of the NAACP do not treat members free; nor do the dentists. The undertakers in the Association do not bury members without remuneration. This same situation holds for all other professional and business people in the Association. In many instances, Negro lawyers have worked unselfishly on behalf of their people in the courts for nothing or close to nothing, and in return have not even been retained on legal affairs by the people for whom they have fought. This policy has been prevalent throughout the South, and I can only give three individual examples contrary to this general rule in the South.

While insisting that our lawyers be paid something, I have on all occasions made it clear that they cannot be paid the prevailing rate for their services, but should be paid a smaller amount, in most instances not exceeding $25.00 per day for actual work. Such an amount could certainly not be considered a fee in any sense of the word.

Not only have NAACP lawyers not been paid the prevailing rate for lawyers, but they have not even been paid the amount that is customary for such work in kindred fields. . . .

You will remember that in the primary case in South Carolina, the lawyers on the other side were paid $50,000 for *losing* the case. In dollars and cents, I wonder what it was worth to win it. . . .

. . .

At times I get a little anxious about people who have no regard whatsoever for the amount of time necessary for lawyers to prepare this involved type of litigation. In these instances, we are not dealing with a divorce case, or a personal injury case, or an action on a promissory note, or any of the run-of-the-mill type of cases that can be prepared in an hour or a day or so. We are dealing with a very involved situation, and we are up against very tough legal opposition, which has at its disposal all of the financial resources of the county, the state, and the Dixiecrat movement.

Finally, I say to you in all frankness that it is difficult for me to understand exactly how we are expected to run this Association and to accomplish a difficult job when so much of our time, which could and should be used in fighting the opposition, is taken up by explaining the *actual facts* to readers of an editorial such as yours. You know as well as I do that our people are usually apt to forget the numerous attributes and achievements of an organization such as ours and to remember only this type of criticism. These critical attitudes, whether valid or not, are used as a rationale for not supporting the basic goals of the Association.

If you want to destroy this Association, I know of no better way than to impute motives of personal gain to lawyers associated with our legal battle. Actually, unfounded assertions on the part of people outside the organization cannot destroy the reputation and strength of the organization itself. This letter is being written to you as a friend, because I wanted you to know how deeply we feel about this first attack ever made on the lawyers of our Association. I do not write in a personal vein, but rather in an attempt to affect future cooperation.

It is probably true that NAACP lawyers have gained considerable recognition from their work on Association cases, but it is my feeling that both Negro and white citizens have gained more than any individual lawyer. Certainly my role in the South Carolina primary case has afforded me great personal satisfaction. But my satisfaction was based solely upon the fact that Negroes in South Carolina now have the right of franchise and that to some degree I was instrumental in securing that right. I do not believe that you really think that any of my satisfaction stemmed from the dollars and cents involved in the litigation.

. . .

Sincerely,

Thurgood Marshall

MARSHALL TO ELIZABETH WARING

In his February 16 memo to Walter White, Marshall called for direct political action, and here he offers lavish praise on the National Emergency Civil Rights Mobilization, a lobbying effort organized by more than fifty national groups to secure passage of Truman's civil rights program. Segregationist politicians, of course, were doing everything within their power to defeat the proposed bills, including one to establish a federal Fair Employment Practices Commission (FEPC) and another to stiffen penalties for lynching. A delegation of the civil rights group headed by Roy Wilkins, the acting secretary of the NAACP, visited Truman at the White House, and when Wilkins began to read a prepared statement, the president interrupted him. "You don't need to make that speech to me," Truman said. "It needs to be made to senators and congressmen." The letter below is additional evidence of Marshall's belief that movement activities (for example, lobbying, rallies, strikes, and so on) were sometimes just as important as legal maneuvering.

JANUARY 23, 1950

Dear Mrs. Waring:

. . .

Our Emergency Civil Rights Mobilization in Washington the weekend of January 15th was a tremendous success. We expected 1200 to 1500 delegates from fifteen states. We had 4,037 delegates from thirty-three states and the District of Columbia. They flooded Capitol Hill, saw their congressmen and senators and made a marvelous impression. They also sent a delegation to see the President and the congressional leaders. They have returned home with a renewed determination to keep up the heat on our civil rights program. All in all, I think it is the finest job by this Association to date. We had a terrific job keeping the communists out of the meetings and out of control of the mobilization. On the other hand, the communists were determined to disrupt everything. I am happy to report that they did not reach first base and we kept most of them out. Those who had credentials from recognized organizations were kept under control by a floor committee.

I am enclosing a press release which will give you a brief idea of the meeting. Thanks again for your speech and your continued cooperation in our very difficult job.

The best of everything to you and our judge. We are all looking forward to seeing the two of you next month.

Sincerely yours,

Thurgood Marshall

MARSHALL TO LOUIS LAUTIER

In this letter to the popular columnist for the National Negro Press of America, Marshall states his reasons for wanting to keep the communists, as well as other "left-wing organizations," out of the civil rights movement. It is the strongest expression in any of his letters of the disdain in which he held the communist movement.

JANUARY 25, 1950

Dear Louis:

As you know, it is not often that I have what I consider to be a quarrel with you about your columns or your reporting, but I hated to see you on the other side in your column this week concerning our Mobilization in Washington. . . .

The exclusion of certain organizations from the mobilization was made by the steering committee composed of fifty-five organizations, of which the NAACP was only one. Prior to that time, the committee of representatives of our branches from all sections of the country met to start the ball rolling for the mobilization, and that committee with only one dissenting vote excluded these left-wing organizations. The reason was obvious. They only wanted those organizations which really want civil rights legislation, rather than organizations which merely use civil rights and the Negro for their own selfish purpose. You will remember that as long as Russia was fighting against the United States in the war, left-wing organizations were fighting for the FEPC and everything else in the hope of crippling the war effort. However, as soon as Stalin and the United States joined hands, the left-wing organizations sold Mose down the river and refused to take part in anything on behalf of Mose because it might hinder the war effort. Since the war, they have used the Negro problem only insofar as it could be tied up with their own personal problems. In other words, they have only used the Negro and civil rights where it was for their own advantage, and they have not demonstrated anything on which we can rely.

In the past two years, they have always tied together our legal cases with their fight for world peace, as they call it. They have no hesitancy in connecting the Sweatt case with the Communist Eleven case in New York, although there is no connection between the two. If they had been permitted to take over at our Mobilization, we would have had them going to Congress hollering about the Marshall Plan, the Atlantic Pact and the Communist Eleven trials at the expense of the civil rights legislation. We have got to part with ideologies and get down to business, and if we don't, Mose will really be sold down the river.

. . .

Finally, as to your cracks about seeking political appointments . . . As for myself, I think that I have given at least as much as I have been hired to give, and I have a suspicion that I have given more than that. I doubt that I would voluntarily have gone into the Deep South so many times on these cases if it were just a matter of business rather than the interest in the problem equal to the others who have worked so hard on this job.

On the other hand, the comrades have never gone into the Deep South at a time when the cases were hot—when there were threats of violence to the lawyers and their clients or when there was real danger involved. Rather, the record will show that they have always waited until the danger has passed, at least in part, before trying by ulterior, underhanded and backdoor methods to get into cases which we have been fighting. I have always been fair and tolerant with them but I do not intend to let them disrupt our work, and I do not intend to be a party to their using our plight and our problem for the purpose of buying the newspaper presses and other items for the benefit of their cause rather than our cause. I prefer to stick with those who consider the Negroes' problem the top problem and the one for major emphasis and to block efforts of selfish interests, whoever they might be, from blocking us at every turn.

. . .

Sincerely yours,

Thurgood Marshall

P.S. Although I consider this letter personal and confidential, I want you to know that I am sharing a copy of it with Bill Hastie because I think the three of us know each other well enough to permit me to do so.

MARSHALL TO THE EDITOR OF *THE NEW YORK TIMES*

When commenting on Sweatt v. Painter, et al., *the case to integrate the University of Texas School of Law, Arthur Krock, a reporter for* The New York Times, *wrote about the "equality" that existed between the University of Texas and the "Negro University" in Houston, and favorably summarized the pro-segregationist arguments of the attorney general of Texas. After reading the article, Marshall sent the following telegram to Maceo Smith and others: "Read Arthur Krock's column in today's* New York Times *and get as many letters of protest as possible air mail to* Times.*" Marshall's own letter of protest is below.*

APRIL 19, 1950

Dear Sir:

Arthur Krock's column in yesterday's *Times* gave a completely one-sided version of several cases now pending before the United States Supreme Court. In presenting the argument of the attorney general of Texas in the case of *Sweatt v. Painter, et al.*, Mr. Krock used arguments of the attorney general as facts rather than as mere argument. In the first place, the University of Texas is not truly a school for "Caucasians." As a matter of fact, the student body of the University of Texas includes all racial and ethnic groups except Negroes.

As one of the lawyers in the case, I do not intend to argue the case in the press while it is pending before the Supreme Court. I do, however, wish to call to your attention briefs filed by representatives other than those directly involved in the litigation. For example, the Solicitor General of the United States in this case and among other arguments stated:

> *Under the Constitution every agency of government, federal and state, must treat our people as Americans, and not as members of particular groups divided according to race, color, region, or national ancestry. All citizens stand equal and alike in relation to their government, and no distinctions can be made among them because of race or color or other irrelevant factors. The color of a man's skin has no constitutional significance. If the Constitution is construed to permit the enforced segregation of Negroes, there would be no constitutional barrier against singling out other groups in the community and subjecting them to the same kind of discrimination.*

. . .

Many other briefs were filed by organizations such as the Federal Council of Churches, the CIO, the AF of L, American Veterans Committee, and others. We believe that in all fairness either Mr. Krock or someone else on the *Times* should have presented both sides of the controversy.

Yours very truly,

Thurgood Marshall

Although the Times *did not run Marshall's letter, the newspaper did publish one written by John Frank, a professor at Yale University Law School and one of the attorneys filing a brief in favor of Sweatt's case against Texas. In his sharp rebuke, Frank wrote: "If the schools are equal, how accept the following facts? (1) . . . in legal education the important matter is to have specialists in charge of the teaching of each subject. Texas (colored) is necessarily manned by jacks of all trades. (2) The faculty at Texas (white) is truly distinguished. . . . The faculty at Texas (colored) has never been heard of before. (3) Texas (white) gives students the choice of seventy-five courses. Texas (colored) cannot approach this choice. (4) The library of Texas (white) is about three times as large as the library of Texas (colored). (5) Texas (white) has law review, moot court, and legal aid work for its students which cannot be equaled or perhaps even attempted at Texas (colored)."*

MARSHALL TO JUDAH CAHN

Judah Cahn, a member of the NAACP's board of directors, had asked Roy Wilkins to wire him a resolution about South Africa that he could put before the Central Conference of American Rabbis, and below is Marshall's reply. The South African government of Premier Daniel Malahan had been passing legislation aimed at widening the segregation of the races, and recent legislation sought to divide the country into separate geographical areas for each race. Marshall's telegram here is especially significant because he so rarely commented on issues of foreign policy.

JUNE 7, 1950

Roy out of office. South Africa racial strife between natives and Indians brought about solely because of intolerable conditions as result of governmentally imposed racial restrictions on natives, Indians and all non-whites. Just checked to present conditions, which are even worse as result of new governmentally imposed restrictions based upon race or color. Organization should adopt forceful resolution condemning governmentally imposed racial restrictions which brought about riots and the refusal to take any steps to prevent recurrences instead of passing new regulations to intensify racial conditions. One informed source reports that "if you think Mississippi is bad for darker people, you should see South Africa."

Thurgood Marshall

In spite of what he wrote above, two months later Marshall would refer to Mississippi as "the worst hole in the world."

MARSHALL TO PAULI MURRAY

On June 5, Charles Elmore Cropley, the clerk of the Supreme Court, wired Marshall this brief message: "Judgments Sweatt and McLaurin cases reversed." A day later, Walter White, back in the helm at the NAACP after his marriage to Poppy Cannon, sent the following wire to NAACP supporters across the nation: "Yesterday the United States Supreme Court in two monumental decisions, Sweatt v. University of Texas *and* McLaurin v. University of Oklahoma, *struck the most devastating blow in American history against educational segregation and discrimination. This marks most advanced position won by forty-one years of struggle by NAACP." The Supreme Court ruled that Texas had to admit Sweatt to the University of Texas Law School and that Oklahoma had to allow McLaurin to sit with white students in classrooms and other social settings at the University of Oklahoma. On behalf of his fellow justices, all of them, Chief Justice Vinson wrote: "A law school, the proving ground for legal learning and practice, cannot be effective in isolation." The justices did not overturn the separate but equal precedent established in* Plessy, *but they came quite close to doing so.*

Like countless others, Anna "Pauli" Murray—a civil rights activist, future cofounder of the National Organization of Women (NOW), and author of States' Laws on Race and Color, *a detailed description of legal discrimination against persons of color (1950)—had sent Marshall a letter of congratulations. In a letter he wrote a day earlier about the Supreme Court victory, an optimistic Marshall stated something similar to what appears below: "The end has not yet been reached but it is most certainly in sight."*

Unfortunately, just two months before the monumental decision, Charles Houston, the original driving force behind school desegregation and Marshall's ongoing consultant and dear friend, died of heart failure. "I don't know of anything I did in the practice of law that wasn't the result of what Charles Houston banged into my head," Marshall stated years later.

JUNE 9, 1950

Dear Pauli:

Thanks for your letter of congratulations on the Sweatt and McLaurin cases. Of course it would have been good for the court to have overruled *Plessy v. Ferguson*, but a careful reading of the opinions will show that for all intents and purposes, *Plessy v. Ferguson* has been gutted. It can be that the Court took the position that *Plessy v. Ferguson* did not actually set out this doctrine which has been used so many times. At any rate and whatever way you look at it, the end is in sight, and in view of the fact that the opinion was unanimous, there is little doubt as to what will happen on future cases to be brought.

Thanks again for your continued cooperation.

Sincerely,

Thurgood Marshall

MARSHALL TO JAMES IVY

Marshall sends Ivy, the new editor of The Crisis, *the NAACP's magazine, a rather harsh memorandum to clarify the significance of the recent Supreme Court rulings in the* Sweatt *and* McLaurin *cases.*

JULY 13, 1950

I hate to interfere with *The Crisis* or any other department of the Association, but the editorial in the July issue on the Supreme Court rulings is to my mind completely off point.

For example, in the second paragraph there is a section that states, "Segregated facilities will not be permitted unless they can be proved equal. And equality and segregation have never been bedfellows." This is followed by the third full paragraph, which states: "Although the Court's decisions are restricted to the two school cases under review, the opinions are applicable to similar cases which might arise in other states. Southern states must either establish equal professional and graduate facilities or admit Negroes to existing white institutions.". . .

This last paragraph would make it appear that the decision in Sweatt and McLaurin cases went no farther than the decision in the Gaines case. This, of course, is not true. As a matter of fact, the decisions in both the Sweatt and the McLaurin cases have been recognized as making it impossible to establish "equality" within the segregated system insofar as graduate and professional schools are concerned. I don't believe anyone doubts that.

All in all, the editorial, to my mind, is going to be used by the "separate but equal" boys as showing that within the NAACP there is serious dispute as to the true meanings of these decisions.

MARSHALL TO ARTHUR SHORES

Arthur Shores was Alabama's most important civil rights attorney during this era, and he worked closely with Marshall on numerous NAACP cases.

OCTOBER 27, 1950

Dear Arthur:

. . .

As to the posse looking for the Negro while we were driving back from Montgomery. You remember I suggested that you slow down passing by the group on the road. I am certainly glad that you did not slow down too much. I am sure what would have happened if they had first charged me with being the one they wanted and I had told them, "I am not him, I am Thurgood Marshall from New York and this is Arthur Shores from Birmingham." I think we would then have had quite a time. At any rate, such is life when you go about doing the Master's business in Alabama.

Sincerely,

Thurgood Marshall

CHAPTER TWELVE

1951

MARSHALL TO ROY WILKINS

At the end of 1950, Marshall had difficulty securing a military clearance so that he could travel to Japan and Korea for the purpose of investigating the army's use of court-martials when dealing with African American soldiers. Marshall had learned from his friends at Baltimore's Afro-American, *especially James Hicks, that African American soldiers in Korea had been arrested and court-martialed in disproportionate numbers. "It is obvious," Marshall had written Bob Ming in November 1950, "that Negro officers are going to be made the 'goats' the same as in World War I and II." Although General Douglas MacArthur did not want Marshall to make the trip, and, with help from the FBI, sought to undermine Marshall's plans, the Truman administration cleared the way for Marshall to travel to Japan and Korea in January 1951. His self-typed letters are among the best in the NAACP Papers for showing not only the gravity of Marshall's work and commitment but also his fun-loving personality.*

FEBRUARY 3, 1951

Dear Roy:

. . .

I leave here early in the morning in a special plane for Korea. I have all my stuff, including four bottles of bourbon for snakebites. Can you imagine it, I had an argument with a general this morning who told me that snakes don't bite in the winter. In case they don't, I can use it for some other purpose.

. . .

Thurgood

Roy:

I almost forgot the most important thing. I need your best advice and badly. I am sure that when I complete this job, the story will be that these boys who were court-martialed got a lousy deal. I doubt that MacArthur will change the segregation policies of the armed forces in Japan, including the honor guard officers in GHQ, officers' and enlisted men's clubs, etc.

> This I will tell when I get back and will pull not a single punch, so help me. On the other hand, we have a war on our hands. It would be my idea to stress the fact that it is the communists who are behind this war. They are killing Negroes right along with the other soldiers. We must not forget who our enemies are. There is no doubt that the communists will play up all of the things I report, so it seems to me that I should make it clear at the outset that the bastards will do that and tell the Negroes to be looking for it but to realize that the same bastards are killing Negro GIs right along with the others. Now . . . is that the right approach and how is the best way to say it? Whatever advice you send, better send a copy c/o Frank Williams just in case I get away from here on schedule, which I seriously doubt.
>
> You know, more and more this trip reminds me of your trip with George through Mississippi. This on-the-spot type of job is what we should do more of (I mean somebody else, not me). I am convinced that this is the most important job I have done. For that reason it is even tougher because I am really up against the best over here. The boys down in GHQ are masters at obfuscation (hope spelled correctly). They must have been trained in some diplomatic school. They are shadow boxing—I am shadow boxing—somebody is going to bump up against his own shadow and get knocked out. Keep your fingers crossed because I have an awfully long shadow.
>
> *TM*

MARSHALL TO THE NAACP OFFICE

Although Truman had issued the executive order to establish equality of treatment and opportunity in the armed forces two years earlier and other branches had begun to desegregate, the army was still segregated in 1950. Indeed, the African American soldiers who had been deployed to Korea were part of the all-black 24th Infantry Regiment. Marshall discovered the reason for the ongoing segregation of the army during his meeting with General Douglas MacArthur, alluded to in the following letter. Years later, Marshall recounted both the meeting with MacArthur and the trials he was investigating:

> *. . . I was given an audience with General MacArthur, and I found it very interesting. I questioned him about the continuation of segregation in the Army and he said he was working on it. And I asked him how many years he'd been working on it, and he didn't really remember how many.*
>
> *I reminded him that at the very time we were talking, the Air Force was completely integrated, and the Navy was quite integrated, and the only group not integrated was the Army. He said that he didn't find the Negroes qualified, and when he found them qualified, they would be integrated.*
>
> *. . .*
>
> *There were records of trials, so-called trials, in the middle of the night where the men were sentenced to life imprisonment in hearings that lasted less than ten minutes. They were the old well-known drumbeat court-martials, done in the heat of passion and in the heat of war. There were fifty or sixty involved. One death penalty case I remember in particular: the record showed that this man was charged with being absent in the presence of the enemy. Instead of being charged with AWOL (Absent Without Leave), he was charged with cowardice in the presence of the enemy. And fortunately for him, he produced two witnesses: a major in the Medical Corps and a lieutenant in the Nurse Corps, both of whom testified that he was in a base hospital the very day that he was supposed to be AWOL.*
>
> *And despite their testimony, he was convicted and given life imprisonment.*

FEBRUARY 12, 1951

Well, I am back in Tokyo. If you don't believe Tokyo is a great place, just go to Korea and Tokyo looks like heaven. They should give Korea "back to the Indians" or somebody. It is almost unbelievable that less than two days ago I was actually north of Seoul at the far north position of our army. I actually flew over and past the front line in a helicopter and looked down on the enemy and then came back to our forward position. You should try it sometime. It is good for my low blood pressure, which is now high. It was higher than that yesterday.

At Kumhae (rear hdq. for the 25th division) we went through all the records of all the court martials of the 25th. The Inspector General and I agreed as to what information we wanted and charts were prepared by the staff. These charts show everything about these trials, the preliminary investigations, race of accused, race of investigator, etc. I have a certified copy of these charts. In addition I checked the actual court-martial records of most of the cases. I also talked to as many men as were behind the line. . . .

The still unanswered question is why so many Negroes are charged with cowardice and so few white soldiers. No one has given me any answer on this yet. I have maintained that Negroes are no more or no less cowards than anyone else.

On Sunday I talked to about seventy key men (enlisted men, including privates, corporals and sergeants) from every company of the 24th and every battalion of the 159th field artillery. We had quite a session. One explanation from these men is that in late July and August they had poor leadership, mostly white officers. Another explanation is that in the white outfits the same types of cases were handled by either reprimanding the man or punishment other than court-martial. (NOTE: See next page for amplification of this paragraph.)

The records also show that in some of the trials ending in life sentences of Negroes four of them took the following trial time: 42 minutes, 44 minutes, and two that took 50 minutes each. Many others took approximately one hour, including all the preliminaries and the other formalities.

Although I am convinced after talking to most of the defense counsel that they were competent, I am equally convinced that they did not have sufficient time to prepare these cases.

We also have undisputed evidence that in several instances the men were questioned about an alleged offense—told to forget about it—put up in the front line and then, after weeks of fighting the enemy day and night, were pulled out of the foxholes, returned to the rear and court-martialed. There are one or two almost unbelievable cases of this.

From Kumhae we hitchhiked a plane ride back to Suwan (cargo plane loaded with gasoline and us). Gasoline was in tanks all around us and we were told not to smoke—not to move around, etc. Suwan is the rear hdq. of the 25th division. Incidentally, I don't understand what they mean by "rear." When we were first there, the rear hdq. was 20 minutes by jeep from the forward hdq.

Saturday was spent in conferences with General Keen and members of his staff, and arrangements were made for Sunday, which was quite a day. At 8 A.M. a helicopter took Col. Martin to the front and returned for me. I left at 8:40; we went almost directly north and actually circled Seoul. It looked rather quiet and peaceful, but a short time after, our artillery again began dropping stuff in the town. We landed at NAERI, which is near KIMPO airstrip, which was taken by our forces early that morning. This had been the new forward command post for the 24th infantry since six that morning.

There were about seventy men from the 24th infantry and the 159th field artillery who had been called back from their positions. There were at least two men from each company and each battery, and I talked to them about what I had been doing and what I had found. We then had questions and it appeared that their main complaint was that they had had inefficient white officers and white officers who resented working with Negro troops. They all believed that the court-martials were excessively harsh. Could not talk to them for more than a couple of hours because the war was still going on and the 24th was not only in the front but was advancing.

Returned to Suwan in a jeep. The helicopter took twenty minutes—the jeep back took more than two hours. I reported to General Keen and gave him my impressions of the whole thing. He made no commitment other than to be sure that I had had an opportunity to investigate everything I wanted to. I ended by giving him our views on integration as the only solution to this problem. Col. Martin and I hitchhiked a plane ride to Taegu Eighth Army Hdq. and waited for transportation back to Tokyo Monday night.

I am to assemble the material I have and make a personal report to Gen. MacArthur and the Chief of Staff on Wednesday. I hope to leave for Honolulu on Thursday night. Will notify you of my address at that time.

TM

ROY WILKINS TO MARSHALL

FEBRUARY 20, 1951

Dear Thurgood:

I think your idea of stressing the fact that the communists are our enemy is an excellent one. The line which they have been striving to get over here in America is that this is a race war of the white nations against the colored nations. Your point, as I understand it, is that the communist soldiers have made no difference between colored and white and that our boys have been treated exactly like the others. In other words, this is not a race war but a war between communists and the western world.

I think, also, that it would be a good tactic to point out that the treatment of the Negro soldiers by their own high command and government will be used by the communists in this country as an argument to weaken resistance to communist armies. In other words, as Americans we have two choices: (a) we can continue to be loyal citizens and defenders of our nation as we have been throughout the years, continuing the fight within our own nation for the correction of inequalities and injustices and the winning of victories, or (b) we can bend an ear to the communists in America and swallow their propaganda that we should not aid our own country in a war against communists. The answer to the latter choice is that Negroes are not communists and never have been, as the record in America shows, and that the communist armies opposing us are killing Negro Americans right and left.

I am not sure this is the best expression of the idea, but I am sure you have a point and the most effective way to get it over will occur to you in the course of your speech. Your audience reaction will tell you whether or not it has been made clear.

You know that during World War I the Germans made special efforts to neutralize American Negro soldiers by throwing over leaflets telling them they should not fight the Germans because, while they were in France, America was lynching their people back home. This trick did not work. There was similar propaganda by the Nazis in World War II but, of course, it had even less effect on American Negroes because the Nazis had made clear their ideas on superior and inferior people so that American Negroes were not impressed. Here it seems to me the line is not as clear as it was in World War II because the communists declare no color line and opportunity for the poor and blah, blah, blah. However, as long as they keep killing Negroes and as long as their system denies the rights of protest, defense of opinion, criticism of the government, freedom of speech, assembly, etc., Sam is smart enough to see that he could not get very far under such a system.

It seems to me your own trip is one indication of the difference in the systems. If, by some miracle, a communist soldier were able to send word back to his family complaining of his treatment, court-martials, conviction and sentence, does anyone imagine that the government would permit a person to come to the front line, examine the records, make a report, return home, institute legal proceedings, speak at protest meetings and in other ways struggle to change the conditions?

It might be that your own trip and the contrast of it to the procedure under the Soviet systems will be the clincher in any arguments with the CP which may be raised at your meetings or in any other discussions. If you choose to do so you might use your trip as a part of your speech, taking a swipe at the commies even if they do not ask any questions that give you an opportunity.

That's all for now.

Sincerely,

Roy

After returning to the United States, Marshall worked with the office of the judge advocate general of the army, and together they "were able to bust every one of the convictions. Although we didn't get them all out scot-free, we got most of them out scot-free, and the others [with] a very short term."

MARSHALL TO MYRTA HARRIS

In this letter to Myrta Harris, of The Annals of the American Academy of Political and Social Science, *Marshall protests changes to his use of "Civil War" in an article he had submitted to the journal.*

MARCH 26, 1951

Dear Miss Harris:

I am returning herewith the proof of the article. You will note that I made very few changes. The most important change occurs in the first sentence. In the original manuscript the words used were "Civil War." In the proof it has come back as the "War between the States." I must insist that the term "Civil War" be used in the published document. The phrase "War between the States" is in vogue, in the main, among Southern officials and adherents to the status quo of the South. In all other sections of the country, the phraseology the "Civil War" is used. I cannot afford to have an article published over my name in which a term associated with pro-segregationists appears. . . .

. . .

Very truly yours,

Thurgood Marshall

Two days later, James Charlesworth, the acting editor of the journal, replied to Marshall's protest. "Your preference for 'the Civil War' as distinguished from 'the War Between the States' is a matter of opinion, and it is therefore your professional privilege to object to a caption which appears under your name and which, in your opinion, reflects a bias. I disagree with you entirely. The so-called 'Civil War' was not a civil war in any respect but has been called one in order to make the acts of Southerners heinous. (In saying this I assure you I have no Southern predilections.) The war which occurred between 1861 and 1865 was a war of independence—the same as the mistitled 'Revolutionary War' of 1776–1783. Now that I have given you my views on this subject, I, nevertheless, hasten to assure you that we shall be glad to change the designation back to 'Civil War,' wherever it appears in your article." Marshall could not let the matter rest, of course, and he replied to Charlesworth two days later: "I am happy and relieved to have your assurance that phrase 'Civil War' will appear in the Annals article as in the original manuscript. The very reasons which you advance for use of the term 'War between the States' make the phrase personally abhorrent to me."

MARSHALL TO OLIVER HILL AND SPOTTSWOOD ROBINSON III

Marshall refers below to the front-page story of the May 12 edition of the Richmond Afro American, *which reported on a petition recently filed by Hill and Robinson to integrate public schools in Prince Edward County, Virginia. Sparking the petition was the bold action of sixteen-year-old Barbara Johns, who had led her fellow students in an April 23 strike protesting inferior condi-*

tions at the segregated Robert Russa Moton High School in Farmville. Because of overcrowding at the school, the local school board had constructed additional structures—tarpaper shacks that lacked proper heating and water-resistant roofs. Frustrated by the board's refusal to construct a new building in a timely manner, the students walked out of school, and Johns, the niece of the militant minister Vernon Johns, appealed for help to Hill and Robinson, the NAACP's attorneys in Richmond. Hill and Robinson did not favor a new all-black school, of course, and although they did not consider Prince Edward County to be the best place to begin their legal campaign against segregated schools in Virginia, the two attorneys filed suit and the case eventually joined four others in the 1954 Brown *decision. In a press release drafted on May 3, Robinson had written: "At a mass meeting held in Farmville, on April 26, attended by approximately 1000 persons, it was unanimously voted by citizens of the county that all future activities with regard to the public high schools of the county would be directed at obtaining opportunities and advantages for the students on a racially non-segregated basis."*

MAY 22, 1951

Dear Peanuts and Spot:

Banks has sent us a copy of the *Afro* for the week of May 12th, and all of us have been busily engaged in singing the praises of the two of you for a marvelous job. We have also been getting copies of the editorials in such great "liberal" newspapers as the Richmond *Times-Dispatch* and the *News Leader*. Things are really moving, and it is apparent that the boys on the other side see the handwriting on the wall.

At any rate, I wanted you to know that all of us in this office send to you our sincerest congratulations on the way the matter has been handled. I hope that Banks or one of you can do a short story which we hope to put in *The Crisis*. We should give as wide publicity as possible to this spontaneous action of the people as well as the legal action.

This gets me to the next point. Both of you should be in Atlanta for our annual convention.

. . .

. . . At any rate, here is the time that we really need all of the help possible. This is going to be the most important convention for the South that we have ever held, and we must make the most of it.

Sincerely,

Thurgood Marshall

ROBERT CARTER TO MARSHALL

With Carter taking the lead, the NAACP filed suit in district court against the board of education of Topeka, Kansas, on February 28, asking the court to invalidate segregation statutes that allowed local school boards to offer segregated education in elementary schools. The attorneys later filed an amendment that sought a permanent injunction that would prevent the school board from establishing separate public schools. In the letter below, Carter describes the financial and administrative difficulties surrounding the case, and his plea at the end of the memo seems ridiculously modest, even amusing, in hindsight. Carter refers below to the NAACP attorney Jack Greenberg and the Topeka attorney Charles Bledsoe.

JUNE 13, 1951

As you know, the trial in Topeka, Kansas, will commence on June 25th. I have written to the Topeka, Kansas, Branch, and to the Kansas State Conference of Branches, telling them that we were attempting to secure a large number of witnesses for this trial and requesting that they be prepared to finance the cost of this case. I have just received a letter from the President of the Topeka, Kansas, Branch, who advises me that up to now they have a total of $10.00, and that they had not heard anything from the Kansas State Conference of Branches, but that they are continuing their efforts to raise money to finance the case. I should think that we would have to proceed on the assumption that the case will have to be handled from the National Office.

. . .

The more I think about this case, the more importance I think it will have on our main objective of securing legal support for our attack on segregation. With the case being tried at the present time, it will either go to the Supreme Court at about the same time the South Carolina case goes to the Supreme Court; or, by the time the South Carolina case reaches the Supreme Court, if we are successful in Topeka, we may have a legal precedent in support of our position that segregation is unconstitutional.

Our possibilities for winning here seem much better than they are in South Carolina, particularly in view of the fact that the statutes involved in this case are permissive and give cities of certain size in Kansas the right to enforce segregation, if they so desire. Thus, the pressure for the maintenance of the segregated system is not as great as it would be in southern communities.

. . . Jack has written Bledsoe and has requested that he make available to us some stenographic help. However, in view of the letter which we received from him, it is highly doubtful that the stenographic help which he makes available will be satisfactory. I would therefore request, in addition to our undertaking the cost of transportation of witnesses and of Jack and myself, that you permit us to take along stenographers from this office to help us in the preparation of this case.

I should think that we ought to be able to do this whole job for a sum not in excess of $1200.00.

I also think that we ought to inform the newspapers—and this can be done at the NNPA meeting, rather than by letter—of this case, and ask that they attempt to have it covered. It would probably help us in that area on the question of fundraising.

I realize that $1200.00 is a big slice of money, but it seems to me that it would be a sum which would be very well invested, in view of the stakes involved.

The court heard the case on June 25, and Carter was quite pleased with the trial. Remarkably, even though the three judges upheld segregation, they ruled that

> *Segregation of white children and colored children in public schools has a detrimental effect upon colored children. The impact is greater when it has the sanction of law; for the policy of separating the races is usually interpreted as denoting the inferiority of the Negro group. A sense of inferiority affects the motivation of a child to learn. Segregation with the sanction of law, therefore, has a tendency to retard the educational development of Negro children and to deprive them of some of the benefits they would receive in a racially integrated school system.*

The NAACP asked the Supreme Court to review the lower court's decision, and this case, like the Virginia case noted above, was ruled into the Brown *decision.*

MARSHALL TO THE EDITOR OF THE *AFRO-AMERICAN*

On May 16, 1950, the NAACP filed suit in federal district court in Charleston, South Carolina, seeking an injunction that would enjoin the local school board from using race as a factor when offering public education to the chil-

dren of Clarendon County. Following conversations with J. Waties Waring, one of the federal judges who would hear the case, Marshall had rewritten his brief at least twice before the sympathetic judge was satisfied that the NAACP was making a direct challenge to segregation. The trial began a year later, on May 28, 1951, before a federal panel of three judges—Waring, George Timmerman, and John Parker—with Marshall and Robert Carter arguing the case for the NAACP. The attorney for South Carolina, Robert McC. Figg, shocked Marshall and his legal team by conceding inequality between white and black schools and asking the panel for time to correct the inequality before ruling on the case. Judge Waring countered by saying that the court still had to address the point in Marshall's brief that questioned the constitutionality of segregated education, and Marshall then launched into his case by calling a wide range of social scientists, including the psychologist Kenneth Clark, to testify about the damaging effects of segregated education on the development of African American children.

JUNE 16, 1951

To the Editor:

Regardless of the decision in the Clarendon County school case, the real heroes are the colored people in South Carolina and especially those in Clarendon County.

Many of us who sit in comfortable and safe homes in other sections of the country will never understand the courage of these people in Clarendon County, a rural, prejudiced, Southern community, who dared the risks involved in their bold challenge to white supremacy.

To their aid came the NAACP state conference under the leadership of James M. Hinton, who has never lost his will to fight for human rights, even after having been almost lynched himself.

The nearest one can get to understanding the enormity of the tasks these people took on is to imagine yourself in their position and to ask yourself the question: "Would I have that much courage?" If you are honest with yourself, the answer would most probably be "No!"

The people of Clarendon County and other sections of South Carolina, Georgia and Alabama crowded the courthouse for the trial knowing that only a small proportion of them could get into the small courtroom.

A very few got seats, a few more stood shoulder to shoulder for hours in the courtroom, which was so crowded that they could not even move.

The others stood outside the door and in the hallway. Many had children with them. All of them were extremely well behaved and were living proof of the determination of our people to seek justice in a lawful manner.

These spectators were neither prosperous nor highly educated. Nor did they come from the big cities. For the most part they came from rural communities and made the trip to Charleston to give their support to the people of Clarendon County.

They knew what havoc segregation wreaks. If anyone ever tells you that colored people want segregation, remind him of these people. It was indeed a wonderful experience to be able to be a witness to this display of greatness in human spirit.

Thurgood Marshall

Robert L. Carter

Five days after Marshall and Carter sent this letter, the three-judge panel upheld segregation in Clarendon County public schools in a 2–1 ruling. Judge Waring was the dissenting voice, and his opinion held little room for interpretation: "We must face without evasion or equivocation the question as to whether segregation in education in our schools is legal or whether it cannot exist under our American system enunciated in the Fourteenth Amendment. If segregation is wrong, then the place to stop it is in the first grade and not in graduate schools. Segregation is, per se, inequality."

On July 21, Marshall and his colleagues filed a petition for appeal to the Supreme Court, asking the Court to rule on the question of whether "racial separation in public elementary and high schools is a constitutionally possible pattern." After initially sending the case back to lower court, the Supreme Court later agreed to review the case, and the Clarendon County case also became one of the landmark cases in the Brown *decision.*

Marshall built quite a reputation during his trials in Charleston throughout the years, and several years later Septima Clark, the leader of SCLC's Citizenship Education Program, wrote of Marshall's alleged wildness in a letter to Elizabeth Waring, the judge's wife: "Later I found that it was a real trait of Marshall's to drink four martinis at lunch and go right back into the courtroom. He could also shoot dice all night and be fresh for his work at 9:00 a.m. in the morning. I was not an eyewitness to these things but the socialites of Charleston and Columbia discussed his ability to think so clearly with little rest."

MARSHALL TO WALTER WHITE

On July 9, the NAACP publicized a telegram that requested that Blatz Brewing Company withdraw its sponsorship of the television show Amos 'n' Andy. *Signed by Walter White, the telegram stated: "In picturization of Negroes as amoral, semi-literate, lazy, stupid, scheming and dishonest, the caricature thus circulated perpetuates and extends a harmful stereotype which went out with the old time minstrel show."*

JULY 11, 1951

Unfortunately I will not be available anytime next week and cannot participate in the preview of the "Amos 'n' Andy" television films. I will be working steadily from tomorrow through Friday of next week on the Clarendon County appeal.

Here are some points which I think should be considered by everyone.

1. "Amos 'n' Andy" shows have been so consistently bad over so long a period of years that I doubt that anything can be done which would be acceptable to me. If, on the other hand, there was a complete, and I mean complete, change, it would be good.
2. Regardless of what CBS is doing for Negroes in the industry and regardless of how many individual jobs they may give to Negroes in the industry on any number of shows, this could not in any form or fashion balance off the injury done by "Amos 'n' Andy."

Say, for example, CBS has put on Negro singers, dancers and other entertainers. This would do no more than to recognize what everyone recognizes, including those in the deepest South, and that is that Negroes are entertainers and good ones. This would accomplish nothing other than to give some people jobs.

On the other hand, the "Amos 'n' Andy" show in its entirety continuously makes it clear that Negroes are no good at anything else and that as a people they are everything that is wrong. At the end of a few years of these types of programs, CBS would merely have established that there are some good Negro entertainers but that all of the Negroes are guilty of everything that is bad. I would not consider this to be a bargain. I think we should stick to our guns that "Amos 'n' Andy" and everything like it has to go and that there is nothing that CBS, Blatz Beer, Schenley or anyone else can do to remedy this continuing harm.

I would like very much to have this view expressed to the group of people who are to see the "Amos 'n' Andy" pictures.

MARSHALL TO THE EDITOR OF *THE NEW YORK TIMES*

In mid-July, Henry Clark, an African American bus driver and veteran of World War II, had attempted to move his family into an apartment in an all-white neighborhood in Cicero, a working-class suburb of Chicago. Clark's attempt provoked three nights of violence by white mobs numbering in the thousands. White rioters broke into Clark's apartment, threw his furniture into the street, and set fire to both the furniture and the apartment building. Governor Adlai Stevenson then deployed five hundred National Guard troops to the scene to establish order. The New York Times *covered the story in detail, and it also carried an editorial, excerpted here, on the outrageous aftermath of the riots:*

> *The convening of a federal grand jury to inquire further into the Cicero riots of last July gives some hope that the persons responsible for this shameful episode may at last be brought to punishment. The rioting itself was bad enough, designed as it was to prevent a peaceful Negro family from occupying a legally rented apartment in an all-white district. But the sequel was, if anything, worse. For instead of cracking down on the leaders of a mob that disgraced the nation, the Cook County grand jury returned two indictments naming just six people, including the lawyer for the Negro family and three persons concerned with the ownership or rental of the apartment house!*

OCTOBER 26, 1951

To the Editor of *The New York Times*:

I have just returned to the office and wish to take this opportunity to thank *The New York Times* for its editorial on Tuesday, October 23rd, entitled "Aftermath in Cicero."

The viciousness of the outbreak in Cicero and the contempt for law and order by the residents of Cicero are violent evidence of the type of bigotry and prejudice which must be eradicated if true democracy is to survive in this country.

Many Americans have been led to believe that all Negro residents destroy or lower property values. This is, of course, not true, and the United States Supreme Court in the Louisville segregation case in 1919 made it clear that this belief could not be used to deprive Negroes of the right to occupy real property.

Public exposure and censure of this type of lawlessness are among the most effective methods of bringing home to the nation as a whole the dangerously anti-democratic nature of racial hatreds and prejudices which are directly responsible for the Cicero incident. In this regard, *The New York Times* has rendered a significant public service.

The action of Criminal Court Judge Wilbert Crowley in quashing the indictments against the owners of the property and other victims of the Cicero rioters is evidence of the determination of many of our judges to place the law of the land above bigotry and prejudice. We doubt that anything will be accomplished to punish the actual rioters by the Cook County authorities. We, therefore, hope that the federal grand jury investigation will lead to prosecution of the guilty parties by the federal government.

Unfortunately, there are too many places like Cicero in the United States, and everyday prejudice and hatred against Negroes and other minority groups result in deprivation of basic civil rights. Most of these incidents, being of a less violent nature than the Cicero outbreak, do not get widespread publicity. It is to be hoped that the exposure of the true nature of the Cicero riot will aid in the effort to eliminate racial prejudice, hatred and discrimination in the United States.

Very truly yours,

Thurgood Marshall

CHAPTER THIRTEEN

1952–1954

MARSHALL TO WINSTON ROBERTSON

Marshall sends an inspiring note to Robertson, the financial secretary of the New Rochelle NAACP, shortly after the December 25 murders of Harry T. Moore, the head of the Florida NAACP, and his wife, Harriet. The two had been celebrating their twenty-fifth wedding anniversary when a bomb exploded in their house in Mims, Florida. Moore, one of the most courageous leaders of the NAACP at the grassroots level, had led a campaign to raise funds for the defendants in the 1949 Groveland rape case in Florida.

JANUARY 8, 1952

Dear Mr. Robertson:

This will acknowledge with sincere appreciation the contribution of $50.00 from the New Rochelle branch toward the work of our Association.

We are moving along and we believe we are getting some things accomplished despite the vicious characters, such as those who bombed the home of one of our main officers in Florida and killed him on Christmas night, and despite other bombings, riots, etc., we are still convinced that the majority of Americans are opposed to such violence and are actually in favor of both justice and equality for all. We will continue to refuse to be intimidated and will continue to press forward. With the cooperation of friends and the NAACP branches, there is always assurance that we will make justice mean something in the world today.

Again many thanks for your contribution.

Sincerely,

Thurgood Marshall

MARSHALL TO TOURIST COURT JOURNAL COMPANY

MARCH 28, 1952

Gentlemen:

One of your readers has forwarded to us a copy of the editorial page of your *Journal* for September 1951, indicating the reply of the editors to letters received by them.

On page 16, at the top of the page, there is a letter which the editors entitled "Color Line," which states as follows:

> *Sirs: We are subscribers to your magazine and enjoy reading it very much. We have found a lot of help through it, in that we are contemplating buying a tourist court. But the colored situation is quite a problem here, and we wondered if you could give us some suggestions on just how to handle it. I understand you cannot turn them down.*

The editors' reply to this letter was as follows:

> *There are many ways to kill a cat. Should undesirable persons come to the desk to register, simply ask them if they have a reservation. If they do not (which of course they will not have) then tell them that you only have accommodations for the reservations which have been made. Use great care in accepting reservations by phone; don't cash the checks or money orders of the paid-in-advance mail reservations until the party arrives and you see that he is acceptable to you. There are many more methods, but using common sense and adaptations to these basic ideas will keep those you don't want out.*

"Detroit 27, Michigan," following the letter received from the reader [the anonymous signature on the published letter], indicates that the letter came from the state of Michigan, where there is a state law prohibiting discrimination in places of public accommodation and a state public policy announced by the courts in the state of Michigan opposing racial discrimination. It, therefore, appears to us that your reply to the writer is one which urges and encourages the writer to violate the law and public policy of the state of Michigan. We question your right to the use of the United States mails to send a publication which urges your readers to violate the laws of their state.

In view of this, we would like to know whether you would reconsider the reply which you made to your reader and whether you will retract your statements and, in place of your original letter, publish a second letter urging the reader to comply with the laws of his or her state.

Yours very truly,

Thurgood Marshall

MARSHALL TO PRESIDENT HARRY TRUMAN

Marshall met with Lieutenant Leon Gilbert, an African American soldier, several times during his trip to Korea, and here he pleads Gilbert's case to Truman. After he had been convicted of "refusing to advance with his command which had been ordered forward," Gilbert appealed the decision. "I did not refuse to obey the order," he protested. "I was trying to explain why it couldn't be carried out. Then I considered it my duty as an officer to show why the order meant certain death." The order, given by the white commanding officer of Gilbert's African American regiment, was to take position on top of a hill that Gilbert knew was heavily guarded by Korean troops. After the case received international attention, Truman commuted Gilbert's death sentence and gave him a prison sentence of twenty years.

APRIL 30, 1952

My Dear Mr. President:

I am writing to you concerning the case of Lt. Leon A. Gilbert, formerly Company A, 24th Infantry Regiment, APO 25, who was sentenced to death on September 6, 1950, and whose sentence was commuted by you to twenty years on November 27, 1950. You may recall that, in essence, the charge against Lt. Gilbert was that he failed to perform his duty in the face of the enemy by refusing to obey a direct order. His defense was that despite his sterling military record up until that time, he was overcome by a psychological inability to act under the circumstance.

You will also remember that you reduced his death sentence to twenty years' imprisonment. The injustice of the sentence which Gilbert now serves is emphasized by recent newspaper reports which tell of the refusal of certain Air Force officers to fly their planes in preparation for combat in Korea. The newspapers tell that one of such officers has been sentenced to two years, in striking contrast to the death sentence originally given Gilbert, and that court-martial charges are not being pressed against some of the others. Yet what immobilized these men was no different from what overcame Gilbert at the time he subjected himself to the death penalty, to which he was actually sentenced.

While we recognize the difference between the circumstances surrounding the conviction of Lt. Gilbert and the refusal to obey direct orders by the Air Force officers, it is difficult to explain this difference to the general public, and as a matter of fact, there is enough similarity between the two to justify reconsideration of the case of Lt. Gilbert by you. We would, therefore, respectfully urge that the sentence of Lt. Gilbert be commuted to the time he has actually served to date and that Lt. Gilbert be given an opportunity to reenlist in the Army as a private, thereby retaining his services for our government.

Respectfully,

Thurgood Marshall

Truman reduced the soldier's sentence once again in September 1952, this time to seventeen years, and Gilbert later gained his release, with a dishonorable discharge, in 1955.

MARSHALL TO PRESIDENT HARRY TRUMAN

In his June 13 commencement speech at Howard University, Truman called upon Congress to enact the civil rights legislation he had submitted in 1948. In words that must have been deeply appealing to Marshall, Truman stated: "I am not one of those who feel that we can leave these matters to the state alone, or that we can rely solely on the efforts of men of good will. Our federal government must live up to the ideals proposed in our Declaration of Independence and the duties imposed upon it by our Constitution. The full force and power of the federal government must stand behind the protection of rights guaranteed by our federal Constitution."

Around the same time, Dwight Eisenhower, who was preparing to run for the Republican nomination for president, commented on a proposed Fair Employment Practices Commission (FEPC) by stating that the issue of fair employment should be left to the states. Eisenhower also suggested that integration of the army would result in diminished opportunities for advancement for African American soldiers. Beyond his dislike of Eisenhower, Marshall also found the Republican platform on civil rights to be "worse than just bad."

JUNE 13, 1952

News reports of your Howard speech are superb. Your reaffirmation of the need for adequate civil rights legislation is most encouraging. All true Americans must be still applauding. During periods when civil rights are being shamelessly kicked around, we need and appreciate your fearless stand as a real President in the true American tradition.

MARSHALL TO JAMES HINTON, HOBART LAGRONE, AND MACEO SMITH

Marshall fires up his lieutenants—Hinton, the president of the South Carolina NAACP; LaGrone, the president of the Albuquerque NAACP; and Smith, the president of the Texas NAACP—so that their presentations at the annual conference of the NAACP will "completely destroy the validity of segregation," especially in terms of education. As his memorandum indicates, even as he was laying the groundwork for Brown, *Marshall was hearing calls for gradualism from some sections of the NAACP. He also makes reference to Governor James Byrnes of South Carolina and Governor Herman Talmadge of Georgia.*

JUNE 18, 1952

. . .

The morning session will do a complete job of knocking down all theories which have been advanced or which could be advanced to justify segregation. In other words, we hope to completely destroy the validity of segregation so that by the afternoon session there will be no question that segregation is unlawful and cannot be tolerated. The afternoon session will be restricted to what we should do about it.

I hope that each of you will stress from your angle what we can do concretely in this field and use your past experience to predict what can be done in the future. Of course all three of you realize that there are some of our delegates who, while opposed to segregation, are nevertheless constantly listening to those who say, "We are moving too fast, we should take the gradual approach—If we open up white schools, all Negro teachers will lose their jobs—If we win these cases, there will be violence and bloodshed"—and there are those who yield to Talmadge and Byrnes et al. about turning the schools over to private groups.

We are all convinced that this matter can be adequately handled, and we have asked experts in NAACP work to do this job rather than some other people who have not worked actively in our work. In other words, at this session we are going to bury segregation once and for all as our work is concerned, and we know you can do it.

NAACP ON PUBLIC SCHOOL SEGREGATION CASES

Marshall's team provides background information on three of the school desegregation cases that would be included in the Brown *decision. It seems that the NAACP used this document to educate branches and other interested parties about the pending Supreme Court debate and decision.*

NOVEMBER 26, 1952

The Issue

At issue in these three cases, one originating in the rural South Carolina County of Clarendon, another in Topeka, Kansas, and a third in Prince Edward County, Virginia, is the validity of state statutes and constitutional provisions pursuant to which Negro and white children are segregated in public elementary and secondary schools. Acting on behalf of the parents and children in each case, the NAACP attorneys contend that segregation *per se* is discrimination and, accordingly, a violation of the equal protection clause of the Fourteenth Amendment to the United States Constitution. In these cases the equality of facilities afforded the two groups is *not* at issue.

All three cases are before the Supreme Court on appeal from lower court decisions which upheld the constitutionality of segregation on the basis of a Supreme Court decision in *Plessy v. Ferguson* handed down in 1896. The Court at that time formulated the "separate but equal" doctrine, which asserted the right of the states to enforce segregation laws provided equal facilities were made available to both races. The present cases challenge this ruling. Two other cases involving this issue, one originating in Delaware and the other in the District of Columbia, will also be heard by the Court at the same time.

The Argument

The lower courts, the NAACP attorneys contend, were in error in basing their decision on *Plessy v. Ferguson.* They maintain that this ruling has been made obsolete by later decisions of the Court, particularly *McLaurin v. Oklahoma State Regents* and *Sweatt v. Painter*, which held that segregation of Negro students at the University of Oklahoma and the University of Texas, respectively, was unconstitutional.

Citing the decisions in the Sweatt and McLaurin decisions, the NAACP brief in the Clarendon County case, filed on September 23, maintains:

> *This rule cannot be peculiar to any level of public education. Public elementary and high school education is no less a governmental function than graduate and professional education in state institutions.*

The brief in the Topeka case, also filed on September 23, asserts:

> *Since 1940, in an unbroken line of decisions, this court has clearly enunciated the doctrine that the state may not validly impose distinctions and restrictions among citizens based upon race or color alone in each field of governmental activity where question has been raised.*

The brief in the Virginia case, filed on September 26, also cites the Sweatt and McLaurin decisions, and adds:

> Experience following these decisions has made manifest that complete and immediate elimination of racial distinctions in public education is feasible as well as proper.
>
> For many years Negro children in Prince Edward County have suffered educational deprivations at the hands of the state. It is clear that they will continue to suffer as long as racial segregation in public schools is practiced.

Segregation, the NAACP points out, impairs the educational development of its victims. Race as a factor in the selection of students for admission to public schools, the Association holds, is a "constitutional irrelevance" which "cannot be justified as a classification based upon any real difference which has pertinence to a valid legislative objective."

. . .

KENNETH CLARK TO MARSHALL

Clark, a psychologist based at the City College of New York, had testified in Briggs v. Elliot, *the Clarendon County school case, that the system of segregation damaged the psyche of black children. In a landmark study of black children playing with dolls, Kenneth and Mamie Clark found that the children often ascribed negative personal characteristics ("bad," for example) to black dolls, and positive ones ("nice," for example) to white dolls. The study also found that black children usually preferred to play with white dolls over black ones. In the letter below, the fun-loving Clark ribs Marshall about an earlier letter of invitation to a conference of specialists working on* Brown.

JANUARY 23, 1953

Dear Mr. Marshall:

I accept with pleasure your invitation to participate in your small conference of "a select group of our lawyers." Your sudden decision to elevate me from the lowly status of a Ph.D. in psychology to the Olympian peak of a member of the legal profession leaves me stunned with happiness. Words almost fail me as I contemplate the implications of this promotion. As I read your memorandum over and over again, the sudden impact of such phrases as: "we need your cooperation and hope that you can arrange your schedule as to be with us . . ." struck me with incredible force. I cannot understand how I could possibly deserve such a warm demonstration of your highest esteem. To be listed among such great minds as Reeves and Carter fills me with humility and awe. I thought to myself, "Look how you have come, Kenneth, since those terrible days of the Clarendon case when you were being continuously told that a Ph.D. was lower than a worm and a Ph.D. in psychology lower than that." With one grand gesture, Mr. Marshall, you have restored my self-esteem. You have freed me from the burdensome feelings of inferiority. In fact, you have undone, with one memorandum, what these many years of racial segregation and discrimination have done to my personality. You have made me a new man. In short, you have performed the miracle of changing me overnight from a psychologist to a lawyer.

Is it too presumptuous to hope that someday I might do the same for you and transform you from a lawyer to a psychologist?

Gratefully yours,

Kenneth B. Clark

P.S. I will be there. Just try to keep me away.

MARSHALL TO THE NAACP OFFICE

On June 8, the Supreme Court ruled that restaurants in the District of Columbia were not legally entitled to refuse service to individuals because of their race or color, and Marshall stated in response that the NAACP was "highly gratified" with the ruling. On the same day, however, the Court called for re-arguing in the fall the highly publicized cases involving racial segregation in the public schools. Reporting for The New York Times, *Luther Huston described the justices as "hopelessly divided on matters of law and public policy involved."*

The Court called for clarifying answers to five questions, and the NAACP board of directors, while regretting the delay, agreed to work on providing the answers. The board also stated: "We urge the people of this country, both white and Negro, North and South, to follow the example of the Supreme Court and to consider the question of the validity of racial segregation on the basis of facts, the law and their moral responsibility rather than upon the irrational rantings and ravings of biased, die-hard 'white supremacist' demagogues."

The following is a statement that Marshall telephoned to the NAACP office. He certainly was not kidding when he stated that the NAACP had "a terrific job ahead." The Court had asked for an enormous amount of dizzying research, and Marshall's legal team set up task forces to answer the questions.

JUNE 11, 1953

Now is the time to be encouraged rather than discouraged. We have a terrific job ahead. The legal staff has the job of intensified research, both legal and scientific, for the preparation of another set of briefs in these cases. Our branches and state conferences have the job of continuing with extra vigor the campaign of educating each community to the full extent of the evil inherent in racial segregation.

Neither the threats of people like Governor Talmadge and Governor Byrnes nor the complacency of other people can deter any unit of the NAACP in this campaign. Rather, we will continue to rely on the wholehearted support of the majority of Americans, white and Negro, North and South, who are convinced that racial segregation is not only illegal but is equally immoral.

MARSHALL TO JAMES HINTON

Marshall politely strong-arms Hinton, the president of the South Carolina NAACP and a driving force behind the Clarendon County case, to come up with $5,000 for the reargument. No matter how embedded he was in the legal preparation for Brown, *Marshall still had to play the role of fund-raiser for the case.*

JUNE 30, 1953

Dear Rev. Hinton:

We certainly enjoyed having you with us at our 44th Annual Convention in St. Louis. On behalf of our entire staff, I want you to know that all of us sincerely appreciated your leadership and advice.

You will remember . . . we discussed the pending reargument of our four cases in the Supreme Court, including the Clarendon County case.

You will remember that I told you that we had set up a minimum budget of $35,000 as the amount necessary to do the necessary research by hiring qualified experts to work with us, travel, and getting these people together, and in getting meetings throughout the country of the best minds on this problem, as well as the preparation and printing of the briefs themselves.

The national office legal staff is giving up its vacations for this summer. Lawyers and experts throughout the country are likewise giving of their services because everyone realizes the importance of this opportunity to make a full presentation to the Supreme Court of what all of us have wanted to document and say in regard to the invalidity and unconstitutionality of racial segregation.

As you know, and as all of your branches know, South Carolina has always paid every cent of its responsibility for its lawsuits. We entered upon the present budget of $35,000 because of the confidence we have always had that South Carolina will bear its share of the burden. I, therefore, have no hesitancy in assigning to South Carolina an apportionment of at least $5,000 toward this $35,000 budget. However, I must plead with you to make every effort to get this $5,000 to us within sixty days from this date because, as you know, the bills on the type of work we are doing cannot be made on a credit basis and we must pay as we go.

We need you as badly as we have ever needed you, and we need your cooperation more so now than ever. From past experience, I know that the only thing I have to do is to send you this letter and wait for the check from the South Carolina state conference of branches. I know we will get that check within sixty days. I know it will be for not less than $5,000. I'm now removing a $5,000 worry from my mind so that it will be free to work on the cases.

With all best wishes to you and every branch in South Carolina.

Sincerely,

Thurgood Marshall

LOREN MILLER TO MARSHALL

Miller wrote some of the most substantive letters about the briefs that Marshall distributed to the legal experts working on Brown, *and below is a letter in which he delivers highly critical comments on the historical section of the draft brief. He refers to Roger Taney, who delivered the majority opinion in* Dred Scott v. Sandford, *and Oliver Morton, a Republican senator from Indiana (1867–1877).*

Paul Freund, a professor of law at Harvard Law School and former clerk to Supreme Court Justice Louis Brandeis, encouraged Marshall to make the point that the Court *left the content of "great guarantees like that of equal protection and due process of law . . . for an expanding future just as in the case of the great grants of affirmative powers." This did not mean that the historical section of the brief was unimportant, but that Marshall should recognize that "the burden should be on the opposition to establish by clear and decisive evidence that in no circumstances was the equal protection clause intended to embrace unsegregated schooling."*

Marshall's work on Brown *was heavily indebted not only to lawyers like Miller and Freund, and social scientists like Kenneth Clark, but also to a group of hardworking secretaries—including Cecelia Suyat, who would later marry Marshall. Interestingly, Marshall also received letters with constructive legal suggestions from everyday citizens not trained in legal matters, and even during this busy and stressful period he would take time to mail them thoughtful replies.*

NOVEMBER 3, 1953

Dear Thurgood:

I received the brief Saturday night and I have confined my attention to part two thus far. I agree with your estimate that it is far more of an historical survey than it is an argument. The survey of education prior to the Civil War seems to me to be very inconclusive. I think that the survey should carry over to the post Civil War period with some material as to the character of the educational system set up in the South by reconstruction legislatures. After all, school segregation developed in that period and developed at a time when every effort was made to keep the Negro in his place.

On page 209, you say "it may be reasonably doubted whether they would have been similarly acquiescent in segregation." That weak and conciliatory statement should be replaced by a positive assertion to the effect that the framers would not have tolerated segregation in a compulsory school system and there should be some contrast between a compulsory school system and the more or less voluntary school system that prevailed in the nineteenth century.

The section devoted to the debates, beginning on page 215, is mamby-pamby. It is hesitant and unconvincing, a fault that seems to me to stem from the fact that too little stress is laid on the underlying philosophy of the proponents of the Civil Rights Acts and framers of the Amendment.
. . .

The constant stress on the citizenship argument, as made in the debates on the Civil Rights Acts, is understandable and meaningful only against the background of Taney's dictum in the Dred Scott case, but that fact is not illuminated. Taney had said in no uncertain terms that there could be no distinction between citizens. Thus if Negroes were citizens they could not be discriminated against. Why not emphasize that point?

. . .

Much is made in the brief of the fact that the separate but equal doctrine had not been devised at the time of the debates. I think that the positive assertion should be made . . . that the proponents of the Civil Rights Acts and the framers of the Amendment would have rejected that doctrine, since they were out to destroy all "class and caste legislation.". . .

Part Two also suffers from a long discussion in Congress as to its right to forbid racial discrimination in public schools because that section might lead to the conclusion that the matter of separate schools rests solely with Congress. If that section is to be effective, there must be stress laid on the fact that these Congressional debates do not indicate that Congress believed that it had sole authority on this matter. . . . I would approach that problem by pointing out that Bingham changed his drafts of the Amendment to avoid that very pitfall. His first drafts all began with the language that "the Congress shall have power, etc," and ended in final formulation that "no state shall, etc.". . .

On page 245, Senator Martin is quoted as saying, "The remedy for the violation of the Fourteenth and Fifteenth Amendments was expressly not left to the courts. The remedy was legislative because in each case, the Amendment distinctly provided that it shall be enforced by legislation on the part of Congress." Such a statement, standing alone and without explanatory material, certainly plays into the hands of those who say that the Court has no authority to intervene in the school cases. . . . It seems suicidal.

. . .

I will read other sections of the brief as soon as possible and send you my view on them.

Loren

On November 16, the NAACP Legal Defense and Educational Fund publicized the conclusion of its work on the new brief: "The filing of the 240-page brief, with 525 footnotes, brings to an end twenty-two hectic weeks of intensive research and study on the part of 130 lawyers and experts scattered across the country, headed by Thurgood Marshall, NAACP Special Counsel and Director of the Legal Defense and Educational Fund, Inc., and his assistant, Robert L. Carter." The news release also quoted this conclusion of the new brief:

> *Under the applicable decisions of this Court the state constitutional and statutory provisions herein involved are clearly unconstitutional. Moreover, the historical evidence surrounding the adoption, submission and ratification of the Fourteenth Amendment compels the conclusion that it was the intent, understanding, and contemplation that the Amendment proscribed all state-imposed racial restrictions. The Negro children in these cases are arbitrarily excluded from state public schools set apart for the dominant white groups. Such a practice can only be continued on a theory that Negroes, qua Negroes, are inferior to all other Americans. The constitutional and statutory provisions herein challenged cannot be upheld without a clear determination that Negroes are inferior and, therefore, must be segregated from other human beings. Certainly, such a ruling would destroy the intent and purpose of the Fourteenth Amendment and the very equalitarian basis of our government.*

MARSHALL, WALTER WHITE, AND HENRY FOSDICK TO NAACP SUPPORTERS AFTER THE *BROWN* RULING

The reargument of Brown *took place on December 7, 8, and 9. After T. Justin Moore, the assistant attorney general of Virginia, delivered his argument on the morning of December 8, a disgusted—and peeved—Marshall rebutted that "the only way that this court can decide this case in opposition to our position . . . is to find that for some reason, Negroes are inferior to all other human beings." On May 17, 1954, the Supreme Court sided with Marshall and unanimously ruled that segregation in public schools was unconstitutional. "In the field of public education, the doctrine of 'separate but equal' has no place," stated Chief Justice Earl Warren. "Separate educational facilities are inherently unequal." Marshall was feeling optimistic after the announcement of the decision and predicted that the people of the South "would not resist the Supreme Court."*

MAY 17, 1954

Historic Supreme Court decision handed down today unanimously rules racial segregation has no place in American life. Five NAACP cases challenging segregated schooling brought this affirmation culminating four decades work to overthrow separate but equal formula enforced since 1896. Yet court issued no decree on how decision shall be implemented. Justices ordered reargument for the fall term on two key constitutional questions: how and when segregated schools shall in fact be abolished. Grossly inferior school facilities continue in sixteen states and nation's capitol until legal action secures practical definition. NAACP attorneys must prepare for rehearing and must file scores of cases state after state lest pronouncement without enabling action mocks aspirations of three million Negro American youngsters. Actions taken within next few months will determine whether America can solve her problem without violent disunity threatened by extremists. . . .

Harry Emerson Fosdick

Walter White

Thurgood Marshall

LESTER GRANGER TO MARSHALL

Congratulations poured into the NAACP offices following the Brown *decision, and one of the notes came from Jean Williams, a resident of New York City. "It is a wonderful feeling," she wrote, "to wake up in the morning and find that you are free-er. This morning I had more self-respect and pride in myself as a person. And I was proud, not only because I am a colored person, but because I am an American. I am grateful first to your organization, The National Association for the Advancement of Colored People, and secondly, to the Supreme Court of the United States. After all, the Supreme Court said that we were 'human beings entitled to equal rights'—we have known this for a long time." Below is another note of congratulations, this one from Lester Granger, the executive director of the National Urban League.*

MAY 18, 1954

I was in Little Rock, Arkansas yesterday when news of the Supreme Court's decision broke. I can therefore testify from first-hand observation as to the healthy effect of the decision upon those who have opposed as well as those who have supported your tremendous leadership effort. Congratulations and thanks of every Urban League staff and board worker are due you and your organization for a supreme contribution to American democracy in helping to produce the most important racial development in this century.

Perhaps surprisingly, Paul Wilson, the assistant attorney general of Kansas, also sent his congratulations to Marshall. "Although it was my duty as an official of the State of Kansas to urge to the Court the judicial precedents that seemed to justify the Kansas statute, I am frank to say that I feel no dismay at the repudiation of those precedents."

On the opposite end of the spectrum, Governor Herman Talmadge of Georgia announced a few days later that he would resist the Supreme Court decision. "We're not going to secede from the union," he said, "but the people of Georgia will not comply with the decision of the court. It would take several divisions of troops down here to police every school building in Georgia and then they wouldn't be able to enforce it. We're going to do whatever is necessary in Georgia to keep white children in white schools and colored children in colored schools."

MARSHALL TO THE EDITOR OF THE DALLAS *MORNING NEWS*

The white backlash was enormous following the Brown *victory, and "forced association" became one of the favorite catchphrases among those who resisted the decision. Marshall explains in the letter below that the phrase does not accurately describe the goals of the NAACP.*

JUNE 10, 1954

Dear Sir:

I have just seen your editorial "NAACP Plans" in the May 26 issue, in which it is asserted that the "key theme" of the coming national convention of the NAACP in Dallas is to be "segregation in fields other than education," and you ascribe this announcement to me.

The *News* says flatly, "the NAACP is not satisfied with the abolition of segregation by law. NAACP wants to abolish segregation in fact, which means that it desires forced association." It is true that the NAACP wants segregation eradicated in fact, but we have not advocated or suggested "forced association" of any kind.

Let's review the record. I might suggest parenthetically that if the *News* had studied with care the policy and program of the NAACP throughout its 45-year history, it would be the first to realize that while we have inveighed against governmentally imposed segregation, we have not contended for governmentally enforced association. We have maintained consistently that the state has no right to make racial distinctions between its citizens as long as the United States continues to live under its Constitution. We have maintained that racial distinctions in the law as to interstate travel, voting, education in tax-supported institutions, recreation in facilities maintained by taxes, and housing built with tax assistance, are all unconstitutional. We have maintained that purchase and occupancy of housing may not be restricted by municipal ordinances and state laws. In addition, we have contended that the courts, as instruments of the state, may not enforce restrictive housing covenants entered into privately between homeowners aimed at the exclusion of others on the basis of race, color or religion. Most of these contentions have been upheld by the United States Supreme Court.

The record, therefore, demonstrates that the NAACP's primary attack has been against use of the machinery of the state to enforce racial segregation. When state force is removed, citizens, both black and white, will remain free to exercise their individual prejudices and preferences. Only then those individual prejudices and preferences would not receive the support of governmental authority. Never has the NAACP maintained that any private citizen should be forced, in his purely private enterprises, to associate with any other citizens. We agree most emphatically with the assertion in the *News* editorial: "The point is that in private life . . . in social contact, both white and Negro are entitled to be secure in prejudices." As for what the *News* terms "private business," we would have to agree first on a definition since there enters here the whole concept of business imbued with the public interest.

Of course, we would be less than candid if we were not to admit that the NAACP will also strive to secure the adherence of individuals to a standard of conduct opposed to restrictions based upon race and color. We believe that in this regard we stand on high moral ground in keeping with religious teaching of the brotherhood of man and the equalitarian basis of our own political philosophy. There is, however, you must admit, a vast difference between advocacy and enforced adherence. Many will never forego racial prejudice, but we are convinced that most Americans, left free to choose, will eventually come to realize the irrelevance of race and color as a criterion for measurement of the individual.

Only the most uninformed or the most misinformed can be blind to the forces that are now moving toward a major readjustment in the traditional pattern of race relations in both the North and the South and, indeed, over the whole world. The transition period will require, above all, appreciation of the honest position and motives of both sides, recognition of the legitimate aspirations of the Negro, as well as of the long-established customs of whites. Little can be gained, it seems to us, from misrepresentation of the aims and objectives of either side. We offer our full cooperation in the tasks ahead, and we invite men and institutions of justice and goodwill to join in the mutual effort.

Very sincerely yours,

Thurgood Marshall

MARSHALL TO NAACP BRANCH PRESIDENTS AND OFFICERS

On June 24, J. E. Stockstill, an attorney from Picayune, Mississippi, wrote Marshall the following note: "We note your braggadocio bigotry statement: 'All diversionary plans will be tested in Court'—meaning any effort to avert non-segregation. The South has heard such blab-mouth statements for the last 80 years, and we want you to know that any law that is applied to the South is enforced by the citizenry of the South—after all, the will of the people is the law. When you or the Supreme Court or either one think you are bigger than the solid South, you will find out different in the long run." Marshall knew that Stockstill—and thousands of white reactionaries like him—were digging in to resist the implementation of Brown, and in the letter below, which he marked "urgent and immediate action," Marshall seeks information on local action. Of course, he also intended for the letter to apply pressure to local NAACP officials to take action in implementing school desegregation.

SEPTEMBER 17, 1954

Now that public schools have opened, we need specific and detailed information as to exactly what has happened in your local community insofar as desegregation of public schools is concerned.

We want a report as to everything you have done and what other groups and individuals have done; what action, if any, has been taken by the school board; whether petitions have been filed and, if so, what action has been taken on the petitions. If no petition has been filed, what other action has been taken in regard to the school board and any other pertinent information you have.

The important thing is that at the earliest possible moment we must have as complete a picture as possible of the present status of our fight against desegregation in public schools. We need full and accurate information and we need it as fast as possible.

. . .

MARSHALL TO ATTORNEY GENERAL HERBERT BROWNELL, JR.

Continuing his efforts to fight against the white backlash, Marshall petitions the attorney general to take action against the National Association for the Advancement of White People.

NO DATE [FALL 1954]

At the beginning of the present school term, areas in eight Southern and border states began to desegregate their public schools pursuant to the opinion of the United States Supreme Court which on May 17 declared that segregation in public education violated the 14th Amendment. In each of these areas, desegregation was proceeding without trouble of any kind. However, during the past two weeks a movement has grown up starting in Milford, Delaware, and now extending to Baltimore, Maryland, and Washington, D.C., whereby white citizens, including parents of school children, have assembled in mobs and on picket lines for the express purpose of threatening local school officials and Negro children to prevent the Negro children from exercising their constitutionally guaranteed rights to attend desegregated schools in these areas. This unlawful action has come about solely by reason of the provocation of an organization known as the National Association for the Advancement of White People. Such action is not only reprehensible within itself but is obviously in direct violation of the civil rights laws of the United States guaranteeing and protecting American citizens in the exercise of their constitutionally protected rights. These Negro children and their parents deserve the protection of the United States Department of Justice in not being prevented from exercising their right to attend non-segregated schools. We therefore strongly urge you as attorney general of the United States to make it clear to all concerned that the full force of the federal government stands behind the local school boards and students involved in effecting a transition from segregated to desegregated schools and that all who unlawfully assemble, picket or use violence to deprive American citizens of their rights will be dealt with vigorously and promptly as violators of the civil rights laws of the United States.

Thurgood Marshall

RUBY HURLEY TO MARSHALL

Hurley, the regional secretary of the NAACP's southeast region, refers to James Hinton, the president of the South Carolina NAACP, in her characterization of the vicious white backlash to Brown.

SEPTEMBER 21, 1954

Dear Thurgood:

Mr. Hinton and I have been discussing the Mississippi situation, which we consider to be of a serious nature both presently and for future repercussions.

As you may know from the press and radio, public officials, including the governor, the attorney general, one U.S. senator and numerous legislators have pledged to do everything in their power to circumvent the Supreme Court decision of May 17. Further, there is a fast-moving organizing effort on a countywide basis over the state, through which organization of white supremacy is to be maintained at any cost.

Our branches have begun to feel the pressure. All credit has been withdrawn from the president of our new branch, a storekeeper, in Lelzoni. Stringer, in Columbus, is being smeared through the American Legion . . . His credit was withdrawn in Columbus several months ago and you know about the nuisance calls he has received. One of our members who signed the now famous petition in Walthall County did not receive renewal of his contract to drive the school bus, and the school for colored children has been closed for fourteen days. You know about Amite County; Roy talked with you about it when you were in Chicago. Dr. Battle, one of our key people in Indianola, says a large number of his patients on nearby plantations are now former patients.

We think that it would be very wise to put someone in the state as soon as is humanly possible and for an extended period of time. Mr. Hinton thinks, and I agree, that Dan Byrd is the best person. We do not have to spell out the reasons to you. Is there any chance of your giving him that assignment? We hope that you will give this favorable consideration.

Sincerely yours,

Ruby Hurley

MARSHALL TO HIS LEGAL TEAM

Throughout the fall of 1954, Marshall was hard at work on yet another Brown*-related brief, this one on the timetable for implementing the Supreme Court's decision. Rather than demanding an immediate end to segregated schools, Marshall's brief proposed that the school boards in the five cases under* Brown *achieve complete desegregation of their schools by the fall of 1956. The key point here is that Marshall was asking for a timetable for the implementation of* Brown, *a request that the Southern school districts strongly resisted. Marshall had learned to expect such resistance, and when commenting at the beginning of the year on the possibility of implementing* Brown, *he stated: "Of course, you and I know that there are some sections of the Black Belt . . . where the Supreme Court decision that we are legally right would have no effect for thirty years."*

Marshall was also unbelievably rushed when preparing for the "re-reargument" of Brown, *as indicated by his November 4 letter to members of his team:*

> *Enclosed is a copy of the rough draft of the major portions of our brief in the school segregation cases. Although it is rough, we believe that it gives a clear consensus of our thinking as of this moment—and the moment is late. We would like very much to have your detailed*

> *criticism of this either on this copy or in a memorandum accompanying the copy and back to us by Monday, November 8th, which is just one week before the brief is due in final form in the Supreme Court. In the meantime, we will also be working this draft over with the hope that between Monday and Wednesday of next week we can put together your ideas with ours. Please bear in mind, however, that you might not get a chance to see the final draft because of the rush of time, so it is imperative that you get your ideas to us now. We are sorry that we are in this jam but it is the best we can do under the circumstances and we hope that you will continue to cooperate.*

As usual, his team members were eager to cooperate and send along their critical comments. One of the more fascinating replies came from Paul Freund of Harvard, who advised Marshall to write of the role of the Supreme Court not "as a decisive force in facilitating positive social attitudes, etc., but simply as a decisive force in maintaining adherence to constitutional standards governing official action. I am afraid that some members of the Court would rebel at the idea that their function was to make Americans more civilized or democratic."

CHAPTER FOURTEEN

1955–1957

CHANNING TOBIAS TO MARSHALL

Channing Tobias, the chair of the NAACP's board of trustees, wires his sympathy to Marshall upon the death of his wife, Buster, who discovered she had terminal cancer while Marshall was arguing Brown. *Vivian "Buster" Marshall died on February 11 at the age of forty-four. She had told Marshall of her cancer shortly before Thanksgiving 1954, and he had taken time off from work so that he could be with his wife during her final days. Their marriage had not always been easy: his long hours on the job, his constant travels, and several miscarriages, among other things, strained the couple at times. But Marshall took Buster's death quite hard, and, according to Jack Greenberg, a member of his legal team, Marshall's work productivity slowed considerably following Buster's death.*

FEBRUARY 14, 1955

Personally and in behalf of the board of directors NAACP I extend to you and other members of the family heartfelt sympathy in the untimely passing of your beloved companion. Aside from her interest in your work and in the general program of our organization she had the welfare of the community at heart as attested by her participation in many social and community activities. She will be missed not only by her inner circle of friends but by those who knew her for her unselfish labor for community uplift.

Channing H. Tobias

Not quite one year after Buster died, Marshall married Cecelia Suyat, and the couple welcomed their first child, Thurgood Marshall, Jr., within the first year of their marriage.

MARSHALL TO THE EDITOR OF *THE NEW YORK TIMES MAGAZINE*

Attorneys for Kansas, Delaware, Virginia, and the District of Columbia appeared before the Supreme Court on April 11 and 12, with a request that the Court not order the end of racial segregation in public schools "forthwith," a word Marshall favored to expedite implementation of the Court's ruling.

Following Brown, *the Topeka school board had taken measures to end some school segregation by September of 1955, but under its plan, children who wished to do so would be able to attend—until their graduation—the public schools they had attended before* Brown—*namely, segregated schools. Robert Carter and Marshall argued against the Topeka plan, urging the Supreme Court to end any and all forms of segregation in the public schools by September 1956.*

The Eisenhower administration disagreed with Marshall and asked the Court to give local communities a reasonable time in which to desegregate their schools. In reply, Marshall stated that the argument for postponing constitutional rights "is never made until Negroes are involved."

In the following letter, Marshall makes the case that what really matters in implementing school desegregation is the will of the local community, not the decision of the Supreme Court. Marshall was no doubt proud that his hometown of Baltimore had taken steps to desegregate its public schools long before the Supreme Court ruled on a timetable for implementing Brown.

MAY 11, 1955

To the Editor:

The New York Times Magazine is to be congratulated upon the timely publication of Gertrude Samuels's excellent article on school desegregation in Baltimore (May 8). To all of us who have been working for the elimination of racial discrimination and segregation in our nation's public schools, this article is most heartening. With singular insight, she makes clear the secret of Baltimore's success in initiating desegregation without awaiting the Supreme Court's decree, namely, the will to comply with the principle of non-segregation laid down by the court in its historic decision of May 17, 1954.

In Baltimore, as Miss Samuels points out, there was not only the will to comply, but also the intelligence to prepare for this important step, the clear statement of policy by the school board, and the firm enforcement and unwavering execution of this policy in face of misguided resistance.

These are the necessary ingredients for success in desegregation. Given these, the public school systems of Richmond or Atlanta or New Orleans can be desegregated as readily as those of Baltimore, Washington and St. Louis.

Sincerely,

Thurgood Marshall

MARSHALL TO RUBEN AND MARY BARKSDALE

On May 31, the Supreme Court refused Marshall's proposal for an exact timetable for desegregating schools and ruled instead that local school boards must desegregate "with all deliberate speed." Although he did not suggest as much in public, the imprecise language infuriated Marshall, and at an NAACP conference following the decision he pledged to fight any school district that would use the Court's decision to postpone desegregation indefinitely. Two weeks later, he announced that, regardless of what the Court had ruled, September 1956 remained the NAACP's deadline for the end of segregation in public schools. Sounding a more realistic note, however, he also added: "The desegregation program will take time, but I guarantee you that it won't be any fifty or 100 years."

The Eisenhower administration was very pleased with the Court's ruling, and three weeks after the decision Eisenhower even dared to send a telegram advising "patience," "perseverance," and "forbearance" to the forty-sixth annual convention of the NAACP. "I trust that in the decade ahead your organization will display both wisdom and patience as it bears its share of the responsibility for the betterment of our country as a whole," he wrote. Contrary to the president, Marshall announced at the same conference that the NAACP would "push ahead without delay in insisting upon desegregation in all of the Southern states."

In spite of the Court's failure to set a timetable, the school board of Hoxie, Kansas, voted on June 25 to integrate its schools, beginning on July 11, and integration proceeded peacefully for the first two weeks. But after this two-week period, some white residents began to circulate a Life *magazine article titled "A 'Morally Right' Decision," which depicted African American and white children studying together without incident in Hoxie. This article, coupled with other factors, added to the resentment felt by local segregationists, and by the end of July they organized themselves, picketed the schools, and distributed racist literature from organizations such as White America, Inc., and the National Association for the Advancement of White People.*

Local African Americans felt threatened, of course, and so did members of the white school board. As tensions mounted, the NAACP sent its field secretary, Mildred Bond, to investigate local conditions, and Marshall pleaded with the attorney general, the Department of Justice, and the White House to help ease tensions in Hoxie. Justice officials took their cue from Marshall this time, and the FBI sent agents to investigate whether federal laws had been violated in Hoxie. While the school board voted on August 19 to end the summer term two weeks early, the board also announced a few weeks later that it would continue integrated education when the school term resumed on October 31.

In the letter below, Marshall encourages the parents of Hoxie schoolchildren to keep their eyes on the prize. Although he enjoyed life on the national stage, Marshall clearly recognized that his efforts succeeded or failed largely because of the efforts of local parents.

AUGUST 12, 1955

Dear Mr. and Mrs. Barksdale:

Miss Mildred Bond, our field secretary, has sent us a most encouraging report of her visit to Hoxie on August 6.

All of us in this office are much impressed with the courageous and intelligent manner in which you handled the current problem involving a strike of some white parents in Hoxie.

The important thing to bear in mind at this time is that you must keep level heads and not be provoked. You should stand firm and insist on your children remaining in the school and not be provoked by any hotheads on the other side.

In doing this, bear in mind that the entire resources of the NAACP are behind you.

With all best wishes.

Very truly yours,

Thurgood Marshall

MARSHALL TO THE EDITOR OF THE COLUMBIA *RECORD*

Marshall corrects the South Carolina newspaper for misrepresenting the NAACP's strategy for desegregating public schools.

SEPTEMBER 9, 1955

Dear Sir:

I have just read a clipping from the Columbia *Record* of August 30th entitled "Negroes May Delay Clarendon Demand." In that story it is stated:

> *Thurgood Marshall, chief NAACP counsel, reportedly informed counsel for the Summerton School trustees he will leave the Summerton district alone in view of the acute problems to be solved in desegregating the schools there.*

And it is also reported:

> *But the present report on the informal meeting held after the court hearing indicates that NAACP will not further attempt to force integration in this district, but apparently will shift their efforts to other areas.*

These statements as well as the whole tenor of the story are completely inaccurate. We have not changed our position one iota from what we stated to the United States Supreme Court at the hearing on July 15th to the effect that: (1) we believed that both sides should work together in a spirit of good faith and cooperation to carry out the order of the Court issued on that day, and (2) if we should "get to the point where either side was dissatisfied and it couldn't be worked out on an amicable basis, then further relief would be sought . . . the Court having retained jurisdiction."

Nothing has been said by me privately or publicly which in any way justifies a contrary conclusion to this position.

It is true that after the hearing on July 15th I talked with the attorneys for defendants. During that conversation I stated that we would not formally present the Negro children to the white schools for admission in September because such an action was not necessary in the present posture of the case and would have no legal significance. During the same conference I made it clear that we would not give up any of our rights.

I sincerely hope that you will correct this obvious misstatement of fact in the aforementioned article in the Columbia *Record.*

Very truly yours,

Thurgood Marshall

Marshall sent a copy of this letter to J. Waties Waring, and the judge replied with a critical tone on September 17. "The article appearing in the Record of August 30th alleging that you were in effect abandoning the Clarendon County School case was of course very damaging to our fight to end segregation," Waring wrote. "This is especially true in those localities where due to various pressures many of the Negro parents are withdrawing their support of the effort to carry out the terms of the Supreme Court's opinion of May 17th, 1954. It is therefore important that a denial of these charges be made by you and even more important that such a denial receive wide publicity."

Waring went on to take a swipe at what he took to be Marshall's naiveté. "I am also taking the liberty of suggesting that I had supposed that you would have known that it is very dangerous to make any so-called private statements to the lawyers representing the Clarendon County School officials," he penned. "I know them and I had supposed that you did also. But the article in 'Time' and your interview on the Tex and Jinx program seem to indicate that you still believe in the sincerity of the Dixiecrat lawyers. Perhaps a few more 'legal lynchings' will enlighten you." This was not the first time Waring criticized Marshall. In letters to White and other NAACP board members in 1952, Waring had questioned Marshall's legal strategy during the appeal stage of the Clarendon County school case and even proposed that the NAACP hire an outside counsel to argue the Clarendon case before the Supreme Court. Waring, of course, lost that battle.

J. EDGAR HOOVER TO MARSHALL

With the death of Walter White in March and the pending promotion of Roy Wilkins to the top spot, Marshall became Hoover's primary contact at the NAACP, and in the letter below Hoover complains about disparaging comments made by T. R. M. Howard, an African American physician and local NAACP leader from Mississippi, and defends the FBI's investigations of race-based crimes. Hoover also refers to George Lee and Lamar Smith, both of them friends of Howard and voter registration organizers in Mississippi. Lee, a minister, grocer, and local NAACP leader, was shot in broad daylight after trying to vote in Belzoni, Mississippi, on August 13, 1955, and Smith, a farmer, was murdered in front of the courthouse in Brookhaven, Mississippi, just after voting on August 13, 1955. The murder of Emmett Till, also referenced below, was one of the catalysts giving rise to the modern civil rights movement. Till, a fourteen-year-old boy from Chicago, was lynched by Roy Bryant and his half brother, J. W. Milam, on August 28, 1955, a few days after Till had made a pass at Carolyn Bryant, Roy's wife, who was working at the time at the Bryants' general store in Money, Mississippi.

SEPTEMBER 30, 1955

Dear Mr. Marshall:

My attention has been called to a news report of a speech given by Dr. T. R. M. Howard before a meeting of the National Association for the Advancement of Colored People at Baltimore, Maryland, on September 25, 1955, in which he reportedly stated "that the FBI can never seem to work out who is responsible for killings of Negroes in the South." Dr. Howard was quoted as making reference to the "unsolved killings of the Rev. Walter W. Lee and Lamar Smith" and the death of Emmett Till and urging that the President, the attorney general "and J. Edgar Hoover, himself" be called into the conference by national Negro leaders to find out "why Southern investigators of the FBI can't seem to solve a crime where a Negro is involved."

I, of course, do not know Dr. Howard's connections with the National Association for the Advancement of Colored People, but since he used your organization as a forum for his most unfair criticisms of the FBI, I am taking the liberty of writing you to set the record straight. I am sure that since you are familiar with the FBI's position in the investigation of civil rights cases you will want to do everything you can to see that the truth is fully understood by everybody.

As you know, the FBI is the investigative arm of the United States Department of Justice. It is responsible, based on instructions issued by the attorney general, for investigating allegations of violations of laws of the United States. If a complaint has been received indicating a violation of the civil rights statutes, the FBI conducts a preliminary inquiry. The results are then immediately furnished the Criminal Division of the Department of Justice. If the Department of Justice requests a full investigation, this is conducted and the results are furnished to it.

In the case involving Reverend George Wesley Lee of Belmont, Mississippi, the FBI did conduct a preliminary investigation as allegations had been received that Lee had been killed because he refused to remove his name from a list of registered voters. Subsequently, at the request of the Department of Justice, the FBI conducted a full investigation. This has now been completed and the results furnished to the Department of Justice.

In the other two cases mentioned by Dr. Howard, the killings of Lamar Smith, of Brookhaven, Mississippi, and Emmett Till, available facts were presented to the Criminal Division of the Department of Justice, which advised that no investigation was desired in either case as the facts did not indicate a violation of any federal statute.

The statements of Dr. Howard criticizing the FBI show a total disregard of the facts. Apparently he has overlooked the investigations which led to prosecutive action against members of the Ku Klux Klan. In October, 1951, for example, a group of Klansmen, organized by the Exalted Cyclops of the Fair Bluff (North Carolina) Klavern, Ku Klux Klan, abducted two victims and drove them across the state line into South Carolina where each was flogged. As a result of the FBI's prompt investigation, ten persons were convicted in United States District Court, Wilmington, North Carolina, in May, 1952, for violation of the federal kidnapping statute.

In another instance, Ku Klux Klansmen demonstrated and burned crosses in Dade County, Georgia. As a result of their activities, several white persons were intimidated and seven Negroes flogged. The FBI promptly instituted an investigation, and two law enforcement officers were convicted in the United States District Court at Rome, Georgia, in March, 1950, for violation of the federal civil rights statute. It is interesting to note that in this case a resolution was directed to the Atlanta and Knoxville offices of the FBI by members of the federal grand jury of the United States District Court commending the investigating agents of the FBI, who "by their great fidelity and singleness of purpose in developing the information in the Dade County, Georgia, conspiracy trials have gone far beyond the line of duty to aid, assist and protect the citizens of the United States and to further the cause of equity and justice in America." The United States attorney, the federal judge and the attorney general also commended the work of the FBI. Surely this is evidence of the thoroughness and impartiality of the FBI's investigations.

I think you will agree that the FBI's fair and prompt investigations have done much to increase public respect for and consciousness of civil rights. In 1954, moreover, for the third straight year there were no lynchings in the United States. In fact, during the last ten years, compared with the previous decade, lynchings dropped from 65 to 16. Lynchings at any time are terrible examples of mob action. These figures indicate, however, a higher respect for law and the processes of democratic government.

Since Dr. Howard's remarks were made at a meeting of the National Association for the Advancement of Colored People, I felt compelled to call them to your attention in view of the widespread dissemination in the press. Moreover, since you are familiar with the record and have knowledge of the diligence with which the FBI applies itself to cases within its jurisdiction, I know that you would not want your organization to put itself in a position of supporting factual inaccuracies.

Sincerely yours,

J. Edgar Hoover

MARSHALL TO J. EDGAR HOOVER

Marshall offers a surprisingly sympathetic reply to Hoover's complaints about T. R. M. Howard—surprising because Howard's words echoed Marshall's own criticism of the FBI in 1947. Clearly, Marshall was becoming less prophetic and far more political in his dealings with the FBI. There were at least two pragmatic reasons underlying this change: Marshall wanted Hoover's help in fighting communists within the NAACP, and he desired protective assistance from the FBI when traveling in the South. Nevertheless, it would be a mistake to make too much of Marshall's sympathy; after all, even in this letter he continues to pass on his concerns about FBI investigations in the South. At once, Marshall was friend and critic.

OCTOBER 7, 1955

Dear Mr. Hoover:

. . . I have explained [to NAACP supporters] that from our information the FBI had done a thorough and complete job in the case of the killing of Rev. Lee and had done as much as had been requested by the criminal division insofar as the killing of Lamar Smith and Emmett Till. I also explained that the real difficulty with federal prosecutions was the need for strong civil rights statutes, increase in budget and status for the civil rights section of the department and increased budget for additional FBI investigators for those tough cases cropping up throughout the South.

. . .

Frankly, I find in Mississippi and throughout the South a feeling among Negroes that the FBI investigators work too closely with local police officials, many of whom have reputations of being anti-Negro. We also find some suspicion brought about by FBI investigators who are former local police officials. I find it most difficult to remove these suspicions from the minds of Negroes who are constantly being oppressed by others, including local police officials. On the other hand, I find it equally difficult to point to actual expressed prejudice on the part of any FBI agent.

During these very tense times, the best I can do is to try and keep the record straight.

I hope that the letters to our Baltimore branch and to the local Negro newspaper in Baltimore will correct the misstatements allegedly made. I hope that we can, through some arm of the government, stem the ever-increasing tide of threats and intimidation against Negroes in Mississippi and other Southern states who are merely seeking in a most lawful manner to obtain their constitutional rights.

Sincerely,

Thurgood Marshall

FBI MEMORANDUM

Marshall considered himself cowardly in relation to potential threats on his life, and although this internal memorandum from Agent Price to Agent Rosen suggests that Marshall provided the FBI with details about his pending trip to Jackson, Mississippi, merely for the FBI's "information," there is little doubt that he hoped that the FBI would somehow look out for him. Marshall had good reason to be concerned, of course. Death threats were all too common in his life, and after racist thugs tried to bomb the house where he was staying during his defense of Autherine Lucy against the University of Alabama, Marshall's concern for his life only deepened.

NOVEMBER 4, 1955

This is to advise you that on instant date Mr. A. Caldwell, Chief, Civil Rights Section, Criminal Division, Department of Justice, advised Special Agent [deleted] of the Civil Rights Unit that he, Caldwell, had received a telephone call from Marshall to the effect that Marshall was flying to Jackson, Mississippi, on November 5, 1955, where he was to address a meeting of the National Association for the Advancement of Colored People there. Mr. Caldwell stated that Mr. Marshall had said that this information was being furnished to the Department of Justice for its information.

Mr. Caldwell was advised that this Bureau could not furnish Mr. Marshall any protection. Mr. Caldwell stated he realized that and he was asking for no action on the part of this Bureau but was merely passing this information along.

. . .

Marshall, of course, was not the only one whose life was threatened at this point. On the evening of January 19, 1956, thugs shot up the entranceway and front window of James Hinton's home in Columbia, South Carolina. The shotgun blast was part of an ongoing campaign of intimidation against local blacks in response to the Supreme Court's ruling against Clarendon County in the Brown *decision. In his January 30 letter to Hinton, Marshall addressed the incident, calling the violent individuals "dirty cowards" who "could have very well saved the shotgun shell if the purpose was to intimidate you and Mrs. Hinton."*

Threatening letters directed at whites also landed on Marshall's desk. The lack of conviction in the Emmett Till case, for example, resulted in a threatening letter, excerpted here, that Marshall would have read in December 1955.

> *You can plainly see that you shouls continue to fight in a leagal way but you need to meake some changes in your program in dealing*

> *with those Southern Crackers. They have wasted too much of your precious time, and now it is time for you to say dam it to hell with them; They will keep you in court until he end of time—why go to the courts of the unrighteous for justice? The European man is know as an unrighteous man and a brute from ancient time until 1955. No need taking hin into court—you and I must soon learn that the only way to handle him is to knock hell out of him. Organize and let him know that you are ready to spill your blood against his dam ignorance and he will stop immediately all his dam foolishness.*

FBI MEMORANDUM

As Marshall's relationship with the FBI grew friendlier—a later letter shows he even acted as an informant—he sought access to privileged information that would assist his efforts to combat communists within the NAACP. The internal FBI memo below, from Agent Nichols to Agent Tolson, refers to an FBI summary on communist infiltration of the NAACP. The domestic intelligence division of the FBI had completed the summary, and Nichols sent it along to Tolson on the same day as the following memo. The rather benign summary concluded: "Our investigation has shown that the Communist Party, while having some success in infiltrating local branches of organization, has been unable to control or dominate the NAACP on a national or state level." The agents agreed that they would share only "public source material," and Marshall received the material at a meeting with Nichols at the FBI headquarters.

More interesting, however, is the memo's stunning suggestion that at this point Marshall was concerned more about communist infiltration of the NAACP than he was about the brewing Montgomery bus boycott led by Martin Luther King, Jr. Early on, E. D. Nixon, a local NAACP leader in Montgomery and one of the leading personalities behind the boycott, had asked his friend Marshall to represent the boycotters, and Marshall, just about to leave for his honeymoon with Cecelia Suyat Marshall, complied by instructing Robert Carter to offer legal counsel to the emerging movement. After he returned from their honeymoon, Marshall then advised Fred Gray, the local attorney for the boycotters, that the NAACP would never support a suit that sought merely what King was asking for at that point—more courteous treatment of African Americans on segregated buses—but that the NAACP would support a suit seeking integrated seating. Gray, in consultation with King and other leaders, then filed a suit that sought exactly that.

FEBRUARY 8, 1956

By reference from the Director's office, I talked to Thurgood Marshall, the National Association for the Advancement of Colored People. He stated that there were several matters which are worrying him and he would like very much to come down on Thursday or Friday to discuss them with the Director and me.

. . .

He then stated that while he was concerned about the Alabama situation and about [deleted], the matter which is worrying him more than anything else right now is the Communist Party's effort to get into the NAACP to forge out to the forefront. I told him he really had a serious situation here, that I knew he was well aware of the dangers and would do well to keep his guard up. He stated this was exactly why he wanted to come to see us.

I told him if the Director were here, I knew that he would be glad to say hello to him.

It is suggested that I see Marshall and then if the situation develops where it would be desirable for the Director to say hello to him, I can then inquiry as to the Director's availability.

I have asked Mr. Belmont to get up a quick summary on Communist activities in connection with the infiltration of the NAACP.

FBI MEMORANDUM

This memorandum from Agent Price to Agent Rosen reveals Marshall's efforts to warn the FBI that potential criticism of the Department of Justice during the NAACP's annual convention in Washington, D.C., would not accurately reflect his own views. Interestingly, Marshall had become a key source of information for the FBI—exactly what Hoover must have wanted. The deleted material in Marshall's comments below refer to T. R. M. Howard, an outspoken critic of the FBI.

FEBRUARY 9, 1956

This is to record that on the afternoon of 2/9/56, Supervisor [deleted] of the Civil Rights Unit went to the Palace Restaurant for lunch. Upon entering the restaurant he was observed by Mr. A. B. Caldwell, Chief of the Civil Rights Section, Criminal Division, who called for [deleted] to join him, which he did. After they had been eating for some time

Caldwell observed Mr. Thurgood Marshall of the National Association for the Advancement of Colored People, who had entered the restaurant. Caldwell, being acquainted with Marshall, invited him to the table and Marshall accepted the invitation. Marshall partook of a cup of coffee while [deleted] and Caldwell finished their meals. Caldwell introduced [deleted] as being with the FBI and in charge of the Civil Rights Unit.

During the course of the conversation Mr. Marshall advised Caldwell that a conference would be held in Washington on the 4th and 5th of March by the National Association for the Advancement of Colored People. He stated that a resolution would probably be proposed which would be critical to the Department of Justice. Marshall indicated that he suspected [deleted] would be at the conference. He stated that he did not know what outfit [deleted] would represent but that he, [deleted], probably would be able to find some branch of the National Association for the Advancement of Colored People to list him as a delegate. He stated that [deleted] is very outspoken and would undoubtedly bring up some resolution criticizing the Department of Justice. Caldwell advised Marshall that he believed there would be some action by the Department prior to March 4, 1956. In his remarks, Mr. Marshall indicated that he was not sympathetic to [deleted].

Action:

The above is for your information. Caldwell undoubtedly was referring to the fact that the Department plans to make a release regarding the filing of a criminal information in the Bolivar County (Mound Bayou) vote case in which a criminal information would be filed against 11 members of the County Democratic Executive Committee for alleged discrimination against Negro voters.

A similar note, this one describing a phone conversation in which Marshall asked Agent Nichols for information on communist infiltration in the NAACP, was written by Nichols to Agent Tolson on June 15, 1956. J. Edgar Hoover eventually agreed to grant Marshall access to confidential FBI files, and Marshall used the material at the NAACP's convention in San Francisco, where he condemned communists and communist sympathizers who were seeking to gain a foothold in the NAACP. The communists, he said, "are no more interested in Negroes or the NAACP than they are in the United States." But he also added that "the wave of anti-Negro terror in the Deep South," "the unwillingness of state officials," and the "inability of the federal government" to protect African Americans provided the substance for communist propaganda.

ASSISTANT ATTORNEY GENERAL WARREN OLNEY III TO MARSHALL

Shortly after warning the Department of Justice that T. R. M. Howard would publicly criticize the department, Marshall himself criticized the department in public. In the letter below, Assistant Attorney General Warren Olney expresses shock and requests an explanation after reading a report of Marshall's criticism in the Washington Post. *The next several pages include a series of letters between Marshall and Olney on the question of whether the specific details of Marshall's criticism were legitimate and fair.*

MARCH 13, 1956

Dear Mr. Marshall:

The Washington Post carried an account of your recent address to a meeting of the National Association for the Advancement of Colored People at the Vermont Avenue Baptist Church in Washington. The *Post* reports that in an hour-long speech you attacked the Justice Department for failing to use "what powers it already has" to check Southern racial extremists. Until someone in Mississippi is found guilty of murdering a Negro, you are reported to have said, "it hasn't done anything."

These remarks are so untrue, so unjustified, and so at variance with other expressions I have heard from you that I am as surprised as much as I am concerned. I would very much like to know whether you are correctly reported. If the *Post* account of your speech is accurate, I would be more than a little interested in having you point out specifically what you think the Justice Department could and should have done in the Till case that it did not do, and what you meant specifically when you described the Justice Department as failing to use "what powers is already has" to check Southern racial extremists.

You were further described in the same article as having warned the National Association for the Advancement of Colored People that the fight for Negro rights will be "mean, nasty and dirty." I have not assumed that you intended this language to describe the methods of the National Association for the Advancement of Colored People.

I am enclosing a copy of the *Washington Post* article.

Sincerely,

Warren Olney III

MARSHALL TO ASSISTANT ATTORNEY GENERAL
WARREN OLNEY III

Marshall refers to, among other things, the famous case of Autherine Lucy, the first African American student to be admitted to the University of Alabama. Shortly after her enrollment on February 1, white mobs gathered in protest, prompting university trustees to suspend her just five days later. The NAACP then protested the suspension, and on February 29 U.S. Judge Hobart Grooms ordered the university to reinstate Lucy. The twenty-six-year-old student boldly announced that she would return to the classroom, and Marshall could not have been more pleased. "That girl sure has guts," he stated.

MARCH 14, 1956

Dear Mr. Olney:

This will acknowledge your letter of March 13 concerning the report in the *Washington Post* of my talk at the meeting of the NAACP in Washington on last Sunday. I read the article for the first time as it was enclosed in your letter, and at the outset I would say that the entire article is the result of an unfortunate emphasis by the reporter. I did not spend an hour attacking the Department of Justice. I don't believe I mentioned the Justice Department more than twice.

I discussed the murders of Rev. G. W. Lee and Lamar Smith and the shooting of Gus Courts. I said from the information we had these cases were entitled to consideration by the Department of Justice and that the violence against them seemed to be connected with the exercise of the right to register and vote. I still believe I am correct on this. I at no time have ever said that the Department of Justice had jurisdiction over the Till case. I didn't say it last Sunday and I never have said it at any time. On several occasions I have said that a good example of the deficiencies of the present civil rights statutes is that they did not cover the Till case.

At the meeting on last Sunday I did say that until the federal government put somebody in jail for denying the right to vote and murder in connection with voting, our government was not doing its duty. This was in connection with the failure of the state of Mississippi to act, and it was my intention to give the audience my opinion that until some concrete action had been accomplished by the federal government, Negroes in Mississippi were without protection from either the state or federal government in the exercise of their right to vote.

In regard to my suggestion as to what the Department of Justice can do within its own powers, I am certain that the Department of Justice can and should prosecute those responsible for denying the vote to Negroes in last year's Mississippi statewide elections. I also believe that it is within the power of the Department of Justice to investigate the actions of individuals and organizations such as the White Citizens Council who deliberately did everything in their power to thwart the order of Judge Grooms in the University of Alabama case. I, of course, cannot overemphasize the need for investigation of the actions of the White Citizens Councils in Mississippi and Alabama. In all frankness, I assume that this is being done. However, I cannot understand why some prosecutions have not been forthcoming especially in regard to the voting situation in Mississippi.

As to the statement that the fight would be "mean, nasty and dirty," this is a complete misstatement or misquote. What I said was that the opposition to this fight for full equality will be mean, nasty and dirty. After this warning, I pointed out specifically to the audience that we did not intend to get down into the gutter with the opposition but would continue to maintain our fight on a high plane. I am enclosing copy of self-explanatory letter to the *Washington Post* on this point.

On reading the clipping you sent, I could very well understand your anxiety but assure you that it is an almost complete job of misemphasis by the reporter and at least one direct misstatement of fact. I hope that you will take my word for what I actually said because I, for one, never intend to be guilty of misstatement of fact concerning any governmental agency and certainly not the Department of Justice. I have spent too much of my time and gotten too much criticism for trying to keep the record straight on the Department to, at this late date, change my position.

Sincerely,

Thurgood Marshall

ASSISTANT ATTORNEY GENERAL WARREN OLNEY III TO MARSHALL

MARCH 19, 1956

Dear Mr. Marshall:

I have received your letter of March 14, 1956, in reply to mine of March 13th, and with which you enclosed a copy of your letter to the *Washington Post* correcting some of the errors in that paper's report of your address to the National Association for the Advancement of Colored People made at the Vermont Avenue Baptist Church in Washington on Sunday, March 11th. I accept without reservation your explanation that the *Washington Post* article is "an almost complete job of misemphasis by the reporter and at least one direct misstatement of fact."

The assurance in your letter to me that you have never said that the Department of Justice had jurisdiction over the Till case is welcome and is consistent with the view you have expressed in private on a number of other occasions. Undoubtedly you are aware that some members and officers of the NAACP, as well as others, have repeatedly made public statements which have been critical of the Department for not taking action in that case. Such criticism is, as I am sure you must realize, unfair to the Department and misleading to the general public, including the NAACP's own membership. When the Director and Counsel of the NAACP Legal Defense and Educational Fund, upon whom the organization has in the past depended for legal advice, appears on the same platform where this untrue and unfair criticism is uttered, and says nothing to correct it, the impression is very naturally created that you concur. I note that in your letter to the editor of the *Washington Post* you were again silent on this subject and that you did not even repeat to him what you were at the same time writing privately to me about your personal realization that there was no federal jurisdiction under which the Department could have taken action in the Till case.

In your letter to me you write concerning your speech of the 11th:

> *I discussed the murders of Rev. G. W. Lee and Lamar Smith and the shooting of Gus Courts. I said that from the information we had these cases were entitled to consideration by the Department of Justice and that the violence against them seemed to be connected with the exercise of the right to register and vote. I still believe I am correct on this.*

I am certain that you are well aware that all three of these cases have been the subject of the most careful consideration by the Department of Justice. In all three cases the Federal Bureau of Investigation was promptly requested by the Criminal Division of the Department to obtain all the facts and evidence in order to determine whether federal jurisdiction existed. It is true, of course, that if the violence in any of these cases arose out of the exercise, or attempt to exercise, the right to register to vote in any federal election, or was perpetrated in any election at all under color of law, federal jurisdiction would be established. However, up to the present time no such evidence has come to light.

In the case of the murder of the Reverend George Wesley Lee the FBI investigation did not substantiate the allegation that he was killed because of his refusal to remove his name from the Humphreys County, Mississippi, list of registered voters. Since the sole jurisdiction to prosecute for the murder lay with the State of Mississippi, the Department's only proper course was to furnish the District Attorney of Humphreys County with the pertinent facts. This has been done.

In the Lamar Smith case there is also a total lack of federal jurisdiction. It is true that Smith had been active in matters relating to an election shortly before he was shot, but the evidence obtained by the FBI does not establish a connection between this activity and the shooting. Moreover, because this was a local election in which there were no federal candidates, no federal jurisdiction would exist to prosecute for the violence unless the perpetrators were state or local officials or were otherwise acting under color of law. The circumstances of the shooting, as developed by the FBI, negate such a possibility.

According to Gus Courts, an effort was made to intimidate him and to compel him to cancel his registration and to refrain from voting in any election, including an election involving federal candidates. Such intimidation, if it occurred, is a violation of federal law, and the FBI has been requested to determine the facts. The investigation has included inquiry into the subsequent shooting of Courts, but it has not been possible to identify his assailant and neither has it been possible to establish that the shooting in actuality originated with anything connected with Courts' registration or with voting. Consequently it cannot be said with any certainty that jurisdiction exists under the federal civil rights statutes. This does not mean that the Courts case has been neglected by the Department. The FBI was requested to investigate the allegations of intimidation, including circumstances of the subsequent shooting, as soon as it was learned that there was a possibility that this violence might have originated in an attempt to prevent registration or voting in an election protected by federal law. The Department is prepared to prosecute whenever the evidence is sufficient to establish the commission of a federal offense and the identity of the perpetrator.

In the Lee, Smith and Court cases the Department has done everything possible to determine whether any crime against the laws of the United States were committed and, if so, by whom. The law and the facts, as you well know, do not permit of anything more. Yet the plain implication of your speech, as reported in your letter to me, is that the Department has failed in its duty in these cases. In your letter to me you go on and say, "At the meeting last Sunday I did say that until the federal government put somebody in jail for denying the right to vote and murder in connection with voting, our government was not doing its duty."

Our government has done and is doing its full duty in its attempt to investigate these cases. If federal jurisdiction can be established and the perpetrators of these crimes identified, the government will prosecute. It is untrue and unfair to say that the government is not doing its duty simply because success has so far eluded its best investigative efforts.

Your letter also says that you are certain that this Department can and should prosecute those responsible for denying the vote to Negroes in last year's Mississippi statewide elections. You are referring no doubt to the alleged disenfranchisement of the Negro voters in Mound Bayou. Yet you know that the Department did investigate this incident thoroughly, and that the question of prosecution is presently under consideration. Is it fair to accuse the Department of having failed in its duty even before a determination has been made as to whether prosecution is legally justified?

I do not comment upon your remarks concerning the White Citizens' Councils since you have not criticized the Department's treatment of them.

In concluding your letter to me you write:

> *. . . I, for one, never intend to be guilty of misstatement of fact concerning any governmental agency and certainly not the*

Department of Justice. I have spent too much of my time and gotten too much criticism for trying to keep the record straight on the Department, to at this late date change my position.

This is a proper sentiment, but I find it difficult to reconcile with what you have said about the Department in the Lee, Smith and Courts cases and with what you left unsaid in public about the Till case.

During the past three years it has been the purpose of the Attorney General and the Criminal Division of the Department of Justice to enforce all the federal and criminal statutes, including the civil rights laws, with equal efficiency and vigor. We have done so. Our actions in all the many civil rights cases that have arisen during these years are the proof. In connection with the enforcement of these laws there is nothing which should have or could have been done which has been left undone by the Department. It would appear to me that the record of your public remarks upon the Department's conduct of civil rights cases is in need of some straightening out.

Sincerely yours,

Warren Olney III

MARSHALL TO ASSISTANT ATTORNEY GENERAL WARREN OLNEY III

MARCH 21, 1956

Dear Mr. Olney:

I have your letter of March 19th and hate to get involved in such a discussion with you. And I say this in good faith.

It is perfectly all right for you as an official of the Department of Justice or for me as an ordinary lawyer to have our views as to the cold instrument of the law. It is another thing to sit idly by and realize that injustices of all types are rampant in Mississippi and Alabama and both the state and federal governments seem powerless to stop this wave of terror ranging from economic pressure to cold-blooded murders.

I did not know the official action in the Lee and Smith cases until after I had made the Washington speech. I still feel that their murders were the result of their insisting on their right to register and vote and for the purpose of intimidation over other Negroes who might exercise their right to vote. I had hoped the Department would have been able to establish this and to bring about the prosecutions under the civil rights statutes. The fact that it couldn't be done because of the apparent lack of trustworthy testimony does not completely eliminate my belief that Negroes are not getting the protection they are entitled to as citizens.

Your answer, of course, that the evidence is just not available, is a good one and one with which I cannot quarrel. However, I do think I have a right to say that there is something wrong that neither state nor federal governments can protect Negroes in the exercise of their constitutionally protected rights. Maybe the answer is stronger federal laws. Maybe the answer is more funds for investigation. Whatever it is, the fact remains that the wave of terror will continue. I do not see how I can be expected to remain quiet on that point.

You also mention in your letter that I did not write to the *Washington Post* about the Till case. The reason I did not do so was because the article you sent me from the *Washington Post* did not mention the Till case and my letter to you was in response to your letter, which was marked "personal."

You also inquire in your letter about the apparent difference between local and federal elections insofar as civil rights statutes are concerned. As a result of the cases of *Smith v. Allwright* and *Terry v. Adams*, I am unable to see any difference between federal and local elections insofar as the Constitution and laws of the United States are concerned.

Finally, I do not for the life of me understand why it is taking so long to set up the prosecution in the Mound Bayou and similar cases of denial of the right to vote in last year's Mississippi elections. When we are completely denied justice in the courts of Mississippi, I think it only right and proper that we look to the federal government for vigorous prosecution in cases involving the denial of a federal right.

Sincerely,

Thurgood Marshall

MARSHALL TO ROBERT NEWBEGIN

Marshall sends rare political commentary to Robert Newbegin, a resident of Roslyn, New York.

MARCH 22, 1956

Dear Mr. Newbegin:

I have your letter of March 16 and have read it very carefully. While I am a registered Democrat, I have always been an independent voter and I do not ever remember voting a straight ticket of any party. Rather, I believe in voting for men and measures rather than for voting for parties as such. It would make no real difference whether I was registered Democrat or Republican. I do not, however, enjoy your emotional regard for either political party. I agree with you that Governor Dewey did a splendid job in getting through the legislature to set up the State Commission Against Discrimination. I and many other Negroes have voted for Governor Dewey as governor for the state of New York.

I also voted for Willkie for President. At the same time I hope you will agree that I did right in voting for Senator Lehman for senator as I voted for Senator Ives for senator. I do not believe that Negroes should blindly follow any political party. If this is the burden of your letter, I agree with you. However, if the burden of your letter is that Negroes should solely support the Republican ticket, I would disagree with you. Why not join us in urging Negro and white Americans to vote for men and measures rather than for party labels?

Sincerely,

Thurgood Marshall

MARSHALL TO B. K. VINE

In this letter to a resident of Flushing, New York, Marshall states his opposition to the notion that African Americans should return to Africa.

MARCH 22, 1956

Dear Mr. Vine:

I have your letter of March 19. I, of course, do not agree with certain statements in your letter, especially the one that "the white man created the South and developed the property." The truth of the matter is that the Negroes by their sweat did more to develop the South than anyone else. At least it was a joint venture with the Negro getting the short end of financial return.

I also did not agree that the solution of the problem is to set up a separate country in Africa or someplace else. There is no more reason to send the Negroes back to their country than there is to send others back to their native countries. As a matter of fact, the Negroes are quite satisfied with this country and the Constitution and the Fourteenth Amendment. It would, therefore, seem better to suggest that those in the South who do not like the Fourteenth Amendment would be the ones to leave.

Sincerely,

Thurgood Marshall

MARSHALL TO ROY WILKINS

Marshall refers to the International News Service (INS), a news wire agency similar to the Associated Press, in this memorandum about the anniversary of Brown.

MAY 8, 1956

This is the first portion of a statement which INS has requested that I do on what has been accomplished since the decision and what remains. I would like you to look this over. I will call Alice from Miami this afternoon and add to it.

> During the past two years, while we have witnessed many disgraceful actions on the part of some Southern Americans, significant and far-reaching progress has been made toward true democracy. In the first place, the solid South has been shattered. Desegregation of public schools is moving ahead in nine of the

seventeen Southern states. More than a quarter of a million Negro children are now attending mixed schools in these nine states and the District of Columbia. Up to two years ago, we had seventeen states against the Union and the world. Now we have but eight. This is significant progress.

. . .

In some areas of the South effective resistance exists solely because the people in those areas do not yet realize the Constitution is supreme and have fears that desegregation will not work. It is just a matter of time until many of these people clarify their thinking on both points and start toward desegregation. "We have nothing to fear but fear itself."

Of course, there will be some who will refuse to face realities. For purely selfish prejudiced reasons they will oppose the law of the land to the bitter end. . . . They have placed themselves in rebellion against the Constitution. For those recalcitrant school officials who refuse to even start, we have no recourse but to pursue the matter through the courts.

FBI MEMORANDUM

The following memorandum from Agent Jones to Agent Nichols shows not only that the FBI was still tracking Marshall rather closely in 1956 but also that Marshall gave a favorable public impression of the Montgomery bus boycott led by Martin Luther King, Jr.—no doubt disappointing news for the King-loathing J. Edgar Hoover. Marshall also commented on King in his speech at the NAACP's annual convention a month later, when he praised the "unblemished forthright Christian leadership of men like Rev. M.L. King, Rev. Abernathy, and E.D. Nixon."

But Marshall's later assessment of the boycott, as recounted by Harris Wofford, the future head of the civil rights office in the Kennedy White House, was not quite that positive: "All that walking for nothing! They could just as well have waited while the bus case went up through the courts, without all the work and worry of the boycott."

Marshall also found himself disagreeing with King's early attitude toward the law. "I used to have a lot of fights with Martin about his theory about disobeying the law," Marshall recalled in 1977. "I didn't believe in that. I thought you did have a right to disobey a law, and you also had a right to go to jail for it." At first, Marshall recalled, King "couldn't see the second part, but eventually he did."

MAY 21, 1956

Thurgood Marshall, special counsel of the NAACP, appeared on the television program, "Youth Wants to Know," on the National Broadcasting Network yesterday afternoon. [Deleted] was the moderator.

. . .

Marshall advocated passive resistance as exemplified by the recent Montgomery, Alabama, bus situation as the best method of operating in the South because the NAACP absolutely refuses to utilize force representative of the force applied against the Negro by the whites in the South. He stated the NAACP was surprised by the development and conditions of the Montgomery situation and he referred to it as a "grass roots upheaval" with which the NAACP had nothing to do. In regard to the present political campaign Marshall denied that there was any such thing as a "Negro vote" but that the Negroes should support the party with the best civil rights platform. He stated that unless the Democrats produce more in the civil rights platform, Negroes might go Republican.

In regard to White Citizens Council (WCC), he said that it represented a threat to the government as a whole and that like the Ku Klux Klan, these councils were a threat to the economic growth of the South and that in addition they controlled the state legislatures in Mississippi and Alabama and that their main reason for existence was to cut down the membership and the flow of funds to the NAACP.

Recommendation:

For information only.

Marshall's warning about the possibility of a weak Democratic platform on civil rights apparently fell on deaf ears. In an August 21 letter, which he wrote shortly after the Democratic convention, Marshall observed: "So far as I am concerned the Democrats' platform on civil rights was not a 'compromise,' it was a 'sell out.'"

MARSHALL TO ASSISTANT ATTORNEY GENERAL WARREN OLNEY III

This is a rare note of appreciation to the assistant attorney general about the Justice Department's brief seeking injunctive protection for the Hoxie school board in its ongoing efforts to desegregate public schools. Hostile whites had created a climate that made desegregation difficult, and the school board obtained a federal injunction that enjoined the segregationists from blocking the board's efforts.

SEPTEMBER 5, 1956

Dear Mr. Olney:

I just came across a copy of the brief for the United States as amicus curiae filed in the case involving the Hoxie school district now pending before the United States Court of Appeals for the Eighth Court. I am taking the liberty of making two comments to you concerning this brief.

In the first place, it is indeed gratifying to see action on the part of the Department of Justice as the legal arm of our government in filing a brief of this type in this most important case involving the right of a local school board to carry out the intent and purpose of the decision of the Supreme Court in the school segregation cases.

The second point I would like to make is that I have gone over the brief with a rather critical eye and there is no question but that it is an exceptionally well done legal document which should go a long way toward bringing about a more thorough understanding of the law on the point of desegregation of schools.

Sincerely,

Thurgood Marshall

The segregationists appealed the injunction against them, but then failed to appear at the September 10 hearing in the federal appellate court. The Department of Justice showed up, however, and the hearing marked the first time that a representative of the Eisenhower administration appeared in court to expedite compliance with Brown. *Representing the Justice Department, Henry Putzel, Jr., stated that the government had entered the case because of "its obligation to ensure respect for fundamental human rights."*

MARSHALL TO PRESIDENT DWIGHT EISENHOWER

During the war years, Marshall had expressed frustration with Eisenhower's failure to respond to numerous NAACP inquiries about the court-martials of African American soldiers, and here he dresses down "My Dear President Eisenhower" for giving support to those who blamed African Americans for racial violence.

SEPTEMBER 6, 1956

My Dear President Eisenhower:

Citizens in our country continue to look to our President for forthright leadership in enforcement of the Constitution and laws of the United States as interpreted by the United States Supreme Court. Likewise, we sincerely hope that our President will take an unequivocal stand against mob action wherever it occurs and regardless of who are the participants. With this in mind, we find views expressed by you at yesterday's press conference which are most disturbing to many of us.

In commenting on the disgraceful situations in Clinton, Tennessee, and Mansfield, Texas, which are the sole result of lawless mobs interfering with lawful governmental procedures, you are quoted as saying:

> But I do believe that we must all, regardless of our calling in this world, help to bring about a change in spirit *so that extremists on both sides* do not defeat what we know is a reasonable, logical conclusion to this whole affair, which is recognition of equality of men.
>
> Now, there—the South is full of people of goodwill, but they are not the ones we hear now. We hear the people that are adamant and are so filled with prejudice that they can't keep still—they even resort to violence; and *the same way on the other side of the thing, the people who want to have the whole matter settled today.* (underscoring ours)

In both of the underscored sections of this quotation, you have given support to many in this country who have sought to confuse the issue by trying to divide responsibility for such situations between lawless mobs and other Americans who seek only their lawful rights in a lawful manner, often after unbelievably long periods of waiting.

In the two instances you were discussing, it is apparent from the record that after considerable litigation in the true American tradition, duly constituted federal courts ordered desegregation of the public schools involved. At the outset there was no immediate opposition from the local people. However, after agitation by hate-mongers from other areas, the local people were swept into a frenzy of open defiance and opposition to the court orders. Please bear in mind that at this stage it is not a question of Negro citizens versus white citizens, but it is a question of unlawful violent opposition against the orders of duly constituted federal courts. These are the only "two [sides]" involved. Surely, you do not mean to equate lawless mobs with federal courts as "extremists."

I am certain that you do not mean to draw this comparison between the courts and the mobs. Rather I fear that you were comparing the lawless mobs with those of us who are trying under most difficult conditions to obtain the rights which have been enjoyed by all other Americans for these many years. If so, we respectfully suggest that the use of this language in this context is most unfortunate. There is nothing that anyone can point to which would in any way justify the use of such phrases in commenting upon Clinton, Tennessee, and Mansfield, Texas. To do so only beclouds the specific issue of whether or not lawlessness shall prevail anywhere in this country and tends to alleviate the full responsibility of the lawless mob by giving the impression that there is someone else or some group of people who are equally guilty of bringing about the lawless situation. Otherwise, the real guilty parties would be the framers of the Declaration of Independence and the Constitution of the United States.

After your press conference yesterday you stated that you had requested further information on these matters.

We, therefore, respectfully suggest that you reexamine your statements of yesterday in the light of facts which you no doubt now have at hand and speak out in forthright terms against anyone who openly and violently interferes with the orderly judicial processes of the federal government.

Respectfully,

Thurgood Marshall

MARSHALL TO MACEO SMITH

After Marshall had begun to provide legal aid to the Montgomery bus boycott, government officials in Alabama sought to ban the NAACP, partly by claiming that the organization engaged in politics and therefore violated its nonprofit status, and in June of 1956, an Alabama judge demanded that the NAACP surrender its membership list to his court as part of a ruling that found the Association guilty of conspiracy in promoting the Montgomery bus boycott. The NAACP refused the demand and appealed after it was found in contempt of court. Political leaders in other Southern states (Louisiana, Texas, Georgia, Virginia, Arkansas, Tennessee, South Carolina, Florida, and North Carolina) also began to plan their own legal attacks on the NAACP. As Robert Carter put it in a May 1957 memorandum, "The form of attack is now reasonably clear—to force the public identification of our members and contributors so that they can be subjected to terrorization; to have our activities declared illegal as constituting barratry, champetry, etc. and to force lawyers to cease handling cases sponsored by the NAACP on threat of disbarment; and to have us defined as a profit-making organization operating in violation of state revenue laws."

Although he seemed to hold a contrary position earlier, Marshall, a firm believer in the rule of law, now disagreed with NAACP leaders, including Roy Wilkins, who favored not disclosing the organization's membership lists, and in his letter to Maceo Smith below, Marshall concedes that it may be necessary for the NAACP to reveal its lists in Southern states that sought to ban the Association. The letter is important also because Marshall uses it to take a swipe at Lyndon Johnson in reply to Smith's argument that because Johnson and Price Daniel, two key political leaders in the state, had begun a "so-called campaign of moderation," the NAACP should not put the Texas NAACP on the list of Southern branches that might have to surrender their lists. Marshall compares Johnson and Daniel to Senator John Sparkman, a segregationist from Alabama.

SEPTEMBER 19, 1956

Dear Maceo:

I have carefully gone over your memorandum of September 13th and hasten to send this note even before discussing it with Roy. I still do not believe that we should exclude any of the Southern states from the proposal which has been agreed upon. All that you say in your memorandum is no doubt true. I am equally certain that your predictions are no doubt accurate. However, we are dealing with a matter of trusteeship, and if by any combination of circumstances your predictions are wrong and we are faced with the problem of giving up the names of Texas members, we will be in a tough spot without any means of retreat and it will be mighty tough to find that we were wrong in our judgment.

The only sure way and, indeed the only honest way, of dealing with this matter is to take the position that despite predictions to the contrary, we might be compelled to give up the names of our members. This is a true and accurate statement and any other statement could not be completely accurate. It has to be looked at from the viewpoint of the board of directors rather than from the viewpoint of any state regardless of how decent the picture might appear. Incidentally, I am sure you will agree that neither Prince Daniel nor Lyndon Johnson can be depended upon to keep their word insofar as Negroes or Negro organizations are concerned. This I assume is true of most of the politicians of the South. Certainly Lyndon Johnson nor Prince Daniel is in any better shape than Sparkman, who is now making pronouncement after pronouncement endorsing segregation.

Sincerely,

Thurgood Marshall

In spite of the harassment of Alabama officials, Marshall and Carter continued to offer legal advice to King and other leaders of the boycott, and the two NAACP legal minds worked together on the petition asking the Supreme Court to let stand a lower court's decision that ruled that bus segregation was unconstitutional. The Supreme Court ruled in favor of the NAACP's petition on November 13, 1956, and shortly after the historic ruling Martin Luther King, Jr., took his seat on an integrated bus in Montgomery. A little more than a year later, King sent a $1,000 donation to the NAACP LDF and once again expressed his thanks. "We will remain eternally grateful to you and your staff for the great work you have done for not only the Negro in particular but American Democracy in general. No sane objective, intelligent individual can deprecate the work of the NAACP."

Nevertheless, Marshall remained wary of King's tactics. Indeed, just three months earlier, Marshall played a significant role in drafting a resolution, adopted by the twenty-ninth annual NAACP convention in San Francisco, which stated that the convention was "not yet ready to take a position on [the technique of nonviolent resistance] as a national project." Marshall's concern for law and order—coupled with his deep suspicions about civil disobedience—was especially evident in the resolution's embrace of "lawful means" in the quest for racial justice. "We are convinced," the resolution stated, "that our program of action to obtain and enforce civil rights for all Americans must be broadened to the point of using all lawful means available to obtain our objectives."

ANONYMOUS TO MARSHALL

This letter, found in the "crank letters" file of the NAACP Papers, refers to an October state court hearing in Tyler, Texas, where Marshall and U. Simpson Tate were fighting the state's attempt to prevent the NAACP and LDF from carrying out their civil rights work within the state. Letters of criticism did not come only from white racists, of course. In July 1956, for instance, a former resident of Georgia wrote: "I am a negroe, and I'm as black as they come. Please why make all this silly fuss over segregation. . . . [Your work] is making things very unbearable for us colored folks. . . . Please leave things be as they were. Segregation is okay as long as its on equal footing. At least its America we live in. Im better off here than the people in some of the other lands segregation or not."

OCTOBER 11, 1956

Sirs,

I have just been listening to the proceedings of The Tyler case in which both of you are taking an active part.

If someone had told me 25 years ago that I would live to see the Dignity of the layw of this or any other state insulted by a NIGGER Cross Questioning one of The States High Officials, I would have thought they were crazy.

HERE,S some information that each of you need the Worst kind. The Niggers have come a long way since the days of Slavery, and No factor has been as much responsible for it as the Generosity of the White folks, and to think that while this was going on and their liveing conditions inproveing as they have, The Niggers were sneaking around under cover trying to create a situation which their habits of Life, Intelegence, and many other factors do not permit.

Here is something just as true as the idea that the Indians will never come back and take over the Country. "The Niggers will never accomplish their purpose, which they are useing as anti segregation, which in fact is

NIGGER EQUALITY. Supreme Court Ruleings, nor any Court Ruleings will never accomplish this idea.

I have lots of friends among the colored race. I have from time to time helped them in many ways as have lots of others of whom I know, But we are not going to have them attending White Schools, or useing White peoples Parks or Batheing Pools for more reasons than ONE.

You must know the Figures on the prevalence of Vanerial amoung your people. You Mustvknow the Lack of Chastity, and last but not least you must know that as a race they are FILTHY, and in practically all cases, especially amoung the one,s who would invade Swimming Pools, and Schools etc, they carry a Body Odor which is almost unbearable. NOT CLEAN and seem to want to be. Not Trustworthy, and do more Dastardly outrageous crimes (Sneaking off with Babies as it were, Rapeing them and then cutting their throats).

Of course you may make a little temporary progress in your Law suits, But there are lots of ways, except through legal process that White folks CAN and Will prevent their haveing to allow to be destroyed a manner of living that they and also most of the Niggers have been enjoying for all these years.

I belong to the KKK, But while they did lots of things I didn't sanction they forestalled lots of things outside the Law and probably delayed these maneuvers of yours for several years. THERE ARE LOTS OF THEM IN THE COUNTRY now. You may also remember 1861? This could easily be repeated if necessary.

You had just as well Call off the Dogs, and disband.

Of course you have already caused a feeling of distrust amoung the races, which none of us will ever outlive, and when you find yourself back where you started without the Friendship of the Whites, or any cooperation from them, you will then Realize what a fool you have been. You CANt Win. The white folks are not going to MIX with Niggers beyond the fair tteatment they have always given them.

God never intended that.

WHITE MAN

PS. I wish you knew that your task is impossible.

PS-This may be a little rough, but I imagine you know that the records show that every THIRD Nigger child is illegitimate.

This matter is already being given attention, and will become universal if necessary. Close all publoc Schools and substitute there for Private Schools. YOU CANT POSSIBLY WIN.

MARSHALL TO ISRAEL GOLDSTEIN

In his December 7 letter, the president of the American Jewish Congress invited Marshall to "an emergency meeting . . . to protest Nasser's reign of terror against Egyptian Jewry. We feel the American public must be made aware of the shocking expulsions, jailings and confiscation of property being perpetrated by the Egyptian dictator against a defenseless minority—in flagrant violation of the human rights provision of the UN Charter." Marshall's reply below provides further evidence that he did not altogether neglect international issues even as he appeared to focus stereoscopically on domestic matters related to racial injustice.

DECEMBER 10, 1956

Dear Dr. Goldstein:

I have just received your letter of December 7th concerning the emergency meeting at the Hotel Statler on December 19th. I do not know of anything more disturbing than Nasser's reign of terror and would welcome the opportunity to join you at this meeting but for the following fact. Our case against segregated schools in Dallas, Texas, is set for hearing beginning on December 19th and is absolutely essential that I be there for many reasons.

Although I cannot be with you at your meeting on December 19th, I hope you will know that I will most certainly be with you in spirit in doing everything possible to register the most vigorous protest against Nasser and all he stands for.

Sincerely,

Thurgood Marshall

MARSHALL TO AUTHERINE LUCY FOSTER

The University of Alabama's board of trustees had refused to comply with an earlier decision enjoining them to reinstate Autherine Lucy Foster, and on

January 18 Judge Hobart Grooms ruled that the board "was justified in expelling" Foster. Board members had expelled her for making "false, defamatory, impertinent and scandalous charges" after she and her attorneys had accused them of allowing campus riots to occur.

FEBRUARY 15, 1957

Dear Mrs. Foster:

The question as to appealing the possibility of appealing the last ruling of Judge Grooms in your case has given us no end of difficulty. In the first place, all of us in this office and, indeed I am certain, that all good Americans feel indebted to you for all that you have done to bring democracy into practice in Alabama. None of this would have been possible but for your determination to secure your rights guaranteed by the Constitution and laws of the United States. Whatever we have been able to do to help along the way on this has been done in the interest and justice for Americans without regard to their race or color.

The main point has been established in your case and that is the right of Negroes to attend the University of Alabama. No one will ever be able to take from you the credit you deserve for bringing this about. There is likewise no doubt in anyone's mind that Negroes will be attending the University of Alabama in the very near future. Thus, the first point to be considered ends up with the fact that you have opened the University of Alabama by this court decision and all that remains is for qualified Negroes to apply. Their rights will be enforced by the courts. This, of course, assumes that our federal government will protect the Negroes who do apply in the future.

As to your particular case: The problem becomes extremely difficult through no fault of your own. The last ruling of Judge Grooms has placed the expulsion order on such technical grounds as to cast considerable doubt on the possibility of a successful appeal in the federal appellate courts where jurisdiction is limited to federal questions. Judge Groom decided the case on the nonfederal ground that the university had the right to discipline a pupil. Even if this ruling would be upset on appeal, there is little doubt but that the University of Alabama officials would merely admit you and then expel you for the same reason, after they had technically complied with the court order. Thus, nothing would be accomplished at that stage. There is also considerable legal opinion that the appeal would not be successful.

We have, therefore, reluctantly come to the position after considering all of the factors that we are advised against appealing the latest ruling of Judge Grooms. I hope you will recognize that this decision was arrived at only after the most careful deliberation and with great reluctance.

Whatever happens in the future, remember from all concerned that your contribution has been made toward equal justice for all Americans and that you have done everything in your power to bring this about. Bearing this in mind, we continue to look to the future.

Sincerely,

Thurgood Marshall

The university would reverse its expulsion order—in 1980.

MARSHALL TO WALTER WINCHELL

Marshall consistently stayed in touch with the media—liberal and conservative, black and white—during his years with the NAACP, and here he sends a telegram of appreciation to Walter Winchell, a white columnist who regularly denounced civil rights violations, for his February 16 column celebrating the arrest of sixteen "yellow members" of the White Citizens Council in Clinton, Tennessee, after their attack on an African American minister who had escorted local black children to public school. Winchell wrote:

> *Now, Mr. Brownell, you ought to put the whole damn organization where it belongs—alongside the name of the KKK on your U.S. Attorney General's subversive list. . . . Their ugly record shows that the White Citizen Councils have adopted a policy of advocating or approving force or violence to deny others their constitutional rights. It shows that they have created a climate of fear in many Southern communities and have promoted group hatred and group violence. In short, it shows they are anti-American and subversive.*

FEBRUARY 18, 1957

Just read your recent column reprinted in Pittsburgh Courier on White Citizens Council, Klan and others. Thanks a million for a marvelous column during a very trying period.

Thurgood Marshall

EPILOGUE

In one of their last acts together as colleagues, Thurgood Marshall and Roy Wilkins invited their friends and supporters to join them in celebrating the third anniversary of *Brown*. On the same day of the celebration—May 16, 1957—the board of the NAACP Legal Defense and Educational Fund, Inc. (NAACP LDF), following Marshall's counsel, passed a resolution that "no person should be a Board member, officer, or employee of this corporation who is also a Board member, officer or employee of the NAACP."

Marshall advocated this formal separation after an IRS investigation, prompted by segregationist politicians, had noted that the tax-exempt NAACP LDF and the taxpaying NAACP were not independent—a ruling that threatened the NAACP LDF's tax exemption. Other reasons, no doubt, fueled Marshall's counsel—for example, his frustrating relationship with Robert Carter (who, conveniently, would leave the NAACP LDF to become the NAACP's general counsel), his resistance to NAACP calls that he develop a more activist legal department, his disagreement with NAACP leaders about the possibility of releasing membership lists to southern courts, and his increasing need for professional independence. But when explaining the move in years to follow, Marshall would consistently point to the IRS decision as the major factor.

The resolution meant that the NAACP LDF and the NAACP were now separate organizations, each with its own board, budget, staff, and program. It also meant that Marshall's stunning career with the NAACP had formally come to an end.

Although the story of Marshall's civil rights letters during his tenure with the NAACP ends here, his career as the nation's most important civil rights lawyer would flourish for several more years. After formally leaving the NAACP, Marshall immediately became director-counsel of the NAACP LDF, and just around the corner waited the school crisis in Little Rock, Arkansas, the second wave of Freedom Riders, and more race-based murders. These, of course, were exactly the type of cases that made Thurgood Marshall what he was and would continue to be—a civil rights rebel.

It should come as no surprise that the rebel Marshall would continue to write pointed civil rights letters during his tenure with the NAACP LDF (1957–1961). Unfortunately, because the papers of the NAACP LDF are closed to the public, we do not have access to most of the letters he wrote during this period. But we are fortunate to have some evidence of such letters in other public papers, especially presidential papers, and these reveal that Marshall's civil rights pen was alive and healthy in his new role with the NAACP LDF. Consider one of my favorite documents in the Dwight D. Eisenhower Library—a telegram that Marshall sent Eisenhower a little more than four months after he left the NAACP, when the 1957 Little Rock school integration crisis was still in crisis mode:

> Today, after withdrawal of federal troops from Central High School in Little Rock, Arkansas, Negro children were harassed by groups of other children inside of school. Their complaints to the National Guard were ignored and laughed at. This is typical of what can be expected if federal troops are withdrawn. As one of the attorneys representing Negro children involved in Little Rock crisis I urge you not withdraw federal troops until you are personally convinced that the safety of these children as well as that of the country is guaranteed. Certainly this cannot be assured until mob hysteria created by Governor Faubus and his agents has had sufficient time to die down under firm hand of government. Past actions of Governor Faubus require that you have absolute assurance that he will protect Negroes involved. Any weakening of the federal government's position in Little Rock will encourage others to risk presence of federal troops if they are only to be there for a week. Negro Americans, while not represented at

> conferences about Little Rock, continue to hope for the continued firm protection of their national government. For these reasons we respectfully urge that no concessions be made.

Predictably, Eisenhower did not reply.

Although they are few in number, at least by comparison to his letters in the NAACP Papers, the public letters of Marshall's career with the NAACP LDF suggest that just as his passion for civil rights flourished after he left the NAACP, so too did his remarkable productivity. Consider this striking report that he mailed to the future Washington, D.C., mayor Marion Barry, then a student leader in the civil rights movement, about the NAACP LDF's defense of the many students involved in the sit-in movement in 1960:

> We are now participating in the defense of between 1,500 and 1,750 individuals. In many cases a single individual is actually involved in more than one proceeding. For example, there are some students who have been arrested for sitting-in or demonstrating on several occasions. In other cases the same individual is charged with several different alleged crimes, such as, trespass, conspiracy and violation of fire ordinances. In at least two cities we have had several lawyers tied up in litigation over a period of more than four months on a daily basis.

Marshall went on to list thirteen states (and many more communities) where the NAACP LDF was defending students from prosecution. And if the litigation demands of the sit-in movement were not enough to fill Marshall's plate in 1960, in this same year he accepted an invitation to serve as legal advisor to the Kenyan nationalists as they met in London to draft their constitution. The Kenyans knew him as the most effective advocate for the constitutional rights of African Americans in the United States, and they, like so many others who had been disenfranchised through the years, craved his expert knowledge and counsel about securing and safeguarding democratic rights.

During his short-lived (not quite five years) but ceaselessly busy tenure with the NAACP LDF, Marshall also carried on his favorite practice of lambasting the media, white and black, when he sensed that it failed in accurately reporting his work as a civil rights leader. Here, for instance, is a blunt telegram he sent to John Johnson, the founder of *Jet* and *Ebony*, in 1961:

> May 25th Jet contains the following statement quote in a Raleigh, N.C. speech given at a time the Freedom Riders were touring the state, "NAACPer Thurgood Marshall rapped the sponsoring group (CORE) for not defending in court its members after the civil rights demonstrations. CORE officials considered the attack 'a low blow' and an example of how the NAACP attempts to embarrass other groups in the civil rights field. P.S. CORE does have legal counsel for any of the members arrested during the ride, but participants are pledged to stay in jail if sentenced as part of the protest." I did speak in Raleigh, North Carolina Sunday, May seventh but did not mention Freedom Riders, CORE or anything in relation to either Freedom Riders or CORE. Your staff could have checked this with me before publication especially in view of innuendo in statement. Unfairness of statement more evidenced by fact that your staff obviously did check with CORE. Would appreciate correction by you.

Make no mistake about it: The old rebel kept rebelling at the NAACP LDF. But Marshall's conservative streaks also remained intact as he transitioned to his new leadership role, and he continued to inform the FBI about African American militants and individuals with leftist leanings. In 1959, for example, he sent the agency a flyer that he had picked up in Detroit. Titled "WHERE DO YOU STAND on the question of SELF-DEFENSE?" the fascinating flyer read:

> Robert Williams, NAACP president in Union County, North Carolina, was suspended from his post by NAACP Secretary Roy Wilkins. Williams' 'crime' is that he said Negroes can't expect justice from Jim Crow courts, and should meet violence with violence. On June 3 he was put on trial before an NAACP committee in New York, whose recommendation will be taken up by the NAACP national board on June 8. Who is right—Williams or Wilkins? Should Negroes defend themselves when attacked or should they turn the other cheek? With school integration still a goal to be reached five years after the Supreme Court decision; with the murder of Mack Charles Parker, dragged from his Mississippi jail cell; with recent court decisions freeing white men accused of assaulting Negro women; with continued violence directed against negroes, North and South—

> the debate now rages: HOW SHALL NEGROES PROTECT THEMSELVES AND THEIR RIGHTS? What program is needed to win the fight for Negro equality? Hear "The Case of Robert Williams," Friday, June 12, 8 PM, Eugene V. Debs Hall 3737 Woodward, SPONSOR Friday Night Socialist Forum.

Marshall, who no doubt favored Wilkins over Williams, sent along a simple note with the flyer in his mailing to the FBI: "I picked this up while it was being distributed in Detroit on Friday night. I thought you might want it." If Marshall was a rebel after leaving the NAACP, then, he was a patriotic rebel committed to U.S. democracy, the resolution of civil rights cases through litigation in the court system, and the work of the FBI in countering individuals and movements deemed to be subversive of the U.S. government.

As for its part, the FBI continued to monitor Marshall throughout his tenure with the NAACP LDF, tracking his travels and speeches. The most attention it granted to Marshall, however, came in 1961, when the Kennedy administration instructed the FBI to conduct a nationwide investigation for the president as he considered nominating Marshall to the U.S. Court of Appeals for the Second Circuit.

Predictably, many of the FBI reports from the South were downright damning. A report from Richmond, Virginia, for instance, quoted a prominent attorney as saying that:

> If Marshall were a white man, he would never be considered for a judgeship. He added that Marshall is a 'run of the mill' attorney in that his legal abilities are below average; his legal experience appears to have been limited to civil rights and racial matters; and he is biased and bigoted in his approach to issues concerning members of his own race. He also noted that Marshall has never, to his knowledge, held any sort of judicial position, and he observed that, in his opinion, Marshall could not judge issues dispassionately and solely on the basis of the issues proven through the admission of legal evidence.

But there was at least one Southern attorney who offered another perspective—Virginia governor J. Lindsay Almond, Jr. In his prior role as the state's attorney general, Almond had argued against Marshall numerous times in federal court, and his knowledge of Marshall's legal temperament was extensive.

The governor did not draw attention to Marshall's obvious lack of a refined pedigree when the FBI interviewed him; nor did he dispute the point about Marshall's stereoscopic focus on civil rights cases. Instead, he characterized Marshall as "a very capable lawyer; level-headed and highly experienced." Almond also stated "that as far as deciding matters concerning racial segregation . . . Mr. Marshall as a judge would lean over backwards in order to decide a case strictly on its merits," and that "many people who might question the qualifications for Mr. Marshall for the judiciary would be highly influenced in their judgments because of Mr. Marshall's race."

The governor was exactly right on this last point—pride and prejudice would and did pollute the judicial politics surrounding Marshall's nomination to the federal bench. Urged on by civil rights advocates like Frank Reeves and William Coleman, President Kennedy nominated Marshall for the federal bench in mid-August of 1961. But it would take the full Senate Judiciary Committee eleven months before voting on his nomination. Unsurprisingly, the committee vote saw four Southern senators, headed by the segregationist James Eastland of Mississippi, opposing the eleven votes to confirm.

With his ascension to the federal bench (where, incidentally, not one of his decisions was overturned), Marshall left behind his role as "Mr. Civil Rights," at least in the sense of serving as the nation's most preeminent legal advocate for first-class citizenship for African Americans. But his reputation, particularly among those who knew him well, followed him for the rest of his life. After he was appointed to the Supreme Court, for example, fellow Associate Justice Lewis F. Powell, steeped in the field of U.S. history, wrote Marshall a letter that included one of the most memorable tributes he must have received in his lifetime: "I have said publicly that, when the proper history is written of our time, you will be recognized as having done more to assure freedom for the Negro race than any other." Marshall's civil rights reputation also came to the fore shortly after he died on January 24, 1993, when his closest colleague on the Supreme Court bench, Associate Justice William Brennan, then retired, offered this glowing tribute: "Thurgood Marshall's commitment to making the Constitution a vehicle to protect the equal rights of all has no match in American history."

How are we to test such high words of praise? Perhaps we might shift our gaze away from the Supreme Court bench for a moment and turn toward everyday life—to the boys and girls of all colors who, right now, are studying in integrated public schools, playing on integrated playgrounds, and swimming in integrated pools. Or to the adults of all colors who are working in integrated businesses, living in integrated neighborhoods, and voting at integrated polling places. And with that last point in mind, perhaps we might look upward again, this time to Capitol Hill, with its resplendent white dome, or even to the White House itself, where pillars of white privilege have begun to fade, crack, and rock back and forth.

Was Lewis Powell right? Did Thurgood Marshall really do more to assure freedom for African Americans than anyone else? And was Brennan right in claiming that Marshall's constitutionally inspired commitment to protecting the equal rights of all was without match in U.S. history?

The case is in your hands.

ACKNOWLEDGMENTS

On June 28, 1946, NAACP delegates and supporters gathered in Cincinnati, Ohio, to honor the man who three weeks earlier had won yet another Supreme Court victory to advance the cause of civil rights, this one securing the right to interstate travel without having to suffer the indignity of racial segregation. As he stood to receive the Spingarn Medal, the NAACP's annual award for distinguished achievement, Thurgood Marshall, beloved for his fun personality, especially his jokes and storytelling and deep laughs, took a serious moment to express his gratitude. "In accepting the medal with sincere appreciation," he stated, "I wish to make it clear that it is accepted with the understanding that it is an award coming to one person in recognition of the work of a large group of lawyers who have always worked together in a spirit of wholehearted cooperation and without any hope of reward other than that of seeing a job done." It was classic Marshall, always quick to tip his hat to his formidable legal team, and he did not take long to widen the circle, either, thanking not only the attorneys but also "all of our delegates present at this convention who have made the victories of these legal cases possible."

Although his understanding was immeasurably richer than mine will ever be, Marshall knew exactly what I have come to sense—the National Association for the Advancement of Colored People is a generous organization. And I could not be more grateful than I am for the NAACP's willingness to share the early civil rights letters of Thurgood Marshall with the wider world. Special thanks to Lynn Slawson and Ned Himmelrich for their assistance with contract matters related to permission to publish the NAACP letters. On a similar note, I must thank those individuals whose family members were closely connected with the NAACP and who kindly granted me permission to publish letters authored by their loved ones: Karen Hastie Williams, Loren Miller, and Rodney Hinton.

I, too, need to widen the circle, and my gratitude immediately extends to five strong women who have played indispensable roles in bringing this book to publication: Linda Loewenthal of the David Black Literary Agency, Dawn Davis and Maya Ziv of Amistad/HarperCollins, Sharon Herr, and Alyson Shade. I have said it before, and I will say it again—Linda is a literary agent extraordinaire, and I cannot even begin to imagine that there is anyone better in the business. Dawn expressed interest in the book early on, and she strengthened the manuscript with a technical precision that Marshall would no doubt join me in admiring and appreciating. Maya kept us on track and brought order out of disorder. Sharon and Alyson were and are beautiful treasures—there are no better words to describe them—and their work in research, typing, and proofreading, coupled with their easy smiles, made my work a lot easier, and far more enjoyable, than it otherwise would have been.

Derrick Bell responded, enthusiastically and energetically, to my invitation to write the foreword, and I am grateful for not only his compelling words but also his thoughts on improving the manuscript and, even more, his ongoing efforts to achieve equal justice for all.

I am also greatly indebted to the professional staff members of the Manuscript Reading Room at the Library of Congress. Many thanks to all of them for their expert assistance as I navigated my way through the NAACP Papers—the most valuable collection of civil rights papers in the world. I looked at the microfilm version of the papers at Pattee/Paterno Library at Pennsylvania State University, and the librarians there were characteristically helpful, especially in advocating for the purchase of new computers for microfilm research.

Numerous other archives and archivists, and libraries and librarians, offered invaluable assistance along the way, including Andrew Salinas of the Amistad Research Center at Tulane; Cynthia Ostroff of Yale University Library; Harlan Greene of the Avery Research Center of African American History and Culture at the College of Charleston; Juliette Smith of Savory Library at Talladega College; Joellen ElBashir of the Moorland Spingarn Research Center at Howard University; Henry Fulmer of the South Caroliniana Library at the University of South Carolina; Louis Jackson at the

Martin Luther King, Jr. Papers Project at Stanford University; Sylvia Morra, Louise Hyder-Darlington, Anna Pilston, and Joan Quinn of High Library at Elizabethtown College; Tom Mooney of the Nebraska State Historical Society; Deborah Dandridge and Tara Wenger of the Kenneth Spencer Research Library at the University of Kansas Libraries; Dorothy Hazelrigg of the Thomas Cooper Library at the University of South Carolina; David Kessler of the Bancroft Library at the University of California, Berkeley; Susan Brady at the Beinecke Rare Book and Manuscript Library at Yale University; Harriet Obus of the American Jewish Historical Society; Wendy Pflug of the University of Pittsburgh; Emily Ferrigno of the Irving S. Gilmore Music Library at Yale University; Jean Cannon of the Harry Ransom Research Center at the University of Texas at Austin; Regine Hebberlein of the Seeley G. Mudd Manuscript Library at Princeton University; Carrie Hintz of the Butler Library at Columbia University; Mary Ann Quinn of the Rockefeller Archive Center; and Harry Miller of the Wisconsin Historical Society.

Thanks, too, to the Federal Bureau of Investigation; the John Jacob Library at Washington and Lee University; Harvard Law Library; the Special Research Library at the University of Kansas; the Special Collections Research Center at Syracuse University Library; the Houghton Library of Harvard University; the Hoover Institution Archives at Stanford University; Schlesinger Library at Harvard University; the Rare Book and Manuscript Library at Columbia University; Wilson Library at the University of North Carolina; the University of Pittsburgh Library; Brown University Library; the W. E. B. Du Bois Library at the University of Massachusetts; and the presidential libraries of Franklin D. Roosevelt, Harry S. Truman, and Dwight D. Eisenhower.

A word of thanks is also due to scholars and journalists whose stellar works I have drawn from when trying to understand Thurgood Marshall and the NAACP, especially Mark Tushnet, Howard Ball, Patricia Sullivan, Carl Rowan, Roger Goldman, Risa Goluboff, Juan Williams, Glenda Elizabeth Gilmore, and Taylor Branch.

Jeff Long, an internationally respected scholar of Hinduism, the chair of the department of religious studies at Elizabethtown College, and an all-around good guy, deserves my thanks for the support and encouragement he sends my way so reliably. My students at Elizabethtown College have heard many an excursus on Thurgood Marshall and his legal quest for equal justice, and I thank them for expressing an interest in my scholarly work or, at the very least, for egging me on to share my interests beyond the topic of the day. My friend Karen Hodges dared to entrust me with her expensive camera, and my research assistant, Sari Mauro, has always stood ready to track down information. Two leaders on campus—Provost Susan Traverso and Dean Chris Bucher—were exceptionally kind in granting funds to help cover costs related to publishing the NAACP letters.

Thanks, too, to the owners of the best coffee shop in the universe—Al and Sue Pera of Cornerstone Coffeehouse in Camp Hill—and the hipsters they attract, most notably Carmen Finestra and Frank and Chris Suran. How the Commonwealth of Pennsylvania can survive with Frank no longer at the helm as state archivist is a question that plagues all concerned researchers.

Connie and Bob Long, and Lis and Jan Hagen-Frederiksen, have offered their inimitable care and concern throughout this project, and I am happily indebted to them.

I could never adequately write these acknowledgments without expressing thanks to Karin and our sons, Jackson Griffith and Nathaniel Finn. It is my hope that one day Jack and Nate, whom Karin mothers with toughness and tenderness, will read this book and come to understand, perhaps more fully than before, that there are boys and girls who are not able to enjoy the good life that we take for granted in Highland Park—with its great schools, safe parks, and affordable homes—and that they in turn will offer their own thanks by somehow marshalling the justice that, in spite of Thurgood Marshall's rich legacy, still eludes us after all these years.

A POSTSCRIPT ON THE MAJOR PLAYERS

Charles Houston.

After leaving his job as special counsel of the NAACP in 1940, Houston returned to his family's law firm in the District of Columbia (Houston & Houston, which later became Houston, Houston, Hastie & Wadie). He continued to advise Thurgood Marshall and the NAACP throughout the rest of his life, and Marshall always pointed to Houston as the most important influence on his legal career. Charles Houston died of a heart attack on April 22, 1950.

Walter White.

White married Poppy Cannon, a white magazine editor, in 1949, sparking a major controversy within the NAACP community. This controversy, as well as other matters, including an article in which he encouraged African Americans to lighten their skin and straighten their hair, gave rise to demands that the Association remove White from office. But with the help of Eleanor Roosevelt, a longtime friend and advocate, White continued on as the Association's executive secretary, although with greatly reduced powers. In effect, Roy Wilkins took charge of everyday administration while White acted as the Association's spokesman. Walter White died of a heart attack on March 21, 1955.

Roy Wilkins.

After White's death, Wilkins became the executive secretary of the NAACP and served in this role until he retired in 1977. Throughout the modern civil rights movement, Wilkins consistently favored advancing civil rights through court decisions, legislation, and executive decrees, and he never warmed to the street protests and mass rallies led by Martin Luther King, Jr. Because of his legalistic approach to social transformation, as well as his unqualified commitment to integration, Wilkins faced sharp criticism from African American militants in the 1960s and

1970s; the Revolutionary Action Movement even plotted to kill him in 1967. Two years earlier, the Young Turks, NAACP board members desiring a more activist approach, were almost successful in engineering his removal as executive secretary. But Wilkins was a survivor, and even as he adopted some reforms advocated by his critics, he continued to focus on law and education as the most effective ways to advance the rights, lives, and common good of African Americans. Roy Wilkins died on September 8, 1981.

William Hastie.

President Harry Truman nominated William Hastie to the U.S. Court of Appeals for the Third Circuit in 1949, eventually making Hastie the first African American federal judge with tenure. After enjoying a recess appointment, Hastie was confirmed in 1950 and served as an appeals judge until 1968, as chief judge from 1968 to 1971, and as senior judge from 1971 until his death in 1976. Hastie wrote decisions in more than four hundred federal cases.

Interestingly, he did not let his judgeship prevent him from serving as a member of the Board of Directors of the NAACP Legal Defense and Educational Fund, Inc., and in this role he often provided Marshall with personal and professional counsel. (Indeed, Hastie was the model Marshall had in mind when he refused, in conversations with Attorney General Robert F. Kennedy, to accept anything but a federal judgeship at the circuit court level in 1961.)

His distinguished career on the federal bench led to Hastie's name appearing on several short lists of Supreme Court nominees through the years. President Johnson even considered him as a candidate for the Court before settling on Marshall as his first choice. Nevertheless, the relationship between Marshall and Hastie remained close, marked by deep respect and fondness, to the end. William Hastie died on April 14, 1976.

Thurgood Marshall.

Marshall served as director-counsel of the NAACP Legal Defense and Educational Fund, Inc., from 1957 to 1961. In 1958 he successfully argued in *Cooper v. Aaron*, perhaps his most famous NAACP LDF case, that the Supreme Court had a constitutional obligation to direct officials in Little Rock, Arkansas, to reopen schools closed by Governor Orval Faubus in defiance of the *Brown* decision.

President John F. Kennedy nominated Marshall as judge of the Second Circuit of the U.S. Court of Appeals in 1961, and Marshall served in this role until 1965. Although his decisions were not especially groundbreaking during his tenure on the appeals court, none of them was overturned by the Supreme Court.

Impressed with Marshall's solid record on the federal bench, as well as his earlier success in arguing cases before the Supreme Court, President Johnson named Marshall as Solicitor General in 1965, and in this role he won fourteen of the nineteen cases he argued before the Supreme Court.

An opening on the Supreme Court occurred after President Johnson knowingly created a conflict of interest for Associate Justice Tom Clark by naming his son, Ramsey Clark, to be U.S. attorney general. Clark's decision to leave the Court left Johnson free to nominate Thurgood Marshall as the first African American Supreme Court justice. Marshall gladly accepted the nomination, and he served the Court as an associate justice from 1967 to 1991.

Marshall was a liberal justice, and his decisions, like those offered by William Brennan, his closest colleague on the bench, sought to advance the rights of persons of color, women, the poor, the disenfranchised, and those facing the death penalty (which he consistently regarded as cruel and unusual punishment). As a firm believer in church-state separation, Marshall never attended the annual Christmas party at the Supreme Court. And as a justice deeply opposed to abstract legal reasoning, Marshall always allowed his life experiences—especially those he gained through his many years with the NAACP—to permeate his legal arguments and decisions. For instance, in a 1976 memorandum he sent to Chief Justice Warren Burger about *Moore v. City of East Cleveland*, Marshall wrote:

> *I cannot agree with your conclusion that there is no constitutionally protected right—whether phrased in terms of association or privacy—for a grandmother to perform the duties of a mother for her grandchildren. I do not agree with you that our cases have narrowly limited the concept of "family" to "parents and their offspring." Personal decisions of individuals bound by family ties to live with each other should not be subject to state interference except to insure that basic health and safety standards are met, as they admittedly are in this case. I have seen too many situations where a strong grandparent literally held the family together and was responsible for the education and upbringing of decent, law-abiding youngsters, to agree as a matter of constitutional law that the "nuclear" family is "the basic building block of our society." That is a middle class norm that government has no business foisting on those to whom economic or psychological necessity dictates otherwise.*

It was this type of advocacy—one that gave the strongest of voices to individuals and groups long ignored, dismissed, and silenced—that became the hallmark characteristic of Marshall's tenure on the nation's highest court.

His efforts to advance equal justice under law for everyone, not just the historically privileged, left him tired and weary—and sometimes angry—as the Supreme Court shifted to the right in the 1980s and especially after William Brennan retired in 1990. When his own health began to decline precipitously, Marshall decided to announce his retirement on June 27, 1991.

Thurgood Marshall—the "old rebel"—died on January 24, 1993.

NOTES

INTRODUCTION

xx "I guess I'm an old rebel anyhow": "The Reminiscences of Thurgood Marshall" (Columbia Oral History Research Office, 1977), *Thurgood Marshall: His Speeches, Writings, Arguments, Opinions, and Reminiscences*, ed. Mark V. Tushnet (Chicago, IL: Lawrence Hill Books, 2001), 480.

xx "a civil rights victory party": Katherine Q. Seelye, "A Civil Rights Victory Party on the Mall," *The New York Times*, January 18, 2009, p. 27.

xx "It is a huge civil rights moment": Seelye, "A Civil Rights Victory Party."

xxiv "No doubt you": Marshall to E. Norman Lacey, December 16, 1941, NAACP Papers, microfilm edition [NAACP MF], 4, reel 7, 203.

xxvi "biased and bigoted": FBI Field Report, Richmond, Virginia, September 14, 1961, FBI File on Thurgood Marshall [FBI TM]. This field report includes statements from individuals interviewed by the FBI's Richmond office as part of a nationwide investigation preceding Marshall's appointment to the federal court.

CHAPTER ONE: 1935–1936

Marshall to Senator Millard Tydings, April 10, 1935

4 "Understand you insist": Marshall to Millard Tydings, April 10, 1935, NAACP MF, 2, reel 3, 394.

4 "Please couch your telegrams": Millard Tydings to Marshall, April 12, 1935, NAACP MF, 2, reel 3, 369.

Marshall to the Maryland State Board of Education, November 14, 1935

7 "injected prejudice throughout": Marshall to Charles Houston, July 13, 1936, NAACP MF, 2, reel 3, 156.

Walter White to Marshall, January 18, 1936

7 "get even with Maryland": "The Reminiscences of Thurgood Marshall," *Thurgood Marshall*, 418.

8 "Start working on this": Charles Houston to Marshall, January 3, 1936, NAACP MF, 3A, reel 13, 707.

Marshall to Charles Houston, January 21, 1936

10 "Accept candidacy but avoid communism": Charles Houston to Marshall, January 23, 1936, NAACP MF, 2, reel 3, 104.

Marshall to President Franklin Roosevelt, April 22, 1936

10 "You can't name one bill": Juan Williams, "Interviews with Thurgood," www.thurgoodmarshall.com/interviews/politics.

Marshall to George Crawford, April 23, 1936

12 "Mr. Marshall, while a student here": William Hastie to Mordecai Johnson, May 29, 1936, William H. Hastie Papers [WHHP], microfilm edition, 2, reel 11, 568.

14 "Emphasize that the opposition": Marshall to George Lawrence, March 6, 1937, NAACP MF, 11B, reel 24, 833.

Marshall to Walter White, October 6, 1936

19 "How very tush-tush": Sidney E. Zion, "Thurgood Marshall Takes a New 'Tush-Tush' Job," *The New York Times Magazine*, August 22, 1965, p. 11.

CHAPTER TWO: 1937–1938

Marshall to Governor James Allred, July 31, 1937

27 "Please hear our cries": Anonymous to the NAACP, July 2, 1937, NAACP MF, 8, reel 15, 415.

28 "I am sure": James Allred to Marshall, August 16, 1937, NAACP MF, 8, reel 15, 426.

Marshall to J. M. Tinsley, August 30, 1937

28 "The petition recites": "NAACP Files Suit to Equalize Teachers' Salaries in Maryland," NAACP news release, December 31, 1936, NAACP MF, 3A, reel 11, 439.

29 "The breaking down": Marshall, untitled document, no date [1937], NAACP MF, 3A, reel 10, 543.

Marshall to the *Afro-American*, March 29, 1938

32 "Wherever there are separate schools": Marshall to Mary Gardner, April 30, 1937, NAACP MF, 3A, reel 2, 758.

Marshall to Governor Fred Cone, July 28, 1938

35 "Please my son": Dinnah Kirkland to the NAACP, June 30, 1939, NAACP MF, 7, reel 10, 21.

37 "there was no sufficient evidence": Fred Cone to Marshall, August 2, 1939, NAACP MF, 7, reel 10, 141.

Marshall to Ruth Perry, December 6, 1938

40 "An investigation by A. T. Walden": "Stay Secured for Two Georgia Men," NAACP news release, NAACP MF, 8, reel 10, 487.

40 "We have received": Marshall to George Munro, December 6, 1938, NAACP MF, 8, reel 10, 622.

CHAPTER THREE: 1939

Marshall to Dartnell Publications, January 4, 1939

42 "[I]f you have just": J. T. Kemp to Customers, NAACP MF, 11, reel 23, 64.

Marshall to Governor W. Lee O'Daniel, February 27, 1939

45 "shot Cherry Conley": Reuben Williams to Marshall, March 29, 1939, NAACP MF, reel 14, 996.

Marshall to Stephen F. Whitman & Son, Inc., April 5, 1939

46 "In the first place": Charles Norris to Marshall, April 22, 1939, NAACP MF, 11, reel 23, 172.

Marshall to Attorney General Frank Murphy, April 15, 1939

49 "The present law": Welly Hopkins to Marshall, May 31, 1939, NAACP MF, 7, reel 21, 691.

Marshall to Roy Wilkins, May 4, 1939

49 "We have noted": Roy Wilkins to William Champion, May 5, 1939, NAACP MF, 11, reel 23, 191.

Marshall to Charles Houston, August 4, 1939

51 "was entitled to be admitted": "Court Backs Negro on Full Education," *The New York Times*, December 13, 1939, p. 1.

Charles Carter to Marshall, October 25, 1939

52 "I am call upon you": James Blackwell to the NAACP, NAACP MF, 8, reel 3, 334.

Marshall to B. M. Amole, October 26, 1939

54 "We have had many complaints": Marshall to Maude Tollefson, September 23, 1938, NAACP MF, 11, reel 29, 196.

54 "take the back seat, boy": Marshall to the Greyhound Bus Lines, September 21, 1939, NAACP MF, 11, reel 29, 238.

Marshall to Grace Corrigan, November 22, 1939

57 "I am sending copies": Grace Corrigan to Marshall, November 28, 1939, NAACP MF, 3B, reel 3, 120.

CHAPTER FOUR: 1940

Marshall to William Hastie, April 23, 1940

65 "I'm just another Negro": Clennon King, Jr., to Walter White, April 18, 1940, NAACP MF, 3B, reel 11, 679.

Marshall to His Wife Vivian Marshall, No date [May 1940]

68 "Despite any views to the contrary": Marshall to Walter White, May 14, 1940, NAACP Papers, Library of Congress [NAACP LOC], Washington, D.C., BII, A533, folder 3.

68 "Yes, I think that we had": "The Reminiscences of Thurgood Marshall," *Thurgood Marshall*, 497.

68 "Take Texas": Quoted in Juan Williams, *Thurgood Marshall: American Revolutionary* (New York: Three Rivers Press, 1998), 108.

Requests for Help to the NAACP, multiple dates

70 "I was told": Anonymous to the ACLU, June 10, 1940. The ACLU forwarded this letter to Marshall, NAACP MF, 7, reel 30, 124.

70 "I am herewith informing you": Anonymous to the NAACP, received May 23, 1939, NAACP MF, 7, reel 13, 529.

71 "I do not know": "Statement Made by Robert Booker," June 5, 1940, NAACP MF, 13C, reel 12, 454.

Marshall to President Franklin Roosevelt, July 23, 1940

72 "No person of any race": Quoted in Marshall to Stewart McDonald, July 23, 1940, NAACP MF, 5, reel 13, 761.

73 "This type of racial discrimination": Marshall to Stewart McDonald, July 23, 1940, NAACP MF, 5, reel 13, 761.

74 "I am today ordering": Stewart McDonald to Marshall, August 20, 1940, NAACP MF, 5, reel 13, 853.

74 "Although the matter": Marshall to Ray Guild, November 26, 1940, NAACP MF, 5, reel 13, 843.

Marshall to Secretary Frank Knox, July 26, 1940

74 "to rescind a recent": Quoted in "President Asked to Stop Job Discrimination in Plane Factories to Aid U.S. Defense," NAACP news release, May 17, 1940, NAACP MF, 9, reel 16, 876.

Marshall to Secretary Henry Stimson, August 7, 1940

77 "The success of": Henry Stimson to Marshall, August 2, 1940, NAACP MF, 9, reel 16, 891.

Secretary Henry Stimson to Marshall, August 20, 1940

77 "the present program": Marshall to Henry Stimson, August 1, 1940, NAACP MF, 9, reel 8, 261.

Marshall to Representative Martin Dies, September 27, 1940

80 "in each instance where": Marshall to Jerome Britchey, April 12, 1940, NAACP MF, 11B, reel 1, 918.

Marshall to Carter Wesley, November 9, 1940

85 "not subject to limitations": *Grovey v. Townsend* 295 U.S. 45 (1935).

Marshall to Secretary Cordell Hull, December 11, 1940

88 "a report has been received": Harold Finley to Marshall, January 13, 1941, NAACP MF, 13C, reel 3, 741.

CHAPTER FIVE: 1941

Marshall to William Hastie, January 17, 1941

90 "the undemocratic and un-American practice": Quoted in "NAACP Protests War Department Plan for Segregated Air Squadron at Tuskegee," NAACP news release, February 14, 1941, NAACP MF, 9B, reel 25, 531.

Marshall to Attorney General Robert Jackson, April 28, 1941

97 "A preliminary investigation": Wendell Berge to Marshall, May 19, 1941, NAACP MF, 4, reel 9, 161.

97 "Since the decision": Marshall to Wendell Berge, July 25, 1941, NAACP MF, 4, reel 9, 169.

97 "[T]here is nothing more important": Marshall to James Hinton, May 16, 1942, NAACP MF, 4, reel 10, 719.

Marshall to Caroline Cuninghame, June 17, 1941

98 "Mary has two daughters": Caroline Cuninghame to Marshall, May 16, 1941, NAACP MF, 18, reel 10, 365.

Marshall to Secretaries of War and Navy, December 30, 1941

107 "So far as the Navy": Ross McIntyre to Walter White, January 15, 1942, NAACP MF, 15B, reel 1, 259.

CHAPTER SIX: 1942–1943

Marshall to Assistant Attorney General Wendell Berge, January 30, 1942

108 "The denial of the right to vote": Marshall to Francis Biddle, January 30, 1942, NAACP MF, 7, reel 24, 293.

110 "Careful consideration": Wendell Berge to Marshall, February 11, 1942, NAACP MF, 7, reel 24, 299.

Marshall to Governor Keen Johnson, May 29, 1942

111 "We have received no word": Marshall to Keen Johnson, June 12, 1942, NAACP MF, 7, reel 30, 1028.

Marshall to Norman Holmes, July 2, 1942

111 "subjected to some terrible things": Norman Holmes to the NAACP, NAACP MF, 9, reel 13, 257.

Marshall to Harry Butler, July 27, 1942

114 "did not conduct himself": Harry Butler to Marshall, July 29, 1942, NAACP LOC, BII, B186, folder 8.

Walter White to Morris Ernst, October 31, 1942

116 "For God's sake": Morris Ernst to Walter White, October 29, 1942, NAACP MF, 18, reel 5, 544.

Marshall to Assistant Attorney General Wendell Berge, April 26, 1943

117 "It seems to us": Marshall to Francis Biddle, April 15, 1943, NAACP MF, 9B, reel 14, 115.

120 "Private Raymond Carr": Marshall to Miss Harper, April 27, 1943, NAACP MF, 9B, reel 11, 152.

120 "maybe one of these days": Marshall to John McKenna, October 1, 1943, NAACP MF, 3B, reel 3, 746.

121 "stating the uniqueness of Thurgood's talents": Walter White to William Hastie, May 4, 1943, NAACP LOC, BII, A524, folder 4.

121 "is worth a million times more": Walter White to William Hastie, May 6, 1943, NAACP LOC, BII, A524, folder 5.

Marshall to Walter White, October 15, 1943

122 "We all hope": Marshall to Walter White, October 2, 1943, NAACP MF, 18, reel 16, 374.

Marshall to George L. P. Weaver, November 30, 1943

122 "the most important elections yet": Marshall to George Schuyler, November 26, 1943, NAACP LOC, BII, B99, folder 4.

Marshall to Walter White, No date [December 1943]

124 "a sentence that": William Hastie to Walter White, NAACP 15B, reel 1, 28.

CHAPTER SEVEN: 1944–1945

Marshall to Senator Claude Pepper, January 28, 1944

127 "I know you don't": William Howard, Jr., to Cynthia Goff, January 1, 1944, NAACP MF, 7, reel 25, 498.

Marshall to Attorney General Francis Biddle, April 3, 1944

129 "At present the Department": Francis Biddle to Marshall, April 10, 1944, NAACP MF, 4, reel 11, 427.

130 "case that started the whole voting": "The Reminiscences of Thurgood Marshall," *Thurgood Marshall*, 427.

Marshall to the NAACP Office, April 15, 1944

131 "I have just returned": Marshall to Maceo Smith, April 30, 1944, NAACP MF, 4, reel 11, 444.

Marshall to Godfrey Cabot, May 1, 1944

131 "As to the question": Marshall to Godfrey Cabot, April 27, 1943, NAACP MF, 16B, reel 3, 162.

Marshall to Assistant Attorney General Tom Clark, May 5, 1944

133 "The facts in the case": "Justice Dept. Will Not Prosecute in Killing of Soldier," NAACP news release, May 11, 1944, NAACP MF, 9B, reel 14, 558.

Marshall to Roger Baldwin, June 9, 1944

137 "The problem of restrictive covenants": Marshall to National Legal Committee, June 13, 1944, NAACP MF, 5, reel 20, 506.

Marshall to Attorney General Francis Biddle, July 5, 1944

138 "NO NEGRO VOTES": Untitled document, No date, NAACP MF, 4, reel 6, 913.

Marshall to Secretary James Forrestal, October 19, 1944

141 "There is no sufficient evidence": "Race, Not Mutiny, Is Issue in Trial of 50 Negro Seamen," NAACP news release, October 13, 1944, NAACP MF, 9B, reel 5, 493.

Marshall to Secretary James Forrestal, July 13, 1945

150 "I should be happy": James Forrestal to Marshall, October 29, 1945, NAACP MF, 9B, reel 6, 406.

Marshall to Attorney General Tom Clark, October 15, 1945

151 "I, Ida McCoy Lee": Untitled document, October 9, 1945, NAACP MF, 18, reel 9, 376.

Marshall to the NAACP Branches, November 14, 1945

155 "an astronomical amount of war stamps": Marshall to Walter White, August 29, 1945, NAACP MF, 18, reel 5, 885.

Marshall to President Harry Truman, November 14, 1945

157 "This is to acknowledge": William Hassett to Marshall, November 24, 1945, Harry S. Truman Library [HSTL], Independence, Missouri, Official File, box 390, folder: OF 286-A (45-46).

CHAPTER EIGHT: 1946

Marshall to Assistant Secretary of War Howard Petersen, January 30, 1946

160 "Enclosed please find photostat": Marshall to Robert Patterson, January 11, 1946, NAACP MF, 9, reel 10, 946.

Marshall to the Trial Committee of the New York City Board of Education, No date [February 1946]

161 "The first American soldier": Quoted in "School Board Acquits May Quinn of Bias, Finds Neglect of Duty," *New York Tribune*, February 28, 1946; accessed at NAACP MF, 3C, reel 23.

Marshall to J. Edgar Hoover, May 10, 1946

163 "the action of the Tennessee state troopers": "Killing of Negroes Is Protested Here: NAACP Tells Truman Shooting of 2 by Tennessee Troopers in Jail Was Worthy of Nazis," *The New York Times*, March 2, 1946, p. 26.

Marshall to Attorney General Tom Clark, May 28, 1946

166 "In my capacity": "Ball Urges Curb on Powers: Denies Right to Abuse Strike Privilege—Clark Attacks Ku Klux Klan 'Resurgence,'" *The New York Times*, May 19, 1946, p. 9.

Walter White to Marshall, June 5, 1946

167 "He put his hand on me": Richard Goldstein, "Irene Morgan Kirkaldy, 90, Rights Pioneer, Dies," *The New York Times*, August 13, 2007, Nation section.

167 "Today we are just emerging": Quoted in Williams, *Thurgood Marshall*, 146.

167 "No more suitable choice": Walter White to Marshall, April 26, 1946, NAACP LOC; quoted in Williams, *Thurgood Marshall*, 143.

167 "The opinion of the United States Supreme Court": "U.S. Supreme Court Strikes Blow at Segregation," NAACP news release, June 3, 1946, NAACP MF, 15, reel 18, 120.

Marshall to the NAACP Office, June 12, 1946

168 "They destroyed the Negro": "Negro Trial Shift Called Necessary," *The New York Times*, June 9, 1946, p. 12.

Walter White to the NAACP Board, September 9, 1946

173 "Boy, I have had the works": Marshall to A. Leon Ransom, August 17, 1946, Leon Ransom Papers, Moorland-Spingarn Research Center, Howard University, Washington, D.C., box 173, folder 1.

173 "a great big, twenty-pound": "The Reminiscences of Thurgood Marshall," *Thurgood Marshall*, 431.

173 "when the christening of Thurgooda": Marshall to William Hastie, October 20, 1944, NAACP MF, 18B, reel 21, 788.

Marshall to Carter Wesley, October 25, 1946

174 "found [Margold] wasn't working": "The Reminiscences of Thurgood Marshall," *Thurgood Marshall*, 423.

Marshall to Attorney General Tom Clark, December 3, 1946

181 "The excessive heat": NAACP press release, quoted in "NAACP Rescues Lynch Victim, Describes 'Sadism' of Attack," NAACP MF, 7, reel 27, 343.

Marshall to Maceo Hubbard, December 4, 1946

182 "We got this Nigger": See Juan Williams's interview at thurgoodmarshall .com.

185 "a disobedience movement": George Streator, "Negroes Cautioned on Resistance Idea," *The New York Times*, November 23, 1946, p. 14.

Marshall to Carter Wesley, December 27, 1946

186 "red-blooded Anglo-Saxon man": "Bilbo Urges Mississippi Men to Employ 'Any Means' to Bar Negroes from Voting," *The New York Times*, June 23, 1946, p. 30.

Marshall to Attorney General Tom Clark, December 27, 1946

189 "The death cries": "The Silent Indictment," *The New York Times*, December 21, 1946, p. 18.

CHAPTER NINE: 1947

Attorney General Tom Clark to Marshall, January 13, 1947

192 "To refute Marshall's charge": J. Edgar Hoover to Tom Clark, January 1947, FBI File on the NAACP [FBI NAACP], microfilm edition, reel 2, 9.

J. Edgar Hoover to Walter White, January 13, 1947

199 "Attached is a self-explanatory letter": Walter White to Thurgood Marshall, January 20, 1947, NAACP MF, 7, reel 27, 35.

Marshall to Ruby Hurley, February 6, 1947

201 "is one of the finest things": Marshall to Gloster Current, January 20, 1947, NAACP MF, 3B, reel 4, 32.

201 "letting them down": Ruby Hurley to Marshall, February 5, 1947, NAACP MF, 3B, reel 4, 36.

Marshall to William Hastie, April 3, 1947

205 "In this particular case": Marshall to Donald Murray, April 9, NAACP MF, 3B, reel 15, 280.

205 "There can be no equality": George Streator, "Negroes Map Fight on Dual Education," *The New York Times*, June 28, 1947, p. 4.

Marshall to the New York *Herald Tribune,* September 18, 1947

210 "was one of the blackest": Harriet Beecher Stowe, *Uncle Tom's Cabin*, A Norton Critical Edition, ed. Elizabeth Ammons (New York: W. W. Norton & Company, 1994), 206–7.

Marshall to John Wrighten, September 29, 1947

211 "For the life of me": Marshall to Hinton, Boulware, and Rev. Beard, December 30, 1947, NAACP MF, 3B, reel 14, 352.

Marshall to the Editor of the Dallas *Morning News,* September 29, 1947

216 "The association's tendency": William Ruggles to Marshall, October 15, 1947, NAACP MF, 3B, reel 4, 1164.

Marshall to Geoffrey Parsons, September 30, 1947

219 "Negroes are entitled": "South Carolina Negroes Win Vote in Democratic Primary Elections," *The New York Times,* July 13, 1947, p. 1.

Marshall to Roy Wilkins, October 30, 1947

226 "very small minority": Samuel A. Towers, "Hollywood Communists 'Militant,' but Small in Number, Stars Testify," *The New York Times,* October 24, 1947, p. 1.

Marshall to Geoffrey Parsons, October 30, 1947

227 "met on hills": Felix Belair, Jr., "Truman Asks Group to Check Bigotry," *The New York Times,* January 16, 1947, p. 1.

227 "In consideration of the present status": Marshall to Channing Tobias, January 14, 1947, NAACP LOC, II, A481, folder 6.

228 "It is clear that racism": Statement of Thurgood Marshall Before President's Committee on Civil Rights, NAACP MF, 15, reel 1, 371.

CHAPTER TEN: 1948

Marshall to the Editor of the Dallas *Morning News,* February 5, 1948

232 "I cannot see": William Ruggles to Marshall, February 23, 1948, NAACP MF, 3B, reel 15, 523.

Marshall to the Press, May 3, 1948

234 "Congratulations on your outstanding victory": James Hinton to Marshall, April 19, 1948, NAACP MF, 4, reel 9, 980.

234 "It has been a long": Marshall to James Hinton, April 20, 1948, NAACP MF, 4, reel 9, 976.

235 "Because of the race or color": "Anti-Negro Pacts on Realty Ruled Not Enforceable," *The New York Times,* May 4, 1948, p. 1.

Marshall to Charles Anderson, June 3, 1948

236 "To the extent that": Charles Anderson to Marshall, May 18, 1948, NAACP MF, 3B, reel 1, 856.

Marshall to Governor M. E. Thompson, September 13, 1948

239 "It is my understanding": M. E. Thompson to Marshall, September 14, 1948, NAACP MF, 4, reel 8, 295.

Marshall to Henry Moon, October 28, 1948

241 "It seems to me": Marshall to William Hastie and Others, October 19, 1948, NAACP MF, 3, reel 13, 845.

CHAPTER ELEVEN: 1949–1950

Marshall to Walter White, February 16, 1949

250 "I guess I'm an old rebel anyhow": "The Reminiscences of Thurgood Marshall," *Thurgood Marshall*, 480.

Marshall to Lemuel Graves, Jr., February 24, 1949

251 "Instead of contributing": Marshall to Harry Truman, February 1, 1949, NAACP MF, 5, reel 7, 644.

Stephen Spingarn to Clark Clifford, May 16, 1949

254 "Well, you knew": "The Reminiscences of Thurgood Marshall," *Thurgood Marshall*, 456.

255 "done more up to date": George Streator, "Truman Defended by Negro Students," *The New York Times*, August 24, 1949, p. 62.

255 "It is hereby declared": See Harry Truman, "The Armed Forces," *The New York Times*, July 27, 1948, p. 4. This reference provides the text of Executive Order 9981.

Marshall to Assistant Attorney General Alexander Campbell, June 1, 1949

260 "inadvisable for us": Alexander Campbell to Marshall, June 14, 1949, NAACP MF, 5, reel 20, 178.

Marshall to Horace Bond, June 13, 1949

261 "To be frank": Horace Bond to Marshall, June 15, 1949, Horace Mann Bond Papers [HMBP], Special Collections and University Archives, W. E. B. Du Bois Library, University of Massachusetts, Amherst, Massachusetts, Series III, box 63, folder 261.

Marshall to Robert Silberstein, August 2, 1949

263 "told the other states": "The Reminiscences of Thurgood Marshall," *Thurgood Marshall*, 427.

A. P. Tureaud to Marshall, August 4, 1949

263 "WELL OLD BUZZARD TUREAUD": KKK TO A. P. Tureaud, Alexander P. Tureaud Papers, microfilm edition, no date, reel 33, 509. Letters in the same area as this one, however, are dated 1960.

Marshall to Elizabeth Waring, January 23, 1950

270 "You don't need to make that": C. P. Trussel, "President Insists on 1950 Showdown in Rights Program," *The New York Times*, January 18, 1950, p. 21.

Marshall to the Editor of *The New York Times*, April 19, 1950

273 "equality": Arthur Krock, "The Segregation Issue as Stated by Texas," *The New York Times*, April 18, 1950, p. 30.

273 "Read Arthur Krock's column": Marshall to Maceo Smith, April 18, 1950, NAACP MF, 3B, reel 16, 441.

275 "If the schools are equal": John Frank, "Letters to the Times: Equality in Education, Texas Claim Disputed on Facilities of Segregated Law School," *The New York Times*, April 25, 1950, p. 30.

Marshall to Judah Cahn, June 7, 1950

276 "the worst hole in the world": Marshall to Gloster Current, August 28, 1950, NAACP MF, 26A, reel 15, 377.

Marshall to Pauli Murray, June 9, 1950

276 "Judgments Sweatt and McLaurin cases reversed": Charles Elmore Cropley to Marshall, June 5, 1950, NAACP MF, 3B, reel 3, 742.

276 "Yesterday the United States Supreme Court": Walter White to NAACP supporters, June 6, 1950, NAACP MF, 3B, reel 16, 694.

276 "A law school": *Sweatt v. Painter* (44) 339 U.S. 629.

276 "The end has not yet been reached": Marshall to W. I. Gibson, June 8, 1950, NAACP MF, 3B, reel 16, 703.

276 "I don't know": "The Reminiscences of Thurgood Marshall," *Thurgood Marshall*, 417.

CHAPTER TWELVE: 1951

Marshall to Roy Wilkins, February 3, 1951

279 "It is obvious": Marshall to Robert Ming, November 28, 1950, Robert Ming Papers, Moorland-Spingarn Research Center, Howard University, Washington, D.C., box 196-3, folder: "Correspondence—Marshall, Thurgood."

Marshall to the NAACP Office, February 12, 1951

281 "I was given an audience": "The Reminiscences of Thurgood Marshall," *Thurgood Marshall*, 443.

Roy Wilkins to Marshall, February 20, 1951

285 "were able to bust": "The Reminiscences of Thurgood Marshall," *Thurgood Marshall*, 443.

Marshall to Myrta Harris, March 26, 1951

286 "Your preference for 'the Civil War' ": James Charlesworth to Marshall, March 28, 1951, NAACP LOC, BII, A72, folder 6.

286 "I am happy and relieved": Marshall to James Charlesworth, March 30, 1951, NAACP LOC, BII, A72, folder 6.

Marshall to Oliver Hill and Spottswood Robinson III, May 22, 1951

287 "At a mass meeting": Press Release, May 3, 1951, Brown Collection, MS 759, Box 9, folder 138. Robinson included this release in a letter to Marshall dated May 2, 1951.

Robert Carter to Marshall, June 13, 1951

289 "Segregation of white children": Quoted in a document that the NAACP used for explaining the various cases wrapped up in *Brown v. Board of Education.* See "Public School Segregation Cases," November 26, 1952, NAACP MF, 3C, reel 3, 223.

Marshall to the Editor of the *Afro-American,* June 16, 1951

291 "We must face without evasion": Albert J. Dunmore, "Waring Blasts Negro Leadership as Being 'Segregation Profiteers,' " *Pittsburgh Courier*, July 7, 1951, p. 1.

291 "racial separation in public": See "Public School Segregation Cases," November 26, 1952, NAACP MF, 3C, reel 3, 223.

291 "Later I found that": Septima Clark to Elizabeth Waring, October 12, 1962, Judge J. Waties and Elizabeth Waring Papers, Avery Research Center for African American History and Culture, College of Charleston, South Carolina, box 1, folder 2.

Marshall to Walter White, July 11, 1951

292 "In picturization of Negroes": "Brewery Company Asked to Drop 'Amos 'n' Andy,' " NAACP news release, July 9, 1951, NAACP MF, 15B, reel 10, 280.

Marshall to the Editor of *The New York Times*, October 26, 1951

293 "The convening of a federal grand jury": "Aftermath in Cicero," *The New York Times*, October 23, 1951, p. 28.

CHAPTER THIRTEEN: 1952–1954

Marshall to President Harry Truman, April 30, 1952

297 "refusing to advance": "Doomed Officer Denies Cowardice," *The New York Times*, October 15, 1950, p. 9.

Marshall to President Harry Truman, June 13, 1952

299 "I am not one of those": "Text of Address by the President on Civil Rights," *The New York Times*, June 14, 1952, p. 10.

299 "worse than just bad": Marshall to Walter White, July 14, 1952, NAACP MF, 18C, reel 23, 965.

Marshall to the NAACP Office, June 11, 1953

303 "highly gratified": "Association Hails Restaurant Ruling," *The New York Times*, June 9, 1953, p. 25.

303 "hopelessly divided": Luther A. Houston, "Supreme Court Lifts Negro Ban by Cafes," *The New York Times*, June 9, 1953, p. 1.

303 "We urge the people": "Association Hails Restaurant Ruling," *The New York Times*, June 9, 1953, p. 25.

Loren Miller to Marshall, November 3, 1953

306 "great guarantees like": Paul Freund to Marshall, November 4, 1953, Paul A. Freund Papers [PAFP], Harvard Law Library, Harvard University, Cambridge, Massachusetts, box 96, folder 8.

308 "The filing of the 240-page": NAACP LDF news release, November 16, 1953, Brown Collection.

Marshall, Walter White, and Henry Fosdick to NAACP Supporters after the *Brown* Ruling, May 17, 1954

308 "the only way": Quoted in Robert J. Cottrol, Raymond T. Diamond, and Leland B. Ware, *Brown v. Board of Education: Caste, Culture, and the Constitution* (Lawrence, KS: University Press of Kansas, 2003).

308 "In the field of public education": Luther A. Huston, "1896 Ruling Upset," *The New York Times*, May 18, 1954, p. 1.

309 "would not resist the Supreme Court": Huston, "1896 Ruling Upset," p. 14.

Lester Granger to Marshall, May 18, 1954

309 "It is a wonderful feeling": Jean Williams to Marshall, May 18, 1954, NAACP MF, 3C, reel 14, 855.

310 "Although it was my duty": Paul Wilson to Robert Carter, May 19, 1954, Brown Collection, MS 759, box 9, folder 137. Wilson sent his congratulations to both Carter and Marshall.

310 "We're not going to secede": Untitled document, May 23, 1954, NAACP MF, 3C, reel 15, 848.

Marshall to NAACP Branch Presidents and Officers, September 17, 1954

312 "We note your braggadocio": J. E. Stockstill to Marshall, June 24, 1954, NAACP MF, 18, R6, 443.

Marshall to His Legal Team, No date

315 "Of course, you and I know": "'Upheaval' Doubted If School Bias Ends," *The New York Times*, January 24, 1954, p. 34.

315 "Enclosed is a copy": Marshall to Paul Freund, November 4, 1954, PAFP, box 96, folder 8.

316 "as a decisive force": Paul Freund to Marshall, November 5, 1954, PAFP, box 96, folder 8.

CHAPTER FOURTEEN: 1955–1957

Marshall to the Editor of *The New York Times Magazine,* May 11, 1955

318 "forthwith": See the Brown documents at loc.gov/exhibits/brown/brown-brown.html.

318 "is never made": Luther A. Huston, "Arguments Ended on Desegregation," *The New York Times*, April 15, 1955, p. 12.

Marshall to Ruben and Mary Barksdale, August 12, 1955

319 "with all deliberate speed": "Text of Desegregation Opinion," *The New York Times*, June 1, 1955, p. 26.

319 "The desegregation program": "Racial Deadline Set," *The New York Times*, June 14, 1955, p. 16.

319 "patience," "perseverance," "forbearance": Emanuel Perlmutter, "President Gives Pledge on Civil Rights," *The New York Times*, June 23, 1955, p. 20.

320 "push ahead without delay": Perlmutter, "President Gives Pledge on Civil Rights."

320 "A 'Morally Right' Decision": "A 'Morally Right' Decision," *Life* (July 25, 1955): 29–31.

Marshall to the Editor of the Columbia *Record*, September 9, 1955

322 "The article appearing in the *Record*": J. Waties Waring to Marshall, September 17, 1955, NAACP LOC, II, B146, folder 15.

FBI Memorandum, November 4, 1955

327 "dirty cowards": Marshall to James Hinton, January 30, 1956, NAACP LOC, III, J5, folder 9.

327 "You can plainly see": Crank Letter to Marshall, December 15, 1955, NAACP LOC, IIB, box 100, folder 1.

FBI Memorandum, February 8, 1956

328 "Our investigation has shown": FBI Memorandum, February 8, 1956, FBI NAACP, reel 4, 543.

FBI Memorandum, February 9, 1956

330 "are no more interested": "Fight Reds, Bias, NAACP Urged," *The New York Times*, June 27, 1956, p. 24.

Marshall to Assistant Attorney General Warren Olney III, March 14, 1956

332 "That girl sure has guts": Wayne Phillips, "U.S. Judge Orders Alabama Co-ed to Be Reinstated," *The New York Times*, March 1, 1956, p. 1.

FBI Memorandum, May 21, 1956

341 "unblemished forthright Christian leadership of men": Quoted in Williams, *Thurgood Marshall*, 251.

341 "All that walking for nothing!" Quoted in Harris Wofford, *Of Kennedys and Kings: Making Sense of the Sixties* (Pittsburgh: University of Pittsburgh Press, 1992), 119.

341 "I used to have a lot of fights": "The Personal Reminiscences of Thurgood Marshall," *Thurgood Marshall*, 471.

342 "couldn't see the second part": "The Personal Reminiscences of Thurgood Marshall," *Thurgood Marshall*, 479.

342 "So far as I am concerned": Marshall to Mickey Levine, August 21, 1956, NAACP LOC, III, J3, folder 8.

Marshall to Assistant Attorney General Warren Olney III, September 5, 1956

343 "its obligation to ensure": "Protection Asked for School Board," *The New York Times*, September 11, 1956, p. 21.

Marshall to Maceo Smith, September 19, 1956

346 "The form of attack": Robert Carter to Paul Freund, May 3, 1957, PAFP, box 96, folder 8.

346 "so-called campaign of moderation": Maceo Smith to Roy Wilkins and Thurgood Marshall, September 13, 1956, NAACP MF, 20, reel 12, 131.

347 "We will remain eternally grateful": Martin Luther King, Jr., to Marshall, February 6, 1958, *The Papers of Martin Luther King, Jr.*, vol. 4, *Symbol of the Movement*, ed. Clayborne Carson, Susan Carson, Adrienne Clay, Virginia Shadron, and Kieran Taylor (Berkeley, CA: University of California Press, 2000), 360.

347 "not yet ready": "NAACP Studies Resistance Move," *The New York Times*, July 1, 1956, p. 60.

Anonymous to Marshall, October 11, 1956

348 "I am a negroe": Rufus Walters to Marshall, July 15, 1956, NAACP LOC, BIII, J2, folder 3.

Marshall to Israel Goldstein, December 10, 1956

350 "an emergency meeting": Israel Goldstein to Marshall, December 7, 1956, NAACP LOC, BIII, J1, folder 1.

Marshall to Autherine Lucy Foster, February 15, 1957

351 "was justified in expelling": Philip Benjamin, "Co-ed's Expulsion Upheld by Court," *The New York Times*, January 18, 1957, p. 10.

Marshall to Walter Winchell, February 18, 1957

352 "yellow members": Walter Winchell, "Winchell Bombards KKK, White Councils, 'Mobocrats,'" *Pittsburgh Courier*, February 16, 1957, p. 7.

EPILOGUE

355 "no person should be a Board member": See National Association for the Advancement of Colored People, aka NAACP v. NAACP Legal Defense & Educational Fund, Inc., Appellant, 753 F.2d 131 (D.C. Cir., 1985).

356 "Today, after withdrawal of federal troops": Marshall to Dwight D. Eisenhower, October 1, 1957, Dwight D. Eisenhower Library, General File, Box 920, GF 124-A-A School.

357 "We are now participating": Marshall to Marion Barry, August 4, 1960, NAACP MF, 21, reel 21, 920–21.

358 "May 25th Jet contains": Marshall to John Johnson, May 19, 1961, NAACP MF, 21, reel 12, 232–33.

358 "WHERE DO YOU STAND": For a copy of this flyer, as well as Marshall's accompanying note, see Marshall to FBI, June 8, 1959, FBI TM.

359 "If Marshall were a white man": FBI Field Report, Richmond, Virginia, September 14, 1961, FBI TM.

360 "a very capable lawyer": FBI Field Report, Richmond, Virginia, September 14, 1961, FBI TM.

360 "I have said publicly": Lewis F. Powell to Marshall, February 20, 1976, Lewis F. Powell, Jr., Archives, Washington and Lee University, School of Law.

360 "Thurgood Marshall's commitment": Untitled document, U.S. Supreme Court news release, January 24, 1992, Harry A. Blackmun Papers, Library of Congress, box 1406, folder 3.

LOCATION OF LETTERS

CHAPTER ONE: 1935–1936

Marshall to Millard Tydings, March 18, 1935, NAACP Papers, microfilm edition [NAACP MF], 2, reel 3, 365. The last number in NAACP MF citations indicates the exact or approximate slide number on the reel.

Marshall to Millard Tydings, April 10, 1935, NAACP MF, 2, reel 3, 368.

Marshall to the Maryland State Board of Education, November 14, 1935, NAACP MF, 2, reel 3, 440.

Walter White to Marshall, January 18, 1936, NAACP MF, 4, reel 13, 713.

Marshall to Charles Houston, January 21, 1936, NAACP MF, 2, reel 3, 532.

Marshall to Franklin Roosevelt, April 22, 1936, NAACP MF, 2, reel 3, 404.

Marshall to Stephen Gambrill, April 22, 1936, NAACP MF, 2, reel 3, 409.

Marshall to George Crawford, April 23, 1936, NAACP MF, 2, reel 3, 122.

Marshall to Roy Wilkins, May 4, 1936, NAACP Papers, Library of Congress [NAACP LOC], Washington, D.C., BII, L38, folder 11.

Marshall to Charles Houston, May 25, 1936, Brown v. Board of Education Collection [Brown Collection], Yale University, MS 759, box 4, folder 6.

Charles Houston to Marshall, September 17, 1936, NAACP MF, 2, reel 3, 591.

Marshall to Walter White, October 6, 1936, NAACP MF, 2, reel 3, 609.

Marshall to Walter White, November 10, 1936, NAACP MF, 12D, reel 7, 75.

CHAPTER TWO: 1937–1938

Marshall to Walter White, February 2, 1937, NAACP MF, 12B, reel 2, 175.

Marshall to Walter White, March 25, 1937, NAACP MF, 11B, reel 22, 860.

Marshall to James Dorsey, April 27, 1937, NAACP MF, 11, reel 15, 36.

Marshall to S. S. Kresge Company, May 20, 1937, NAACP MF, 12C, reel 19, 421.

Marshall to James Allred, July 31, 1937, NAACP MF, 8, reel 15, 417.

Marshall to J. M. Tinsley, August 30, 1937, NAACP MF, 3A, reel 1, 896.

Marshall to the NAACP Office, October 17, 1937, NAACP LOC, BI, C179, folder 6.

Marshall to Walter White, November 1, 1937, NAACP MF, 6, reel 8, 11.

Marshall to the *Afro-American,* March 29, 1938, NAACP MF, 3A, reel 10, 492.

Marshall to the NAACP Executive Staff, June 23, 1938, NAACP MF, 3A, reel 11, 685.

Marshall to Fred Cone, July 28, 1938, NAACP MF, 7, reel 5, 654.

Marshall to Sylvia Frank, October 1, 1938, NAACP MF, 10, reel 19, 975.

Marshall to Ruth Perry, December 6, 1938, NAACP MF, 8, reel 10, 623.

CHAPTER THREE: 1939

Marshall to Dartnell Publications, January 4, 1939, NAACP MF, 11, reel 23, 61.

Marshall to W. Lee O'Daniel, February 27, 1939, NAACP MF, 8, reel 14, 997.

Marshall to Stephen F. Whitman & Son, Inc., April 5, 1939, NAACP MF, 11, reel 23, 146.

Marshall to Frank Murphy, April 15, 1939, NAACP MF, 7, reel 21, 677.

Marshall to Roy Wilkins, May 4, 1939, NAACP MF, 11, reel 23, 188.

Marshall to Mrs. E. W. Grant, July 25, 1939, NAACP MF, 10, reel 13, 19.

Marshall to Charles Houston, August 4, 1939, NAACP MF, 3A, reel 15, 209.

Charles Carter to Marshall, October 25, 1939, NAACP MF, 8, reel 1, 283.

Marshall to B. M. Amole, October 26, 1939, NAACP MF, 11, reel 29, 250.

Marshall to Grace Corrigan, November 22, 1939, NAACP MF, 3B, reel 3, 119.

CHAPTER FOUR: 1940

Marshall to Morris Glickfeld, January 3, 1940, NAACP MF, 3C, reel 11, 315.

Marshall to Frank Hines, No date [January 1940], NAACP MF, 9, reel 14, 937.

Marshall to Roy Wilkins, January 26, 1940, NAACP MF, 16B, reel 2, 412.

Marshall to Jerome Britchey, March 28, 1940, NAACP MF, 15B, reel 2, 653.

Marshall to Carter Wesley, April 2, 1940, NAACP MF, 18, reel 9, 87.

Marshall to William Hastie, April 19, 1940, NAACP MF, 16B, reel 5, 603.

Marshall to William Hastie, April 23, 1940, NAACP MF, reel 11, 677.

Charles Houston to Marshall, April 24, 1940, NAACP MF, 9, reel 12, 16.

Marshall to His Wife Vivian Marshall, No date [May 1940], NAACP MF, 15B, reel 4, 78.

Marshall to Walter White, May 22, 1940, NAACP LOC, BII, A533, folder 3.
Requests for Help to the NAACP, see Notes.
Marshall to Franklin Roosevelt, July 23, 1940, NAACP MF, 5, reel 13, 851.
Marshall to Frank Knox, July 26, 1940, NAACP MF, 9, reel 16, 888.
Marshall to Henry Stimson, August 7, 1940, NAACP MF, 9, reel 16, 895.
Henry Stimson to Marshall, August 20, 1940, NAACP MF, 9, reel 16, 890.
Robert Patterson to Marshall, August 29, 1940, NAACP MF, 9, reel 16, 892.
Marshall to A. F. Whitney, September 5, 1940, NAACP MF, 18B, reel 1, 622.
Marshall to Martin Dies, September 27, 1940, NAACP MF, 5, reel 6, 841.
Marshall to O. John Rogge, October 9, 1940, NAACP MF, 7, reel 30, 705.
Marshall to William Hastie, October 21, 1940, NAACP MF, 16B, reel 7, 761.
Marshall to Carter Wesley, November 9, 1940, NAACP MF, 18, reel 9, 167.
Marshall to Cordell Hull, December 11, 1940, Franklin D. Roosevelt Library, Hyde Park, New York.

CHAPTER FIVE: 1941

Marshall to William Hastie, January 17, 1941, NAACP MF, 9B, reel 25, 524.
Marshall to Robert Jackson, January 20, 1941, NAACP MF, 18C, reel 28, 980.
Marshall to Walter White, February 2, 1941, accessed at americanradioworks.publicradio.org.
Marshall to Godfrey Cabot, April 25, 1941, NAACP MF, 16B, reel 3, 167.
Marshall to Robert Jackson, April 28, 1941, NAACP MF, 4, reel 9, 155.
Marshall to Caroline Cuninghame, June 17, 1941, NAACP MF, 18, reel 10, 364.
Marshall to the American Civil Liberties Union, July 28, 1941, NAACP MF, 5, reel 6, 951.
Marshall to J. E. Andrews, August 8, 1941, NAACP MF, 15B, reel 14, 8.
Marshall to the NAACP Office, November 17, 1941, NAACP MF, 18, reel 5, 409.
Marshall to E. Norman Lacey, December 16, 1941, NAACP MF, 4, reel 7, 203.
Marshall to Secretaries of War and Navy, December 30, 1941, NAACP MF, 15B, reel 1, 237.

CHAPTER SIX: 1942–1943

Marshall to Wendell Berge, January 30, 1942, NAACP MF, 7, reel 24, 291.
Marshall to Keen Johnson, May 29, 1942, NAACP MF, 7, reel 30, 1026.
Marshall to Norman Holmes, July 2, 1942, NAACP MF, 9, reel 13, 251.

Marshall to Harry Butler, July 27, 1942, NAACP LOC, BII, B186, folder 8.

Marshall to Walter White and William Hastie, September 30, 1942, NAACP MF, 3B, reel 5, 998.

Walter White to Morris Ernst, October 31, 1942, NAACP LOC, BII, B99, folder 3.

Marshall to Wendell Berge, April 26, 1943, NAACP MF, 9B, reel 14, 118.

FBI Field Report, September 9, 1943, FBI File on the NAACP [FBI NAACP], reel 1, 495.

Marshall to Walter White, October 15, 1943, NAACP MF, 3B, reel 3, 734.

Marshall to George L. P. Weaver, November 30, 1943, NAACP MF, 4, reel 7, 383.

Marshall to the NAACP Office, December 7, 1943, NAACP MF, 18, reel 5, 665; NAACP LOC, BII, B99, folder 4.

Marshall to Walter White, No date [December 1943], NAACP MF, 15B, reel 1, 27.

Marshall to Maceo Smith, December 31, 1943, NAACP MF, 18, reel 9, 286.

CHAPTER SEVEN: 1944–1945

Marshall to Claude Pepper, January 28, 1944, NAACP MF, 7, reel 25, 490.

Marshall to Francis Biddle, April 3, 1944, NAACP MF, 4, reel 11, 395.

Marshall to the NAACP Office, April 15, 1944, NAACP MF, 18, reel 5, 812.

Marshall to Godfrey Cabot, May 1, 1944, NAACP MF, 16B, reel 3, 182.

Marshall to Tom Clark, May 5, 1944, NAACP MF, 9B, reel 14, 556.

Marshall to Sam Winter, May 10, 1944, NAACP MF, 4, reel 11, 469.

Marshall to George Schuyler, May 25, 1944, NAACP LOC, BII, B99, folder 5.

Marshall to Roger Baldwin, June 9, 1944, NAACP MF, 5, reel 22, 790.

Marshall to Francis Biddle, July 5, 1944, NAACP MF, 4, reel 8, 133.

Marshall to Carolyn Moore, September 7, 1944, NAACP MF, 9B, reel 14, 624.

Marshall to the NAACP Office, September 20, 1944, NAACP MF, 3B, reel 9, 1068.

Marshall to James Forrestal, October 19, 1944, NAACP MF, 9, reel 17, 783.

Marshall to Roy Wilkins, March 12, 1945, NAACP LOC, BII, B99, folder 6.

Marshall to Henry Stimson, May 24, 1945, NAACP MF, 15A, reel 7, 27.

Marshall to Henry Stimson, July 6, 1945, NAACP MF, 9B, reel 24, 1135.

Marshall to James Forrestal, July 13, 1945, NAACP MF, 9B, reel 6, 387.

Walter White to Marshall, July 17, 1945, NAACP MF, 18, reel 5, 887.

Marshall to Tom Clark, October 15, 1945, NAACP MF, 18, reel 9, 367.

Marshall to the NAACP Branches, November 14, 1945, NAACP MF, 3C, reel 6, 200.

Marshall to Harry Truman, November 14, 1945, Harry S. Truman Library

[HSTL], Independence, Missouri, Official File, box 390, folder OF 286-A (45-46).

CHAPTER EIGHT: 1946

Marshall to Amos Hall, January 24, 1946, NAACP MF, 3B, reel 13, 350.

Marshall to Howard Petersen, January 30, 1946, NAACP MF, 9, reel 10, 943.

Marshall to the Trial Committee of the New York City Board of Education, No date [February 1946], NAACP MF, 3C, reel 23, 339.

Marshall to J. Edgar Hoover, May 10, 1946, NAACP MF, 7, reel 22, 256.

J. Edgar Hoover to Marshall, May 14, 1946, NAACP MF, 7, reel 22, 259.

Marshall to Tom Clark, May 28, 1946, HSTL, Papers of Tom Clark, box 58, folder Mark-Marsh.

Walter White to Marshall, June 5, 1946, NAACP MF, 15, reel 18, 125.

Marshall to the NAACP Office, June 12, 1946, NAACP MF, 7, reel 21, 1116.

Marshall to the Editor of *The New York Times*, July 2, 1946, NAACP MF, 7, reel 23, 435.

Walter White to the NAACP Board, September 9, 1946, NAACP MF, 18, reel 5, 1000.

Marshall to Carter Wesley, October 25, 1946, NAACP MF, 18, reel 9, 422.

Marshall to Eleanor Roosevelt, October 28, 1946, NAACP MF, 7, reel 22, 693.

Marshall to Lulu White, November 6, 1946, NAACP MF, 4, reel 11, 656.

Marshall to Tom Clark, November 19, 1946, NAACP MF, 7, reel 22, 168.

Marshall to Tom Clark, December 3, 1946, NAACP MF, 7, reel 27, 252.

Marshall to Maceo Hubbard, December 4, 1946, NAACP MF, 7, reel 22, 169.

Marshall to Carter Wesley, December 27, 1946, NAACP MF, 18, reel 9, 441.

Marshall to Tom Clark, December 27, 1946, J. Edgar Hoover [JEH] Confidential Files, reel 11, 938.

CHAPTER NINE: 1947

Tom Clark to Marshall, January 13, 1947, NAACP MF, 7, reel 27, 28; JEH Confidential Files, 11, 940.

J. Edgar Hoover to Walter White, January 13, 1947, NAACP MF, 7, reel 27, 33.

Marshall to Walter White, January 23, 1947, NAACP LOC, BII, A410, folder 7.

J. Edgar Hoover to Walter White, January 28, 1947, NAACP LOC, BII, A410, folder 7.

Marshall to Ruby Hurley, February 6, 1947, NAACP MF, 3B, reel 4, 35.

Marshall to Howard Johnson Restaurants, February 7, 1947, NAACP MF, 15A, reel 6, 19.

Marshall to William Hastie, April 3, 1947, NAACP MF, 3B, reel 15, 268.

Marshall to Frank DeCosta, July 1, 1947, NAACP MF, 3B, reel 13, 322.

Marshall to Gloster Current, July 8, 1947, NAACP MF, 18, reel 6, 53.

Statement of Policy Concerning the NAACP's Education Cases, September 1947, NAACP MF, 18, reel 6, 121.

Marshall to the New York *Herald Tribune*, September 18, 1947, NAACP MF, 15B, reel 12, 115.

Marshall to John Wrighten, September 29, 1947, NAACP MF, 3B, reel 14, 340.

Marshall to the Editor of *Life*, September 29, 1947, NAACP MF, 3B, reel 16, 359.

Marshall to the Editor of the Dallas *Morning News*, September 29, 1947, NAACP MF, 3B, reel 4, 1157.

Marshall to Heman Sweatt, September 30, 1947, NAACP MF, 3B, reel 15, 429.

Marshall to Geoffrey Parsons, September 30, 1947, NAACP MF, 4, reel 7, 488.

Marshall to Geoffrey Parsons, October 4, 1947, NAACP MF, 3C, reel 17, 589.

Marshall to the NAACP Committee on Administration, October 27, 1947, NAACP MF, 16B, reel 5, 186.

Marshall to Roy Wilkins, October 28, 1947, NAACP MF 18, reel 6, 102.

Marshall to Roy Wilkins, October 30, 1947, NAACP MF, 18, reel 3, 64.

Marshall to Geoffrey Parsons, October 30, 1947, NAACP LOC, BII, A481, folder 4.

CHAPTER TEN: 1948

Marshall to the Editor of the Dallas *Morning News*, February 5, 1948, NAACP MF, 3B, reel 15, 517.

Marshall to Walter White, February 13, 1948, NAACP MF, 18, reel 6, 132.

Marshall to Roscoe Dunjee, April 20, 1948, NAACP MF, 3B, reel 13, 676.

Marshall to the Press, May 3, 1948, NAACP MF, 5, reel 22, 2.

Marshall to George Beaver, Jr., May 13, 1948, NAACP MF, 5, reel 21, 814.

Marshall to Charles Anderson, June 3, 1948, NAACP MF, 3B, reel 1, 854.

Marshall to Erwin Griswold, June 14, 1948, NAACP MF, 3B, reel 13, 749.

Marshall to M. E. Thompson, September 13, 1948, NAACP MF, 4, reel 8, 293.

Marshall to the Editor of the *Dallas News*, September 21, 1948, NAACP MF, 4, reel 7, 547.

Marshall to Henry Moon, October 28, 1948, NAACP MF, 3B, reel 13, 855.

Marshall to Seth Richardson, No date [1948], NAACP MF, 13C, reel 5, 863.

Marshall to Walter White, December 20, 1948, NAACP MF, 18, reel 3, 83.

Marshall to Roscoe Dunjee, December 29, 1948, NAACP MF, 3B, reel 13, 903.

CHAPTER ELEVEN: 1949–1950

Marshall to Herbert Swope, January 12, 1949, NAACP MF, 18C, reel 9, 728.

Marshall to Walter White, February 16, 1949, NAACP MF, 18, reel 6, 219.

Marshall to Lemuel Graves, Jr., February 24, 1949, NAACP MF, 5, reel 13, 1125.

Marshall to J. Waties Waring, May 4, 1949, NAACP MF, 18, reel 4, 254.

Stephen Spingarn to Clark Clifford, May 16, 1949, HSTL, Official File, box 782, folder OF 208-I.

James Hinton to Marshall, May 26, 1949, NAACP MF, 26A, reel 19, 73.

Marshall to Maceo Smith, June 1, 1949, NAACP MF, 5, reel 15, 938.

Marshall to Alexander Campbell, June 1, 1949, NAACP MF, 5, reel 20, 166.

Marshall to Horace Bond, June 13, 1949, Horace Mann Bond Papers [HMBP], Special Collections and University Archives, W. E. B. Du Bois Library, University of Massachusetts, Amherst, Massachusetts, Series III, box 63, folder 261.

Marshall to William Winston, July 27, 1949, NAACP MF, 13A, reel 20, 429.

Marshall to Robert Silberstein, August 2, 1949, FBI File on Thurgood Marshall [FBI TM].

A. P. Tureaud to Marshall, August 4, 1949, Alexander P. Tureaud Papers, microfilm edition, reel 8, 872.

Walter White to Marshall, November 16, 1949, NAACP MF, 18, reel 3, 100.

Marshall to Franklin Richards, December 7, 1949, NAACP MF, 5, reel 14, 81.

Marshall to John McCray, December 12, 1949, J. Waties Waring Papers, Howard University, Washington, D.C., box 110-15, folder Marshall, Thurgood.

Marshall to Elizabeth Waring, January 23, 1950, NAACP MF, 4, reel 11, 152.

Marshall to Louis Lautier, January 25, 1950, NAACP MF, 13B, reel 7, 227.

Marshall to the Editor of *The New York Times*, April 19, 1950, NAAP MF, 3B, reel 16, 444.

Marshall to Judah Cahn, June 7, 1950, NAACP MF, 15A, reel 5, 409.

Marshall to Pauli Murray, June 9, 1950, NAACP MF, 3B, reel 16, 749.

Marshall to James Ivy, July 13, 1950, NAACP MF, 3B, reel 16, 716.

Marshall to Arthur Shores, October 27, 1950, NAACP MF, 5, reel 19, 182.

CHAPTER TWELVE: 1951

Marshall to Roy Wilkins, February 3, 1951, Roy Wilkins Papers [RWP], Library of Congress, box 3, folder 1951 (M-Z).

Marshall to the NAACP Office, February 12, 1951, NAACP MF, 17, reel 29, 276.

Roy Wilkins to Marshall, February 20, 1951, RWP, box 3, folder 1951 (M-Z).

Marshall to Myrta Harris, March 26, 1951, NAACP LOC, BII, A72, folder 6.

Marshall to Oliver Hill and Spottswood Robinson III, May 22, 1951. Copy of letter in editor's possession.

Robert Carter to Marshall, June 13, 1951, Brown Collection, MS 759, box 9, folder 137.

Marshall to the Editor of the *Afro-American*, June 16, 1951, p. 4. This is the date of publication.

Marshall to Walter White, July 11, 1951, NAACP MF, 15B, reel 10, 210.

Marshall to the Editor of *The New York Times*, October 26, 1951, NAACP MF, 5, reel 19, 727.

CHAPTER THIRTEEN: 1952–1954

Marshall to Winston Robertson, January 8, 1952, NAACP MF, 26B, reel 6, 221.

Marshall to Tourist Court Journal Company, March 28, 1952, NAACP MF, 15B, reel 12, 820.

Marshall to Harry Truman, April 30, 1952, HSTL, Official File, box 1711, folder OF 2715-M.

Marshall to Harry Truman, June 13, 1952, HSTL, General File, box 1578, folder Marshall, Thurgood.

Marshall to James Hinton, Hobart LaGrone, and Maceo Smith, June 18, 1952, NAACP MF, 1 Supp (51-55), reel 5, 908.

NAACP on Public School Segregation Cases, "Public School Segregation Cases," November 26, 1952, NAACP MF, 3C, reel 3, 223.

Kenneth Clark to Marshall, January 23, 1953, Kenneth Clark Papers, Library of Congress, Washington, D.C., box 61, folder 6.

Marshall to the NAACP Office, June 11, 1953, NAACP MF, 3C, reel 15, 623.

Marshall to James Hinton, June 30, 1953, NAACP MF, 3C, reel 2, 418.

Loren Miller to Marshall, November 3, 1953, Brown Collection, MS 759, box 9, folder 140.

Marshall, Walter White, and Henry Fosdick to NAACP Supporters, May 17, 1954, NAACP MF, 3C, reel 15, 137.

Lester Granger to Marshall, May 18, 1954, NAACP MF, 3C, reel 14, 911.

Marshall to the Editor of the Dallas *Morning News*, June 10, 1954, NAACP MF, 3C, reel 3, 854.

Marshall to NAACP Branch Presidents and Officers, September 17, 1954, NAACP MF, 3C, reel 5, 212.

Marshall to Herbert Brownell, Jr., No date [Fall 1954], NAACP MF, 3C, reel 15, 947.

Ruby Hurley to Marshall, September 21, 1954, NAACP MF, 3C, reel 1, 782.

Marshall to His Legal Team, see Notes.

CHAPTER FOURTEEN: 1955–1957

Channing Tobias to Marshall, February 14, 1955, NAACP MF, 18, reel 6, 485.

Marshall to the Editor of *The New York Times Magazine*, May 11, 1955, NAACP MF, 3C, reel 4, 579.

Marshall to Ruben and Mary Barksdale, August 12, 1955, accessed at www.crossroadstofreedom.org.

Marshall to the Editor of the Columbia *Record*, September 9, 1955, NAACP MF, 3C, reel 3, 824.

J. Edgar Hoover to Marshall, September 30, 1955, FBI NAACP, reel 3, 1239.

Marshall to J. Edgar Hoover, October 7, 1955, FBI NAACP, reel 3, 1329.

FBI Memorandum, November 4, 1955, FBI TM.

FBI Memorandum, February 8, 1956, FBI TM.

FBI Memorandum, February 9, 1956, FBI TM.

Warren Olney III to Marshall, March 13, 1956, Papers of Warren Olney III [WOP], The Bancroft Library, University of California, Berkeley, California, BANC MJS, 99/171C.

Marshall to Warren Olney III, March 14, 1956, WOP, 99/171C.

Warren Olney III to Marshall, March 19, 1956, WOP, 99/171C.

Marshall to Warren Olney III, March 21, 1956, NAACP LOC, BIII, J3, folder 6.

Marshall to Robert Newbegin, March 22, 1956, NAACP LOC, BV, 2923, folder 6.

Marshall to B. K. Vine, March 22, 1956, NAACP LOC, BIII, J7, folder 5.

Marshall to Roy Wilkins, May 8, 1956, NAACP MF, 3D, reel 3, 691.

FBI Memorandum, May 21, 1956, FBI TM.

Marshall to Warren Olney III, September 5, 1956, NAACP MF, 3D, reel 1, 148.

Marshall to Dwight Eisenhower, September 6, 1956, DDEL, General File, box 916, GF 124-A-1.

Marshall to Maceo Smith, September 19, 1956, NAACP MF, 20, reel 12, 412.

Anonymous to Marshall, October 11, 1956, NAACP LOC, BIII, J2, folder 3.

Marshall to Israel Goldstein, December 10, 1956, NAACP LOC, BIII, J1, folder 1.

Marshall to Autherine Lucy Foster, February 15, 1957, Arthur D. Shores Papers, Talladega College, Talladega, Alabama.

Marshall to Walter Winchell, February 18, 1957, NAACP LOC, BIII, J6, folder 8.

INDEX